ALSO BY NICK MALGIERI

PERFECT
COOKIES, CAKES,
AND CHOCOLATE

NICK MALGIERI

PHOTOGRAPHS BY TOM ECKERLE

HarperCollins books may be purchased for educational, business, or sales promotional use. For information, please write: Special Markets Department, HarperCollins Publishers, 10 East 53rd Street, New York, NY 10022.

FIRST EDITION

Designed by Joel Avirom and Jason Snyder
Illustrations by Laura Hartman Maestro
Photography by Tom Eckerle

Printed on acid-free paper

Library of Congress Cataloging-in-Publication Data is available upon request.

ISBN 10: 0-06-123347-1
ISBN 13: 978-0-06-123347-0

06 07 08 09 10 ❖/   10 9 8 7 6 5 4 3 2 1

To my cousin, Karen Ludwig, a great baker

CONTENTS

INTRODUCTION

WHEREVER I TRAVEL, PEOPLE BUYING ONE of my books invariably ask, "Which are your favorite recipes in this book?" Not wanting to impose my taste on anyone else, I usually answer something non-committal, since I really do love all the recipes I put in my books. If I didn't really love them, they wouldn't be there. But within every book there are some recipes that are special to me – they might come from a dear friend or relative, or from a place where I worked happily in the past when I still worked in hotels and restaurants. Or they might be recipes from a beloved cookbook of the past or present or a colleague whose work I especially admire. This is why I've had such a good time choosing the recipes for this anthology of three of my books. *Cookies Unlimited, Perfect Cakes,* and *Chocolate.* I went through each of the books marking my most favorite recipes to include here. I also made sure to choose as many recipes as possible illustrated with color photographs since they not only make the recipes look appetizing, but also give valuable pointers on the appearance of the finished dessert.

I hope you enjoy the recipes in *Perfect Cookies, Cakes, and Chocolate* as much as I did while choosing them. They all taste as good as they look!

Nick Malgieri
New York City
May 2006

Perfect COOKIES, Cakes, and Chocolate

INTRODUCTION TO COOKIES

I WAS GENETICALLY PROGRAMMED WITH a passion for cookies. When my mother was a little girl in Italy, she loved all types of little sweets so she got the nickname *biscottini e taralluzzi (biscottini* are little biscotti, or cookies in general; *taralli* are ring cookies that are usually salty, but diminutive ones, *taralluzzi,* are usually sweet). I never had a chance. I have always loved cookies, though I don't eat nearly as many as I would like to. I can never resist them. Whether they are offered at the end of a cocktail party as a signal it's time to leave, or at the end of a meal in a fancy restaurant, no matter how sated I am, I always have room for a cookie or two.

When I was a child, my maternal grandmother, who loved to bake, lived with us. Her repertoire was limited to the southern Italian recipes she had grown up with but she made biscotti and her other specialties often. Though I never got a recipe from my grandmother, I'm sure her influence was what led me to dedicate my life to baking.

The other great cookie and baking influence in my early life was my father's sister, whose given name was Rachel, but who was always called Katy or Kitty. She was the American baker in our family. The first chocolate chip cookies I tasted were from her oven as were almond crescents, love knots, and many of her other specialties.

Of course, growing up in the 1950s, it was impossible not to see (and taste) the increasing number of industrially made cookies then coming on the market. My parents were never afraid to try something new and though we made occasional forays to bakeries and the cookie aisle of the supermarket, we preferred our homemade baked goods.

My first real exposure to European cookies came when I was an apprentice in Switzerland. As the Christmas holidays approached, the pastry shop of the hotel where I was working was filled with the scent of chocolate, nuts, and spices. The pastry chef and his assistants were busy preparing traditional Swiss *Weinachtsguetzli* (literally, Christmas goodies)–various cookies with many shapes, textures, and flavors. There were *Spitzbueben, Anisbroetli,* and *Basler Leckerli,* all traditional *Guetzli,* and you'll find recipes for them in this book. Swiss baking reaches its apogee with small things such as cookies; and you can see the perfect uniformity when they are lined up on trays in pastry shop showcases and windows. The beautiful precision the Swiss bring to baked goods in general had a lasting influence on both my taste and my vision of how desserts should be presented.

I didn't discover the delicate little cookies known as petits fours until I had left Switzerland and gone to Monaco to work at the Sporting Club in Monte Carlo. In fact a large part of my job as a *commis patissier* (pastry chef's assistant) during the first season I worked there was to arrange platters of dainty petits fours served in the restaurant after dessert. On gala evenings, when we had as many as a thousand guests for a set menu, every table received such a platter. One of the great rewards of working there was seeing and then learning the elaborate presentations made when Prince Rainier and Princess Grace attended a soiree at the Sporting Club. The pastry chef and his staff would spend the better part of a week getting ready and much of that time was spent preparing the great platter of petits fours presented after dessert. The recipes in this book for champagne fingers and tuiles date from those days.

I began collecting Italian cookie and biscotti recipes around the same time, because from Monaco I often had the chance to visit Italy. Later, when I was doing research for my Italian dessert book, I spent several months in Italy, looking around for interesting recipes, buying cookbooks (I came home with 200), and tasting lots of cookies. Many of those recipes are in that book, but some others are here.

I started teaching in 1979 and the most popular classes of the year have remained those about holiday baking, especially holiday cookies. People love cookies because the recipes are usually simple, they don't require a lot of time to make, and, let's face it—hardly anyone ever refuses a cookie.

There are lots of those simple straightforward recipes in this book but there is also the occasional challenging one that will require a bit more from the baker than dropping dough onto a pan from a teaspoon. You'll see, they can be fun to do if you approach them patiently with a relaxed attitude.

I love collecting recipes and then fine-tuning them to my taste and style. The recipes that follow are the result of a lifetime spent collecting from family, friends, colleagues, and anywhere cookie recipes are found—they are like cookies themselves, diverse, sweet, and fun and I hope you enjoy them.

COOKIES

A SHORT HISTORY
OF COOKIES

WE KNOW THAT SMALL CAKES HAVE BEEN served since baking as we know it began. The Romans celebrated important events such as weddings and fertility rites with cakes made with honey and rye flour and studded with nuts and dried fruit. These were the ancestors of fruitcake, *panforte* (an Italian fruit and nut cake), certain kinds of cookies such as *mostaccioli* in Italy and *Lebkuchen* in German-speaking countries, and many of the baked goods we still make today.

The Greeks also produced small cookie-like cakes made from flour and honey. These were called *boen* and that's how we got the word "bun."

The word "cookie" first appeared in an English dictionary in the eighteenth century, in a reference to the Dutch word *koekje*, which means "little cake." The word became common in America where Dutch settlers baked *koekjes* in indoor and outdoor ovens or on a griddle set over hot coals. This may also be one of the origins of the cookie sheet.

French petits fours (meaning "little ovens") are small fancy cookies also originating sometime in the eighteenth century. These elegant cookies, small sweet items, were baked at a lower oven temperature and placed in the oven after the larger ones had been removed.

By the end of the nineteenth century, wood- and coal-burning iron stoves had made cookie baking more accessible for home cooks. Cookies rapidly became a standard snack and lunch box item.

Soon to follow was commercial cookie production, and within the first 15 years of the twentieth century, several industrial cookie companies had introduced a wide variety of packaged cookies.

Brownies, which are a close relation of the cookie, first emerged before 1910. Although the term "brownie" had been seen in print prior to this, there is no documentation on who actually invented it. It may have even been a mistake when a chocolate cake accidentally collapsed.

By the middle of the twentieth century, cookies were a staple in every household kitchen. The chocolate chip cookie was first introduced by Ruth Wakefield at her Toll House Inn in the 1930s. Chocolate chip cookies still have the lead among cookie popularity, and over 90 million bags of chocolate chips are sold annually.

Though commercially and industrially made cookies are finding wider and wider audiences, there is still no replacement for a homemade cookie, fresh from the oven and made with care in a small quantity.

MAKING COOKIES

THE COOKIE PANTRY

Though cookie ingredients are not really different from the ingredients needed for any kind of baking, the following is a list of items you need to have on hand for the recipes in this book.

BUTTER: The first and foremost ingredient in cookie recipes. It's true that not every cookie recipe contains butter, but most do and it's important not to skimp. Use good, fresh unsalted butter; it provides a fragility, a depth of flavor, and a delicacy that no other fat can duplicate. By the way, there are a few recipes that call for oil—for those use a mild, bland oil, such as canola, peanut, or corn oil.

MILK is whole milk in all the recipes that call for it.

CREAM is heavy whipping cream.

BUTTERMILK is the cultured low-fat variety easily found in the supermarket.

EGGS: Whenever eggs are called for they should be graded large.

FLOUR: The recipes here call for either all-purpose or cake flour. Use either bleached or unbleached all-purpose flour—it will make no difference in these recipes. Cake flour should be plain cake flour, not the self-rising type. To substitute all-purpose flour for cake flour, subtract 2 tablespoons from each cup of cake flour called for. Remember to measure all flour with nested, graduated-size dry-measure cups, not the clear glass or plastic cups meant for measuring liquids. And even more important, gently scoop or spoon the flour into the dry-measure cup, then level it off with the straight side of a metal or rubber spatula or the back of a knife. Don't dip and sweep.

CORNSTARCH: In certain very tender cookie recipes cornstarch is used in combination with flour. This is done to lower the flour's protein content, so the dough will have a weaker gluten formation, and consequently the cookies will be more tender.

BREAD CRUMBS: Make your own by pulverizing day-old French or Italian bread in the food processor. If you buy commercial bread crumbs in the supermarket, be sure to get the unflavored variety.

SUGAR: Plain granulated sugar is called for in most of the recipes in this book.

COARSE OR SANDING SUGAR: This is a coarser-textured white sugar for decorating or coating some cookies before baking. Coarse sugar is not readily available in the supermarket, but is easy to get from mail-order sources.

BROWN SUGAR: Remember that the difference between light and dark brown sugar is only the amount of molasses added to the sugar. There is more in dark brown than in light. Granulated light brown sugar may be substituted for moist light brown.

CONFECTIONERS' SUGAR: This very finely ground sugar with some cornstarch added so it doesn't clump is used to sprinkle on cookies or to make glazes. Confectioners' sugar may also be an ingredient in some very delicate doughs used for making tender, fragile cookies. Before sprinkling confectioners' sugar on cookies, make sure they have cooled thoroughly or the sugar will melt. Also, be sure to sprinkle the sugar lightly—too heavy a coating is cloyingly sweet and messy to boot.

MOLASSES: Molasses comes in mild (unsulphured) and robust flavors. I don't find a great deal of difference between the two and use them interchangeably.

CORN SYRUP: Corn syrup, either light or dark, figures mostly in recipes for fillings and glazes rather than in cookie recipes. In certain British and Australian recipes, I have used corn syrup rather than golden syrup with very good results. Golden syrup is a very thick sugar syrup, originally developed as a honey substitute. You can also use honey.

HONEY: Be sure to use a dark, robust-flavored honey.

DECORATIVE COLORED SUGARS AND NONPAREILS: The former are coarse sugar crystals like sanding sugar but they come in a variety of different colors and mixed multicolored assortments. They are sometimes available in the supermarket. Nonpareils are tiny spheres of opaque sugar that come in white or multicolored assortments. The same type of sugar used to make nonpareils is used to make little colored season-specific decorations such as green Christmas trees or orange pumpkins. All these decorations should be used sparingly on cookies to avoid an unappetizing and overburdened look.

LEAVENERS: I always use double-acting baking powder. Several nonaluminum-based brands on the market give results as good as the standard types. Baking soda, called for in a few recipes, is used if the recipe contains an acid ingredient, such as honey, cocoa, molasses, brown sugar, citrus, or a cultured dairy product. The acidity reacts with the alkalinity of the baking soda to make carbon dioxide form and foam up and leaven the dough or batter. Bicarbonate of ammonia is an unusual leavener. It not only causes rising during baking but also promotes the complete desiccation of the dough or batter to which it is added, making very dry and crisp cookies. It is called for in only a few recipes here, and regular baking powder may always be substituted.

SALT: Fine sea salt has been used to test all these recipes. Never substitute kosher or other coarse salt. The crystals of these salts are larger, so measurements will not be accurate.

NUTS: Nuts provide flavor, tenderness, and textural variety in many cookie recipes. Try to purchase nuts in vacuum cans or in a store where you can taste them to be sure they are fresh and sweet-tasting, not rancid. Nuts should be stored in a plastic bag in the freezer. For best results, bring the nutmeats to room temperature before grinding them.

To blanch almonds or pistachios, bring them to a boil in a pan of water and drain. Rub the nuts in a coarse-textured towel to loosen the skins, then go over each one to separate the nuts from the skins. Place blanched nuts on a jelly roll pan and dry them out in a 300 degree oven for about 5 to 10 minutes (don't let them color) and cool before using.

To blanch hazelnuts, toast them at 350 degrees on a jelly roll pan until the skins have loosened, then proceed with the towel as for almonds. It is not necessary to dry out hazelnuts.

To chop nuts, pulse them briefly in the food processor, or to get uniformly larger pieces, chop by hand using a large chopping knife on a cutting board. To grind nuts, pulse them repeatedly in the food processor until they are ground very fine. Stop the machine occasionally and scrape down the inside bottom of the bowl where the finest particles may accumulate.

CANDIED FRUIT: Best quality candied fruit is usually only found in import and specialty stores. The type available in the supermarket at holiday time for typical fruitcake baking is usually bitter and undercandied, resulting in an inexpensive product which lacks flavor and sweetness. If you don't plan ahead and order fine quality candied fruit from one of the mail-order sources, wait until you can, rather than use the supermarket type.

GINGER IN SYRUP: A type of candied ginger suspended in a thick syrup, usually sold in jars. Crystallized ginger is not a substitute.

CRYSTALLIZED GINGER: Candied ginger dried and rolled in granulated sugar. Taste it first to see if it is tender, sweet, and peppery, not dry and tough.

CHOCOLATE: Unsweetened, semisweet, or bittersweet, milk and white chocolates are used in recipes in this book. Make sure any chocolate you use tastes good on its own, because the chocolate is what gives the cookies their taste. I use a serrated knife to chop chocolate into ¼-inch pieces before using it in a recipe or melting it.

To melt chocolate, place pieces in a heatproof bowl, then bring a saucepan half filled with water to a boil. Turn off the heat and put the bowl over the pan of hot water. Stir occasionally with a spoon or spatula until the chocolate is melted. Remove the bowl from the pan and cool the chocolate slightly before using. Or place the chocolate in a microwave-safe bowl and microwave, on half-power if possible, for about 20 to 30 seconds at a time, removing the bowl and stirring the chocolate occasionally, until it is melted.

COCOA: Both nonalkalized and alkalized cocoa are called for in my cookie recipes. The difference between the two is that alkalized (Dutch process) cocoa has been treated with alkali to make it darker and slightly less bitter. In these recipes, they may be used interchangeably.

FLAVORINGS: Always purchase pure flavoring extracts, not artificial ones. Nowadays, unfortunately, there are mixtures of the two. I like to purchase vanilla extract at a cooking specialty store—it may be a little more expensive, but premium brands of vanilla have the strongest flavor. If you use vanilla beans, make sure they are plump and moist. I like Madagascar Bourbon vanilla extract and beans the best. Other extracts called for in the recipes are almond, anise, lemon, and orange.

FLAVORING OILS: There are excellent ones available. Follow the manufacturer's guidelines about substituting for extracts. Generally, use half as much oil as extract.

SPICES AND HERBS: Make sure spices are strong and fragrant when you purchase them. Remember to keep spices in a cool, dark place and discard them after a year or so when their aroma begins to weaken.

EQUIPMENT

MIXER: I love my Kitchen-Aid mixer and wouldn't know what to do without it. When you use a heavy-duty stand mixer, remember that the paddle attachment is for all general mixing purposes, such as beating butter–always softened to room temperature–or incorporating flour into a dough. The wire whisk is used only to incorporate air into whipped cream or whipped eggs or egg whites.

FOOD PROCESSOR: This propeller-bladed mixing and chopping machine was first introduced here in the early seventies and has since become standard home kitchen equipment. It is essential for chopping and grinding nuts, and also great for mixing pastry doughs and other preparations that don't need to be aerated.

ROLLING PIN: I prefer a straight wooden rolling pin about 24 inches long with no handles. My friend Dorie Greenspan recently gave me a new French pin that is made from hard white nylon (it looks just like plastic) and it works very well because it has such a smooth surface. Whatever type of rolling pin you use, make sure to scrape off any little pieces of dough stuck to it and wipe it with a damp cloth after each use. Never wash a rolling pin by immersing it in water.

BRUSHES: I like natural bristle brushes and am particularly fond of black-bristled ones because the stray hairs are easy to spot if the brush begins to shed.

GRATERS: A standard box grater works well. Just be sure to look for one that has diagonally placed holes–citrus zest will not stick as it does in the standard round nail holes. There is a relatively new grater on the market that looks like a carpenter's rasp, which works really well for citrus zest.

CUTTERS: I have a collection of cookie cutters going back to my childhood, but I keep using the same ones over and over. My favorites are the sets of round plain and crinkled cutters that come in several increasing diameters. These are also now available in hard plastic. Of course, there are hundreds of specialty shapes available from most kitchenware and hardware stores.

Ice Cream Scoops: These can be very handy for forming cookies. Look for these in a serious kitchenware store or restaurant supply store for the best quality and the largest selection of sizes; 1-tablespoon and ½-tablespoon sizes are practical for most of the cookies here.

Molds: Cookie molds are used to make shortbread; anise cookies, such as Swiss *Anisbroetli* or German *Springerle*; or spicy Dutch *speculaas*. If you don't find these in a specialty cookware store, see Sources. By the way, I think individual *Springerle* molds, like little tiles, do a better job of marking the dough than the *Springerle* rolling pins.

Pans: Because I visit cooking schools to teach all over North America, I have used and continue to use all types of pans for baking cookies. I don't think it matters whether the pan has sides or not: A classic cookie sheet of 12 × 15 inches usually only has one raised side, and jelly roll pans, available in sizes between 10 × 15 inches to 12 × 18 inches, usually have four sides and are about an inch deep. Remember that shiny pans promote light baking and dark pans encourage cookies to bake darker, especially on the bottom.

The bar cookies are baked in 9 × 13 × 2-inch or 10 × 15 × 1-inch pans. The ones I use are aluminum and are standard home-style ones you can buy in any kitchen or hardware store. If your pans of this type are particularly thin, place them on a cookie sheet or jelly roll pan or double them. This will prevent the bottoms of cookies from burning. I almost always bake cookies on pans lined with parchment or foil—it makes both removing or unmolding cookies or bars and cleanup so easy. The only other pans I use are a pair of heavy steel nonstick-coated 9 × 14-inch French pans, with slightly raised sides. These are great for tuiles or any other cookies that need to spread and become very thin during baking. Though I don't own any, I have used insulated cookie sheets often at the many cooking schools I visit. These pans are wonderful because they prevent the bottoms of cookies from burning. This is exactly the same result you get by stacking two cookie sheets or jelly roll pans together.

Silicon Mats: These are all the rage in professional baking circles. They are thin mats of pure silicon that are placed on a baking pan (they come in the sizes that commercial pans measure, 12 × 18 inches being the smallest) to provide a perfectly nonstick surface for baking. Fairly expensive, they may be used thousands of times and only need to be wiped clean after each use. If you like to collect every new kitchenware item that emerges, then by all means get some, though I don't find that they are so useful for home baking.

Racks: I like sturdy stainless steel racks the same size as the pans I use. I usually slide the paper or foil that the cookies have been baked on directly off the sheet and onto the rack to cool. If you have baked bars, just place the whole pan on the rack until completely cooled. When you need to cool cookies over a cylindrical form to curve them, steady a rolling pin on a jelly roll pan by bunching a kitchen towel underneath it. If you are going to make a lot of curved cookies, save the cardboard cores from inside rolls of paper towels, foil, plastic wrap, or wax paper, cover them with foil, and use these to curve cookies.

KNIVES: My favorite knife is the offset serrated knife. It makes cutting bars and chopping chocolate a real breeze. In general I use stainless steel knives when I'm baking cookies.

SPATULAS: Large and small offset spatulas are the best for spreading batter in pans, or spreading thin disks of batter on sheets for tuiles or tulipes.

TECHNIQUES

BAKING COOKIES After mixing up excellent ingredients to make a batch of cookies, you certainly don't want to burn them while they are baking. Follow these simple rules to avoid burning cookies:

Use an oven thermometer to make sure your oven is actually running at the temperature it's set for. Bake cookies in the middle level of the oven for even coloring and best results. As the cookies are baking reverse the position of the pan from front to back once or twice. If you are baking more than one pan of cookies at a time, place racks so they divide the oven into thirds. Double the pan or use an insulated cookie sheet on the lower rack. About a third of the way during the baking time, switch the pan from the bottom of the oven to the top and vice versa (remember the pan on the bottom of the oven should be doubled when you switch racks). Also rotate the pans back to front for even coloring. Work quickly so the oven doesn't lose too much heat while you are switching the pans around.

COOLING COOKIES See "Racks" page 9.

COOKIE STORAGE Keep cookies in a tin or plastic container with a tight-fitting cover. If you must stack cookies on top of each other, put sheets of wax paper or parchment between the layers—this will keep filled, sandwich, or iced cookies from sticking together. Use the same method for freezing cookies (though, if I am going to freeze cookies, I prefer to sandwich or ice them before serving for neatest results).

FREEZING COOKIES Everyone likes to get ahead and get a few batches of cookies into the freezer before the year-end holidays or another big event. Whether the cookies survive freezing depends more on your own freezer than anything else. If the freezer is very clean, not too crowded, and you don't open it often, your cookies will come through the freezing process relatively unscathed. Crisp cookies may become somewhat limp upon defrosting—if possible, preheat the oven to 300 degrees and reheat them on a cookie sheet for less than 10 minutes, then let them cool before serving.

Perhaps the best choices for freezing are bar and refrigerator cookies. For bars, bake and cool the large cake without cutting it. Wrap and freeze, then cut into individual cookies according to the recipe after you have defrosted the cake. Rolls of refrigerator cookie dough that have been frozen only need to come up a little in temperature before being sliced and baked—a great way to utilize the freezer and get freshly baked cookies at the same time. In any case, if you want to prepare a large assortment of cookies, choose some bar and refrigerator cookies that may be frozen, but don't confine the whole list to frozen cookies.

SHIPPING COOKIES There are two keys to shipping cookies successfully: Wrap them loosely and individually in plastic wrap and use small containers. If you want to ship a lot of cookies, get a lot of small containers and nestle them in Styrofoam (or real) popcorn in a large box. This has recently become easier and less expensive with the availability of the multiple-use disposable plastic containers.

What to Do If You Have Only Two Cookie Sheets

Many of the recipes here call for making several dozen cookies. If you don't have a lot of cookie sheets, here's a simple solution: Cut parchment or foil sheets the same size as your pans. Line the pans and bake the first batch of cookies. While they are baking, form more cookies on the precut sheets. When the first cookies are baked, slide the papers off the pans, cool the pans until they are no longer hot, then slide the papers with more cookies onto the pans to bake. Also remember that cookie sheets and jelly roll pans are relatively inexpensive and that with two cookie sheets and two each jelly roll pans of two different sizes you can tackle almost any recipe here and not have to wait for pans to cool between baking batches of cookies.

BAR COOKIES

PERHAPS THE EASIEST OF ALL COOKIES TO PREPARE, bar cookies are really a large cake, divided. The dough or batter is poured into a large pan (all the bar cookie recipes here use a 13 × 9 × 2-inch or a 10 × 15 × 1-inch pan), then spread flat. The baked cake is then cut into bars or squares. Some recipes call for dough used as a base for a topping, yet others have fillings like large rectangular pies or tarts cut into squares.

Perhaps the richest and most elegant bar cookies are brownies, and they are in a special section at the end of this chapter.

HINTS FOR BAR COOKIES

1 Prepare the pan carefully to ensure that the baked cake will be easy to unmold. I like to butter the pan, then line it completely, bottom and sides, with a large piece of parchment paper or foil. The butter on the pan holds the paper in place. I also butter the paper, just to be extra careful.

2 On a rack, cool the baked cake in the pan for 10 minutes. Then remove it from the rack. Using the paper lining, lift it from the pan, and transfer back to the rack to cool completely.

3 After the cake has cooled, lift it, again by the paper lining, to a board to cut it. If necessary, slide a knife or spatula between the cake and the paper to loosen, then slide the cake from the paper to the board.

4 I usually trim away the edges before cutting bar cookies so that the cookies will be more uniform.

5 Neatness counts! Use a ruler to mark the cake into 2-inch squares (or any other size squares or rectangles you wish) before you cut.

6 Use a sharp knife and wipe it frequently with a damp cloth for neatest cutting.

7 Finally, to prevent the bars from drying, store them between layers of wax paper or parchment in a tin or plastic container with a tight-fitting cover

8 For longer storage, wrap individually in cellophane or plastic wrap and freeze.

QUANTITY BAKING HINT: A double recipe calling for a 9 × 13 × 2-inch pan will fit perfectly in a 12 × 18 × 1-inch half sheet pan as will 1½ times a recipe for a 10 × 15 × 1-inch pan.

MOTHER B's

THIS NUTMEG-SCENTED BAR COOKIE comes from my old friend Stephanie Weaver. They are named for her suburban Detroit childhood neighbor, Mrs. Barnes, who gave the recipe to Stephanie's mother in the 1960s. A variation of an old-fashioned Southern cookie called a pound cake cookie, these will quickly become favorites.

1 Set a rack in the middle level of the oven and preheat to 350 degrees.

2 Measure the flour, nutmeg, baking soda, and salt into a mixing bowl and stir well to combine.

3 In the bowl of an electric mixer, beat the butter and sugar together, using the paddle attachment on medium speed. Beat in the egg and continue beating until the mixture is smooth.

4 Lower the mixer speed and beat in half the dry ingredients. When this is incorporated, slowly add the buttermilk and beat until smooth. Then beat in the rest of the dry ingredients.

5 Remove the bowl from the mixer and stir the batter well with a rubber spatula. Scrape the batter into the prepared pan and smooth the top evenly.

6 Bake the cake about 25 to 30 minutes, until well risen and a light golden color, and a toothpick or small knife inserted in the center emerges clean. Remove from the oven and cool on a rack for 10 minutes, then, using the paper, lift the cake from the pan onto a rack and let cool completely.

1¾ cups all-purpose flour

1½ teaspoons freshly grated nutmeg

½ teaspoon baking soda

¼ teaspoon salt

8 tablespoons (1 stick) unsalted butter, softened

1 cup sugar

1 large egg

½ cup buttermilk or sour milk

One 9 × 13 × 2-inch pan, buttered and lined with buttered parchment or foil

7 To cut the bars, use the paper to transfer the cake onto a cutting board. Slide a long knife or spatula under it to loosen the paper or foil, then pull it away. Use a ruler to mark, then cut the cake into 2-inch squares.

8 The squares will keep between sheets of parchment or wax paper in a tin or plastic container with a tight-fitting cover for several days. Freeze for longer storage.

MAKES ONE 9 × 13 × 2-INCH PAN, ABOUT TWENTY-FOUR 2-INCH SQUARES

COOKIES

ELEGANT ALMOND BARS

~⌃ ⌃~

THIS IS A DECIDEDLY FANCY COOKIE, great with ice cream or sherbet as the dessert for an elaborate or plain meal. The recipe comes from my friend Gary Peese of Austin, Texas, who is always sending me wonderful recipes—even when I forget they were from him.

1 Set a rack in the middle level of the oven and preheat to 350 degrees.

2 Combine the flour, salt, and baking powder in a bowl and stir well to combine.

3 In the bowl of an electric mixer fitted with the paddle attachment, beat together on low speed, until smooth, the almond paste, sugar, and one of the eggs, about 2 minutes.

4 Add the butter, lemon zest, and vanilla and continue beating on medium speed for about another 5 minutes, until the mixture is very smooth and light. Add the remaining eggs, one at a time, scraping the bowl and beater after each addition. Remove the bowl from the mixer and use a large rubber spatula to stir in the flour mixture by hand.

5 Scrape the batter into the prepared pan and spread it evenly with a large offset spatula. Scatter the sliced almonds uniformly over the batter.

6 Bake the cake for about 30 to 40 minutes, until well risen, and a toothpick or small knife inserted in the middle emerges clean.

7 Cool on a rack for 10 minutes, then remove the pan from the rack. Use the paper to transfer the cake from the pan back onto the rack to cool completely.

1 cup all-purpose flour

¼ teaspoon salt

1 teaspoon baking powder

One 8-ounce can almond paste,
    cut into ½-inch pieces

1 cup sugar

6 large eggs

16 tablespoons (2 sticks) unsalted butter,
    softened

1 teaspoon finely grated lemon zest

1 teaspoon vanilla extract

4 ounces (about 1 cup) blanched sliced
    almonds

Confectioners' sugar for finishing

One 10 × 15 × 1-inch pan, buttered and
lined with buttered parchment or foil

8 Use the paper to move the cake onto a cutting board. Slide a long knife or spatula under it to loosen the paper or foil and pull it away. Use a ruler to mark, then cut the cake into 2-inch squares.

9 For up to several days, store the squares between sheets of parchment or wax paper in a tin or plastic container with a tight-fitting cover. Freeze for longer storage. Dust with confectioners' sugar before serving.

MAKES ONE 10 × 15 × 1-INCH PAN,
ABOUT THIRTY-FIVE 2-INCH SQUARES

CHEWY ALMOND BARS

⤺ ໑ ෬ ⤻

THIS IS A GREAT RECIPE FOR USING leftover nuts. It's great with one type of nut, but it's just as good with a mixed bag of chopped nuts. This recipe comes from Patsye Hardin of Dallas, Texas.

1 Set a rack in the middle level of the oven and preheat to 350 degrees.

2 Melt the butter in a small pan over low heat and pour it into the baking pan. Tilt the pan so the butter coats the sides, too. Set aside.

3 In a large bowl whisk together the eggs and vanilla just until whites and yolks are combined. Combine the brown sugar, flour, baking soda, and nuts, then fold into the egg mixture. Scrape the batter into the prepared pan. Don't stir the batter and butter together.

4 Bake about 30 to 35 minutes, until firm and golden. Cover a rack with aluminum foil and invert the baked bar onto it. Lift off the pan and allow to cool completely.

5 Transfer the cake onto a cutting board and slide away the foil. Using a ruler as a guide, cut into 2-inch squares. Just before serving, dust lightly with confectioners' sugar.

3 tablespoons unsalted butter

3 large eggs

2 teaspoons vanilla extract

1½ cups dark brown sugar

½ cup all-purpose flour

¾ teaspoon baking soda

1½ cups slivered almonds or other nuts, cut into ¼ inch pieces

Confectioners' sugar for finishing

One 9 × 13 × 2-inch pan, buttered and lined with buttered parchment or foil.

6 For up to several days, store the squares between sheets of parchment or wax paper in a tin or plastic container with a tight-fitting cover. Freeze for longer storage.

MAKES ONE 9 × 13 × 2-INCH PAN, ABOUT TWENTY-FOUR 2-INCH SQUARES

Elegant Almond Bar (LEFT) *and Chewy Almond Bar*

CHOCOLATE-ICED PEANUT SQUARES

I LOVE PEANUT BUTTER COOKIES of all kinds—especially when they have chocolate icing on them. Sometimes I vary these by using chunky peanut butter, or by adding a handful of chopped honey-roasted peanuts to the dough. They are great unfrosted, but adding the chocolate icing and the chopped peanuts really makes them extraordinary.

1 Set a rack in the middle level of the oven and preheat to 350 degrees.

2 In the bowl of an electric mixer fitted with the paddle attachment, beat the butter and peanut butter about half a minute on medium speed until well mixed. Beat in both sugars and continue beating until the ingredients are combined, about another half a minute. Beat in the egg, yolk, and vanilla extract.

3 Remove the bowl from the mixer and stir in the flour with a wooden spoon. Scrape the dough into the prepared pan and use your floured palms to press it evenly into the pan.

4 Bake the cake about 20 to 25 minutes, or until firm and lightly brown. Cool in the pan on a rack.

5 To make the topping, stir the soft butter into the melted chocolate with a small rubber spatula.

6 Use the paper to transfer the cake to a cutting board. Slide a long knife or spatula under the cake to loosen the paper, then pull it away. With a small offset spatula spread the icing evenly over the top. Sprinkle immediately with the chopped peanuts.

PEANUT BUTTER DOUGH

12 tablespoons (1½ sticks) unsalted butter, softened

⅓ cup peanut butter

⅔ cup light brown sugar

½ cup granulated sugar

1 large egg

1 large egg yolk

1½ teaspoons vanilla extract

2½ cups all-purpose flour

TOPPING

4 tablespoons (½ stick) unsalted butter, softened

6 ounces semisweet or bittersweet chocolate, melted and cooled

½ cup coarsely chopped honey-roasted peanuts

One 9 × 13 × 2-inch pan, buttered and lined with buttered parchment or foil

7 Let the cake stand at room temperature for several hours to set the glaze, or place briefly in the freezer or refrigerator to hasten the process.

8 Using a ruler as a guide, cut into 2-inch squares.

9 For up to several days, store the squares between sheets of parchment or wax paper in a tin or plastic container with a tight-fitting cover. Freeze for longer storage

MAKES ONE 9 × 13 × 2-INCH PAN, ABOUT TWENTY-FOUR 2-INCH SQUARES

CURRANT SQUARES

～⤳⤳～

NOTHING IS HOMIER OR MORE COMFORTING than these old-fashioned moist squares loaded with currants. Of course, you may substitute dark or golden raisins or a combination, if you choose. By the way, the standard supermarket currants called for here are really very tiny raisins, not dried, tart red, black, or white currants, which are related to gooseberries. The French name for the tiny raisins used here is *raisins de Corinthe*, or Corinthian raisins, and the English word "currant" is a corruption of "Corinth."

1 Combine the water and currants in a medium saucepan. Bring to a full boil over medium heat. Remove from the heat, stir in the baking soda, and set aside to cool completely.

2 Set a rack in the middle level of the oven and preheat to 350 degrees.

3 Place the flour, baking powder, and nutmeg into a bowl. Stir well to mix.

4 In the bowl of an electric mixer fitted with the paddle attachment, beat the butter and sugar on medium speed until well mixed, about a minute. Beat in the vanilla extract, then the eggs, one at a time, beating until smooth after each addition.

5 Remove the bowl from the mixer and with a large rubber spatula stir in the currants and water. Then stir in the flour mixture.

6 Scrape the batter into the prepared pan and smooth the top with an offset spatula.

⅔ cup water

1½ cups currants

1 teaspoon baking soda

2 cups all-purpose flour

1½ teaspoons baking powder

½ teaspoon freshly grated nutmeg

12 tablespoons (1½ sticks) unsalted butter, softened

1 cup sugar

1 teaspoon vanilla extract

2 large eggs

One 9 × 13 × 2-inch pan, buttered and lined with buttered parchment or foil

7 Bake the cake for about 30 to 40 minutes, or until it is well risen, well colored, and a toothpick or a small knife inserted in the center emerges clean. Cool on a rack for 10 minutes, then remove the pan from the rack. Use the paper to transfer the cake from the pan to the rack to cool completely.

8 Place the cake on a cutting board and slide a long knife or spatula under it to loosen the paper or foil and remove it. Use a ruler to mark, then cut the cake into 2-inch squares.

9 For up to several days, store the squares between sheets of parchment or wax paper in a tin or plastic container with a tight-fitting cover. Freeze for longer storage.

MAKES ONE 9 × 13 × 2-INCH PAN,
ABOUT TWENTY-FOUR 2-INCH SQUARES

COOKIES

DOREEN'S GINGER SQUARES

～❀～

THIS RECIPE IS A WONDERFUL SOUTH African import from my friend Kyra Effren in Dallas. Doreen was Kyra's mother's best friend, who died unexpectedly soon after passing the recipe on to Kyra. So thanks to Kyra, the recipe wasn't lost.

You'll need some ginger preserved in syrup to make this recipe.

1 Set a rack in the middle level of the oven and preheat to 375 degrees.

2 Combine the flour, sugar, ground ginger, and baking powder in a bowl and stir well to combine.

3 Melt the butter in a 2-quart saucepan over low to medium heat. Off the heat stir in the flour and sugar mixture.

4 Beat the egg, preserved ginger, cherries, and ginger syrup into the dough, beating with a wooden spoon.

5 Scrape the dough onto the prepared pan and use the floured palm of your hand to press the dough evenly into all corners of the pan. Use the back of a spoon to smooth the top of the dough if necessary.

6 Bake the cake about 20 to 30 minutes, or until lightly browned and firm to the touch.

7 Place the cake on a rack and immediately mix the confectioners' sugar and lemon juice for the glaze. Add water, a teaspoon at a time, if the icing is too thick to spread. Brush the glaze over the hot ginger cake so the glaze will set as the cake cools. Allow to cool completely.

8 To cut the ginger squares, slide the whole

GINGER SQUARES

2½ cups all-purpose flour

1 cup sugar

2 tablespoons ground ginger

2 teaspoons baking powder

16 tablespoons (2 sticks) unsalted butter

1 large egg

¼ cup drained preserved ginger, finely chopped (reserve the drained syrup)

¼ cup finely chopped candied cherries

2 tablespoons reserved ginger syrup

LEMON GLAZE

2 cups confectioners' sugar

3 tablespoons strained lemon juice

One 10 × 15 × 1-inch pan, buttered and lined with buttered parchment or foil

cake on the paper to a cutting board. Slide a long knife or spatula under the cake to loosen the paper or foil, then pull it away. Use a ruler to mark, then cut the cake into 2-inch squares.

9 For up to several days, store the squares between sheets of parchment or wax paper in a tin or plastic container with a tight-fitting cover. Freeze for longer storage.

MAKES ONE 10 × 15 × 1-INCH PAN,

ULTIMATE LEMON SQUARES

~ ୬ ୧ ~

THIS GREAT VERSION OF A CLASSIC comes from my friend and former student, Cara Tannenbaum. Cara now works with us at Peter Kump's New York Cooking School and is one of our star baking teachers.

1 Set a rack in the middle level of the oven and preheat to 350 degrees.

2 For the base, in a standing mixer fitted with the paddle attachment, beat the butter on medium speed. Beat in the confectioners' sugar and vanilla and continue beating a minute or two, until light. Lower the speed and beat in the flour.

3 Spread the dough over the bottom of the prepared pan, using a small offset spatula or the back of a spoon to smooth it. Bake the base about 20 to 25 minutes, until golden and baked through.

4 While the base is baking prepare the topping. Be careful not to overmix the topping, or it will have a coarse- textured foam on the top when baked. In a large mixing bowl, whisk the eggs just to break them up. Whisk in the sugar, then the lemon juice and zest.

5 As soon as the base is baked, remove it from the oven and pour on the topping. Immediately return the pan to the oven and continue baking the squares another 25 to 30 minutes, or until the topping is set and firm.

6 Cool on a rack until completely cooled.

7 To cut the cake, use the paper to transfer it to a cutting board and slide a long knife or

COOKIE BASE

16 tablespoons (2 sticks) unsalted butter, softened

½ cup confectioners' sugar

1 teaspoon vanilla extract

2 cups all-purpose flour

LEMON TOPPING

4 large eggs

2 cups sugar

6 tablespoons strained lemon juice

1 tablespoon finely grated lemon zest

Confectioners' sugar for finishing

One 9 × 13 × 2-inch pan, buttered and lined with buttered parchment or foil

spatula under it to loosen the paper or foil, then pull it away. Trim the edges, use a ruler to mark, then cut the cake into 2-inch squares.

8 Dust with confectioners' sugar before serving. For up to several days, store the squares in a tin or plastic container with a tight-fitting cover.

MAKES ONE 9 × 13 × 2-INCH PAN, ABOUT TWENTY-FOUR 2-INCH SQUARES

HONEY PECAN SQUARES

~⤴ ⤵~

THIS IS A RICH AND EASY RECIPE GIVEN to me by Jayne Sutton of Darien, Connecticut. I'm proud to say that Jayne has been coming to my classes for more than 20 years, recently bringing her daughter Leslie, too.

1 For the dough, combine the flour, granulated sugar, salt, and baking powder in the bowl of a food processor and pulse several times to mix. Cut the butter into about sixteen pieces and add to the work bowl. Continue pulsing until the butter is finely worked into the dough and the mixture is a fine powder again. Add the eggs; continue pulsing until the dough forms a ball.

2 Place the dough on a floured surface. Roll into a roughly 9 × 13-inch rectangle. Fold the dough in half (to make it easier to handle) and transfer it to the prepared pan. Unfold the dough and press it out evenly over the bottom of the pan. Use the back of a spoon to smooth it if necessary. With your fingertips, press the dough about an inch up the sides of the pan all the way around. Chill the dough while you prepare the filling.

3 Set a rack in the middle level of the oven and preheat to 350 degrees.

4 For the filling, combine the butter, brown sugar, honey, and salt in a medium saucepan and bring to a simmer, stirring occasionally with a metal spoon. Pour in the cream and allow the mixture to boil up once. Remove from the heat and stir in the pecans. Let cool for about 15 minutes, then pour over the

COOKIE DOUGH

2 cups all-purpose flour

⅓ cup granulated sugar

¼ teaspoon salt

1 teaspoon baking powder

8 tablespoons (1 stick) cold unsalted butter

2 large eggs

FILLING

12 tablespoons (1½ sticks) unsalted butter

¾ cup light brown sugar, firmly packed

3 tablespoons dark honey

Pinch salt

2 tablespoons heavy whipping cream

3 cups pecan halves or a mixture
   of halves and pieces

One 9 × 13 × 2-inch pan, buttered and lined with buttered parchment or foil

chilled crust. With the point of a spoon, spread the pecans evenly over the dough. Bake for about 25 to 30 minutes, or until the pastry is baked through and the filling is bubbling.

5 Place on a rack until completely cooled.

6 Transfer the pastry to a cutting board and slide a long knife or spatula under it to loosen the paper or foil, then pull it away. Trim the edges, use a ruler to mark, then cut the pastry into 2-inch squares.

7 For up to several days, store the squares in a tin or plastic container with a tight-fitting cover for longer storage.

MAKES ONE 9 × 13 × 2-INCH PAN,
ABOUT TWENTY-FOUR 2-INCH SQUARES

OSGOOD SQUARES

⁓ ◦ ⌣

THIS IS AN ADAPTATION OF A RECIPE for Osgood pie, recently shared by Bennie Sue Dupy, originally from Mart, Texas, near Waco. These rich raisin and pecan squares are like a combination of pecan pie and a rich butter raisin custard.

1 Set a rack in the middle level of the oven and preheat to 350 degrees.

2 For the dough, combine the flour, salt, baking powder, and sugar in the bowl of a food processor and pulse several times to mix. Cut the butter into about sixteen pieces and add to the work bowl. Continue pulsing until the mixture is a fine powder again. Add the eggs and pulse repeatedly. Continue pulsing until the dough forms a ball.

3 On a floured surface, roll the dough into a roughly 9 × 13-inch rectangle. Fold the dough in half for easier handling and transfer it to the prepared pan. Unfold the dough into the pan and press it evenly against the bottom of the pan. Use the back of a spoon to smooth the surface if necessary. Using your fingertips, press the dough about an inch up the sides of the pan. Chill the dough while preparing the filling.

4 For the filling, in the bowl of a standing electric mixer fitted with the paddle attachment, combine the butter and sugar. Beat several minutes on medium speed until light. Beat in the egg yolks, one at a time, and continue to beat until the mixture is smooth. Remove from the mixer and stir in the pecans and raisins.

COOKIE DOUGH

2 cups all-purpose flour

¼ teaspoon salt

1 teaspoon baking powder

⅓ cup sugar

8 tablespoons (1 stick) cold unsalted butter

2 large eggs

FILLING

8 tablespoons (1 stick) unsalted butter, softened

1 cup sugar

4 large eggs, separated

4 ounces (about 1 cup) coarsely chopped pecan pieces

1 cup dark raisins

Pinch salt

One 9 × 13 × 2-inch pan, buttered and lined with buttered parchment or foil

5   In a mixer fitted with the whisk attachment, in a clean, dry mixer bowl, whip the egg whites with the salt on medium speed until they are white, opaque, and beginning to hold their shape. Continue whipping the egg whites until they hold a soft peak. With a rubber spatula, fold the egg whites into the pecan and raisin mixture, until no streaks of white remain. Scrape the filling into the chilled pan and bake for about 35 to 40 minutes, or until the pastry is baked through and the filling is set and a deep gold.

6   Cool completely on a rack.

7   Place the pastry on a cutting board and slide a long knife or spatula under it to loosen the paper or foil, then pull it away. Trim the edges, use a ruler to mark, then cut the pastry into 2-inch squares.

8   For up to several days, store the squares in a tin or plastic container with a tight-fitting cover. Freeze for longer storage.

MAKES ONE 9 × 13 × 2-INCH PAN, ABOUT TWENTY-FOUR 2-INCH SQUARES

HUNGARIAN APRICOT BARS

THIS WONDERFUL RECIPE FOR A TRIPLE decker bar was shared by an old friend, Nancy Berzinec, who lives out in Pennsylvania Dutch country. I met Nancy in 1985 when she was the cooking school director at Sue and Lynn Hoffman's Kitchen Shoppe in Carlisle, Pennsylvania, where I taught. Nancy says that this is a favorite Christmas cookie in her family.

APRICOT FILLING
12 ounces dried apricots, coarsely chopped
1½ cups water to cover apricots
½ cup sugar

COOKIE BASE
1 cup all-purpose flour
Pinch salt
½ teaspoon baking powder
8 tablespoons (1 stick) unsalted butter, softened
½ cup sugar

1 teaspoon finely grated lemon zest
2 large egg yolks (you'll be using the whites for the topping)
Nut Meringue Topping
2 large egg whites
Pinch salt
½ cup sugar
4 ounces (about 1 cup) finely chopped blanched almonds
One 10 × 15 × 1-inch pan, buttered and lined with buttered parchment or foil

1 Combine the apricots, water, and sugar in a 1½ -quart saucepan. Bring to a simmer, cooking over medium heat, for about 25 to 30 minutes, or until the apricots are soft and somewhat thickened. Use a small whisk to break up the cooked apricots further. Pour the filling into a bowl to cool. (You may cover and refrigerate the filling for several days before proceeding.)

2 When you are ready to bake the bars, set a rack in the middle level of the oven and preheat to 350 degrees.

3 For the base, mix together the flour with the salt and baking powder. In a standing mixer fitted with the paddle attachment, beat the butter on medium speed. Beat in the sugar and lemon zest and continue beating a minute or two, until light. Beat in the egg yolks, then lower the speed and beat in the flour mixture.

4 Spread the dough over the bottom of the prepared pan. Use a small offset spatula or the back of a spoon to smooth it

5 Spread the cooled apricot filling evenly over the base and set aside while preparing the topping.

6 In the bowl of an electric mixer fitted with the whisk attachment, whip the egg whites and salt on medium speed. Continue whipping until the egg whites are very white and opaque

and beginning to hold their shape. Increase the speed to the maximum and add the sugar in a steady stream. Continue whipping until the egg whites hold a firm peak. Remove from the mixer and gently fold in the almonds.

7 Spread the almond meringue over the filling. Bake the pastry for about 45 minutes, or until it is baked through and the almond meringue is a deep golden color.

8 Place on a rack until completely cool

9 To cut the pastry, transfer it to a cutting board and slide a long knife or spatula under it to loosen the paper or foil, then pull it away. Trim the edges, use a ruler to mark, then cut the pastry into 2-inch squares. (Use a very sharp knife—the topping is sticky.)

10 For up to several days, store the squares in a tin or plastic container with a tight-fitting cover.

MAKES ONE 10 × 15 × 1-INCH PAN, ABOUT THIRTY-FIVE 2-INCH SQUARES

VIENNESE LINZER SQUARES

~⟋⟍~

THE COMBINATION OF RICH, spicy dough is excellent with the slight sharpness of the raspberry preserves. This is an adaptation of an authentic Viennese recipe so the result is a cakey-textured torte. Really, the only difference between this and a typical Linzertorte is the shape. I adapted this from the bible of Viennese baking, *Wiener Süssspeisen* ("*Viennese Sweets*") (Trauner Verlag, Linz, Austria, 1968) by Eduard Mayer.

1 Set a rack in the middle level of the oven and preheat to 350 degrees.

2 Combine the flour, ground hazelnuts, granulated sugar, spices, and baking powder in the work bowl of a food processor and pulse to mix. Add the butter and pulse again until the butter is finely incorporated, but stop before the mixture becomes pasty. Add the eggs and pulse until a soft dough forms.

3 Use an offset spatula to spread half of the dough evenly over the bottom of the pan.

4 Leaving a ½-inch margin all around spread the preserves on top of the dough.

5 Place half the remaining dough in a pastry bag fitted with a ½-inch plain tube (Ateco #806) and pipe five equidistant lines of the dough along the length of the pan. Use the remaining dough to pipe six or seven lines diagonally across the first ones.

6 Scatter and press the sliced almonds on top of the lattice. Bake the cake for about 40 minutes, or until it is well risen, well colored, and firm to the touch. Cool the cake in the pan on a rack for 10 minutes. Use the paper to

2½ cups all-purpose flour

6 ounces (about 1½ cups) whole
    unblanched hazelnuts, finely ground in
    the food processor

1 cup granulated sugar

1½ teaspoons ground cinnamon

½ teaspoon ground cloves

1½ teaspoons baking powder

16 tablespoons (2 sticks) cold unsalted
    butter, cut into 16 pieces

2 large eggs

1 cup seedless raspberry preserves or jam

1 ounce (about ¼ cup) sliced almonds

Confectioners' sugar for finishing

One 9 × 13 × 2-inch pan, buttered and lined
with buttered parchment or foil

transfer the cake from the pan to the rack and let it cool completely.

7   To cut the cake, place it on a cutting board and slide a long knife or spatula under it to loosen the paper or foil, then pull it away. Use a ruler to mark, then cut the cake into 2-inch squares. Dust lightly with confectioners' sugar immediately before serving.

8   For up to several days, store the squares between sheets of parchment or wax paper in a tin or plastic container with a tight-fitting cover. Freeze for longer storage.

MAKES ONE 9 × 13 × 2-INCH PAN, ABOUT TWENTY-FOUR 2-INCH SQUARES

COOKIES

DATE AND WALNUT BARS

THIS RECIPE CHUGGED IN THROUGH my fax machine one day from Tina Korting at the Western Reserve Cooking School in Hudson, Ohio. Tina wrote that this cookie was a holiday tradition in her family and that her grandmother wrapped the bars in colored cellophane to give as gifts. I've been to Hudson to teach dozens of times, first at my friend Zona Spray's cooking school, then later when Zona sold the school to Carol Ferguson.

1 Set a rack in the middle level of the oven and preheat to 350 degrees.

2 Measure the flour and baking powder into a mixing bowl and stir well to mix.

3 In a mixing bowl, whisk the eggs until whites and yolks are combined. Whisk in the sugar in a stream and continue whisking for a few seconds, so that the mixture is well blended. Fold in one third of the flour mixture, then half the butter. Add half the remaining flour and all the remaining butter. Finally fold in the last of the flour.

4 Fold in the dates and walnuts and scrape the batter into the prepared pan.

5 Bake about 30 to 35 minutes, until the cake is well risen and a light golden color and until a toothpick or a small knife inserted in the center emerges clean. Cool on a rack for 10 minutes, then remove the pan from the rack. Use the paper to transfer the cake to the rack to cool completely.

1 cup all-purpose flour

1 teaspoon baking powder

2 large eggs

1½ cups sugar

16 tablespoons (2 sticks) unsalted butter, melted and cooled

1 cup chopped pitted dates

1 cup coarsely chopped walnut pieces

One 9 × 13 × 2-inch pan, buttered and lined with buttered parchment or foil

6 To cut the bars, use the paper to place the cake on a cutting board and slide a long knife or spatula under it to loosen the paper or foil and then pull it away. Use a ruler to mark, then cut the cake into 2-inch squares.

7 For up to several days, store the squares between sheets of parchment or wax paper in a tin or plastic container with a tight-fitting cover. Freeze for longer storage.

MAKES ONE 9 × 13 × 2-INCH PAN, ABOUT TWENTY-FOUR 2-INCH SQUARE

BROWNIES

LOTS OF STORIES EXIST TRYING TO EXPLAIN THE ORIGIN of the brownie. One even states that they were invented in upstate New York by a college student whose nickname was Brownie. Whatever their origin, they are certainly the most popular of all bar cookies. Although for my other books I've written numerous recipes for brownies, I still have a few unusual ones for this volume.

Though many bar cookies are just thinner versions of cakes, brownies are in a special category. They are richer and chewier than any cake would ever be. I don't think I would like a wedge of a round brownie covered with a rich frosting and eaten with a fork like a cake—brownies are casual and meant to be eaten out of hand. And besides, they are easier to make than almost any cake.

PECAN BROWNIES

THESE ARE A VARIATION OF ONE OF MY favorite recipes: Supernatural Brownies in my chocolate book. I could eat a pan of these every week, but so that I don't, mostly I make them to bring to parties or to put in Christmas cookie baskets.

16 tablespoons (2 sticks) unsalted butter

8 ounces bittersweet chocolate, cut into ¼-inch pieces

4 large eggs

1 cup dark brown sugar, firmly packed

1 cup granulated sugar

2 teaspoons vanilla extract

½ teaspoon salt

1 cup all-purpose flour

10 ounces (about 2½ cups) coarsely chopped pecan pieces

One 9 × 13 × 2-inch pan, buttered and lined with buttered parchment or foil

1 Set a rack in the middle level of the oven and preheat to 350 degrees.

2 Melt the butter in a saucepan over medium heat. Off the heat add the chocolate. Let stand 2 minutes, then whisk smooth. If all the chocolate has not melted, return the pan to very low heat and stir constantly until the chocolate melts.

3 In a large bowl, use a rubber spatula to stir one egg into the brown sugar. Make sure any lumps in the sugar are dissolved. Add the remaining eggs, one at a time, stirring each in with the rubber spatula in the same way. Stir in the granulated sugar, then the vanilla and salt. Stir in the chocolate mixture.

4 Finally, fold in the flour, then 2 cups of the pecans.

5 Scrape the batter into the prepared pan and smooth the top with an offset spatula. Scatter the remaining chopped pecans over the top of the batter and with your fingertips gently press them in.

6 Bake for about 30 to 35 minutes, or until a toothpick or a small knife inserted into the center emerges clean. Cool completely on a rack.

7 Wrap and refrigerate the pan so that the cake solidifies completely—at least 4 hours; overnight is best. This also makes the cake easier to cut.

8 Transfer the whole cake to a cutting board and slide a long knife or spatula under it to loosen the paper or foil, then pull it away. Use a ruler to mark, then cut the cake into 2-inch squares.

9 For up to several days, store the brownies between sheets of parchment or wax paper in a tin or plastic container with a tight-fitting cover. Freeze for longer storage. If you plan to keep the brownies for any length of time, it is better to wrap them individually.

MAKES ONE 9 × 13 × 2-INCH PAN,
OR ABOUT TWENTY-FOUR 2-INCH SQUARES

WEST TENTH STREET BROWNIES

~೧ ೧~

THE NAME OF THIS RECIPE IS THE result of my finding it in Greenwich Village a few blocks from where I live. As I walked east on Tenth Street, I saw a yellowed index card lying on the sidewalk. When I picked it up I saw written in a spidery hand in blue fountain pen ink a recipe for "The Best Brownie's [sic] in the World." Well, I put it aside in a miscellaneous recipe file, and a few months later tried it. They turned out to be sensational and certainly a contender for the title. If you like very sweet brownies, these will be your favorites

1 Set a rack in the middle level of the oven and preheat to 350 degrees.

2 In a medium saucepan, melt the butter over medium heat. Off the heat add the chocolate. Let stand 2 minutes, then whisk until smooth. If all the chocolate has not melted, return the pan to low heat and stir constantly until the chocolate melts.

3 In a large bowl, whisk the eggs with the salt and vanilla, just until mixed. Whisk in the sugar in a stream, then whisk in the chocolate and butter mixture. Switch to a rubber spatula and fold in the flour.

4 Set the batter aside until it has cooled to room temperature (test it with your fingertip). Fold in the chocolate chips and nuts.

5 Scrape the batter into the prepared pan and smooth the top with an offset spatula.

16 tablespoons (2 sticks) unsalted butter

3 ounces unsweetened chocolate,
    cut into ¼-inch pieces

4 large eggs

½ teaspoon salt

1 teaspoon vanilla extract

2 cups sugar

1 cup all-purpose flour

1 cup (a 6-ounce bag) semisweet chocolate
    chips

4 ounces (about 1 cup) coarsely chopped
    pecan or walnut pieces

One 9 × 13 × 2-inch pan, buttered and lined with buttered parchment or foil

6 Bake the cake for about 30 to 35 minutes, or until a toothpick or a small knife inserted in the center emerges clean. Cool completely on a rack.

7 Wrap and refrigerate the pan so that the cake solidifies—at least 4 hours; overnight is best. This also makes the cake easier to cut.

8 Transfer the whole cake to a cutting board and slide a long knife or spatula under it to loosen the paper or foil, then pull it away. Use a ruler to mark, then cut the cake into 2-inch squares.

9 For up to several days, store the brownies between sheets of parchment or wax paper in a tin or plastic container with a tight-fitting cover. Freeze for longer storage. If you plan to keep the brownies for any length of time, it is better to wrap them individually in cellophane.

MAKES ONE 9 × 13 × 2-INCH PAN, ABOUT TWENTY-FOUR 2-INCH BROWNIES

DROP COOKIES

I'VE INCLUDED TWO TYPES of drop cookies here. The first are the simplest—you merely drop the batter from a spoon onto a pan and the cookies are ready as soon as they are baked.

Some drop cookies, however, need to be shaped after they are baked—these are the whole family of tuile- (French curved roofing tile) type cookies. They are really just drop cookies, and in most cases you could leave them flat as they emerge from the oven, but traditionally the warm cookies are draped over a rolling pin or some other cylindrical form to make them curve.

HINTS FOR DROP COOKIES

1 Don't overmix the dough or batter, especially if the recipe begins by mixing butter and sugar. Overmixing drop cookie batters can overaerate them. If that happens the cookies puff up too much in the oven then fall miserably into flat, greasy pancakes. Your objective is gently risen, light cookies.

2 Make sure you drop only as much dough or batter as the recipe tells you. Otherwise your cookies could become gigantic. Space the cookies far enough apart on the baking sheets so there is room for them to spread. Most drop cookies spread quite a bit while they are baking.

3 If you drop too much batter on the pan too close together, all the cookies may run together into one vast rectangular cookie—maybe that's how some bar cookies were invented!

4 Review the rules for baking in "Baking Cookies" (page 10)—most drop cookies are delicate and need to be handled carefully and the pans moved around often for even baking.

5 Drop cookies will keep at room temperature for up to a week or so. Freeze for longer storage. It is not recommended to freeze delicate drop cookies such as tuiles or they will soften.

PENNSYLVANIA DUTCH
SOFT MOLASSES COOKIES

ANOTHER OLD-FASHIONED NINETEENTH-century recipe, straight from the middle of Pennsylvania Dutch country, Carlisle, Pennsylvania. It comes from Esther Hoffman, mother of my friend Lynn Hoffman.

1 Set the racks in the upper and lower thirds of the oven and preheat to 350 degrees.

2 In a large bowl, combine the flour, baking soda, salt, and spices; stir well to mix.

3 In the bowl of a standing electric mixer fitted with the paddle attachment, beat together the butter and the sugar. Beat in the egg, then continue to beat until smooth. Beat in the molasses.

4 Lower the speed and beat in half the flour mixture, then all the hot water. Scrape the bowl and beater well, then beat in the remaining flour mixture. Remove the bowl from the mixer and give the dough a final mixing with a large rubber spatula.

5 Drop tablespoons of the dough 3 or 4 inches apart on the prepared pans.

6 Bake the cookies for 12 to 15 minutes, or until they rise and become firm.

7 Slide the papers off the pans onto racks.

3 cups all-purpose flour

1 teaspoon baking soda

½ teaspoon salt

½ teaspoon ground cinnamon

½ teaspoon ground ginger

8 tablespoons (1 stick) unsalted butter, softened

½ cup sugar

1 egg

¾ cup molasses

⅓ cup hot water

2 or 3 cookie sheets or jelly roll pans covered with parchment or foil

8 After the cookies have cooled, detach them from the paper and store them between sheets of parchment or wax paper in a tin or plastic container with a tight-fitting cover.

MAKES ABOUT 40 COOKIES

ANZAC BISCUITS

ANZAC IS AN ACRONYM FOR AUSTRALIA and New Zealand Army Corps and these cookies (or, as the British call them, "biscuits") were made during the Second World War by everyone Down Under to send to soldiers at the front. My friend Melbourne food stylist Maureen McKeon, who gave me the recipe, wrote that she remembers helping her Irish grandmother pack large tins of the cookies.

1 Set the racks in the upper and lower thirds of the oven and preheat to 325 degrees.

2 In a large bowl, combine the oatmeal, coconut, and flour; stir well to mix.

3 In a medium saucepan over low heat, melt the butter. Still over low heat, stir in the sugar and the honey. Cook until the mixture is beginning to simmer, stirring occasionally until the sugar melts.

4 Combine the water and baking soda in a little bowl, then off the heat stir into the simmered mixture—be careful, it will bubble up. Just keep on stirring and the foam will abate.

5 Stir the warm liquid into the oatmeal and flour mixture to make an evenly moistened batter.

6 Drop teaspoonfuls of the batter 2 or 3 inches apart on the prepared pans.

7 Bake the cookies for 12 to 15 minutes, or until they spread and color evenly.

1 cup rolled oats (regular oatmeal)

I cup firmly packed shredded sweetened coconut

1 cup all-purpose flour

8 tablespoons (1 stick) unsalted butter

1 cup sugar

2 tablespoons honey or Lyle's Golden Syrup

2 tablespoons hot water

1½ teaspoons baking soda

2 or 3 cookie sheets or jelly roll pans covered with parchment or foil

8 Slide the papers off the pans onto racks.

9 After the cookies have cooled, detach them from the paper and store them between sheets of parchment or wax paper in a tin or plastic container with a tight-fitting cover.

MAKES ABOUT 45 COOKIES

PERFECT COOKIES, CAKES AND CHOCOLATE

CHEWY OATMEAL
RAISIN COOKIES

I KNEW I COULD COUNT ON MY FRIEND Sheri Portwood, Dallas caterer and all-around great baker, for a chewy, sweet, homey oatmeal cookie recipe. This recipe fulfills all the requirements you want in such a cookie—and is chock-full of raisins, nuts, and chocolate chips. If you want plainer cookies, make them just with raisins—or with any combination of the raisins, nuts, and chips. Just make sure to add a total of 3½ cups of whichever ingredient.

Set the racks in the upper and lower thirds of the oven and preheat to 350 degrees.

2 In a large bowl, combine the flour, baking powder, salt, and oatmeal; stir well to mix.

3 In the bowl of a standing electric mixer fitted with the paddle attachment, beat together the butter, granulated sugar, and brown sugar until well mixed, about a minute. Beat in the eggs, one at a time, beating smooth after each addition, then beat in the vanilla.

4 Lower the mixer speed and beat in the flour and oatmeal mixture, then add the raisins, nuts, and chips.

5 Drop tablespoons of the batter about 3 to 4 inches apart on the prepared pans. Flatten the mounds with the back of a fork.

6 Bake the cookies for 15 to 20 minutes, or until they spread and color evenly and become firm.

7 Slide the papers off the pans onto racks.

2 cups all-purpose flour

1 teaspoon baking powder

1 teaspoon salt

2 cups rolled oats (regular oatmeal)

16 tablespoons (2 sticks) unsalted butter, softened

1 cup granulated sugar

1 cup firmly packed dark brown sugar

2 large eggs

1 teaspoon vanilla extract

1½ cups dark raisins

4 ounces (about 1 cup) coarsely chopped walnut or pecan pieces

1 cup (one 6-ounce bag) semisweet chocolate chips

3 or 4 cookie sheets or jelly roll pans covered with parchment or foil

8 After the cookies have cooled, detach them from the paper and store them between sheets of parchment or wax paper in a tin or plastic container with a tight-fitting cover.

MAKES ABOUT 60 COOKIES

O
K
I
E
S

AUNT IDA'S
POPPY SEED COOKIES

~ ⌐ ⌐

THE AUNT IN THIS CASE IS NOT MINE. She belongs to those relentless cookbook, recipe, and kitchenware collectors, Marilynn and Sheila Brass of Cambridge, Massachusetts. My friend Sandy Leonard makes these and adds the grated zest of an orange. The Brass sisters prefer a pure old-fashioned Jewish cookie with lots of old-country poppy seed flavor without the orange zest—you can decide for yourself. Thanks also to my friend, cookbook dealer Bonnie Slotnick, who shared an almost identical recipe.

1 Set the racks in the upper and lower thirds of the oven and preheat to 325 degrees.

2 In a bowl, combine the flour, baking powder, and salt; stir well to mix. Stir in the poppy seeds.

3 In a large mixing bowl, whisk the eggs to break them up. Whisk in the sugar, then the oil and the vanilla extract. Use a rubber spatula to fold the dry ingredients in thoroughly.

4 Drop teaspoonfuls of the dough 2 or 3 inches apart on the prepared pans. Before you bake the cookies, flatten them slightly with the back of a fork or a small spatula.

5 Bake the cookies for 12 to 15 minutes, or until they spread, become firm, and are lightly colored around the edges.

6 Slide the papers off the pans onto racks.

3 cups all-purpose flour
2 teaspoons baking powder
Pinch salt
½ cup poppy seeds
3 large eggs
1 cup sugar
1 cup peanut or other mild oil
1 teaspoon vanilla extract

2 or 3 cookie sheets or jelly roll pans covered with parchment or foil

7 After the cookies have cooled, detach them from the paper and store them between sheets of parchment or wax paper in a tin or plastic container with a tight-fitting cover.

MAKES ABOUT 60 COOKIES

*Aunt Ida's Poppy Seed
Cookie (LEFT) and
Pecan Wafer, page 43*

PENNSYLVANIA DUTCH SOFT
SUGAR COOKIES

THIS DELICIOUS, HOMEY RECIPE COMES from veteran baker and recipe collector Nancy Berzinec. Though buttermilk works well in the recipe, in the past these were probably a vehicle for using up milk that had soured.

1 Set the racks in the upper and lower thirds of the oven and preheat to 375 degrees.

2 In a bowl, combine the flour, baking powder, baking soda, and salt; stir well to mix.

3 In the bowl of a standing electric mixer fitted with the paddle attachment, beat together the butter and the sugar until combined, then beat in the vanilla. Add the eggs, one at a time, beating smooth after each addition. Lower the speed and beat in a third of the flour mixture, then half the buttermilk, and another third of the flour mixture. Scrape the bowl and beater often. Beat in the remaining buttermilk, then the remaining flour mixture.

4 Scrape the bowl and beater, then remove the bowl from the mixer, and give the dough one final mixing with a large rubber spatula.

5 Drop tablespoons of the dough 3 or 4 inches apart onto the prepared pans.

6 Bake the cookies for about 15 minutes, or until they spread and rise—they should be lightly golden.

4 cups all-purpose flour

2 teaspoons baking powder

1 teaspoon baking soda

Pinch salt

16 tablespoons (2 sticks) unsalted butter, softened

2 cups sugar

3 teaspoons vanilla extract

3 large eggs

1 cup buttermilk or sour milk (see Note)

3 or 4 cookie sheets or jelly roll pans covered with parchment or foil

7 Slide the papers off the pans onto racks.

8 After the cookies have cooled, detach them from the paper and store them between layers of parchment or wax paper in a tin or plastic container with a tight-fitting cover.

NOTE: To make a cup of fresh milk sour add a teaspoon of some acidic liquid such as vinegar or lemon juice.

MAKES ABOUT 60 COOKIES

PECAN WAFERS

THESE ARE SUBLIME AS IS OR COUPLED around some melted milk chocolate. Either way, they are crisp, delicious, and easy to prepare.

1 Set the racks in the upper and lower thirds of the oven and preheat to 375 degrees.

2 In the bowl of a standing electric mixer fitted with the paddle attachment, beat together the butter, brown sugar, and granulated sugar until combined, then beat in the egg and vanilla. Beat until smooth without overbeating.

3 Remove the bowl from the mixer and, with a large rubber spatula, stir in the flour and pecans.

4 Roll rounded teaspoonfuls of the dough into balls, then place them 2 or 3 inches apart on the prepared pans, and press them slightly to flatten.

5 Bake the cookies for 12 to 15 minutes, or until they have spread and are deep gold around the edges but still fairly pale on top.

6 Slide the papers off the pans onto racks.

7 After the cookies have cooled, detach them from the paper and store them between sheets of parchment or wax paper in a tin or plastic container with a tight-fitting cover.

8 tablespoons (1 stick) unsalted butter, softened

1 cup firmly packed light brown sugar

½ cup granulated sugar

1 large egg

1 teaspoon vanilla extract

1½ cups all-purpose flour

4 ounces (about 1 cup) pecan pieces, finely chopped but not ground

2 or 3 cookie sheets or jelly roll pans lined with parchment or foil

VARIATION

For a change, substitute walnuts or macadamia nuts for the pecans.

MAKES ABOUT 50 COOKIES,
HALF THAT MANY IF SANDWICHED

LOADED WITH CHIPS CHOCOLATE CHIP COOKIES

～◦∂ ⌒ ∂◦～

I USED TO MAKE THESE SO OFTEN THAT now, when I taste chocolate chip cookies without double the amount of chips to the amount of batter, I'm disappointed. For a standard chocolate chip cookie, halve the weight of the chips.

1 Set the racks in the upper and lower thirds of the oven and preheat to 375 degrees.

2 In a bowl, combine the flour, salt, and baking soda; stir well to mix.

3 In the bowl of a standing electric mixer fitted with the paddle attachment, beat together the butter, brown sugar, and granulated sugar until combined, then beat in the egg and vanilla, beating until smooth. Don't overbeat.

4 Remove the bowl from the mixer and with a large rubber spatula stir in the flour mixture. Stir in the chips and the optional nuts.

5 Drop teaspoonfuls of the dough 2 or 3 inches apart on the prepared pans.

6 Bake the cookies for 12 to 15 minutes, or until they are deep gold and firm.

7 Slide the papers off the pans onto racks.

8 After the cookies have cooled, detach them from the paper and store them between sheets of parchment or wax paper in a tin or plastic container with a tight-fitting cover.

1¼ cups all-purpose flour

½ teaspoon salt

½ teaspoon baking soda

8 tablespoons (1 stick) unsalted butter, softened

½ cup firmly packed light brown sugar

¼ cup granulated sugar

1 large egg

1 teaspoon vanilla extract

2 cups (one 12-ounce bag) semisweet chocolate chips

3 ounces (about ¾ cup) coarsely chopped walnut or pecan pieces, optional

2 or 3 cookie sheets or jelly roll pans covered with parchment or foil

VARIATION

CHOCOLATE CHUNK COOKIES: Instead of chocolate chips, use 12 ounces of dark, milk, or white chocolate, cut into ¼-inch pieces. Or try combining two kinds of chips or chunks in the same batch of cookies.

MAKES ABOUT 35 COOKIES

EASY COCONUT DROPS

~୨ ୨ ୧~

I CAN NEVER HAVE ENOUGH COCONUT, whether it's in cakes, cookies, or custards. This easy cookie with lots of coconut flavor and texture is my idea of perfection.

1   Set the racks in the upper and lower thirds of the oven and preheat to 375 degrees.

2   In the work bowl of a food processor fitted with the steel blade, place the coconut and pulse for 1-second intervals about a dozen times. Your object is to make the coconut smaller but not to grind it too fine.

3   In a bowl, mix the flour with the baking powder and salt.

4   Combine the butter and sugar in the bowl of an electric mixer fitted with the paddle. Beat on medium speed for about half a minute, then beat in the vanilla, then the egg. Beat until smooth again.

5   Lower the speed and beat in the flour mixture, then the coconut.

6   Remove the bowl from the mixer and complete the mixing with a large rubber spatula.

7   Drop teaspoonfuls of the batter on the prepared pans about 2 or 3 inches apart. Bake the cookies about 12 to 15 minutes, until they have spread and are golden around the edges.

8   Slide the papers from the pans onto racks.

One 7-ounce bag sweetened shredded coconut

1 cup all-purpose flour

1 teaspoon baking powder

¼ teaspoon salt

8 tablespoons (1 stick) unsalted butter, softened

¾ cup sugar

1 teaspoon vanilla extract

1 large egg

2 cookie sheets or jelly roll pans lined with parchment or foil

9   After the cookies have cooled, detach them from the paper and store them between sheets of parchment or wax paper in a tin or plastic container with a tight-fitting cover.

MAKES ABOUT 40 COOKIES

TUILES

I NEVER UNDERSTOOD WHY THESE CURVED COOKIES WERE CALLED TILES, because all the floor and wall tiles I had ever seen were square or rectangular and flat. It wasn't until I was working at the Sporting Club in Monte Carlo that I asked my chef, Alexandre Frolla, how the cookies got their name. My question was greeted with peals of laughter from all the Frenchmen who heard it. It seems that the French word tuile specifically means a curved clay roofing tile—very common on the Riviera, had I only looked up. A wall or floor tile would be called a *carreau*, or "square." I'm sure everyone was thinking: Americans!

Tuiles are among the most elegant and delicate of all cookies. A very thin drop cookie, a warm tuile is usually draped over a rolling pin or other cylindrical form to create the characteristic curve. This adds a lot of elegance to their appearance, but does nothing to alter the taste. So if you have to save time, leave them flat.

HINTS FOR PERFECT TUILES

1 Don't beat the batter a lot; aeration only makes the batter puff up. Tuile batters should just be stirred together.

2 When you are spooning the batter out onto the baking sheet, keep stirring up the batter as you spoon it out so the nuts stay in suspension.

3 Watch the cookies closely as they are baking—these are so thin that a minute can make the difference between perfect and burned.

4 Bake only one pan of tuiles at a time. You'll need time to curve the cookies and if you bake two pans simultaneously, one will either be burning or cooling to the point that the cookies will be too stiff to bend.

5 If you want to make lots of tuiles, enlist the help of a second person so that one can place the batter on the pan and the other can watch the oven. Both should do the curving: One person can remove the tuiles from the pans while the other places them on and removes them from the curved forms.

ALMOND LACE COOKIES

⟋⟍⟋⟍

THIS EXQUISITELY DELICATE AND FRAGILE cookie is well worth the little trouble it takes to make. Usually with drop cookies, you can do other things while the cookies are baking, but with these, you must stand guard at the oven—a minute too long and they will burn. Also, if you wish to curve them, you have to time them carefully. Because they are so delicate they must be removed from the pan immediately after they are baked, so I recommend baking only one pan at a time.

By the way, it's no mistake that there is no flavoring in this recipe—the flavor comes from the delicate combination of the caramelized sugar blended with toasted almonds and butter.

Many thanks again to Jayne Sutton for another delicious recipe from her endless collection.

1 Set a rack in the middle level of the oven and preheat to 375 degrees.

2 Place the butter in a small saucepan and melt it over low heat.

3 Remove the pan from the heat, and stir in the sugar, cream, almonds, and flour. Return the pan to low heat and stir constantly with a wooden spoon, until the mixture thickens and bubbles. Remove the pan from the heat.

4 Drop the batter by small teaspoonfuls onto the prepared pans, leaving at least 3 inches between each cookie. Prepare all your pans even though you are only going to bake one at a time.

5 Have a thin-bladed spatula, pancake turner, or thin, flexible plastic scraper ready to remove the cookies from the pan, and several rolling pins or other forms (see page 8) to curve the cookies over, if you intend to do that. If you want the cookies flat, have ready a couple of pans covered with foil to cool the baked cookies—they are much too fragile to put on a rack. Finally, have another jelly roll

8 tablespoons (1 stick) butter

½ cup sugar

2 tablespoons cream

3 ounces (about ¾ cup) finely ground blanched almonds

¼ cup flour

2 or 3 cookie sheets or jelly roll pans, well buttered or covered with foil

pan to receive the cooled, curved cookies. If you intend to leave the cookies flat, tear off some sheets of wax paper or foil to put between the layers of cookies on the pan.

6 Place a single pan in the oven and bake the cookies for 6 to 8 minutes, until they come to a simmer, spread and become thin, and take on a deep golden color.

7 Remove the pan from the oven and immediately replace it with another. Leave the cookies you just removed for a few seconds to firm up, then quickly slide the spatula under each one and detach it. Either place over the rolling pin to curve or put on one of the

cooling pans. Move on to the next cookie immediately. If the cookies become too cold and hard to remove from the pan without shattering them, replace the pan in the oven to soften the cookies again.

8   Continue until all the cookies are baked. To reuse the pans, wipe them well, or line with a fresh sheet of foil. Just make sure the pans are cool when you spoon the batter onto them.

9   Store the flat cookies between sheets of parchment or wax paper in a tin or plastic container with a tight-fitting cover. I don't recommend trying to store curved tuiles more than a few hours before serving—they are so fragile they would turn into a tin of very delicious crumbs.

REFRIGERATOR COOKIES

WHEN I WAS A CHILD IN THE FIFTIES, these cookies were still known as icebox cookies—and there were even a few actual iceboxes still in use. This type of cookie is made from a dough shaped into a cylinder or rectangle—or other compact form—then chilled. Right before baking, the dough is cut into thick or thin slices and placed on the pans. These cookies are the original convenience foods. You can mix up the dough today and slice and bake cookies tomorrow—or even next week or next month if you freeze the dough.

HINTS FOR REFRIGERATOR COOKIES

1 Make the shaped log of dough uniform so the cookies will be all the same size when they are sliced. Use a ruler to verify the size of the log given in the recipes.

2 Make sure the shaped dough is thoroughly chilled before attempting to cut it. Otherwise the dough will compress and lose its shape and the resulting cookies will not look neat.

3 Slice the cookies to the thickness specified in the recipe. If necessary, use a ruler and mark the piece of dough before you cut.

4 As you slice, rotate or turn the piece of dough so you aren't starting to cut at the same place every time—this is to keep the dough from getting squashed down and distorted.

5 If the dough softens while you are cutting it, replace it in the refrigerator until it becomes firm again before continuing.

Each individual recipe has specific instructions for forming the dough. What follows is a general procedure for most recipes.

1   Scrape the dough from the mixer bowl onto a lightly floured work surface and shape and squeeze into a rough cylinder, about 10 inches long and 2 inches in diameter (individual recipes may specify different lengths or more than one roll).

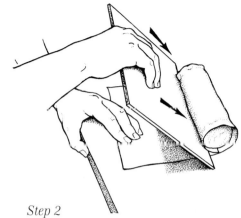

2   Wrap a piece of parchment or wax paper around the dough and use the side of a cookie sheet or a piece of stiff cardboard to press the paper tight around it, as in the illustration. Chill the dough until firm.

Step 2

3   If you want square or rectangular cookies, press the dough into a plastic or foil-lined 8- or 9-inch square pan, then chill. Unmold the dough, cut it into 1½- to 2-inch wide lengths—depending on the depth of the dough in the pan—and slice across the rectangular bars to make individual cookies.

4   Another shape variation that makes good-looking refrigerator cookies is a finger (as in a lady finger). Form the dough into cylinders, and press down on the length of the cylinder so that when viewed from one of the narrow ends the dough appears to be a narrow oval. Chill, and cut finger-shaped cookies.

FRENCH VANILLA SABLÉS

~⌒◡⌒~

THESE ARE EASY-TO-MAKE AND elegant cookies. *Sablé* means "sandy" in French and refers to the crumbly texture of this cookie. They may be varied infinitely by adding solid elements, such as nuts, chocolate chips, or diced dried or candied fruit to the dough. Or you could roll the formed dough in cinnamon sugar or chopped nuts to encrust the outside—use your imagination.

1 In the bowl of a standing electric mixer fitted with the paddle attachment, beat the butter and sugar on medium speed until well mixed, light colored, and fluffy, about 4 or 5 minutes, then beat in the vanilla and egg yolk. Continue beating until very smooth, about 2 more minutes.

2 Scrape the bowl and beater well and beat in the flour.

3 Scrape the dough from the mixer bowl onto a lightly floured work surface and shape and squeeze it into a rough cylinder, about 10 inches long and 2 inches in diameter.

12 tablespoons (1½ sticks) unsalted butter, softened

⅓ cup sugar

1 teaspoon vanilla extract

1 egg yolk

1½ cups all-purpose flour

2 cookie sheets or jelly roll pans lined with parchment or foil

4 Roll a piece of parchment or wax paper around the dough. Tighten the paper around by pressing in with the side of a cookie sheet or a piece of stiff cardboard, as in the illustration on page 5. Chill the dough until firm. Or, at this stage, it can be double-wrapped in plastic, frozen, and kept for up to several weeks.

5   When you are ready to bake the cookies, set the racks in the upper and lower thirds of the oven and preheat to 350 degrees. Slice the cookies ¼ inch thick, rotating the roll of dough often so it won't become squashed and misshapen from the weight of the knife.

6   Arrange the cookies on the prepared pans with about an inch between them in all directions. Bake for about 12 to 15 minutes, until the cookies have puffed somewhat and become dull and are firm to the touch. Slide the papers from the pans onto racks.

7   After the cookies have cooled, store them between sheets of parchment or wax paper in a tin or plastic container with a tight-fitting cover.

MAKES ABOUT 40 COOKIES

53

PALM BEACH LEMON COOKIES

THIS ZINGY COOKIE COMES FROM MY old friend, veteran cooking teacher and renowned hostess Myrtle Singer, of Palm Beach, Florida.

1   In a bowl, combine the flour, baking powder, baking soda, and salt; stir well to mix.

2   In the bowl of a standing electric mixer fitted with the paddle attachment, beat the butter and sugar together on medium speed until well mixed, about a minute, then beat in the lemon zest.

3   Beat in the egg yolks, one at a time, beating until smooth after each addition. Lower the mixer speed and beat in half the flour mixture, then all the lemon juice. Scrape the bowl and beater well; beat in the remaining flour mixture.

4   Scrape the dough onto a lightly floured work surface and shape and squeeze it into two rough cylinders, each about 8 inches long and 2 inches in diameter.

5   Roll a piece of parchment or wax paper around each piece of dough and tighten the paper by pressing it in with the side of a cookie sheet or a piece of stiff cardboard, as in the illustration on page 51. Chill the dough until firm. Or, at this stage, it can be double-wrapped in plastic, frozen, and kept for up to several weeks.

3 cups all-purpose flour

½ teaspoon baking powder

½ teaspoon baking soda

¼ teaspoon salt

10 tablespoons (1¼ sticks) unsalted butter, softened

1 cup sugar, plus more for sprinkling the cookies before baking

Finely grated zest of 1 large lemon

3 large eggs, separated

4 tablespoons strained lemon juice

3 or 4 cookie sheets or jelly roll pans lined with parchment or foil (you will need to cool and reuse them)

6   When you are ready to bake the cookies, set the racks in the upper and lower thirds of the oven and preheat to 350 degrees.

7 In a small bowl, beat the egg whites with a fork, just until mixed. Cut each log into approximately 48 cookies (six slices per inch). Make sure to rotate the roll of dough often so it doesn't become squashed from the weight of the knife.

8 Arrange the cookies on the prepared pans about an inch apart in all directions. Brush the surface of each cookie with the egg white, then sprinkle each cookie with a pinch of sugar. Bake the cookies for about 10 to 12 minutes, until they have spread slightly and are a very pale golden color. Slide the papers from the pans onto racks.

9 After the cookies have cooled, store them between sheets of parchment or wax paper in a tin or plastic container with a tight-fitting cover.

MAKES ABOUT 100 SMALL THIN COOKIES

TENNESSEE ICEBOX COOKIES

WHEN I WAS ON TOUR PROMOTING MY book *Chocolate*, I made a stop in Nashville and was invited to be on the radio with Mindy Merrell, whom I've known for many years in her capacity as publicist for the Jack Daniel's distillery. Mindy's other guest that day was Tammy Algood from the University of Tennessee's Agricultural Extension Service and Tammy had brought a basket of treats to the studio. One of them was this cookie, which was so good I immediately begged for the recipe. It comes from her grandmother Betsey McPherson and the cookies are heavenly.

1 In a bowl, combine the flour, baking soda, and salt; stir well to mix.

2 In the bowl of a standing electric mixer fitted with the paddle attachment, beat the butter and brown sugar together on medium speed until well mixed, about a minute, then beat in the vanilla.

3 Beat in the eggs, one at a time, beating smooth after each addition. Scrape the bowl and beater well and beat in the flour mixture followed immediately by the almonds.

4 Scrape the dough onto a lightly floured work surface and shape and squeeze it into two rough cylinders, each about 10 inches long and 2 inches in diameter.

5 Roll a piece of parchment or wax paper around each piece of dough and tighten by pressing it in with the side of a cookie sheet or a piece of stiff cardboard, as in the illustration on page 51. Chill the dough until firm. Or, at this stage, it can be double-wrapped in plastic, frozen, and kept for up to several weeks.

3 cups all-purpose flour

1 teaspoon baking soda

¼ teaspoon salt

16 tablespoons (2 sticks) unsalted butter, softened

2½ cups firmly packed light brown sugar

1 tablespoon vanilla extract

2 large eggs

4 ounces (about 1 cup) coarsely chopped slivered almonds

3 or 4 cookie sheets or jelly roll pans lined with parchment or foil (you will need to cool and reuse them)

6 When you are ready to bake the cookies, set the racks in the upper and lower thirds of the oven and preheat to 350 degrees. Slice the cookies ¼ inch thick, rotating the roll of dough often as you slice so it doesn't become squashed from the weight of the knife.

7 Arrange the cookies on the prepared pans about an inch apart in all directions and bake them for about 12 to 15 minutes, until they have puffed somewhat and have become dull and are firm to the touch. Slide the papers from the pans onto racks.

8 After the cookies have cooled, store them between sheets of parchment or wax paper in a tin or plastic container with a tight-fitting cover.

MAKES ABOUT 80 COOKIES

PISTACHIO THINS

Any recipe is always dressed up by the aromatic flavor and striking appearance of pistachios. Here, the nuts are in a meltingly tender dough and create a delicious cookie. Make sure when you bake the cookies to leave them pale, or the color of the pistachios will be obscured.

1 In a bowl, combine the flour, cornstarch, and salt; stir well to mix.

2 In the bowl of a standing electric mixer fitted with the paddle attachment, beat together the butter and confectioners' sugar at medium speed until well mixed, about a minute.

3 Beat in the egg yolk and lemon zest until they are well incorporated and the mixture is smooth. Scrape the bowl and beater well and beat in the flour mixture. Finally, beat in 1 cup of the chopped pistachios.

4 Scrape the dough onto a lightly floured work surface and shape and squeeze it into a rough cylinder, about 10 inches long and 2 inches in diameter.

5 Roll a piece of parchment or wax paper around the dough and tighten it by pressing in with the side of a cookie sheet or a piece of stiff cardboard, as in the illustration on page 51. Quickly unwrap the dough and roll it out onto the work surface. Paint the dough all around with the reserved egg white and roll it in the remaining ½ cup pistachios. The outside of the dough should be completely

1¼ cups all-purpose flour

½ cup cornstarch

¼ teaspoon salt

12 tablespoons (1½ sticks) unsalted butter, softened

⅔ cup confectioners' sugar

1 large egg, separated

1 teaspoon finely grated lemon zest

6 ounces (about 1½ cups) finely chopped unsalted pistachios, divided

2 or 3 cookie sheets or jelly roll pans lined with parchment or foil

covered. Rewrap the dough in parchment or wax paper and repeat the tightening if the shape has become distorted. Chill the dough until firm. Or, at this stage, it can be double-wrapped in plastic, frozen, and kept for up to several weeks.

6 When you are ready to bake the cookies, set the racks in the upper and lower thirds of the oven and preheat to 350 degrees. Slice the cookies ¼ inch thick, rotating the roll often so it doesn't become squashed from the weight of the knife.

7 Arrange the cookies on the prepared pans about an inch apart in all directions and bake them for about 10 to 12 minutes, until they have puffed somewhat and become dull and feel firm to the touch. Slide the papers from the pans onto racks.

8 After the cookies have cooled, store them between sheets of parchment or wax paper in a tin or plastic container with a tight-fitting cover.

MAKES ABOUT 40 COOKIES

"TRUFFLED" BRETON SHORTBREADS

⌒◝◞ ◝◞⌒

BRETON SHORTBREADS OR SABLÉS ARE very popular in France, and this amusing variation with chunks of milk chocolate was created by one of France's best-known pastry chefs, Frédéric Bau. "Truffled" in recipes usually refers to foods studded with black Périgord truffles, an aromatic fungus, sort of a subterranean mushroom. The chopped chocolate throughout the cylinder of cookie dough makes the roll of dough resemble a sweet trompe l'oeil version of a rich sausage. This recipe is loosely adapted from *Caprices de Chocolat* ("*Chocolate Fantasies*") (Editions Albin Michel, 1998) by Bau.

2 cups all-purpose flour

½ teaspoon baking powder

¼ teaspoon salt

10 tablespoons (1¼ sticks) unsalted butter, softened

¾ cup sugar

4 egg yolks

4 ounces milk chocolate cut into ¼-inch pieces, sifted after chopping to remove all the tiny particles

2 cookie sheets or jelly roll pans lined with parchment or foil

1 In a bowl, combine the flour, baking powder, and salt; stir well to mix.

2 In the bowl of a standing electric mixer fitted with the paddle attachment, beat together the butter and sugar on medium speed until well mixed and fluffy, about 4 or 5 minutes, then beat in the egg yolks, one at a time, beating smooth after each addition.

3 Scrape the bowl and beater well and beat in the flour mixture. Then, using a large rubber spatula, mix in the chocolate.

4 Scrape the dough onto a lightly floured work surface and shape and squeeze it into a rough cylinder, about 12 inches long and 2 inches in diameter.

5 Roll a piece of parchment or wax paper around the dough and tighten the paper by pressing it in with the side of a cookie sheet or a piece of stiff cardboard, as in the illustration on page 51. Chill the dough until firm. Or, at this stage, it can be double-wrapped in plastic, frozen, and kept for up to several weeks.

6 When you are ready to bake the cookies, set the racks in the upper and lower thirds of the oven and preheat to 350 degrees. Slice the cookies ¼ inch thick, rotating the roll of dough often as you slice so it doesn't become squashed from the weight of the knife.

7 Arrange the cookies on the prepared pans about an inch apart in all directions and bake them for about 12 to 15 minutes, until they have puffed somewhat and have become dull and are firm to the touch. Slide the papers from the pans onto racks.

8 After the cookies have cooled, store them between sheets of parchment or wax paper in a tin or plastic container with a tight-fitting cover.

MAKES ABOUT 48 COOKIES

61

SICILIAN FIG PINWHEELS

~ഗ്ഗ~

THERE ARE LOTS OF POPULAR RECIPES around for a refrigerator cookie with a date filling. They gave me the idea of using a Sicilian-inspired fig filling in a similar type cookie. These are perfect for the holidays—they have that requisite spicy flavor we always associate with Christmas cookies.

1 For the dough, in the work bowl of a food processor fitted with the steel blade, combine the flour, sugar, salt, and baking powder. Pulse several times to mix. Add the butter and the orange zest and pulse repeatedly at 1-second intervals until the mixture is fine and powdery. Add the eggs through the feed tube and continue to pulse until the dough forms a ball. Scrape the dough onto a lightly floured work surface and shape it into a 6-inch square. Wrap in plastic and chill while you prepare the filling.

2 Place the stemmed and diced figs in a saucepan and cover with water. Bring to a full boil over medium heat. Drain and cool the figs.

3 In the work bowl of a food processor fitted with the steel blade, combine the cooled figs with the remaining filling ingredients except the walnuts. Pulse until the mixture is finely ground, but not a puree. Scrape the filling into a bowl and stir in the walnuts. If the filling is very thick and difficult to spread, stir in 1 to 2 tablespoons water.

4 To form the cookies, remove the dough from the refrigerator and unwrap it. Place it on a floured work surface and knead it briefly until smooth and malleable. Flour the dough and the work surface and roll it out into a

COOKIE DOUGH

2 cups all-purpose flour

⅓ cup sugar

¼ teaspoon salt

½ teaspoon baking powder

8 tablespoons (1 stick) cold unsalted butter, cut into 10 pieces

1 tablespoon finely grated orange zest

2 large eggs

FIG FILLING

One 12-ounce package dried Calimyrna figs, stemmed and diced (about 2 cups)

⅓ cup apricot preserves

2 ounces semisweet chocolate, cut into ¼-inch pieces

½ teaspoon ground cinnamon

¼ teaspoon ground cloves

3 ounces (about ¾ cup) finely chopped walnut pieces

2 or 3 cookie sheets or jelly roll pans covered with parchment or foil

12-inch square. Cut the square in half to make two 6 × 12-inch rectangles. Spread half the filling evenly over each, then roll them up, jelly roll fashion from a long side. Try not to lengthen the rolls as you roll or the eventual sliced cookies will be too small.

5 Wrap each cylinder in plastic wrap or wax paper. Chill again for from 2 hours to 3 days.

6 When you are ready to bake the cookies, set the racks in the upper and lower thirds of the oven and preheat to 350 degrees. Slice the cookies ¼ inch thick, rotating the roll often so it doesn't become squashed from the weight of the knife.

7 Arrange the cookies on the prepared pans about an inch apart in all directions and bake them for about 12 to 15 minutes, until they are no longer shiny and the bottoms are light brown. Slide the papers from the pans onto racks.

8 After the cookies have cooled, store them between sheets of parchment or wax paper in a tin or plastic container with a tight-fitting cover.

MAKES ABOUT 96 COOKIES

ZALETI BOLOGNESI

〜

I SAW THE LEGENDARY ITALIAN BAKER and teacher Margherita Simili prepare these when she came to give a class at Peter Kump's New York Cooking School in the late eighties. Though unfortunately I long ago lost Margherita's recipe, my re-creation here is very much like hers in flavor and texture. Zaleti (*gialetti* in Italian) means "little yellow things" in Emilian dialect.

Stone-ground cornmeal will assure you of a better cornmeal flavor. Most other cornmeal has been degerminated so it keeps but loses a lot of corn flavor in the process.

1 In a bowl, combine the flour, cornmeal, salt, and baking powder; stir well to mix.

2 In the bowl of a standing electric mixer fitted with the paddle attachment, beat together the butter and sugar on medium speed until soft and light, about 3 or 4 minutes. Beat in the vanilla, then the eggs, one at a time, beating until smooth after each addition. On low speed, beat in the dry ingredients.

3 Scrape the dough onto a lightly floured work surface and shape and squeeze it into two rough cylinders, each about 8 inches long and 2 inches in diameter.

4 Roll a piece of parchment or wax paper around each piece of dough and tighten it by pressing it in with the side of a cookie sheet or a piece of stiff cardboard, as in the illustration on page 51. Chill the dough until firm. Or, at this stage, it can be double-wrapped in plastic, frozen, and kept for up to several weeks.

5 When you are ready to bake the cookies, set the racks in the upper and lower thirds of the oven and preheat to 350 degrees. Slice the cookies ¼ inch thick, rotating the roll often so it doesn't become squashed from the weight of the knife.

1½ cups all-purpose flour

1½ cups stone-ground yellow cornmeal

¼ teaspoon salt

1 teaspoon baking powder

12 tablespoons (1½ sticks) unsalted butter, softened

½ cup sugar

1 teaspoon vanilla extract

2 large eggs

2 or 3 cookie sheets or jelly roll pans covered with parchment or foil

6 Arrange the cookies on the prepared pans about an inch apart in all directions and bake them for about 10 to 12 minutes, until they have puffed somewhat and become dull and feel firm to the touch. Slide the papers from the pans onto racks.

7 After the cookies have cooled, store them between sheets of parchment or wax paper in a tin or plastic container with a tight-fitting cover.

MAKES ABOUT 60 THIN COOKIES

DARK CHOCOLATE SABLÉS

THIS IS AN EXTREMELY DARK AND chocolaty cookie for one made with cocoa powder rather than melted chocolate. Though the cookie is splendid on its own, I also like to add nuts or chocolate chips to the dough, just for variety.

1   In a bowl, combine the flour, cocoa, baking soda, and salt; stir well to mix.

2   In the bowl of a standing electric mixer fitted with the paddle attachment, beat together the butter and sugar on medium speed until well mixed and fluffy, about 4 or 5 minutes, then beat in the vanilla and egg. Continue beating until the mixture is very smooth, about 2 minutes longer.

3   Scrape the bowl and beater well and beat in the flour mixture.

4   Scrape the dough onto a lightly floured work surface and shape and squeeze it into a rough cylinder, about 10 inches long and 2 inches in diameter.

5   Roll a piece of parchment or wax paper around the dough and tighten the paper by pressing it in with the side of a cookie sheet or a piece of stiff cardboard, as in the illustration on page 51. Chill the dough until firm. Or, at this stage, it can be double-wrapped in plastic, frozen, and kept for up to several weeks.

6   When you are ready to bake the cookies, set the racks in the upper and lower thirds of the oven and preheat to 350 degrees. Slice the cookies ¼ inch thick, rotating the roll of dough often as you slice so it doesn't become squashed from the weight of the knife.

1½ cups all-purpose flour

⅓ cup alkalized (Dutch process) cocoa powder, sifted after measuring

½ teaspoon baking soda

⅛ teaspoon salt

8 tablespoons (1 stick) unsalted butter, softened

½ cup sugar

1 teaspoon vanilla extract

1 large egg

2 cookie sheets or jelly roll pans lined with parchment or foil

7   Arrange the cookies on the prepared pans about an inch apart in all directions and bake them for about 10 to 12 minutes, until they have puffed somewhat and become dull and feel firm to the touch. Slide the papers from the pans onto racks.

8   After the cookies have cooled, store them between sheets of parchment or foil in a tin or plastic container with a tight-fitting cover.

MAKES ABOUT 40 COOKIES

CHECKERBOARD COOKIES

THIS FUN COOKIE IS EASY TO MAKE when you have equal amounts of vanilla and chocolate doughs. Follow the directions below exactly, especially with regard to the chilling times, and your reward will be perfect checkerboard cookies.

1 Press the French Vanilla Sablés dough into a 1-inch-thick square, then wrap and chill. Do the same with the Dark Chocolate Sablés dough. Chill the doughs for several hours or up to several days.

2 When you are ready to form the cookies, remove the vanilla dough from the refrigerator, unwrap it, and on a floured surface roll it out to an 8 × 12-inch rectangle, about ⅜ inch thick. Slide the dough onto a cookie sheet, cover it with plastic wrap, and chill it until firm again, about 30 minutes. Repeat with the chocolate dough. The dough may remain chilled for several days at this point as long as you have not already chilled it for a long time; if it is adequately covered, it won't dry out.

3 Remove the vanilla dough from the refrigerator and paint it with lightly beaten egg white. Slide the chocolate dough over it and put a jelly roll pan or cookie sheet on top of the stack of dough. Gently press the pan down so the two layers of dough adhere.

4 Immediately cut the layered dough in half, making two 8 × 6-inch rectangles. Paint the top of one rectangle with egg white and place the second one over it. You now have four alternating layers of vanilla and chocolate dough. Repeat the gentle pressing with the

1 batch French Vanilla Sablés (page 52)
1 batch Dark Chocolate Sablés (page 165)
1 egg white for adhering the dough

3 or 4 cookie sheets or jelly roll pans lined with parchment or foil

pan, then wrap and chill the dough several hours before continuing.

5 Remove the dough from the refrigerator and place it on a cutting board. Using a long sharp knife, cut the dough across the 6-inch side into sixteen ⅜-inch-thick slices.

6 Place one of the slices of dough cut side down on the work surface, so that the four alternating stripes of dough are facing upward. Paint the dough with egg white and stack another slice of dough on top of it, making sure that the slices alternate: If the first slice is chocolate, white, chocolate, white from left to right, turn the second slice so it is white, chocolate, white, chocolate from left to right. Moisten the top slice and stack another slice on top of it. Again make sure they alternate in colors. Moisten the top slice and stack a fourth and final slice on top of it, again making the colors alternate. Repeat with the remaining slices of dough. You will have four stacks.

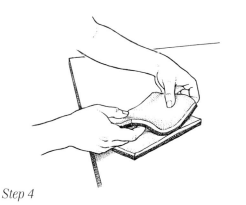

Step 4

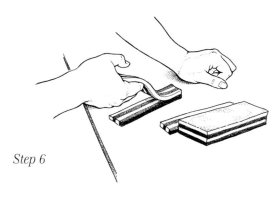

Step 6

Step 8

7 Gently press each side of each stack of dough to square it and wrap and refrigerate for several hours. They may be well wrapped and frozen at this point—defrost in the refrigerator before continuing.

8 When you are ready to bake the cookies, set the racks in the upper and lower thirds of the oven and preheat to 350 degrees. Slice the cookies ¼ inch thick, turning the stack of dough often so it doesn't become squashed from the weight of the knife.

9 Arrange the cookies on the prepared pans about an inch apart in all directions and bake them for about 10 to 12 minutes, until they have puffed somewhat and become dull and feel firm to the touch. Slide the papers from the pans onto racks.

10 After the cookies have cooled, store them between sheets of parchment or wax paper in a tin or plastic container with a tight-fitting cover.

MAKES ABOUT 100 COOKIES

COOKIES

ROLLED COOKIES

ROLLED COOKIES ARE ALL MADE from doughs that are usually chilled after mixing, then rolled out on a floured surface with a rolling pin, cut into shapes, and baked.

HINTS FOR ROLLED COOKIES

1 When you are ready to chill the dough, form it into a rectangular cake about ½ inch thick. In that shape the dough will chill quickly and will also be easier to roll because you will be starting with a fairly thin piece.

2 Always place chilled dough on a floured work surface and also lightly flour the dough itself. Use pinches of flour on the work surface and the dough. When you use pinches of flour, you may reflour the dough and work surface as often as necessary and not worry about adding too much flour to the dough. But if you use handfuls of flour, the dough will happily absorb it (which you don't want because handfuls of flour toughen the dough by making it dry and tasteless).

3 If the dough is chilled too hard, pound it gently with the rolling pin to soften it. Don't just slam away, pound in precise strokes close together over the top of the dough. Pounding dough in this way softens it and also makes it thinner. Rolling the hard, thick, chilled dough might make it break apart.

4 Roll out only small pieces of chilled dough. A large piece of dough may soften too much before it is all cut and be difficult to handle. It is far better to roll out small pieces of dough and cut them rapidly, than risk ruining a whole batch of dough by having to reroll it.

5 After cutting out the cookies, save all the scraps and gently mass them together; chill again before rolling out. You'll find that if you allow the scraps to chill before you roll them out again, the second batch of cookies will be just as tender as the first. To avoid having more scraps, use a knife or pizza cutter to cut the rolled sheet of scraps into squares or rectangles. Another way to deal with scraps is to form them as refrigerator cookies: gently knead them into a cylinder and wrap and chill as in directions for making refrigerator cookies. When it is cold, slice and bake the cookies—this method will also leave no scraps.

6 Don't place rolled cookies too close together on the baking pans—although they do not spread, they still puff a little and, if they are too close, could stick together.

CRISPY ST. NICHOLAS COOKIES

So what could be wrong with a cookie named after my patron saint? These are a typical Hungarian Christmas cookie; the recipe comes from my friend Nancy Berzinec.

1 In a bowl, combine the flour, cinnamon, baking powder, and salt; stir well to mix.

2 In the bowl of a standing electric mixer fitted with the paddle attachment, beat together on medium speed the butter and sugar until light and whitened, about 5 minutes. Beat in the egg and lemon zest and continue beating until smooth and light, another 2 minutes.

3 Scrape down the bowl and beater with a large rubber spatula and, on low speed, add the flour mixture. Continue mixing until the dough is smooth.

4 Remove the bowl from the mixer and complete the mixing with a large rubber spatula.

5 Scrape the dough onto a piece of plastic wrap and press it into a square or rectangle about ½ inch thick. Wrap and chill the dough until it is firm, about an hour or two.

6 When you are ready to bake the cookies, set racks in the upper and lower thirds of the oven and preheat to 350 degrees.

7 On a floured surface, roll out a third of the dough at a time until it is about ⅛ inch thick. Use a fluted cutter between 2 and 3 inches in diameter, or any kind of decorative cutter you wish. Just be sure to dip it frequently in flour. As they are cut, place the cookies on

2½ cups all-purpose flour

1 teaspoon ground cinnamon

½ teaspoon baking powder

½ teaspoon salt

8 tablespoons (1 stick) unsalted butter, softened

1 cup sugar

1 large egg

2 teaspoons finely grated lemon zest

2 or 3 cookie sheets or jelly roll pans covered with parchment or foil

the prepared pans about an inch apart in all directions. Repeat with the remaining dough. Save, press together, chill, and reroll the scraps to make more cookies.

8 Bake the cookies about 15 to 20 minutes, or until they first become dull and dry-looking and feel slightly firm when pressed with a fingertip. If you overbake the cookies, they will be very dry. Slide the papers from the pans onto racks.

9 Store the cooled cookies between sheets of parchment or wax paper in a tin or plastic container with a tight-fitting cover.

Makes about 36 cookies, depending on the size of the cutter used

SCOTTISH SHORTBREAD

THIS REALLY EASY VERSION OF THIS cookie is also the best one I have ever tasted. I've had the recipe for years and it comes from Peggy Pinckley, a native of Scotland, who now lives in Springfield, Missouri. I met Peggy in the late 1980s when she came to an afternoon demonstration class I was teaching at Peter Kump's. After class she invited me to come to teach at her school, the Parisian Pantry. I visited Springfield and taught several times at the school, which no longer exists.

Many recipes for shortbreads contain rice flour—a starch like cornstarch—and there are those who think that shortbreads without rice flour are not "the real thing." Industrially made shortbreads contain rice flour to weaken the flour—that is, to lower its protein content. In large industrial batches it takes a long time to incorporate the flour and all-purpose flour would be too strong—it would make the dough tough and elastic. In the small batches we make at home using a home-model electric mixer to beat in the flour, no such danger exists.

A note about butter: All the flavor in your shortbreads will come from the butter. You can make sure that the butter you are using is perfectly fresh with this little test: Unwrap a stick of the butter and use a table knife to scrape an inch-long shaving off one side of the stick. The butter revealed under the scraping should be the same color. If the outside is darker than the inside it means that the butter has oxidized—has been exposed to air and has become stale—and it won't have the same fresh taste as butter that is a uniformly light color inside and out.

1 Set racks in the upper and lower thirds of the oven and preheat to 325 degrees.

2 In the bowl of a standing electric mixer fitted with the paddle attachment, beat the butter and sugar on medium speed for 5 to 10 minutes, or until the mixture becomes light in color and very soft and fluffy.

3 Remove the bowl from the mixer and fold in the flour by hand. The dough will be soft.

20 tablespoons (2½ sticks) unsalted butter, softened

⅔ cup sugar

3¼ cups all-purpose flour

2 or 3 cookie sheets or jelly roll pans covered with parchment or foil

4 Place a handful of the dough at a time on a lightly floured work surface. Use the floured palm of your hand to press out the dough until it is about ⅜ inch thick—don't make the dough too thin. If the dough seems to be sticking, run a long thin knife or spatula under it to loosen it: whatever you do, do not use a lot of flour or the shortbreads will be dry and tough. Cut out the shortbreads using a fluted round cutter anywhere from 2 to 4 inches in diameter, dipped in flour. With a spatula or pancake turner transfer them to the prepared pans, spacing them about 1½ inches apart—they don't spread, but they puff a little.

5 Continue until all the dough has been cut and you have a large pile of scraps. Continue pressing out and cutting the scraps until they have all been used. The key here is to use very little flour on the work surface and on the dough. This way the last shortbread you cut out will be just as tender and fragile as the first.

6 Bake the shortbreads about 15 to 20 minutes, making sure they are just a very pale golden color. Slide papers from pans onto racks.

7 Pack the cooled cookies between sheets of parchment or wax paper in a tin or plastic container with a tight-fitting cover.

VARIATION

BROWN SUGAR SHORTBREAD: Substitute light brown sugar for all or half the sugar.

MAKES ABOUT 36 COOKIES, DEPENDING ON HOW LARGE THEY ARE CUT

PECAN SAND TARTS

Supposedly these cookies got their name from their postbaking coating of sugar, which gives them a sandy texture. This recipe comes from a great friend and cookie lover, Peggy Tagliarino.

1 Set racks in the upper and lower thirds of the oven and preheat to 325 degrees.

2 In the bowl of a standing electric mixer fitted with the paddle attachment, beat together the butter, sugar, and salt on medium speed for 5 to 10 minutes, until very light, fluffy, and whitened.

3 Beat in the egg and vanilla and continue beating until smooth. Lower the mixer speed and beat in the pecans. Then beat in the flour, about a third at a time, scraping the bowl and beater between each addition.

4 Scrape the dough out onto a floured work surface and divide into three pieces.

5 Flour one piece of dough and roll it out about ⅜ inch thick, moving it continually so it doesn't stick to the surface. If it does stick, slide a long, thin-bladed knife or a long spatula under the dough to detach it. Cut the dough with a 2-inch fluted cutter and place the cookies on a prepared pan, about an inch apart on all sides. Repeat with the remaining dough. Save all the scraps until the end, then reroll them and cut more cookies.

6 Bake the cookies about 20 or 25 minutes, until they are light golden on the bottom but still very pale on top. Slide the papers from the pans onto racks.

16 tablespoons (2 sticks) unsalted butter, softened

½ cup sugar

½ teaspoon salt

1 large egg

1 teaspoon vanilla extract

4 ounces (about 1 cup) pecan pieces, finely ground in the food processor

2½ cups all-purpose flour

Sugar for coating the baked cookies

2 or 3 cookie sheets or jelly roll pans covered with parchment or foil

7 After the cookies have cooled, carefully roll them in grabulated sugar.

8 Store the cooled cookies between sheets of parchment or wax paper in a tin or plastic container with a tight-fitting cover.

MAKES ABOUT 50 COOKIES, DEPENDING ON HOW LARGE YOU CUT THEM

BERNER HASELNUSS STAENGELI
Swiss Hazelnut Bars from Berne

THIS IS A TYPICALLY SWISS RECIPE shared by my friend, cooking teacher and caterer Thea Cvijanovich. Thea was born in Berne, Switzerland, and this recipe is like many from the region. Though I don't think these were originally made without flour for religious reasons, they make a great Passover cookie.

1 In the work bowl of a food processor fitted with the steel blade, combine the hazelnuts and half the sugar. Pulse repeatedly at 1-second intervals until finely ground. Add the lemon zest and cinnamon and pulse again.

2 In a large bowl, whisk the egg whites to break them up. Whisk in the remaining sugar in a stream. Add the hazelnut mixture and with a large rubber spatula combine the ingredients to form a very firm dough. Cover the bowl with plastic wrap and set it aside to let the dough mature for about 30 minutes. (This resting time is to get all the sugar melted so that the dough doesn't change consistency while it is being rolled or baked.)

3 When you are ready to bake the cookies, set racks in the upper and lower thirds of the oven and preheat to 350 degrees.

4 Scatter granulated sugar on a work surface and scrape the dough onto it. Use the palm of your hand to flatten the dough and scatter sugar over it. Roll out and press the dough until it is about ¼ inch thick—it should make a 12-inch square. Using a ruler for accuracy, cut the dough into 1-inch wide strips. Then cut across at 3-inch intervals to make 48 cookies.

4½ cups (about 18 ounces) whole
  unblanched hazelnuts
1½ cups sugar, plus more for rolling out the
  dough
Finely grated zest of 1 lemon
1 teaspoon ground cinnamon
4 large egg whites (a little more than ½ cup)

2 cookie sheets or jelly roll pans covered
with parchment or foil

5 Transfer the cookies to the prepared pans, leaving about an inch all around each. Bake the cookies for about 15 to 20 minutes, until they are slightly puffed but still soft to the touch of a fingertip. Cool on the pans on racks.

6 Store the cooled cookies between sheets of parchment or wax paper in a tin or plastic container with a tight-fitting cover.

MAKES ABOUT 48 COOKIES

GINGERBREAD PEOPLE

〜っつ〜

OF COURSE YOU DON'T HAVE TO CUT these cookies into any particular shape, but if you want to make gingerbread people this is the recipe to use. And the cookies are ideal for decorating—I usually use Royal Icing for that purpose. A bonus: This dough is so tender you can roll and reroll the scraps without having to worry that the last batch of cookies you roll will be tough.

This recipe makes a lot of dough—but it's easy to halve if you need less.

1 In a large bowl, combine the flour, spices, salt, and baking soda, stir well to mix.

2 In the bowl of a standing electric mixer fitted with the paddle attachment, beat together the butter and brown sugar on medium speed until well mixed, about 1 minute. Beat in the eggs, one at a time, beating smooth after each addition. Scrape down the bowl and beater.

3 Lower the speed and beat in about half the flour mixture. Beat in all the molasses, then scrape the bowl and beater. Add the remaining flour mixture, about a cup at a time, and beat after each addition until it has all been absorbed.

4 Remove the bowl from the mixer and give the dough a final mixing with a large rubber spatula. Scrape half the dough onto a large piece of plastic wrap and press it to about a ½ inch thickness. Wrap the dough securely and repeat with the remaining dough. Chill the dough for at least 2 hours or for up to 3 days.

5 When you are ready to bake the cookies, set racks in the upper and lower thirds of the

5 cups all-purpose flour

4 teaspoons ground ginger

1 tablespoon ground cinnamon

1 teaspoon freshly grated nutmeg

½ teaspoon ground cloves

1 teaspoon salt

½ teaspoon baking soda

16 tablespoons (2 sticks) unsalted butter, softened

⅔ cup firmly packed dark brown sugar

2 large eggs

⅔ cup molasses

Royal Icing

Raisins, nut meats, and candies for decorating (optional)

2 or 3 cookie sheets or jelly roll pans covered with parchment or foil

oven and preheat to 350 degrees.

6 Unwrap one of the pieces of dough and cut it in half. Rewrap one of the halves and return it to the refrigerator.

7 On a floured surface, roll out the dough until it is about ¼ inch thick. Use a floured gingerbread "man" or "woman" cutter to cut

cookies on the prepared pans about an inch apart in all directions. Repeat with remaining dough. Save, press together, and reroll the scraps to make more cookies (they don't need to be chilled before rerolling).

8   Bake the cookies about 12 to 15 minutes, or until they become dull and dry-looking and feel slightly firm when pressed with a fingertip. If you overbake the cookies, they will be very dry. Slide the papers from the pans onto racks to cool.

9   After the cookies have cooled decorate them with the Royal Icing and other decorating ingredients if desired.

10   Store the cooled cookies between sheets of parchment or wax paper in a tin or plastic container with a tight-fitting cover.

MAKES ABOUT 30 LARGE COOKIES, DEPENDING ON THE SIZE CUTTER USED

OLD-FASHIONED MOLASSES COOKIES

THESE ARE ONE OF THE FEW AMERICAN cookies I remember my maternal grandmother, Clotilda Lo Conte, baking when I was a child. In fact, I still have the tattered 1930s molasses company recipe pamphlet from which she got the recipe.

These are a little less delicate than the Gingerbread People on page 75, but for all practical purposes the recipes may be used interchangeably.

1 In a large bowl, combine the flour, salt, soda, and spices; stir well to mix.

2 In the bowl of a standing electric mixer fitted with the paddle attachment, beat together, on medium speed, the butter and sugar until well mixed, about a minute. Lower the speed and beat in a third of the flour mixture, then half the molasses; stop and scrape the bowl and beater. Beat in another third of the flour, then the remaining molasses; stop and scrape again. Finally, beat in the remaining flour.

3 Remove the bowl from the mixer and stir up the dough, scraping it from around the inside of the bowl with a large rubber spatula.

4 Place the dough on a piece of plastic wrap and form it into a square or rectangle about ½ inch thick. Wrap the dough and chill it until you are ready to use it—1 hour or up to 3 days.

5 When you are ready to bake the cookies, set racks in the upper and lower thirds of the oven and preheat to 375 degrees.

3 cups all-purpose flour

1 teaspoon salt

1 teaspoon baking soda

1 teaspoon ground cinnamon

1 teaspoon ground ginger

½ teaspoon ground cloves

12 tablespoons (1½ sticks) unsalted butter, softened

⅓ cup sugar

⅔ cup molasses

2 or 3 cookie sheets or jelly roll pans lined with parchment or foil

6   Divide the dough into three parts and place one on a floured work surface. Refrigerate the remaining dough until needed. Press and pound the dough gently with the rolling pin to soften it, then roll it out into a 10-inch square. Use a floured 3- to 4-inch cutter to cut the dough. As each cookie is cut, place it immediately on one of the prepared pans, leaving about 1½ inches between each cookie in all directions. (If you don't have a lot of pans, you can place the cookies on pieces of parchment or foil and stack up the papers. When one pan of cookies is baked, slide the paper off the pan onto a rack and replace with a paper of unbaked cookies.) Repeat with the remaining pieces of dough. Save, press together, chill, and reroll the scraps to make more cookies.

7   Bake the cookies for about 10 to 15 minutes, or until they are light golden all over.

8   Slide the papers from the pans onto racks.

9   Store the cooled cookies between sheets of parchment or wax paper in a tin or plastic container with a tight-fitting cover.

MAKES ABOUT 36 COOKIES,
DEPENDING ON THE SIZE CUTTER USED

PERFECT COOKIES,
CAKES AND CHOCOLATE

UTZIGER HASELNUSS LECKERLI
Swiss Hazelnut Cookies from the Château of Utzigen

THIS TRADITIONAL RECIPE ALSO CAME to me from Thea Cvijanovich, a native of Berne. I met Thea when I was teaching in Winston-Salem, North Carolina, where she lives and does catering. The ingredients for these seem similar to those of the *Berner Haselnuss Staengeli* (Swiss Hazelnut Bars from Berne) on page 73, but the texture and flavor are entirely different.

1 Set a rack in the middle level of the oven and preheat to 325 degrees.

2 In the work bowl of a food processor fitted with the steel blade, combine the hazelnuts and almonds and pulse at 1-second intervals until finely ground. Stop the machine occasionally and scrape down the inside bottom of the bowl with a metal spatula or table knife to loosen any ground nuts caking there. When the nuts are finely ground, pour them into a large roasting pan; place the pan in the oven and toast the nuts until they are golden brown, stirring often with a large wide spatula or pancake turner. Be careful—ground nuts burn a lot more quickly than whole ones.

3 Remove the ground nuts from the oven and pour them onto a clean pan or work surface to cool. Turn off the oven.

4 When the nuts are cool, place them in a large bowl and stir in the sugar, candied fruit, spices, and flour. In another bowl, whisk together the egg whites, lemon juice, and honey, and using a rubber spatula, scrape this into the nut mixture. Fold the ingredients together until they form a stiff dough. Cover the bowl with plastic wrap and allow the dough to rest an hour.

6 ounces (about 1½ cups) whole
 unblanched hazelnuts

6 ounces (about 1½ cups) whole
 unblanched almonds

1 cup granulated sugar

2 tablespoons candied orange rind,
 chopped very fine

2 tablespoons candied lemon rind, chopped
 very fine

1½ teaspoons ground cinnamon

½ teaspoon ground star anise or aniseed

3 tablespoons flour

2 large egg whites

1 tablespoon strained lemon juice

1 tablespoon honey

Confectioners' sugar for rolling out
 the dough

GLAZE

½ cup confectioners' sugar mixed with
 2 tablespoons kirsch or lemon juice

2 cookie sheets or jelly roll pans covered
with parchment or foil

5 When you are ready to bake the cookies, set a rack in the upper third of the oven and preheat to 425 degrees. It is traditional to bake these cookies with mostly top heat, so only one pan at a time will be baked—but they bake quickly, so the whole procedure doesn't take too long.

6 Strew the work surface with confectioners' sugar and place the dough on it. Sprinkle the dough with more confectioners' sugar and press and roll out the dough into a 12-inch square about ¼ inch thick. Cut the dough into 1½-inch strips with a knife or pizza wheel, then cut across at 3-inch intervals. Straight lines will make rectangles, diagonal ones will make diamonds. As the cookies are cut, place them on the prepared pans, leaving about an inch around all the sides. While the cookies are baking prepare the glaze.

7 Bake for about 8 to 10 minutes, or until the cookies puff slightly and look dry. Remove the cookies from the oven and immediately brush with the glaze. Cool on the pans on racks.

8 Store the cooled cookies between sheets of parchment or wax paper in a tin or plastic container with a tight-fitting cover.

MAKES ABOUT 32 COOKIES

Utziger Haselnuss Leckerli (LEFT)
and Berner Haselnuss Staengeli, page 73

APRICOT ALMOND RUGLACH

IF YOU'VE NEVER TRIED RUGLACH, now is the time. It's one of the world's best cookies, made from a rich cream cheese wrapped around sugar, nuts, and jam. The cookies always caramelize a little while they're baking, creating a combination of sweet, buttery flavors not duplicated in any other cookie I know. I could make (and eat!) ruglach once a week.

This version comes from my friend Bonnie Stern, Canada's top food authority. It is from her book *Desserts* (Random House of Canada, 1998).

1 Set racks in the upper and lower thirds of the oven and preheat to 350 degrees.

2 In the work bowl of a food processor fitted with the steel blade, combine the flour, butter, and cream cheese. Pulse until the dough forms a ball. Remove the dough from the work bowl and divide into two pieces. Place each on a piece of plastic wrap and press each out into a 6-inch disk. Wrap in plastic and refrigerate while preparing the filling.

3 To make the filling, stir the jam until it is spreadable; stir together the almonds, sugar, and zest in a bowl.

4 Remove one of the pieces of dough from the refrigerator and place it on a lightly floured surface. Flour the dough and roll it out into a 9- to 10-inch circle. Using a pizza wheel, cut the circle in twelve equal wedges. Spread with half the jam and evenly scatter on half the almond mixture. Roll up each triangle of dough into a small crescent from the outside inward. As the ruglach are formed, place them on the prepared pan. Repeat with the other piece of dough and the remaining filling.

CREAM CHEESE PASTRY

1 cup all-purpose flour

8 tablespoons (1 stick) cold unsalted butter, cut into 12 pieces

4 ounces cold cream cheese, cut into 12 pieces

FILLING

¼ cup apricot jam

2 ounces (about ½ cup) chopped toasted almonds

¼ cup sugar

1 teaspoon finely grated lemon zest

TOPPING

1 egg

¼ cup sugar

1 ounce (about ¼ cup) chopped almonds

2 cookie sheets or jelly roll pans covered with parchment or foil

5 To make the topping, beat the egg in a small bowl until well broken up. In another bowl, mix the sugar and almonds. Brush the top of each pastry with beaten egg, then sprinkle with the almond sugar.

6 Bake for about 30 minutes, or until golden and slightly caramelized. Slide the papers from the pans to racks.

7 Ruglach are best on the day they are baked, but they will certainly keep between sheets of parchment or wax paper in a tin or plastic container with a tight-fitting cover.

MAKES ABOUT 24 COOKIES

CHOCOLATE SHORTBREAD

THIS IS AN INTERESTING VARIATION of the classic Scottish shortbread. One word of caution: Unlike the plain shortbread dough on page 70, this dough needs to chill thoroughly before being rolled.

1   Mix the flour with the salt in a medium bowl.

2   In another bowl, stir the softened butter with a rubber spatula until it is smooth. Scrape the chocolate into the butter and continue mixing until the dough is all one color. Fold in the flour to make a smooth, soft dough.

3   Scrape the dough onto a piece of plastic wrap and press it into a square or rectangle about ½ inch thick. Wrap and chill the dough until it is firm, about an hour or two.

4   When you are ready to bake the cookies, set racks in the upper and lower thirds of the oven and preheat to 350 degrees.

5   On a lightly floured surface, roll out a third of the dough at a time until it is between ⅛ and ¼ inch thick. Cut the cookies with a fluted cutter between 2 and 3 inches in diameter, dipping it frequently in flour. Place the cookies, as they are cut, on the prepared pans about an inch apart in all directions. Repeat with the remaining chilled dough. Save, press together, chill, and reroll all the scraps to make more cookies.

2⅓ cups all-purpose flour

¼ teaspoon salt

16 tablespoons (2 sticks) unsalted butter, softened

6 ounces semisweet chocolate, melted and cooled

2 or 3 cookie sheets or jelly roll pans covered with parchment or foil

6   Bake the shortbreads about 15 to 20 minutes, or until they become dull and dry-looking and feel slightly firm when pressed with a fingertip. Place the pans on racks to cool the cookies. If you overbake these cookies, they will be lethally dry.

7   Pack the cooled cookies between sheets of parchment or wax paper in a tin or plastic container with a tight-fitting cover.

MAKES ABOUT 40 COOKIES

PIPED COOKIES

VERSATILE PIPED COOKIES ARE AS DECORATIVE as they are delicious. The name refers to the process of making them. They either are made extruded in decorative designs from a cookie press or are piped out of a pastry bag. We'll consider each separately.

COOKIE PRESS COOKIES: A cookie press is a hand-operated extruding machine. It is a cylinder with a metal die at one end (presses come with a variety of these, each creating different designs). The dough is held in the cylinder and pushed down and through the die by a plate at the top when the handle is pressed. Cookie presses work the way a gun does: One pull of the trigger pushes a uniform quantity of dough through the die every time—all the cookies emerge the same size.

PIPED COOKIES: Not as precise as pressed cookies, they are formed by squeezing the dough through a pastry bag. The shape and design come from whatever plain or decorative tube you put on the end. Firm doughs are the easiest to pipe because they hold their shape and the bag must be firmly squeezed to force them through. Looser mixtures, such as the batter for ladyfingers, are a little more difficult to pipe because the flow is more difficult to control.

MERINGUES: The ones in this chapter are all piped cookies, although some meringues may be spooned out onto the pans like drop cookies.

HINTS FOR PIPED COOKIES

1 Follow the instructions on pages 86-88 for piping and you will get good results even on the first try.

2 Use a nylon and plastic-coated canvas bag. Disposable bags are good, but sometimes they split if you try to use them to pipe a firm dough.

3 For best results, use the size and type tube specified in the recipe. A smaller tube could crush delicate mixtures and cause them to liquefy or, if the dough is firm, may make it impossible to pipe. Conversely, if you use too large a tube, a soft mixture may flow through it too quickly and if the dough is firm the result will be gigantic cookies. The cookies in the following recipes will keep for a week or so. Freeze them for longer storage.

How to Pipe

The purpose of a pastry bag is to make the process of shaping cookies easier, though many first-timers find it awkward. Follow the simple rules below and you won't have trouble.

1 Inserting the tube into the bag: When you insert the tube, make sure it is firmly seated in the narrow end of the bag. If the batter you are going to pipe is soft and thin, close off the end of the bag before you begin to fill it. Twist some material from right behind the wide end of the tube and press it into the tube from the outside, as in illustration 1. This will keep the batter from leaking out as you are pouring it in. This is not necessary if the dough is firm.

Step 2

2 Filling the bag: From the wide end of the bag fold back about the top third to the outside and hold it in your nonwriting hand, under the cuff, fingers poised around it as if they were holding a glass. (See illustration 2.) Use your writing hand to fill the bag, not more than half full. Or stand the bag in a large jar or measuring cup and fold the top of the bag down over the outside. This way you can use both hands to fill.

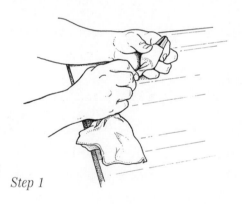

Step 1

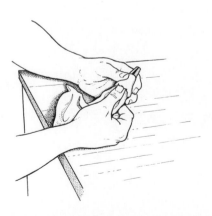

3 Closing the top of the bag: After you have filled half (or less) of the bag, twist the top right above the batter or dough. This closes off the top of the bag so the batter will only come out the end with the tube.

4 Opening the bottom of the bag: Right before you start piping, undo the twisted fabric closing the bottom of the bag.

5 Beginning to pipe: Always hold the bag in the hand you use to write. (If you are left-handed and write back-handed, pipe the same way.) Hold the bag only at the top and, with one hand, grip the top of the bag as though it were an orange half you are about to press over a hand juicer. Use only the index finger of your other hand against the side of the bag to steady it. Do not grip the bag with both hands.

6 Piping half-spheres: To pipe most cookies, hold the bag perpendicular to the pan with the tube about an inch above the surface. Tighten your writing hand to squeeze out some batter or dough. When the cookie is the size you want it, stop squeezing and pull the bag away straight upward. This is the same method you would use to pipe stars or simple flower shapes with a star tube.

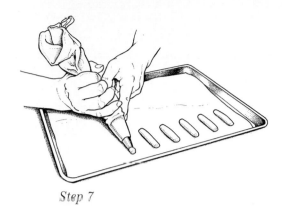

Step 7

7 Piping fingers: To make a long shape, hold the bag at a 45-degree angle to the pan and touch the tube to the surface. Begin to squeeze gently as you pull the tube toward you. When the line of batter on the pan is as long as the recipe states, stop squeezing, then lift the bag away, but back over the shape you have just piped. Don't pull the bag away, or you risk leaving a tail.

8 Piping shells or teardrops: This is done the same way as the fingers above, but to leave a pointed shape gradually release the pressure as you pipe.

9 Cleaning the bag and tube: As soon as you finish piping, remove the tube from the bag, wash it in hot, soapy water, and dry it thoroughly. Wash the bag in hot soapy water and rinse it thoroughly. Sometimes I send a pastry bag through the dishwasher cycle stretched around several of the prongs, wide end down, on the upper rack. Occasionally wash pastry bags in the washing machine with detergent and bleach when you are doing other kitchen laundry.

BUTTER ALMOND FINGERS

⁓ ⁓

THESE COOKIES BRING OUT THE DELICACY of an almond-butter combination better than any other cookie I know. The covering of sliced almonds on these crisp, delicate cookies gives them a little extra crunch. Marilyn Miller was kind enough to share this recipe for which I had been searching for years.

1 Set racks in the upper and lower thirds of the oven and preheat to 350 degrees.

2 In the bowl of a standing electric mixer fitted with the paddle attachment, beat the butter, sugar, salt, and vanilla on medium speed until soft and light, about 5 minutes.

3 Add the egg and continue beating until smooth.

4 Lower the speed and add the flour in several additions, beating smooth after each.

5 Remove the bowl from the mixer and with a large rubber spatula, give the dough a final mixing.

6 Using a pastry bag fitted with a ⅜-inch plain tube (Ateco #804), pipe the dough into 2½- to 3-inch fingers on the prepared pans. Leave about an inch around each cookie in all directions. After the cookies are all piped, sprinkle them with the sliced almonds, then with your fingertips gently press the almonds into the cookies.

18 tablespoons (2¼ sticks) unsalted butter, softened

1¼ cups sugar

⅛ teaspoon salt

1 teaspoon vanilla extract

1 large egg

2½ cups all-purpose flour

8 ounces (about 2 cups) blanched sliced almonds for covering the outside of the cookies

3 cookie sheets or jelly roll pans covered with parchment or foil

7 Bake for about 15 to 20 minutes, until the cookies are firm and the almonds are a light golden color.

8 Slide the papers from the pans onto racks.

9 Store the cooled cookies between sheets of parchment or wax paper in a tin or plastic container with a tight-fitting cover.

MAKES ABOUT 120 SMALL COOKIES

LANGUES DE CHAT

"Sid and Sis" Cat's Tongues

THESE COOKIES ARE A FAVORITE throughout Europe. The loose batter is piped through a small tube; it spreads and becomes thin and delicate in the oven. To make sure the cookies don't become distorted, I rub the foil lining flat with a soft cloth or paper towel. Then it's easy to brush the foil with soft, not melted, butter.

To get best results with this recipe, measure the egg white very accurately. If three egg whites are less than ½ cup, beat a fourth in a small bowl with a fork until it breaks up and add enough to the measuring cup to make exactly ½ cup.

Sid and Sis are my two black cats, ages 16 and 11, respectively.

1 Set racks in the upper and lower thirds of the oven and preheat to 400 degrees.

2 In the bowl of a standing electric mixer fitted with the paddle attachment, beat together on medium speed the butter, confectioners' sugar, and vanilla until well mixed and smooth, about 2 minutes.

3 Add the egg whites in about five or six additions, beating smooth after each.

4 Remove the bowl from the mixer and with a large rubber spatula stir in the flour.

5 Fit a pastry bag with a ¼-inch plain tube (Ateco #802). Fill the pastry bag and pipe the batter in 2½-inch fingers. Leave about 1½ inches all around each to allow for spreading.

6 Bake for about 6 or 7 minutes, or until the cookies have spread and are golden around the edges.

6 tablespoons (¾ stick) unsalted butter, softened

1¼ cups confectioners' sugar

1 teaspoon vanilla extract

½ cup egg white (from about 3 to 4 large eggs)

1 cup all-purpose flour

4 cookie sheets or jelly roll pans lined with buttered foil

7 Slide the foil sheets from the pans to racks. Carefully pry off the cooled cookies.

8 Store the cookies between sheets of parchment or wax paper in a tin or plastic container with a tight-fitting cover.

MAKES ABOUT 150 COOKIES

SPRITZ COOKIES

~ ⚬ ~

THESE ARE A CLASSIC. THE GERMAN verb *spritzen* means "to squirt" and it is also the term used for piping with a pastry bag. Though these cookies may be formed in that way, this recipe is really meant for use with a cookie press. Look around at garage sales for the old-fashioned ones with a screw mechanism. I got my spiffy new Swiss cookie press at Williams-Sonoma and was assured that the store always carries them.

1 Set racks in the upper and lower thirds of the oven and preheat to 375 degrees.

2 In the bowl of a standing electric mixer fitted with the paddle attachment, beat together on medium speed the butter, sugar, salt, and vanilla until very light and fluffy, about 5 minutes. Beat in the egg yolks, one at a time, beating smooth after each addition.

3 Scrape down the side of the bowl and beater. On low speed, add the flour and mix only until it is completely absorbed. Remove the bowl from the mixer and finish mixing the dough with a large rubber spatula.

4 Insert a die into the cookie press, then fill it with about a quarter of the dough. Press the cookies out onto the prepared pans, leaving an inch all around between cookies.

5 Bake the cookies for 10 to 12 minutes, or just until they are a very pale golden color.

6 Slide the papers from the pans onto racks.

7 Store the cooled cookies between sheets of parchment or wax paper in a tin or plastic container with a tight-fitting cover.

16 tablespoons (2 sticks) unsalted butter, softened

¾ cup sugar

¼ teaspoon salt

1 teaspoon vanilla extract

3 large egg yolks

2½ cups all-purpose flour

2 or 3 cookie sheets or jelly roll pans covered with parchment or foil

NOTE: Spritz cookies, depending upon their shape, are often decorated with bits of candied fruit, raisins, or nuts. They may also be made into sandwiches with ganache (page 285) or with melted milk chocolate. Some may be dipped partially or halfway in chocolate. Dipped cookies may also have the dipped ends further dipped in chopped nuts or shaved chocolate.

MAKES ABOUT 75 COOKIES, ACCORDING TO THE SIZE DIE USED

W'S

These pretty cookies are the signature cookie of Wittamer, the best pastry shop in Brussels. The traditional shape is a wavy W, but of course they may be piped in any shape. The recipe is adapted from *Les heures et les jours Wittamer* ("*The Hours and Days at Wittamer*") by Jean-Pierre Gabriel (Editions Lannoo, 1994).

This recipe uses a typically European method: scraping out and using the seeds of a vanilla bean rather than vanilla extract.

1 Set racks in the upper and lower thirds of the oven and preheat to 350 degrees.

2 In the bowl of a standing electric mixer fitted with the paddle attachment, combine the butter and granulated sugar.

3 Use the point of a paring knife to remove the black seeds from the inside of the piece of vanilla bean and add them to the bowl. Beat on medium speed until well mixed, about 2 minutes. Add the egg white and continue to beat until smooth.

4 Lower the mixer speed and beat in the flour, just until it is absorbed. Remove the bowl from the mixer and finish mixing the dough with a large rubber spatula.

5 Using a pastry bag fitted with a ½-inch star tube (Ateco #824), pipe the dough onto the prepared pans in a series of W's (or whatever initial or shape you prefer). Leave about an inch in all directions around each.

6 Bake the cookies for about 15 minutes, or until they are firm and very light golden. Slide the papers from the pans onto racks.

14 tablespoons (1¾ sticks) unsalted butter, softened
⅓ cup granulated sugar
½ vanilla bean, split, or 1 teaspoon vanilla extract
1 large egg white
2 cups all-purpose flour
Confectioners' sugar for sprinkling

2 cookie sheets or jelly roll pans covered with parchment or foil

7 Just before serving the cookies, dust them with confectioners' sugar.

8 Store the cooled cookies between sheets of parchment or wax paper in a tin or plastic container with a tight-fitting cover.

MAKES ABOUT 30 COOKIES

PASTE DI MELIGA

Italian Cornmeal Butter Cookies from Piemonte

I RECENTLY HAD THE OCCASION TO spend a long weekend in Asti in the Piedmont area of northern Italy. Of course, the first thing I did was to take a walk and look at all the pastry shops. There was one cookie in all of them: a delicately flavored but coarse-textured piped butter cookie with delicious tastes of cornmeal and vanilla. I came home and experimented with duplicating them. This recipe is the result.

1 Set racks in the upper and lower thirds of the oven and preheat to 325 degrees.

2 In the bowl of a standing electric mixer fitted with the paddle attachment, beat together on medium speed the butter, sugar, and vanilla until very soft, fluffy, and whitened, about 5 minutes.

3 Add the egg yolks, one at a time, beating smooth after each addition.

4 Remove the bowl from the mixer and use a large rubber spatula to stir in the flour and cornmeal by hand.

5 Using a pastry bag fitted with a ½-inch star tube, (Ateco #824), pipe the cookie dough onto the prepared pans in double S curves about 2½ inches long, as in the illustration. Leave about 1½ inches around each cookie in all directions. These spread quite a bit.

6 Bake the cookies for about 15 minutes, or until they are firm and very light golden.

10 tablespoons (1¼ sticks) unsalted butter, softened

½ cup sugar

1 teaspoon vanilla extract

2 large egg yolks

1 cup all-purpose flour

⅔ cup stone-ground yellow cornmeal

2 cookie sheets or jelly roll pans covered with parchment or foil

7 Slide the papers from the pans onto racks.

8 Store the cooled cookies between sheets of parchment or wax paper in a tin or plastic container with a tight-fitting cover.

MAKES ABOUT 20 COOKIES

Step 5

WALNUT BOULDERS

THIS IS AN AMAZING VARIATION ON meringue cookies. They are giant kiss shapes filled with pieces of walnut and chewy raisins. The nuts and fruit make an excellent contrast to the crisp meringue.

1 Set racks in the upper and lower thirds of the oven and preheat to 300 degrees.

2 In the bowl of a standing electric mixer fitted with the whip attachment, whip the egg whites and salt on medium speed for about 3 or 4 minutes or until white and opaque and beginning to hold their shape.

3 In a bowl, stir ½ cup sugar with the walnuts, raisins, and cornstarch.

4 When the egg whites are ready, increase the mixer speed to the maximum and add the remaining ½ cup sugar a tablespoon at a time. Beat until the egg whites are stiff but not dry.

5 Remove the bowl from the mixer and add the nut and raisin mixture. With a large rubber spatula fold it in thoroughly.

6 Using a pastry bag without a tube, pipe out kiss shapes 1½ inches in diameter on the prepared pans, leaving an inch all around each.

7 Bake the meringues for about 30 minutes, or until they are firm on the outside and still somewhat soft within. The best way to tell is to poke one with a fingertip—if there is only a wet area the size of a hazelnut in the center, they are ready. They will finish crisping as they cool.

4 large egg whites (a bit more than ½ cup)

Pinch salt

1 cup sugar

4 ounces (about 1 cup) walnut pieces, chopped into ¼-inch pieces

1 cup dark raisins, chopped into ¼-inch pieces

2 tablespoons cornstarch

2 cookie sheets or jelly roll pans covered with parchment or foil

8 Cool the meringues on the pans on racks.

9 Store the cooled cookies between sheets of parchment or wax paper in a tin or plastic container with a tight-fitting cover. (Store them only one-layer deep if you want to preserve the points on top.)

MAKES ABOUT 80 COOKIES

MOLDED COOKIES

MOLDED COOKIES FALL INTO SEVERAL CATEGORIES: Some are made by pressing dough into a mold or form or pressing a mold or form onto a piece of dough to imprint a design or shape on it (Swiss and German Springerle and Dutch speculaas are made this way). Others are made by actually baking dough or batter in a plain or decorative mold, like *financiers* and madeleines. Still others are molded by hand into simple or complex shapes, the way a simple gingersnap is rolled into a ball before being placed on the pan to bake.

Whether you want to press a design into the cookie or to bake the dough or batter in a mold, kitchenware stores and mail-order sources make them widely available.

HINTS FOR MOLDED COOKIES

Hand-Molded Cookies

1 Use a small ice cream scoop, measuring spoon, or other consistent measure for the dough to keep the cookies uniform in size.

2 When you are rolling cookie into balls it's better to oil or butter your hands than to flour them. The flour on your hands could bake on the cookies and make an unattractive crust.

3 When a recipe says to roll dough into narrow, pencil-like strands, use very little flour on the work surface or the dough might just slide around rather than rolling into a cylinder.

4 Use a ruler if a recipe calls for cutting dough to specific dimensions. You'll be a lot happier with the resulting neat and uniform cookies

Cookies Formed, but Not Baked, in Mold

1 Make sure the surface of the dough is lightly floured before you press the mold into it.

2 The face of the mold should also be lightly floured.

3 Press the mold lightly but firmly. Too much pressure may make the dough stick to the mold.

4 Remove the mold before you cut around the cookie. A mold left on dough for a long time might stick.

5 If the molds are sticking, try letting the dough dry at room temperature for 20 minutes before pressing with the mold.

6 If the cookies are to be pressed *into* and emerge from a mold, generously flour the inside of the mold first. Try to form a piece of dough so it is roughly the shape of the

cavity into the mold, trim it even with the top of the form. To ease the dough out of the mold, start by digging loose one corner, then inverting the mold over a baking pan. The cookie should drop out of the mold. If the dough doesn't drop even with a pulled-up corner, hold the mold at a 45-degree angle away from you and gently, but smartly, tap the far end of the mold against the work surface a few times. This should encourage the cookie to drop.

Cookies Baked in Molds

1 Prepare molds by buttering and flouring them. Use soft not melted butter and apply it with a brush. It will coat the inside of the mold more thickly.

2 To flour the molds, apply a thin coat of flour and tap it around in the mold so all surfaces are covered. Then turn the mold over and rap it smartly against the work surface to knock out excess flour.

3 After cookies baked in molds emerge from the oven, let them stand a minute or two, then unmold them and arrange them right side up on racks to cool.

Cookies Formed in Molds

Some of the most beautiful cookies possible are those given a decorative design or shape by molds. Some molds are designed to be pressed into dough and lifted off. The cookie is cut out around the shape the mold has imprinted. Others are designed to have dough pressed into the cavity and either removed to bake on a pan or left to bake right in the mold. The resulting cookie not only has a design imprinted on it but also the particular shape. Review the hints on page 97 before you start any of the following recipes.

PECAN BUTTER BALLS

～⁓⁓

THIS RECIPE COMES FROM MY OLD friend Peter Fresulone, who, along with Bill Liederman, was my partner in the Total Heaven Baking Company in the early eighties. We must have sold at least a ton of these cookies a year—they were one of our most popular items. At the time Peter said the recipe had come from his aunt so we always jokingly called them Zi' Rosa's cookies. The joke was that there is absolutely nothing Italian about them.

When Peter went to look for the recipe so that I could reprint it here, he found out that it had actually been given to him by his sister, Carol Pascarella. Belatedly, thanks, Carol, after all these years.

1 Set racks in the upper and lower thirds of the oven and preheat to 325 degrees.

2 In the bowl of a standing electric mixer fitted with the paddle attachment, beat together on medium speed the butter, granulated sugar, and salt until soft and fairly light, about 3 minutes.

3 Beat in the vanilla and water and continue beating until smooth.

4 Remove the bowl from the mixer and stir in the flour and pecans with a large rubber spatual. Keep mixing until the dough holds together.

5 Use a small ice cream or melon ball scoop to separate pieces of the dough for the cookies. Roll the dough between the palms of your hands to make a ball and place on the baking pan leaving about an inch around each. They don't spread, but they do puff slightly. Repeat until all the dough has been used.

16 tablespoons (2 sticks) unsalted butter, softened

⅓ cup granulated sugar

½ teaspoon salt

1 teaspoon vanilla extract

1 tablespoon water (or dark rum, bourbon, or brandy)

2 cups all-purpose flour

8 ounces (about 2 cups) pecan pieces, finely chopped, but not ground, in the food processor

1 cup confectioners' sugar for finishing

2 cookie sheets or jelly roll pans covered with parchment or foil

6 Another method is to roll pieces of the dough under the palms of your hands to make a cylinder about an inch thick. Cut off ¾-inch pieces of the dough and roll as above.

7 Bake the cookies for about 15 to 20 minutes, or until they are firm and golden. Slide the papers from the pans to racks.

8 After they are cold, sift the confectioners'
sugar into a shallow bowl and roll the cookies
in it.

9 Store the cooled cookies between sheets
of parchment or wax paper in a tin or plastic
container with a tight-fitting cover.

MAKES ABOUT 50 COOKIES

VARIATION

VANILLA BALLS: This is an interesting variation on the pecan ball theme sent to me by
my friend Sheri Portwood. She uses cream to
replace some of the butter, which makes an
extremely tender and fragile cookie. I'll just
give the ingredient list, because mixing, shaping, and baking are the same as the recipe
above with one notable exception. Sheri rolls
the cookies in the confectioners' sugar while
they're still warm—it makes more sugar stick
to the cookies.

MAKES ABOUT 40 COOKIES

12 tablespoons (1½ sticks) unsalted butter,
    softened

⅓ cup confectioners' sugar, plus 1 cup for
    finishing

1 teaspoon vanilla extract

¼ cup heavy whipping cream

1¾ cups all-purpose flour

3 ounces (about ¾ cup) lightly toasted
    pecans or other nuts, finely chopped,
    but not ground, in the food processor

WIENER MANDELGIPFERL

Little Viennese Almond Crescents

THESE FRAGILE NUT COOKIES ARE similar to but more delicate than the Pecan Butter Balls on page 99. There are recipes for this cookie that call for either walnuts, hazelnuts, or almonds. I prefer almonds—their delicate flavor seems most in keeping with this very subtle cookie. Thanks to Nancy Berzinec, Paul Kinberg, and Phil Krampetz, who shared their various recipes

1 Set the racks in the upper and lower thirds of the oven and preheat to 350 degrees.

2 In the bowl of a standing electric mixer fitted with the paddle attachment, beat together on lowest speed the butter and the 1 cup confectioners' sugar until combined. Raise the speed to medium and continue beating until soft and smooth, about 2 minutes. Beat in the vanilla.

3 Lower the speed and beat in the almonds, then the flour.

4 Remove the bowl from the mixer and finish mixing with a large rubber spatula.

5 Scrape the dough onto a floured work surface and divide it into four equal pieces. Use the palms of your hands to roll each into a cylinder. Cut each cylinder into twelve equal pieces. Shape each piece into a 2-inch cylinder, then taper the ends slightly. Place on one of the prepared pans, then curve the ends slightly to make a crescent shape. Repeat with the rest of the dough.

18 tablespoons (2¼ sticks) unsalted butter, softened

1 cup confectioners' sugar, plus more for finishing

2 teaspoons vanilla extract

4 ounces (about 1 cup) blanched almonds, finely ground in the food processor

2½ cups all-purpose flour

2 cookie sheets or jelly roll pans covered with parchment or foil

6 Bake the cookies for about 20 to 25 minutes, or until they are firm and very pale. Cool the cookies on the pans on racks (they are too delicate to move when they are hot). When the cookies are cool, sift confectioners' sugar generously over them.

7 Store the cooled cookies between sheets of parchment or wax paper in a tin or plastic container with a tight-fitting cover. Be careful—even cold they are extremely fragile.

MAKES ABOUT 48 COOKIES

SONJA HENIES

NO ONE SEEMS TO KNOW WHY THIS cookie was named for the Norwegian champion skater and movie star of the thirties. The recipe comes from Alexis Grossman, who cuts my hair. One day when I was in her chair we were talking about cookies and she gave me her grandmother's recipe for these. This fragile cookie is covered in walnuts, and has a "thumbprint" or small cavity in the top filled with jam. I don't know if the late movie star ever tasted one of these, but they have star quality of their own.

COOKIE DOUGH

16 tablespoons (2 sticks) unsalted butter, softened

¼ cup granulated sugar

¼ cup firmly packed light brown sugar

2 large egg yolks

1 teaspoon vanilla extract

2 cups all-purpose flour

FINISHING

2 large egg whites

4 ounces (about 1 cup) walnut pieces, finely ground in the food processor

½ cup seedless raspberry jam

2 cookie sheets or jelly roll pans covered with parchment or foil

1 In the bowl of a standing electric mixer fitted with the paddle attachment, beat together on medium speed the butter, granulated sugar, and brown sugar until soft, light, and fluffy, about 5 minutes. Beat in the egg yolks and vanilla and continue beating until smooth.

2 Lower the speed and beat in the flour.

3 Remove the bowl from the mixer and finish mixing with a large rubber spatula. Scrape the dough onto a piece of plastic wrap and press it into a rectangle about ½ inch thick. Wrap well and refrigerate about 1 hour. The dough should become more firm, but do not refrigerate so long that the dough hardens.

4 When you are ready to bake the cookies, set racks in the upper and lower thirds of the oven and preheat to 350 degrees.

5 Cut the chilled dough into 1-inch strips. Cut across the strips every ½ inch. Roll each piece into a ball between the palms of your hands. Repeat with all the dough, lining up the balls of dough on your work surface.

6 In a shallow bowl, beat the egg whites until broken up and place the ground walnuts in another shallow bowl nearby. With your left hand, pick up a ball of the dough and roll it around in the egg white. Use the same hand to lift it out of the egg white and place it in the ground walnuts. With your clean right hand, roll the cookie around in the walnuts to coat it evenly, then place it on one of the prepared pans, spacing the cookies about 1 inch apart.

7 After all the cookies have been coated with the walnuts and arranged on the pans, use the end of a wooden spoon handle or a fingertip to press a cavity into the top of each cookie. The indentation should be about half the cookie's depth. Fill the dimple with a little of the jam.

8 Bake the cookies for about 15 to 20 minutes, or until they are a very light golden and somewhat firm. Cool the cookies on the pans on racks. If the jam has boiled out of the cookies, or they just don't seem full enough, bring more jam to a boil in a small saucepan, lower it to a simmer, let it reduce for a minute or two, then use a small spoon to refill the cookies.

9 Store the cooled cookies between sheets of parchment or wax paper in a tin or plastic container with a tight-fitting cover.

MAKES ABOUT 40 COOKIES

KOURABIETHES

Greek Almond Cookies

THESE CRUMBLY, FRAGRANT COOKIES, staples of the Greek baking repertoire, are perhaps the world's best-known Greek sweet. The delicate texture comes from the large quantity of butter and the ground nuts added to the dough. Michelle Tampakis, my Greek connection, shared this recipe.

1 Set racks in the upper and lower thirds of the oven and preheat to 300 degrees.

2 In the bowl of a standing electric mixer fitted with the paddle attachment, beat together on medium speed the butter and confectioners' sugar until well mixed, about 1 minute.

3 Beat in the egg yolk, brandy, and cloves and continue beating until smooth.

4 Lower the mixer speed and beat in the almonds, then the flour.

5 Remove the bowl from the mixer and complete the mixing with a large rubber spatula.

6 With a small ice cream scoop or measuring spoon, scoop out a piece of dough. Roll it into a ball between the palms of your hands, then pinch the ends to make a football shape. Place on the prepared pans. Repeat, making sure the pieces are all the same size. Leave about an inch all around each cookie.

16 tablespoons (2 sticks) unsalted butter, softened

¼ cup confectioners' sugar, plus more for finishing

1 large egg yolk

1 tablespoon Metaxa (Greek brandy) or other brandy

Pinch ground cloves

2 ounces (about ½ cup) blanched almonds, finely ground in the food processor

2½ cups all-purpose flour

2 cookie sheets or jelly roll pans covered with parchment or foil

7 Bake the cookies for about 15 to 20 minutes, until they are firm and beginning to color only on the bottom. Place the pans on racks, then immediately sift a thick coat of confectioners' sugar over the hot cookies. (These cookies are too fragile to move while they are hot.) Allow them to cool completely, then sift over another coat of confectioners' sugar.

8 Store the cooled cookies between sheets of parchment or wax paper in a tin or plastic container with a tight-fitting cover.

MAKES ABOUT 30 COOKIES

THE GOOD COOK'S
GINGERSNAPS

In 1998, I was invited by Pat Adrian, director of the Good Cook division of the Book-of-the-Month Club, to judge its annual office baking contest. There were luscious cakes, pies, and cookies of all types, but these gingersnaps were the hands-down winners. Julie Ellis-Clayton, the winner of the contest, was kind enough to share her recipe with me. It was adapted from a recipe in *The New England Cookbook* (Culinary Arts Institute, no date).

1   Set the racks in the upper and lower thirds of the oven and preheat to 350 degrees.

2   Combine the flour, baking soda, salt, and spices in a bowl; stir well to mix.

3   In the bowl of a standing electric mixer fitted with the paddle attachment, beat together on medium speed the butter and 1 cup sugar for about 5 minutes until very light, fluffy, and whitened. Add the egg and continue beating until smooth.

4   Lower the speed and beat in half the dry ingredients, then the molasses. Stop the mixer and scrape down the bowl and beater. Beat in the remaining dry ingredients.

5   Remove the bowl from the mixer and use a large rubber spatula to finish mixing the dough.

6   Place the remaining ½ cup sugar in a shallow bowl.

7   Use a small ice cream scoop to form 1-inch-diameter pieces of dough. Roll the pieces into balls between the palms of your hands, then roll them in the sugar. Place the balls of dough

2 cups all-purpose flour

2 teaspoons baking soda

½ teaspoon salt

2 teaspoons ground ginger

1 teaspoon ground cinnamon

½ teaspoon ground cloves

12 tablespoons (1½ sticks) unsalted butter

1 cup sugar, plus ½ cup for finishing

1 large egg

¼ cup molasses

2 or 3 cookie sheets or jelly roll pans covered with parchment or foil

on the prepared pans, leaving about 3 inches all around each, to allow for spreading.

8   Bake the cookies for about 15 to 20 minutes, or until they have spread, colored, the surface has crackled, and they are firm to the touch. Slide the papers from the pans to racks. The cookies become crisp as they cool.

9   Store the cooled cookies between sheets of parchment or wax paper in a tin or plastic container with a tight-fitting cover.

Makes about 40 cookies

CHUNKY PEANUT BUTTER COOKIES

THESE ARE MY FAVORITE VARIATION ON classic peanut butter cookies. They have a real peanut crunch. My friend Jennifer Migliorelli developed this recipe when she was working as a chef in an American restaurant in Hong Kong.

1 Set the racks in the upper and lower thirds of the oven and preheat to 350 degrees.

2 In the bowl of a standing electric mixer fitted with the paddle attachment, beat on medium speed the butter, the sugars, salt, and peanut butter just until smooth. Add the eggs, one at a time. Beat only until smooth after each addition. Beat in the vanilla.

3 Separately, in a small bowl, mix the flour with the baking soda, then beat into the peanut butter mixture, scraping the bowl and beaters. Stir in the peanuts.

4 Roll 1-teaspoon portions of the dough between the palms of your hands to form rough balls and place them on the prepared pans. Leave 3 inches in all directions around each cookie. Flatten the cookies with the bottom of a glass. Bake about 12 to 15 minutes, until the cookies are well risen and golden.

5 Slide the papers from the pans to racks.

6 Store the cookies between layers of wax paper in a tin or plastic container with a tight-fitting cover.

MAKES ABOUT FIFTY 3-INCH COOKIES

8 tablespoons (1 stick) unsalted butter, softened

1 cup firmly packed dark brown sugar

1 cup granulated sugar

½ teaspoon salt

⅔ cup smooth peanut butter

2 large eggs

1½ teaspoons vanilla extract

2½ cups flour

2 teaspoons baking soda

8 ounces (about 2 cups) chopped honey-roasted peanuts

2 or 3 cookie sheets or jelly roll pans lined with parchment or foil

COOKIES

Chunky Peanut Butter Cookie (LEFT) *and The Good Cook's Gingersnap*

LOVE KNOTS

I REMEMBER MY AUNT, KITTY ROCCO, making these cookies during my childhood. Fortunately, her daughter, my cousin Karen Ludwig, saved all her mother's recipes and gave me this one.

1 Set the racks in the upper and lower thirds of the oven and preheat to 375 degrees.

2 Combine the flour and baking powder in a bowl; stir well to mix.

3 In a large mixing bowl, whisk the eggs to break them up. Whisk in the granulated sugar in a stream, then whisk in the butter and lemon extract.

4 Add the flour to the egg mixture and use a large rubber spatula to mix it into the liquid until a soft dough forms.

5 Scrape the dough onto a lightly floured work surface and press into a rectangle. Cut the dough into four equal pieces.

6 Roll each piece of dough into a rough cylinder, then cut it into three equal pieces. Repeat with the remaining pieces of dough to make twelve pieces in all. Take one piece of dough and roll it under your palms to a cylinder 10 inches long. Slice the cylinder into 2-inch rolls. To form a cookie, hold one end of a roll in your left hand and make a loop by crossing the right end over it; tuck the right end of the roll under the cookie so it looks like a knot, as in the illustrations.

COOKIE DOUGH

4½ cups all-purpose flour

4 teaspoons baking powder

6 large eggs

1 cup granulated sugar

8 tablespoons (1 stick) unsalted butter, melted

1 teaspoon lemon extract

ICING

One 1-pound box confectioners' sugar (about 4 cups)

⅓ cup water

½ teaspoon lemon extract

3 cookie sheets or jelly roll pans lined with parchment or foil

7 Arrange the cookies on the prepared pans as they are formed, and repeat the dividing and forming with the remaining dough.

8 Bake the cookies for about 10 minutes, until they are lightly colored on the bottom, but still pale on top, and feel firm, but not dry, when they are poked with a fingertip. Slide the papers from the pans to racks.

9 To make the icing, combine the confectioners' sugar, water, and lemon extract in a medium saucepan. Place over low heat and cook, stirring constantly, until the icing is lukewarm—about 100 to 110 degrees. Hold one of the cookies by the bottom and dip the top third into the icing. Let the excess icing drip back into the pan for a few seconds, then place the iced cookie, right side up, on the paper that it baked on. Continue with the other cookies until they are all iced—it may be necessary to reheat the icing once or twice to keep it liquid.

10 Let the icing dry for several hours at room temperature before packing up the cookies. Store the cooled cookies between sheets of parchment or wax paper in a tin or plastic container with a tight-fitting cover.

MAKES ABOUT 60 COOKIES

VARIATION

ANISE LOVE KNOTS: Substitute 1 tablespoon anisette for the lemon extract in the dough and 1 tablespoon anisette for the lemon extract in the icing. Put 1 tablespoon less water into the icing or it will be too thin.

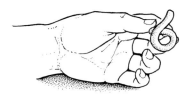

Step 6

TARALLI DOLCI DI PASQUA

Easter Ring Cookies

THESE LARGE COOKIES ARE A TRADITIONAL southern Italian Easter specialty, though they are good any time of the year. If you prefer a plainer cookie, omit the icing and brush the outside with an Egg Wash (page 159). Thanks to Marie Ciampi for sharing the recipe on which this is loosely based.

1 Set the racks in the upper and lower third of the oven and preheat to 350 degrees.

2 In a medium bowl, combine the flour and baking powder; stir well to mix.

3 Break the eggs into a large bowl and whisk them by hand until broken up. Whisk in the granulated sugar in a stream, then the melted butter and vanilla, whisking smooth after each addition. Use a large rubber spatula to fold in the dry ingredients.

4 Turn the dough out onto a floured surface and knead lightly. Divide it into sixteen equal pieces. Roll each piece under your palms into an 8-inch rope, then pinch the ends together to form a circle. Place five or six circles on each pan.

5 Bake the *taralli* about 30 minutes, or until well puffed and deep golden. Cool on racks.

COOKIE DOUGH

5½ cups all-purpose flour

1½ tablespoons baking powder

6 eggs

1 cup granulated sugar

12 tablespoons (1½ sticks) unsalted butter, melted

1½ tablespoons vanilla extract

ICING

3 cups confectioners' sugar

4 tablespoons water

1 tablespoon lemon juice

1 teaspoon vanilla extract

Multicolored nonpareils, optional

3 cookie sheets or jelly roll pans covered with parchment paper or foil

6 To make the icing, combine all the icing ingredients in a saucepan and heat gently until lukewarm, stirring often. Hold one of the cookies by the bottom and dip the top third into the icing. Let the excess icing drip back into the pan for a few seconds, then place the iced cookie, right side up, on the paper that it was baked on. Immediately sprinkle with multicolored nonpareils, if desired, before the icing has a chance to dry. Repeat with the other cookies; it may be necessary to reheat the icing before all the cookies are iced.

7 Store the cooled cookies between sheets of parchment or wax paper in a tin or plastic container with a tight-fitting cover.

VARIATION

If you prefer smaller cookies, divide the dough into 32 or 40 pieces. Roll the dough out to only 5 inches before making it into a circle. And bake the cookies only about 20 minutes; because they are smaller they will be done more quickly.

MADELEINES
French Shell Cookies

THESE LITTLE SHELL-SHAPED CAKES are one of the glories of French baking. Light, delicate, and buttery, they are surprisingly easy to prepare. This recipe calls for two madeleine pans each with twelve cavities. The ones I have are standard and make a 3-inch madeleine. If you only have one pan or your molds are smaller, you can keep reusing the same pan. These bake fairly quickly. If you don't have madeleine pans, try using mini muffin pans; the madeleines won't look the same, but they will taste as good.

1 Set a rack in the middle level of the oven and preheat to 375 degrees.

2 In a medium bowl, by hand, whisk together the eggs and salt until frothy, about 15 seconds. Whisk in the granulated sugar in a stream, then the orange zest and orange flower water, if used.

3 Use a rubber spatula to fold in the flour, then the melted butter.

4 Use a large soup spoon to fill the cavities in the molds about two-thirds full.

5 Bake the madeleines for about 20 minutes, until they are well risen, firm, and a golden color.

6 Remove the pans from the oven and unmold the madeleines immediately onto racks to cool. If you want to reuse the pan, wash it, then butter and flour it again.

7 Dust the madeleines lightly with confectioners' sugar, just before serving.

2 large eggs

Pinch salt

½ cup granulated sugar

Finely grated zest of 1 large orange

1 teaspoon orange flower water, optional

1 cup all-purpose flour

8 tablespoons (1 stick) unsalted butter, melted

Confectioners' sugar for finishing

Two madeleine pans, buttered and floured

8 Store the cooled madeleines between sheets of parchment or wax paper in a tin or plastic container with a tight-fitting cover.

MAKES 24 SHELL-SHAPED COOKIES

LEMON MADELEINES: Substitute the finely grated zest of one large or two small lemons for the orange zest and ½ teaspoon pure lemon extract for the orange flower water.

CHOCOLATE MADELEINES: Substitute ⅔ cup all-purpose flour and ¼ cup unsweetened cocoa powder, sifted after measuring, for the flour. Omit the orange flower water and replace with 1 teaspoon vanilla extract; do not omit the grated orange zest.

SPECULAAS

~ ๑ ๑ ~

THESE MOLDED COOKIES ARE POPULAR throughout the Low Countries as well as in Germany. They are called *speculoos* in Belgium and *Speculatius* in Germany, but apart from a few differences in seasonings, they are the same cookies. The name derives from the word for mirror and refers to the fact that the cookie "mirrors" its mold.

This is a traditional Dutch version of the cookie. To make these you will need a speculaas mold—a flat plate with one side carved into a cavity usually representing a knight, a horse and rider, or some elaborately dressed antique figure. Unlike Swiss *Anisbroetli* (page 119), for which the molds are just pressed against the dough to imprint it, speculaas dough is pressed into the mold and emerges in the shape of the figure. If you don't have a special mold, you may use an *Anisbroetli* mold, or just roll the dough out and cut it into rectangles—the cookies will taste just as good.

1 In a bowl, combine the flour, baking soda, salt, and spices; stir well to mix.

2 In the bowl of a standing electric mixer fitted with the paddle attachment, beat together on medium speed the butter and brown sugar until mixed, about 2 minutes. Lower the speed and beat in half the flour mixture. Stop the mixer and scrape down the bowl and beater with a rubber spatula.

3 Beat in the milk, then the remaining flour. Continue to mix until a firm dough forms.

4 Remove the bowl from the mixer and scrape the dough onto a floured work surface. Fold the dough over on itself several times, then place it on a piece of plastic wrap and press it into a rectangle about ½ inch thick. Wrap and chill the dough several hours or overnight.

5 When you are ready to bake the cookies, set the racks in the upper and lower thirds of the oven and preheat to 350 degrees.

6 Remove the dough from the refrigerator and divide it into twelve pieces. Use one piece of dough at a time; put the rest on a pan and place it in the refrigerator. On a floured work surface, use the palm of your hand to press the piece of dough to roughly the shape of the cavity in the mold. Generously flour the cavity in the mold, then quickly press the dough into the mold, and with a long thin knife, scrape away the excess dough. Invert the mold over the pan and rap the far end of the mold against the pan, holding it at an angle to release the formed cookie. Reflour the mold and repeat with the remaining

3 cups all-purpose flour

½ teaspoon baking soda

½ teaspoon salt

2 teaspoons ground cinnamon

1½ teaspoons freshly grated nutmeg

1 teaspoon ground coriander

1 teaspoon ground ginger

½ teaspoon ground cloves

¼ teaspoon freshly ground white pepper

12 tablespoons (1½ sticks) unsalted butter, softened

1 cup firmly packed light brown sugar

⅓ cup milk or water

2 or 3 cookie sheets or jelly roll pans covered with parchment or foil

pieces of dough. As you accumulate scraps of dough, press them together and chill them to mold again.

7 When all the cookies are formed, bake them for about 15 to 20 minutes, or until they are firm and golden. Slide the papers from the pans to racks.

8 Store the cooled cookies between sheets of parchment or wax paper in a tin or plastic container with a tight-fitting cover.

MAKES ABOUT 24 COOKIES; DEPENDING ON THE SIZE OF THE MOLD USED

ANISBROETLI

Swiss Anise Cookies

~୨ ୧~

THESE ARE EXACTLY THE SAME AS German Springerle—rich anise-flavored dough imprinted with special molds to give the cookies beautiful designs. In Germany, to imprint the dough with designs, they are usually rolled with a special carved rolling pin. The Swiss tend to imprint using individual molds. The Swiss system is more reliable because you are working with only a small portion of the dough at a time. Molds were difficult to find at one time, but now there are many antique-reproduction molds, cast from the Swiss originals, easily available. The molds may be carved to represent domestic, architectural, agricultural, or religious scenes. Or the shape of the mold may be the main design—a heart, diamond, flower—and the surface may be decorated with a geometric design.

1 Combine the flour, cornstarch, baking powder, and half the optional aniseed in a bowl; stir well to mix.

2 Half-fill a medium saucepan with water and bring it to a boil over medium heat. Reduce to a simmer.

3 Break the eggs into the bowl of a standing electric mixer and whisk in the sugar by hand. Place the bowl over the pan of simmering water and warm the mixture, whisking constantly, until it is lukewarm (100 to 110 degrees), about a minute or two. Place the bowl on a mixer fitted with the whisk attachment and whip the mixture on medium speed until cooled to room temperature. Whip in the anise extract.

4 Remove the bowl from the mixer and fold in the flour mixture about a third at a time, until a dough forms.

3 cups all-purpose flour

⅔ cup cornstarch

1½ teaspoons baking powder

2 tablespoons aniseed, optional

4 large eggs

2 cups sugar

3 teaspoons anise extract

2 or 3 cookie sheets or jelly roll pans covered with parchment or foil

5 Scrape the dough onto a floured work surface and lightly flour the top of the dough. Press the dough into a rectangle and divide it into four parts.

6 Strew the rest of the optional aniseed on the prepared pans. With the palms of your hands, press and pat each piece of dough into an 8-inch square. Keep moving the dough and sprinkling more flour under it so it doesn't

stick to the surface. Flour the mold or molds and gently press one into the dough. Cut around the printed dough and use a spatula or pancake turner to transfer it to the prepared pan. Continue with the remaining dough.

7 Allow the cookies to dry, uncovered, at room temperature for 2 or 3 hours.

8 When you are ready to bake the cookies, set the racks in the upper and lower thirds of the oven and preheat to 300 degrees. Bake the cookies for about 20 minutes, until risen and very white on the surface. Do not allow the tops of the cookies to take on any color. They may become a light golden color on the bottom.

9 Slide the papers from the pans to racks.

10 Store the cooled cookies between sheets of parchment or wax paper in a tin or plastic container with a tight-fitting cover.

MAKES 15 TO 20 COOKIES,
DEPENDING ON THE SIZE OF THE MOLDS

BISCOTTI

IF THERE IS ONE COOKIE THAT CAN be identified definitively with America in the last decade of the twentieth century, it is biscotti. The name biscotti means "twice-cooked" and it refers to the way these cookies are made. First the dough is formed into loaves and baked. Then after these cool, they are sliced and baked again. Many nationalities have twice-baked specialties, though they tend to be a little blander than the Italian version.

Many biscotti are enriched with nuts. The recipes in this chapter don't call for the nuts to be toasted in advance because I find that they toast quite enough during the second baking.

HINTS FOR BISCOTTI

1 If the dough seems soft, it is right. It is meant to be that way. Do not add extra flour to the biscotti doughs in this chapter or the resulting cookies will be cement-like. Review the instructions for measuring flour on page 15.

2 If you need to flour the work surface to handle the dough more easily, do so. When the dough is safely on the pan just brush off the excess flour with a dry pastry brush.

3 Make sure you bake the biscotti enough the first time around. If the centers of the logs are not baked through, they will compress when you slice them and harden during the second baking.

4 Use a really sharp knife to slice the biscotti. Cutting with a dull knife will make the baked log shatter.

5 The thinner you slice the biscotti, the more pan room you will need for the second baking. I usually count on one cookie sheet or jelly roll pan per log of biscotti.

6 Watch the biscotti carefully during the second baking. Most biscotti have a fairly high sugar content and will burn easily if left unattended.

7 Cool biscotti on their pans—the extra bit of drying time will help make them even crisper.

8 Biscotti are the perfect "keeping" cookie— just be sure to store them airtight and away from humidity.

CANTUCCINI
Classic Tuscan Biscotti

THESE CLASSIC TUSCAN BISCOTTI ARE very popular all over Italy. They are harder than most biscotti Americans are accustomed to and are made to be dunked in sweet wine or coffee.

1 Set a rack in the middle level of the oven and preheat to 350 degrees.

2 In a bowl, combine the flour, sugar, baking powder, and cinnamon; stir well to mix. Stir in the almonds.

3 In another bowl, whisk the eggs with the vanilla, then use a rubber spatula to stir the eggs into the dry ingredients. Continue to stir until a stiff dough forms.

4 Scrape the dough out onto a lightly floured work surface and divide it in half. Roll each half under the palms of your hands into a cylinder a little shorter than your baking sheet. Place the logs of dough on the baking sheet, making sure they are not too close to each other or to the sides of the pan. Press down gently with the palm of your hand to flatten the logs.

5 Bake for about 25 to 30 minutes, or until the logs are well risen and have also spread to about double their original size. The logs are done if they feel firm when pressed with a fingertip. Place the pan on a rack and let the logs cool completely.

6 Reset the racks in the upper and lower thirds of the oven but leave the temperature at 350 degrees. Place each of the cooled logs

2 cups all-purpose flour

I cup sugar

1½ teaspoons baking powder

½ teaspoon ground cinnamon

6 ounces (about 1½ cups) whole
  unblanched almonds

3 large eggs

2 teaspoons vanilla extract

2 cookie sheets or jelly roll pans covered
  with parchment or foil

on a cutting board and cut it diagonally into slices ⅓ inch thick. Arrange the biscotti on the prepared pans, cut side down. It isn't necessary to leave space between them. Bake the biscotti for about 15 or 20 minutes or until they are well toasted. Cool the pan on a rack.

7 Store the cooled biscotti between sheets of parchment or wax paper in a tin or plastic container with a tight-fitting cover.

MAKES ABOUT 60 BISCOTTI

CHOCOLATE CHUNK
BISCOTTI

THESE ARE A VARIATION ON ELLEN Baumwoll's recipe for chocolate biscotti, which appeared in my book *Chocolate*. Here chunks of dark and milk chocolate are added for a subtle richness.

1 Set a rack at the middle level of the oven and preheat to 325 degrees.

2 In a bowl, combine the flour, cocoa, baking powder, and salt; stir well to mix. Stir in the sugar and chocolates.

3 In another bowl, whisk together the eggs and vanilla and using a large rubber spatula stir the eggs into the flour mixture to form a dough.

4 On a lightly floured surface, press the dough together—it will be sticky. Flour your hands and the surface lightly, but do not add any more flour to the dough. Divide the dough in half and roll each half into a log the length of your pan (14 to 18 inches). Place the logs on a pan, making sure they are not too close to each other or to the sides of the pan. Press down gently with the palm of your hand to flatten the logs. (Use a dry brush to remove excess flour, if necessary.) Bake for about 30 minutes, until they are well risen and have also spread to about double in size. The logs are done when, pressed with a fingertip, they feel firm. Cool the logs on the pan.

5 Reset the racks in the upper and lower thirds of the oven. Using a sharp serrated knife, slice the baked logs diagonally about

1¾ cups all-purpose flour

⅔ cup unsweetened cocoa powder, sifted after measuring

2 teaspoons baking powder

Pinch salt

1¼ cups sugar

6 ounces bittersweet or semisweet chocolate, cut into ¼-inch pieces

6 ounces milk chocolate, cut into ¼-inch pieces

4 large eggs

1 teaspoon vanilla extract

2 cookie sheets or jelly roll pans covered with parchment or foil

every ¼ to ½ inch. Return the biscotti to the pans, cut side down, and bake up to 20 minutes longer, or until the biscotti are dry and crisp.

6 Store the cooled biscotti between sheets of parchment or wax paper in a tin or plastic container with a tight-fitting cover.

MAKES ABOUT 60 BISCOTTI

ALMOND AND HAZELNUT BISCOTTI

〜୨ ৎ〜

THIS COMBINATION WORKS PARTICULARLY well and makes nutty, fragrant biscotti. Of course you may also make them with all hazelnuts or all almonds. Don't be confused by the two quantities for each nut in the ingredient list. The first is for ground nuts, the second for whole ones.

1 Set a rack in the middle level of the oven and preheat to 350 degrees.

2 In a large bowl, combine the flour, sugar, ground nuts, baking powder, baking soda, and cinnamon; stir well to mix. Stir in the whole nuts.

3 Pour the honey into the water in the measuring cup; you will have ⅔ cup of the liquid. Stir the water and honey together, then add them to the bowl.

4 Stir the ingredients together until they form a stiff dough.

5 Scrape the dough onto a lightly floured work surface and divide it in half. Roll each half under the palms of your hands into a cylinder a little shorter than your baking sheet. Place the logs of dough on the baking sheet, making sure they are not too close to each other or to the sides of the pan. With the palm of your hand press down gently to flatten the logs.

6 Bake the logs of dough for about 30 minutes, or until they are well risen and have also spread to about double in size. The logs are done when, pressed with a fingertip, they feel firm. Place the pan on a rack to cool the logs completely.

2 cups all-purpose flour

⅔ cup sugar

2 ounces (about ½ cup) whole unblanched almonds, finely ground in the food processor

2 ounces (about ½ cup) whole unblanched hazelnuts, finely ground in the food processor

1 teaspoon baking powder

½ teaspoon baking soda

1 teaspoon ground cinnamon

3 ounces (about ¾ cup) whole unblanched almonds

3 ounces (about ¾ cup) whole unblanched hazelnuts

⅓ cup honey

⅓ cup water (in a 1-cup glass measuring cup)

2 cookie sheets or jelly roll pans covered with parchment or foil

7   Reset the racks in the upper and lower thirds of the oven but leave the temperature set at 350 degrees. Place each of the cooled logs on a cutting board and slice it diagonally every ⅓ inch. Arrange the biscotti on the prepared pans, cut side down. Bake the biscotti for about 15 or 20 minutes or until they are well toasted. Cool on the pan on a rack.

8   Store the cooled biscotti between sheets of parchment or wax paper in a tin or plastic container with a tight-fitting cover.

MAKES ABOUT 60 BISCOTTI

GINGERY MACADAMIA BISCOTTI

~ ⊙ ⊙ ~

THESE ARE INSPIRED BY BUT NOT BASED on a recipe called Gingerful Biscotti by my friend and mentor Maida Heatter. Please note the two different macadamia nuts in the ingredients: 4 ounces are ground and 6 ounces are chopped.

1 Set a rack in the middle level of the oven and preheat to 350 degrees.

2 In a large bowl, combine the flour, sugar, ground macadamia nuts, baking powder, baking soda, and spices; stir well to mix. Stir in the chopped nuts.

3 In another bowl, whisk the eggs; whisk in the honey and add the mixture to the dry ingredients.

4 Use a rubber spatula to stir the ingredients together until they form a stiff dough. At first it will seem too dry, but keep mixing and it will eventually hold together.

5 Scrape the dough onto a lightly floured work surface and divide it in half. Roll each half under the palms of your hands into a cylinder a little shorter than your baking sheet. Place the logs of dough on the baking sheet, making sure they are not too close to each other or to the sides of the pan. Press down gently with the palm of your hand to flatten the logs.

2 cups all-purpose flour

¾ cup sugar

4 ounces (about 1 cup) unsalted raw macadamia nuts, finely ground in the food processor, plus 6 ounces (about 1½ cups), coarsely chopped

1 teaspoon baking powder

½ teaspoon baking soda

4 teaspoons ground ginger

1 teaspoon ground cinnamon

½ teaspoon freshly ground white pepper

¼ teaspoon ground cloves

2 large eggs

⅓ cup honey

2 cookie sheets or jelly roll pans covered with parchment or foil

6   Bake the logs of dough for about 30 minutes, or until they are well risen and have also spread to about double in size. The logs are done when, pressed with a fingertip, they feel firm. Place the pan on a rack to cool the logs completely.

7   Reset the racks in the upper and lower thirds of the oven but leave the temperature at 350 degrees. Place each of the cooled logs on a cutting board and slice it diagonally every ⅓ inch. Arrange the biscotti on the prepared pans, cut side down. It isn't necessary to allow any space between them. Bake the biscotti for about 15 or 20 minutes or until they are well toasted. Cool on the pan on a rack.

8   Store the cooled biscotti between sheets of parchment or wax paper in a tin or plastic container with a tight-fitting cover.

MAKES ABOUT 60 BISCOTTI

DARK CHOCOLATE
HAZELNUT BISCOTTI

～ᧄ ᧄ～

THE DIFFERENCE BETWEEN THESE AND the Chocolate Chunk Biscotti on page 123 is that these use two different sugars and a lot of hazelnuts.

1 Set a rack at the middle level of the oven and preheat to 325 degrees.

2 In a bowl, combine the flour, cocoa, baking powder, cloves, and salt; stir well to mix. Stir in the hazelnuts.

3 In another bowl, whisk together the eggs, rum, and vanilla. Whisk in first the brown then the white sugar, one at a time. Stir in the flour mixture to form a dough.

4 On a lightly floured surface, press the dough together—it will be sticky. Flour your hands and the surface lightly, but do not add any more flour to the dough. Divide the dough in half and roll each half into a log the length of your pan (14 to 18 inches). Place the logs on a pan and flatten slightly. (Use a dry brush to remove excess flour, if necessary.) Bake for about 25 to 30 minutes, until well risen and firm. Cool the logs on the pan.

1¾ cups all-purpose flour

¾ cup unsweetened cocoa powder, sifted after measuring

2 teaspoons baking powder

¼ teaspoon ground cloves

Pinch salt

8 ounces (about 2 cups) hazelnuts, toasted, skins rubbed off, and coarsely chopped

4 large eggs

1 tablespoon dark rum

1 teaspoon vanilla extract

½ cup firmly packed dark brown sugar

⅔ cup granulated sugar

2 cookie sheets or jelly roll pans covered with parchment or foil

5 Using a sharp serrated knife, slice the baked logs diagonally about every ¼ to ½ inch. Return the biscotti to the pans, cut side down, and bake up to 20 minutes longer, or until the biscotti are dry and crisp.

6 Store the cooled biscotti between sheets of parchment or wax paper in a tin or plastic container with a tight-fitting cover.

MAKES ABOUT 60 BISCOTTI

COOKIES

ALL-CORN BISCOTTI

These delicate, crunchy biscotti are wheat- and gluten-free. Be careful to let the baked cake cool after the first baking or it will be difficult to slice.

1 Set a rack in the middle level of the oven and preheat to 350 degrees.

2 In the work bowl of a food processor fitted with the steel blade, place 1 cup of the almonds and pulse repeatedly until finely ground. Transfer to a bowl with the remaining whole almonds, cornmeal, cornstarch, baking soda, and cinnamon. Stir well to mix.

3 In a separate bowl, whisk the egg, add the sugar, honey, butter or oil, and vanilla, whisking as you add each one. Stir in the dry ingredients with a rubber spatula until a stiff dough forms.

4 Scrape the dough onto the 9 × 13-inch pan and press with palm of your hand until the dough is an even layer completely covering the bottom of the pan, about ½ inch thick.

5 Bake for about 30 minutes, until firm. Cool in the pan for 5 minutes, then invert onto a cutting board and cool completely. Reset the racks in the upper and lower thirds of the oven. Leave the oven on.

6 Cut into three 3 × 13-inch strips, then slice each strip every ½ inch. Arrange the biscotti on the prepared cookie sheets or jelly roll pans and bake again for about 15 minutes.

8 ounces (about 2 cups) whole
    unblanched almonds

1 cup yellow cornmeal

1 cup cornstarch

½ teaspoon baking soda

½ teaspoon ground cinnamon

1 egg

⅔ cup sugar

¼ cup honey

2 tablespoons melted butter or vegetable oil

1 teaspoon vanilla extract

One 9 × 13 × 2-inch pan, buttered and the bottom lined with parchment or foil

2 cookie sheets or jelly roll pans covered with parchment or foil

7 Store the cooled biscotti between sheets of parchment or wax paper in a tin or plastic container with a tight-fitting cover.

MAKES ABOUT 70 BISCOTTI

TRADITIONAL
JEWISH MANDELBROT

MANDELBROT, THE MOST TRADITIONAL Jewish cookie, is really a type of biscotti. This recipe is a combination and variation of excellent recipes sent to me by Rhonda Kaplan of Toronto and Michele Lifshen-Reing, who was a student in my career baking course at Peter Kump's New York Cooking School.

1 Set a rack in the middle level of the oven and preheat to 350 degrees.

2 In a bowl, combine the flour, baking powder, and salt; stir well to mix. Stir in the almonds.

3 In another bowl, whisk the eggs by hand until well mixed. Add the sugar and whisk until smooth. Whisk in the extracts and oil.

4 Fold the flour mixture into the egg mixture until all the flour is absorbed.

5 On a lightly floured surface, press the dough together. Divide the dough in half and roll each half into a log the length of your pan (14 to 18 inches). Place each log on a pan and flatten slightly. Bake for about 25 to 30 minutes, until the are well risen and firm. Cool the logs on the pans and racks.

6 Reset the racks in the upper and lower thirds of the oven. Using a sharp serrated knife, slice the baked logs diagonally about every ½ inch. Place the cinnamon sugar in a shallow bowl and turn the cut biscotti in it. Return the biscotti to the pans, cut side down, and bake up to 20 minutes longer, or until the biscotti are dry and crisp.

2 cups all-purpose flour

1 teaspoon baking powder

¼ teaspoon salt

4 ounces (about 1 cup) whole blanched almonds, coarsely chopped

2 large eggs

½ cup sugar

1 teaspoon vanilla extract

1 teaspoon almond extract

½ cup mild vegetable oil

½ cup sugar mixed with 1 teaspoon cinnamon for finishing

2 cookie sheets or jelly roll pans covered with parchment or foil

7 Store the cooled biscotti between sheets of parchment or wax paper in a tin or plastic container with a tight-fitting cover.

MAKES ABOUT 48 BISCOTTI

COOKIES

CAROLE WALTER'S
ETHEREAL MANDELBROT

THESE ARE COOKIES I COULD MAKE (and eat) daily and never tire of them. They are fine and delicate and I think the best version of this cookie I have ever tried. Sometimes I cheat and substitute a stick of melted butter for the oil—they are even better. Carole told me that this recipe came from a friend in North Carolina and that she always uses pecans in them as a tribute to its Southern origin.

1 Set a rack in the middle level of the oven and preheat to 350 degrees.

2 In a bowl, combine the flour, baking powder, optional cinnamon, and nuts; stir well to mix.

3 In a medium bowl, whisk the eggs and salt by hand until well mixed. Whisk in the sugar and vanilla and when the mixture is smooth whisk in the oil.

4 Fold the flour mixture into the egg mixture until all the flour is absorbed—the dough will be very soft.

5 Spoon the dough onto the prepared pan in two strips, each about 2 inches wide and the length of the pan, making sure they are not too close to each other or to the sides of the pan. Smooth and even off the sides, if necessary.

2½ cups all-purpose flour

1 tablespoon baking powder

1 teaspoon ground cinnamon, optional

4 ounces (about 1 cup) coarsely chopped
    pecan pieces

3 large eggs

Pinch salt

1 cup sugar

1 teaspoon vanilla extract

½ cup mild vegetable oil or 8 tablespoons
    (1 stick) unsalted butter, melted

2 cookie sheets or jelly roll pans covered
with parchment or foil

6 Bake the logs of dough about 25 to 30 minutes, or until they are well risen and have also spread to about double in size. The logs are done when, pressed with a fingertip, they feel firm. Cool on the pan on a rack to room temperature.

7 Using a sharp serrated knife, slice the baked logs diagonally about every ¼ to ½ inch. Return the biscotti to the pan, cut side down, and bake up to 20 minutes longer, or until the biscotti are a deep golden color.

8 Store the cooled biscotti between sheets of parchment or wax paper in a tin or plastic container with a tight-fitting cover.

MAKES ABOUT 60 BISCOTTI, DEPENDING ON HOW THINLY THEY ARE SLICED

COOKIES

TOTEBEINLI

〜◦ჿ◦〜

THE NAME OF THESE ESPECIALLY CRISP and fragile biscotti means "dead men's bones" in Swiss German dialect. Thanks to Thea Cvijanovich from Berne for sharing this interesting variation on standard biscotti.

1 Set a rack in the middle level of the oven and preheat to 350 degrees.

2 In a bowl, combine the flour and baking powder; stir well to mix, then stir in the nuts.

3 In a medium bowl, beat the butter by hand with a rubber spatula, then beat in one third of the sugar. Add one egg and continue beating until smooth. Add another third of the sugar, then another egg, and beat again until smooth. Finally, add the remaining sugar and the last egg, and beat until smooth. Beat in the salt, lemon zest, and cinnamon.

4 Stir in the flour mixture to form a smooth dough.

5 Scrape the dough out onto the prepared 10 × 15-inch pan and press it into an even layer using a rubber spatula or the floured palm of your hand. Make sure the dough reaches into all the corners of the pan and that the top is flat and even.

6 Bake the dough for about 30 minutes, or until it is firm and well colored. Place the pan on a rack to cool for about 15 minutes.

2⅓ cups all-purpose flour

1 teaspoon baking powder

4 ounces (about 1 cup) whole unblanched almonds, cut in half

4 ounces (about 1 cup) whole unblanched hazelnuts, cut in half

2 tablespoons (¼ stick) unsalted butter, softened

1¼ cups sugar

3 large eggs

Pinch salt

Finely grated zest of 1 medium lemon

1 teaspoon ground cinnamon

One 10 × 15 × 1-inch baking pan buttered and lined with parchment or foil

2 cookie sheets or jelly roll pans covered with parchment or foil

7 Set the racks in the upper and lower thirds of the oven and adjust the temperature to 300 degrees. Turn the warm baked slab out onto a cutting board and with a large, sharp knife cut down the length of the slab to make three 3- to 3½-inch-wide lengthwise strips. Then slice each strip across into ½-inch-wide biscotti. Place the biscotti, cut side down, on the prepared pans and bake them for another 20 minutes, or until they are dry and crisp and golden in color.

8 Cool the biscotti on the pans on racks.

9 Store the cooled biscotti between sheets of parchment or wax paper in a tin or plastic container with a tight-fitting cover.

Makes about 90 biscotti

135

COOKIES

AUSTRALIAN ALMOND TOASTS

THIS IS A RECIPE THAT MY FRIEND Kyra Effren brought back from a visit to Australia. Kyra says they are everywhere Down Under, made with all different types of nuts. To be successful, these must be very thin, so get out your sharpest serrated knife. And like the Australians, use any type of nut you like.

1 Set a rack in the middle level of the oven and preheat to 350 degrees.

2 In a bowl combine the flour, baking powder, and salt; stir well to mix, then stir in the almonds.

3 Pour the egg whites into the bowl of an electric mixer fitted with the whip attachment and whip on medium speed until they become white, opaque, and begin to hold their shape, about 2 or 3 minutes. One tablespoon at a time, beat in the sugar, then continue beating until the egg whites hold a firm peak. Beat in the vanilla.

4 Remove the bowl from the mixer and fold in the flour mixture. Continue to fold until the mixture forms a soft dough.

5 Scrape the dough into the prepared loaf pan and smooth the top.

6 Bake the loaf for about 35 to 40 minutes, or until it is well risen and a knife or toothpick inserted in the center emerges clean. Turn off the oven and unmold the loaf onto a rack, roll it onto its side, cover it with a piece of aluminum foil (to conserve moisture and make it easier to cut later), and allow it to cool to room temperature.

1 cup all-purpose flour

1 teaspoon baking powder

½ teaspoon salt

6 ounces (about 1½ cups) whole blanched almonds, coarsely chopped

3 large egg whites (a little less than ½ cup)

½ cup sugar

1 teaspoon vanilla extract

One 8½ × 4½ × 2¾-inch loaf pan, buttered and the bottom lined with parchment or foil

2 or 3 cookie sheets or jelly roll pans covered with parchment or foil

7 When you are ready to slice and rebake the biscotti, set the racks in the upper and lower thirds of the oven and preheat to 275 degrees.

8 Using your sharpest serrated knife, slice the loaf about every ⅛ inch. Arrange the slices on the prepared pans and bake them for about 15 minutes or until they are light golden and dry. Be careful—these burn easily. If they are not all the exact same thickness some may color faster than others and you may have to remove them from the pans one at a time as they are done.

9 Cool the biscotti on racks.

10 Store the cooled biscotti between sheets of parchment or wax paper in a tin or plastic container with a tight-fitting cover. These keep indefinitely.

MAKES ABOUT 60 VERY THIN BISCOTTI

FRIED COOKIES

Deep-frying is not what you think of when you think of making cookies, though it produces some delicate and interesting ones. Fried pastries and cookies were originally the only type made at home, because until well into the twentieth century, most homes in Europe and many in America did not have ovens. Ovens were at the local bakery or belonged to a business. When you needed baking done, you brought the food to be baked to the oven and paid a fee to use it.

When I first visited my cousins in southern Italy in the early seventies, there was still a communal oven down the street from their house. I had a chance to visit once or twice, then unfortunately it was destroyed in a disastrous 1980 earthquake.

Carnival, the season of feasting that precedes the beginning of Lent, was traditionally a time for fried cookies and pastries. Many of the ones we eat today were originally prepared only for Carnival. Meat and meat products had to be avoided during the Lenten fasting, so fried pastries would also have been forbidden. They were usually fried in lard or beef suet—two animal fats with a high smoking point still widely used in Europe for deep-frying.

Fried cookies and pastries are not necessarily heavy or greasy. When foods are properly fried, they absorb only a minute amount of fat. So don't resist trying fried cookies—their textures vary from rich and creamy to shatteringly crisp, and are fun to make and eat on a cold winter night.

Hints for Fried Cookies

1 Fry in a large pan, such as a Dutch oven, and don't fill it more than half full of oil: If the oil breaks down and begins to foam, there will still be room so it doesn't overflow. A pan with a cover is best. The cover isn't used during frying but it helps after the frying is finished. You can move the pan off the burner and cover it, thereby stopping the hot fat fumes from continuing to saturate the air. Leave the covered pan off the heat but on the stove until the oil is cold. Never pick up and move a pan filled with hot oil—it is too dangerous. An electric frying pan, especially one of the deeper models, is ideal for deep-frying.

2 Before you start to fry always have everything ready. Have all the cookies lined up on pans, then have other pans covered with paper towels to receive and drain the fried cookies. Also get out a skimmer or slotted spoon for removing the cookies from the oil. Trying to roll dough, cut out cookies, and fry at the same time will only result in burned cookies, and the temperature of the unmonitored oil can become dangerously high. When you are frying, don't do anything else.

3 Use a good deep-frying thermometer so you know the exact temperature of the oil. Then you can adjust the heat under the frying kettle according to any changes in temperature you read on the thermometer. A deep-frying thermometer is also known as a candy thermometer. Use the kind that looks like a ruler, not the less accurate stem with a round dial at the top.

4 The oil is ready when a bit of dough dropped in rises to the surface and begins to color almost immediately. Before you add large amounts of dough to the frying oil, test a few to see how quickly they will cook through.

5 Don't crowd the pan—too many cookies in the pan at once will bring down the temperature of the oil and make the cookies absorb fat.

6 If the cookies have been rolled out in flour, brush off any excess or it will accumulate in the oil and burn.

7 Remember, hot oil can be extremely dangerous. Banish the curious from the kitchen and keep distractions to a minimum so you can concentrate on the frying.

GALANI

Venetian Carnival Fritters

THESE LITTLE KNOTS OF DELICATE fried dough are similar to *bugnes*, but more elaborate both in flavor and in presentation.

1 In a large bowl, beat together the butter, sugar, and salt with a medium rubber spatula. Whisk in one egg, then the other; the mixture may appear separated—that's all right. Use the rubber spatula to stir in the flour and form a soft dough.

2 Scrape the dough onto a floured work surface, and using a bench scraper or spatula, fold it over on itself several times. Keep folding the dough over on itself and pushing it away, then turning and repeating the operation. Continue to knead for a minute or two, or until the dough is smooth.

3 Coat the outside of the dough generously with flour and place it on a piece of plastic wrap. Form it into a rectangle about ½ inch thick and wrap it up. Let the wrapped dough rest at room temperature for about an hour before you continue.

3 tablespoons unsalted butter, softened

3 tablespoons granulated sugar

½ teaspoon salt

2 large eggs

2 cups all-purpose flour

4 cups vegetable oil for frying

Confectioners' sugar for sprinkling

2 cookie sheets or jelly roll pans covered with parchment or other paper to hold the *galani* before they are fried, and 2 more pans covered with paper towels or brown paper on which to drain the fried *galani*

4 After the dough has rested, divide it into three equal parts. Generously flour both the work surface and the dough. Roll one piece of the dough out into a 9-inch square and with a pizza wheel cut it into 1½ × 3-inch rectangles.

Step 4

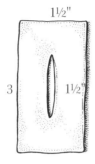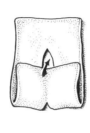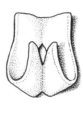

As each piece is cut, place it on one of the prepared pans. Be careful not to let them overlap. Make a slash in the center of each rectangle of dough and thread one end back through it, as in the illustration. Repeat with the remaining dough.

5 Heat the oil in a large kettle to 375 degrees. Fry the *galani* a few at a time, moving them constantly in the hot fat so they color evenly. Fry to a light golden color and drain on the prepared pans.

6 Cool the *galani* to room temperature and sprinkle them generously with confectioners' sugar before serving.

7 As with all fried pastries, these are best the day they are made, but leftovers may be kept for a while at room temperature, loosely covered with plastic wrap.

MAKES ABOUT 50 SMALL *GALANI*

SFINGI
Cream Puff Pastry Fritters

THESE ARE THE EASIEST AND MOST impressive of all fried specialties. They are as sweet and creamy as a small cream puff filled with sweetened pastry cream, even though they are made from a completely unsweetened dough and just rolled in cinnamon sugar.

Sfingi were one of the pastries my maternal grandmother, Clotilda Lo Conte, was famous for. She never gave out recipes, so everyone thought these were so much harder to make than they are. You'll see what I mean when you try them.

1   In a medium saucepan, bring the water, salt, and butter to a boil over low heat. Remove from the heat and sift in the flour all at once. Use a wooden spoon to stir the flour in smoothly.

2   Return the pan to low heat and stir the paste vigorously until it holds together in one piece and the bottom of the pan is lightly filmed. Scrape the paste into a bowl and let it cool for 5 minutes.

3   Beat in the eggs one at a time, beating smooth after each addition.

4   To fry the *sfingi*, in a 4-quart saucepan, heat the oil to 350 degrees. To form the *sfingi*, use two teaspoons. Dip one teaspoon into the oil, then spoon up some of the dough with it. Use the other spoon to scrape the dough off the first one into the oil. Work quickly and fry six or eight *sfingi* at a time. Fry until the *sfingi* crack open and are a deep golden color. Drain on the prepared pans. Just before serving, mix the cinnamon and sugar together in a shallow

1 cup water

Pinch salt

6 tablespoons (¾ stick) unsalted butter, cut into 8 pieces

1 cup all-purpose flour

4 large eggs

4 cups vegetable oil for frying

1 teaspoon ground cinnamon

½ cup sugar

2 cookie sheets or jelly roll pans covered with paper towels or brown paper for draining the *sfingi*

bowl and roll each of the *sfingi* in it. Arrange the *sfingi* on a platter.

5   As with all fried pastries, these are best the day they are made, but leftovers may be kept for a while at room temperature, loosely covered with plastic wrap.

MAKES ABOUT 30 *SFINGI*

SOUR CREAM
DOUGHNUT HOLES

~⚬ ⚬~

NOWADAYS WE AMERICANS NO LONGER eat doughnuts as regularly as our ancestors did. But once in a while indulge. Doughnut holes are a great way to enjoy doughnuts on a small scale. If you're a doughnut aficionado try to find a copy of Sally Levitt Steinberg's *Donut Book* (Knopf, 1987). You can't miss it—it has a hole in the cover! Seriously, it is filled with amusing doughnut lore and even a few recipes.

1 In a large mixing bowl, combine the flour, baking powder, baking soda, salt, and spices; stir well to mix. In another bowl, whisk the egg, then whisk in the granulated sugar. Whisk in the melted butter and sour cream.

2 Pour the liquid ingredients into the flour mixture and with a large rubber spatula mix gently until just combined. Do not overwork. The dough will be sticky. Turn the dough onto a lightly floured work surface and knead gently. Add pinches of flour, if necessary, until the dough just holds together. Cover the dough with plastic wrap and chill for about 1 hour.

3 On a floured surface, roll the dough out to ½-inch thickness. With a 1¼-inch round cutter, cut out the doughnut holes.

4 Heat the oil to 365 degrees, then fry the doughnut holes, a few at a time, turning them once. Try to keep the temperature of the oil between 360 and 375 degrees. It should take about 3 minutes for the doughnut holes to become nicely browned on both sides. Transfer them to one of the prepared pans to cool. Dust lightly with confectioners' sugar just before serving.

2 cups all-purpose flour

2 teaspoons baking powder

½ teaspoon baking soda

½ teaspoon salt

½ teaspoon ground cinnamon

½ teaspoon freshly grated nutmeg

1 egg

½ cup granulated sugar

3 tablespoons melted butter

⅔ cup sour cream

4 cups oil for frying

Confectioners' sugar for sprinkling

1 cookie sheet or jelly roll pan covered with parchment or other paper to hold the doughnut holes before they are fried, and 2 more covered with paper towels or brown paper on which to drain the fried doughnut holes

5   As with all fried pastries, these are best the day they are made, but leftovers may be kept for a while at room temperature, loosely covered with plastic wrap.

MAKES ABOUT TWENTY-FOUR 1I/2-INCH DOUGHNUT HOLES

CHOCOLATE SOUR CREAM DOUGHNUT HOLES: Substitute 1½ cups flour and ⅓ cup unsweetened cocoa powder, sifted after measuring, for the flour in the recipe. If you wish, use Sugar-Based Chocolate Glaze for Cookies to streak the doughnut holes or half-dip them.

145

COOKIES

SHENKELI

Little Thighs

I FIRST ENCOUNTERED THESE WHEN I worked at a hotel in Zurich in the early seventies. The Christmas season had arrived and the hotel's pastry chef, Armand, and his assistants (I was working in the garde-manger department at the time), set about preparing all sorts of *Guetzli* (see page 2 for a full explanation of Swiss Christmas cookies). Because Armand was from Fribourg and came from a French-speaking family, his culinary practices were more those of western Switzerland—not a land of *Guetzli* traditions. So no one was surprised when Armand made a big pan of *Shenkeli*, heretofore exclusively Carnival cookies, for the Christmas holidays.

By the way *Shenkeli* means "thighs" and are sometimes called *Dameshenkeli*, or "ladies' thighs." This makes making and eating *Shenkeli* seem vaguely naughty to the conservative Swiss Germans.

This recipe is adapted from *Guetzli* (Manus Verlag, 1987) by Marianne Kaltenbach, a popular Swiss German food writer and TV personality.

4 tablespoons (½ stick) unsalted butter, softened

½ cup sugar

2 large eggs

Pinch salt

1 tablespoon kirsch

Finely grated zest of 1 small lemon

2¼ cups all-purpose flour

4 cups vegetable oil for frying

2 cookie sheets or jelly roll pans covered with parchment or other paper to hold the *Shenkeli* before they are fried, and 2 more covered with paper towels or brown paper on which to drain the *Shenkeli*

1 In a medium bowl, beat the butter until it is soft and smooth with a large rubber spatula. Beat in the sugar. Switch to a whisk and beat in the eggs, one at a time. Then beat in the salt, kirsch, and lemon zest.

2 Use the rubber spatula to stir in the flour and make a soft dough. Scrape the dough onto a floured work surface, and using a bench scraper or spatula, fold it over on itself several times. Keep folding the dough over on itself and pushing it away, then turning and repeating the operation. Continue to knead for a minute or two, or until the dough is smooth.

3 Coat the outside of the dough generously with flour, then place it on a piece of plastic wrap. Form it into a rectangle about ½ inch thick and wrap it up. Let the wrapped dough rest in the refrigerator for about an hour before you continue.

4 After the dough has rested, divide it into four equal parts. Roll each part into a 12 inch length and cut into twelve equal pieces. Roll over each piece again with the palm of the hand to make it a cylinder about 2 inches long. Repeat with the remaining dough. Place the *Shenkeli* on the prepared pans.

5 Heat the oil to 350 degrees in a large kettle. Fry a few *Shenkeli* at a time, moving them constantly in the hot fat so they color evenly. Fry to a light golden color, then drain on the prepared pans.

6 Cool the *Shenkeli* to room temperature before serving; they are traditionally not covered with sugar since the dough itself is sweet.

7 As with all fried pastries, these are best the day they are made, but leftovers may be kept for a while at room temperature, loosely covered with plastic wrap.

MAKES ABOUT 48 *SHENKELI*

ZEPPOLE
Italian Bread-Dough Fritters

THOUGH *ZEPPOLE* IS THE GENERIC Italian name for fritters of all kinds, it specifically refers to those chewy fritters of fried unseasoned bread dough covered with sugar and eaten outdoors during Italian street festivals.

When I was a child on Fourteenth Avenue in Newark there was a "feast" every weekend from July Fourth to Labor Day in our all-Italian neighborhood. Each feast involved processions of members of a saint's society bearing his or her statue through the streets. After the processions there were enormous street fairs that went on into the night with food stalls, games of chance, and several bandstands playing corny music. To this day if my mother hears loud, bad music or just a lot of noise she says: "It sounds like the feast on Fourteenth Avenue."

These *zeppole* are a delicate version of the greasy wads of fried dough you get at a feast. The taste of them never fails to bring back a flood of memories of my childhood and the closed little world of our immigrant neighborhood.

1 Pour the water into a medium bowl. Whisk in the yeast. Use a rubber spatula to stir in the flour, but add the salt before the flour is completely absorbed. Continue stirring until the ingredients form a very wet dough.

2 Cover the bowl with plastic wrap. Let the dough rise at room temperature for about an hour, or until it is about double in bulk and very puffy.

3 To fry the *zeppole*, heat the oil to 375 degrees in a 4-quart saucepan. Use two soup spoons to form them (at the feast the *zeppole* makers snatched off pieces of dough with one hand): Dip one spoon into the hot oil, then spoon up some of the risen dough with it. Use the other spoon to scrape the dough off the first and drop it into the oil. Work quickly and fry six or eight of the *zeppole* at a time. Fry until

1 cup warm tap water, about 105 degrees
1 envelope (2½ teaspoons) active dry yeast
1¾ cups all-purpose flour
½ teaspoon salt
4 cups vegetable oil for frying
Confectioners' sugar for sprinkling

2 cookie sheets or jelly roll pans covered with paper towels or brown paper on which to drain the *zeppole*

the *zeppole* are a deep golden color. Drain on the prepared pans. When the *zeppole* are cool, dust generously with the confectioners' sugar.

4 As with all fried pastries, these are best the day they are made, but leftovers may be kept for a while at room temperature, loosely covered with plastic wrap.

MAKES ABOUT 24 ZEPPOLE

OLLIEBOLLEN
Dutch Currant Fritters

THESE ARE LIKE LITTLE CLOUDS OF brioche dough, scented with lemon zest and cinnamon and studded with currants. Like so many Dutch specialties, they really deserve to be better known. Many thanks to my Dutch connections: Bonnie Slotnick, who supplied me with a couple of excellent Dutch baking books, from which this recipe is adapted, and Hans Polleman, who, with Bonnie, helped with translation while I struggled through those all but unintelligible recipes.

1   To make the sponge, heat the milk in a small saucepan over low heat until just lukewarm—about 105 degrees at the most. Pour the milk into a small bowl. Whisk in the yeast, then stir in the flour. This will still be very liquid. Cover the sponge with plastic wrap and let it ferment at room temperature for about 30 minutes, or until it is very well risen and foamy.

2   After the sponge has risen, make the dough: In the bowl of a standing electric mixer fitted with the paddle attachment, beat together on medium speed the butter, brown sugar, salt, cinnamon, and lemon zest until smooth. Beat in the egg (the mixture will appear separated—that's okay). Beat in the risen sponge. Stop the mixer and add the 1 cup flour, then beat on low speed until the dough is smooth, about 3 minutes. Beat in the currants.

3   Remove the bowl from the mixer, cover it with plastic wrap, and let the dough rise at room temperature for about an hour, or until it has almost doubled in bulk and is very puffy.

SPONGE

⅔ cup milk

1 envelope (2½ teaspoons) active dry yeast

1 cup all-purpose flour

DOUGH

3 tablespoons unsalted butter, softened

2 tablespoons firmly packed dark brown sugar

¼ teaspoon salt

½ teaspoon ground cinnamon

Finely grated zest of 1 small lemon

1 large egg

Risen sponge (see above)

1 cup all-purpose flour

⅔ cup currants (or ⅓ cup each currants and golden raisins)

4 cups vegetable oil for frying

Confectioners' sugar for sprinkling

2 cookie sheets or jelly roll pans covered with paper towels or brown paper on which to drain the *olliebollen*

4 To fry the *olliebollen*, in a 4-quart saucepan, heat the oil to 350 degrees. Use two soup spoons to form the fritters: Dip one spoon into the hot oil, then spoon up some of the risen dough with it. Use the other spoon to scrape the dough off the first and drop it into the oil. Work quickly and fry six or eight of the fritters at a time. Fry until the *olliebollen* are a deep golden color. Drain on the prepared pans. When the *olliebollen* are cool, dust generously with the confectioners' sugar.

5 As with all fried pastries, these are best the day they are made, but leftovers may be kept for a while at room temperature, loosely covered with plastic wrap.

MAKES ABOUT 30 SMALL *OLLIEBOLLEN*

151

FILLED AND SANDWICH COOKIES

FILLED COOKIES, THE ARISTOCRATS OF THE COOKIE WORLD, involve a little extra effort. They are usually composed of a dough enclosing a rich filling. Like sandwich cookies, later on in this chapter, they provide an interesting contrast between their tender or crisp cookie component and creamy filling.

HINTS FOR FILLED COOKIES

1 Make sure the dough is firm but malleable before trying to shape filled cookies. Success depends on having the dough and filling approximately the same consistency so they do not oppose each other as you are trying to shape the cookies.

2 Be accurate about dimensions. Use a ruler for best results.

3 Prepare both dough and filling in advance—then you can concentrate on shaping the cookies on the following day, or whenever you plan to do it.

4 Apply egg wash sparingly to the outsides of cookies. I dip a brush into the beaten egg, then wipe several times against the rim of the bowl or cup containing the egg. This is to make the excess egg drip off so that when you paint the wash onto the cookies it will not dribble down and puddle underneath them.

CUCIDATI
Sicilian Fig-Filled Cookies

NO ONE SEEMS TO AGREE ABOUT EXACTLY what—besides figs—goes into the filling for these classic Sicilian cookies. There are two distinct versions: One is for a small cookie, made from a filled cylinder of dough, as here, or formed as "ravioli" with the filling enclosed between two layers of the dough and shaped with a decorative cutter. The other is for a large ring-shaped cake about 6 inches in diameter referred to as a *bucellato*, or bracelet. I have read about them in Sicilian cookbooks but have never seen one, either in an Italian pastry shop in the United States or anywhere in Sicily. The following recipe makes a lot of cookies, but they keep indefinitely—so they are a good choice for holiday giving.

PASTA FROLLA

4 cups all-purpose flour

⅔ cup sugar

1 teaspoon baking powder

1 teaspoon salt

16 tablespoons (2 sticks) cold unsalted butter, cut into 16 pieces

4 large eggs

FIG FILLING

12 ounces (about 2 cups) dried Calimyrna figs

½ cup raisins

⅓ cup candied orange peel, diced

⅓ cup whole almonds, chopped and lightly toasted

3 ounces semisweet chocolate, cut into ¼-inch pieces

⅓ cup apricot preserves

3 tablespoons dark rum

1 teaspoon instant espresso coffee granules

½ teaspoon ground cinnamon

¼ teaspoon ground cloves

EGG WASH

1 large egg, well beaten with 1 pinch salt

Multicolored nonpareils for finishing before baking

2 or 3 cookie sheets or jelly roll pans covered with parchment or foil

1 To make the dough, in the work bowl of a food processor fitted with the steel blade, combine the flour, sugar, baking powder, and salt. Pulse two or three times to mix. Add the butter and pulse repeatedly until it is finely incorporated and the mixture is cool and powdery. Add the eggs, all at once, and continue to pulse until the dough forms a ball.

Scrape the dough onto a floured surface, then place it on a piece of plastic wrap. Press the dough into a square about an inch thick and wrap it. Chill the dough while preparing the filling.

2 For the filling, in a large bowl, stem and dice the figs. If they are hard, place them in a saucepan, cover them with water, and bring

them to a boil over medium heat. Drain the figs in a strainer and allow them to cool before proceeding.

3 In a bowl, combine the diced figs with the rest of the filling ingredients and stir them together. In the work bowl of a food processor fitted with the steel blade, pulse to grind the filling mixture finely. Scrape the filling back into the bowl used to mix it.

4 When you are ready to bake the *cucidati*, set the racks in the upper and lower thirds of the oven and preheat to 350 degrees.

5 Take the dough out of the refrigerator, unwrap it, and place it on a floured surface.

Knead the dough lightly to make it malleable again and roll it up into a cylinder. Cut the cylinder into twelve equal pieces. One at a time, on a floured surface, flatten each and make it into a rectangle 3 inches wide and 12 inches long. Paint the wash on the dough and evenly distribute ⅓ cup filling down its length. Bring the edges of dough up around the filling to enclose it, then press the edges of the dough together firmly to seal in the filling. Use your palms to roll over the filled cylinder of dough until it extends to 15 inches, then cut it into 3-inch lengths. Set the filled cylinders aside while filling, rolling, and cutting the other pieces of dough.

6 To finish shaping the *cucidati*, use the point of a sharp paring knife to slash six or eight diagonal cuts in the top of each filled cylinder of dough. Place each slashed cookie on one of the prepared pans, and curve it into a horseshoe shape. Leave about an inch all around between the cookies.

7 After all the *cucidati* are on pans, paint the outsides lightly with the egg wash and sprinkle them sparingly with the nonpareils.

8 Bake the cookies for about 20 minutes, or until they are a light golden color. Slide the papers from the pans to racks.

9 Store the cooled cookies between sheets of parchment or wax paper in a tin or plastic container with a tight-fitting cover.

MAKES ABOUT 60 COOKIES

VARIATION

FIG X'S: These are an amusing alternative way to shape the *cucidati*. After you cut the filled cylinders of dough into 3-inch lengths, make a 1-inch-long cut in the middle of each end and pull the cut sides apart to make the cookie an X, as in the illustration. Do not slash the tops of these cookies. Arrange them on the pans and brush them with egg wash, but do not sprinkle them with the nonpareils. If you wish, dust them with a little confectioners' sugar right before serving.

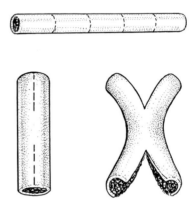

INFASCIADEDDE
Sicilian Twisted Cookies

THESE COOKIES ARE PART OF MY childhood memories. My great aunt Elvira Pescatore Basile, who married my maternal grandmother's brother Michele, always made them at the holidays. Although Zi' Elvira was not Sicilian herself, she had learned to make them from an unidentified Sicilian woman. Back then, in the days before food processors, the almonds were crushed to a paste with a rolling pin!

1 Wrap the Pasta Frolla in plastic and chill the dough in the refrigerator while you prepare the filling.

2 For the filling, place the almonds in a food processor fitted with the steel blade and pulse until finely ground. Add the honey and the cinnamon and pulse to make a smooth paste. Scrape the filling into a shallow bowl.

3 When you are ready to bake the cookies, set the racks in the upper and lower thirds of the oven and preheat to 350 degrees.

4 Take the dough out of the refrigerator, unwrap it, and place it on a floured surface. Knead the dough lightly to make it malleable again and roll it up into a cylinder. Cut the cylinder into four equal pieces.

5 Place one piece of the dough on a floured surface and roll it out to a 12-inch square. Cut the dough into eight strips, each 1½ × 12 inches. Spread about 1½ tablespoons of the filling in a narrow line down the middle

1 batch Pasta Frolla, page 153

ALMOND FILLING

12 ounces (about 3 cups) whole
    unblanched almonds
1 cup honey
½ teaspoon ground cinnamon

FINISHING

Honey
About 2 ounces (½ cup) toasted sliced
    almonds

3 or 4 cookie sheets or jelly roll pans
covered with parchment or foil

of each strip of dough, then fold the strip of dough so the two long ends meet, but do not press them together. Cut the folded strip into 4-inch lengths and twist each once or twice. Arrange the cookies on the prepared pans about an inch apart in all directions. Repeat with the other pieces of dough and the remaining filling.

6 Bake the cookies for about 15 minutes, or until they are golden. Slide the papers onto racks to cool the cookies.

7 Right before serving, drizzle the cookies with the honey and sprinkle with the toasted sliced almonds. (Put the honey and the almonds only on the cookies that will be eaten then—the cookies are awkward to store once the honey is on them.) The honey and almonds make the cookies a little sloppy to eat, but they add an extra dimension to the flavor—the cookies would be bland without them.

8 Store the cooled cookies between sheets of parchment or wax paper in a tin or plastic container with a tight-fitting cover.

MAKES ABOUT 96 NARROW 4-INCH COOKIES

PORTLAND FIG COOKIES

◦———◦

IN APRIL 1998 I WAS IN PORTLAND, Oregon, along with about a thousand other cookbook authors, chefs, and cooking teachers at a convention of the International Association of Culinary Professionals. I went to visit Greg Mistell's Pearl Bakery with my friend Jeffrey Steingarten, the bread maven, and as soon as we got there several friends rushed over and exclaimed: "Try the fig cookies–they're out of this world."

Jeffrey and I were fortunate enough to get a tour of the production area from the owner and while we were in the back, I met the creator of the cookies, Lee Posey, then the pastry chef in charge of all the sweets made in the bakery. I brazenly asked for her recipe without even having tasted one of the cookies and to my surprise she gave it to me. Here it is–one of the best cookies I have ever tasted.

By the way, this recipe differs from the *Cucidati* on page 153 in that the dough here is much thinner and the filling more plentiful.

FLAKY BROWN SUGAR DOUGH

2¼ cups all-purpose flour

⅔ cup firmly packed light brown sugar

Pinch salt

1 teaspoon baking powder

10 tablespoons (1¼ sticks) cold unsalted
butter, cut into 12 pieces

1 large egg

1 teaspoon vanilla extract

FIG FILLING

12 ounces (about 2 cups) Calimyrna figs,
stemmed and diced

⅔ cup currants

5 ounces (about 1¼ cups) walnut pieces,
toasted

Finely grated zest of 1 large orange

¼ cup firmly packed light brown sugar

3 tablespoons unsweetened cocoa powder,
sifted after measuring

1 teaspoon freshly grated nutmeg

1 teaspoon ground coriander

½ teaspoon ground cloves

⅔ cup honey

EGG WASH

1 large egg, well beaten with 1 pinch salt

2 cookie sheets or jelly roll pans covered
with parchment or foil

1 To make the dough, in the work bowl of a food processor fitted with the steel blade, combine the flour, brown sugar, salt, and baking powder. Pulse half a dozen times to mix. Add the butter and pulse about a dozen times, or until the butter is in ¼-inch pieces. In a small bowl, whisk the egg and vanilla together and add to the processor. Continue to pulse just until the dough holds together. Scrape the dough onto a piece of plastic wrap,

form it into a square, and wrap well. Chill the dough while preparing the filling.

2 For the filling, place the figs in a saucepan and cover them with water. Bring to a boil over medium heat. Drain and cool the figs. Combine them with the currants, walnuts, and orange zest and pulse in the food processor until finely minced. Add the remaining filling ingredients and pulse to combine. Scrape the filling into a bowl.

3 Unwrap the dough on a floured work surface. Flour the dough and roll it to a 12 × 16 ¼-inch rectangle. Use a ruler to measure, then cut the dough into five strips, each a little less than 3¼ inches wide by 12 inches long. Use a pastry bag with no tube in it to pipe the filling down the middle of each rectangle of dough. Pull the dough up around the filling to enclose it, then pinch it together firmly. Roll the filled cylinders of dough around so that the seam is on the bottom and roll over them with the palms of both hands to make sure the dough sticks to the filling. Arrange them on the same pans you will later use to bake them and refrigerate the filled cylinders for an hour.

4 When you are ready to bake the cookies, set the racks in the upper and lower thirds of the oven and preheat to 400 degrees.

5 Remove the filled dough cylinders to a cutting board and use a sharp paring knife to cut them into 2-inch lengths. Arrange them on the prepared pans leaving about an inch in all directions, and brush them with the egg wash.

6 Bake the cookies for about 12 to 15 minutes, or until they are a deep golden brown. Slide the papers from the pans onto racks.

7 Store the cooled cookies between sheets of parchment or wax paper in a tin or plastic container with a tight-fitting cover.

MAKES ABOUT 30 COOKIES

MAMOUL
Syrian and Lebanese Date-Filled Cookies

THIS IS A CLASSIC MIDDLE EASTERN pastry of a light dough wrapped around a rich filling. I first learned about *mamoul* from my friend Dahlia Bilger, who kept pressing me to make some with her when she was a student at the New York Restaurant School in the early eighties. Alas, in the intervening years I lost the recipe Dahlia and I concocted. This one is loosely based on a recipe in Claudia Roden's *A Book of Middle Eastern Food* (Knopf, 1972).

When you buy *mamoul* in Middle Eastern markets, they have usually been decorated with a kind of pastry pincer to make an attractive pattern of raised ridges on the surface of the dough. Presumably this is in order to hold the confectioners' sugar with which they are sprinkled. I find that pricking the tops with a fork in a regular pattern accomplishes the same thing.

1 For the filling, put the dates and water in a medium saucepan over low heat. Bring to a simmer, stirring occasionally, and reduce, stirring often, until the consistency is thick and jam-like. Spread the filling out on a plate or shallow bowl to cool.

2 When you are ready to make the cookies, set the racks in the upper and lower thirds of the oven and preheat to 350 degrees.

3 To make the dough, in the work bowl of a food processor fitted with the steel blade, place the flour. Add the butter and pulse about a dozen times, or until it is finely mixed in. Take the cover off the machine and sprinkle the flour and butter mixture with the rose water and milk. Replace the cover and pulse until the dough just forms a ball. Scrape the dough onto a floured work surface, then press it together and roll it into a cylinder 15 inches long. Slice the dough every ½ inch to make 30 pieces of dough.

DATE FILLING

½ pound pitted dates, finely chopped

3 tablespoons water

DOUGH

1¾ cups all-purpose flour

12 tablespoons (1½ sticks) cold unsalted butter, cut into 20 pieces

2 teaspoons rose or orange flower water

2 tablespoons milk

Confectioners' sugar for finishing

2 cookie sheets or jelly roll pans covered with parchment or foil

4 To form a *mamoul*, roll a piece of dough into a sphere, then insert an index finger into the sphere to make a hole. Use your thumbs to enlarge the hole so that the dough becomes a little cup. Fill with a spoonful of the filling, then close the dough around the filling. Place each cookie seam side down on one of the pans. Leave about 1½ inches around in all directions.

5 Repeat with the remaining dough and filling. After all the *mamoul* have been formed, press each gently to flatten it, and use a fork to pierce the surface in a decorative design.

6 Bake the *mamoul* for about 20 to 25 minutes, making sure they remain very white. They should take on no color at all. Cool on the pans on racks. Dust heavily with confectioners' sugar just before serving.

7 Store the cooled cookies between sheets of parchment or wax paper in a tin or plastic container with a tight-fitting cover.

MAKES ABOUT 30 COOKIES

RAILROAD TRACKS

I DON'T KNOW IF THESE COOKIES — composed of a roll of dough flattened and filled with jam—are called this in the United States, but it is the standard European name for them. This is the special occasion for which you've been saving that jar of homemade or fine-quality jam or jelly. This delicate dough is a perfect foil for a subtly flavored filling. Thanks to Paul Kinberg for this recipe.

1 In a bowl, combine the flour, baking powder, and salt; stir well to mix.

2 In the bowl of a standing electric mixer fitted with the paddle attachment, beat together on medium speed the butter and granulated sugar until well mixed, about 1 minute. Beat in the vanilla, then the egg, and continue beating until the mixture is smooth.

3 Remove the bowl from the mixer and stir in the flour mixture with a large rubber spatula. Scrape the dough onto a floured work surface.

4 Press the dough together and roll it into a cylinder. Divide the dough into six equal pieces and roll each to a narrow cylinder the length of your baking pan.

5 Transfer the dough to the pans (to move it easily you can coil it up, then uncoil it on the pan). Arrange three pieces of dough on each pan, equidistant from one another and from the sides of the pan. Use the side of your hand to press a ½-inch-wide trough down the middle of each piece of dough.

6 Set the racks in the upper and lower thirds of the oven and preheat to 350 degrees.

2 cups all-purpose flour

½ teaspoon baking powder

Pinch salt

12 tablespoons (1½ sticks) unsalted butter, softened

⅔ cup granulated sugar

2 teaspoons vanilla extract

1 large egg

½ cup seedless raspberry jam or other jam or jelly of your choice

Confectioners' sugar for finishing, optional

2 cookie sheets or jelly roll pans covered with parchment or foil

7 Beat the jam or jelly with a fork to liquefy it, then use a small spoon, a paper cone, or the snipped corner of a nonpleated plastic bag to fill the trough in each piece of dough with about 2 tablespoons of the jam. Only fill it about two-thirds full or the jam will overflow while the cookies are baking.

8 Bake the cookies for about 20 minutes, or until they are a light golden color. Transfer the pans to racks to cool.

9 Cut each of the cooled cookie logs into about six or eight diagonal slices. Right before serving, dust the cookies very lightly with confectioners' sugar, if you wish.

10 Store the finished cookies between sheets of parchment or wax paper in a tin or plastic container with a tight-fitting cover.

MAKES ABOUT 40 COOKIES

SUVAROFFS

~o o c~

THIS IS A FANCY NAME THE SWISS HAVE given to a fairly simple cookie. It is composed of two diamond shapes sandwiched with a kirsch-flavored almond paste filling–definitely an adult cookie.

To cut these cookies into the traditional size and shape, you'll need a 2- to 2½-inch diamond-shaped cutter, either plain or fluted. If you can't find one, make a pattern from a piece of stiff cardboard; then you can use a knife to cut out the cookies, and they'll be all the same size. Of course, you can also use another 2- to 2½-inch shape for these.

1   To make the dough, in the bowl of an electric mixer fitted with the paddle attachment, beat together the butter, sugar, lemon extract, and lemon zest on medium speed until soft and light, about 5 minutes.

2   Remove the bowl from the mixer and use a rubber spatula to incorporate the flour. Scrape the dough onto a piece of plastic wrap and form it into a square about ½ inch thick. Wrap and chill the dough until firm–several hours to several days.

3   Cut the dough in half and refrigerate one piece. Place the other on a floured surface and flour it lightly. Press and pound the dough gently with a rolling pin to soften it, then roll the dough about 3/16 inch thick. Use a plain or fluted 2- to 2½-inch diamond-shaped cutter to cut the dough. Place the cookies on the prepared pans leaving about 1 inch around each in all directions.

COOKIE DOUGH

14 tablespoons (1¾ sticks) unsalted butter, softened

¼ cup granulated sugar

½ teaspoon lemon extract

Finely grated zest of 1 small lemon

2¼ cups all-purpose flour

FILLING

4 ounces almond paste

4 tablespoons (½ stick) unsalted butter, softened

½ cup confectioners' sugar

1 tablespoon kirsch

Green food coloring

2 cookie sheets or jelly roll pans covered with parchment or foil

4 When you are ready to bake the cookies, set the racks in the upper and lower thirds of the oven and preheat to 350 degrees. Bake the cookies for about 15 minutes, or until they are a very pale golden color. Cool them on the pans on racks.

5 While the cookies are baking, prepare the filling. In the bowl of a standing electric mixer fitted with the paddle attachment, beat together on medium speed the almond paste and butter until soft and very light, about 5 minutes. Lower the mixer speed and add the confectioners' sugar. Beat for another 2 or 3 minutes on medium speed. Beat in the kirsch, then stop the mixer and scrape down the bowl and beater. Beat in just enough food coloring to tint the filling a light, tender green.

6 After the cookies have cooled, invert half of them, so that the bottoms are facing up. Pipe or spoon about 1 teaspoon of the almond filling on each. Top with another cookie, bottom to bottom. Gently press them together.

7 Store the finished cookies between sheets of parchment or wax paper in a tin or plastic container with a tight-fitting cover.

MAKES ABOUT 20 SANDWICHED COOKIES

LINZER HEARTS

THOUGH THIS RECIPE CALLS FOR GROUND hazelnuts, almonds or pecans will work just as well. And the raspberry jam that sandwiches the rich nut dough can be changed to apricot, which would be just as good.

1 In a bowl, combine the flour and spices; stir well to mix.

2 In the bowl of a standing electric mixer fitted with the paddle attachment, beat together on medium speed the butter and sugar until soft and light, about 5 minutes. Lower the mixer speed and beat in the almonds and the flour and spice mixture, one at a time.

3 Remove the bowl from the mixer and use a large rubber spatula to finish mixing the dough. Scrape the dough onto a piece of plastic wrap and shape it into a rectangle about ½ inch thick. Wrap and chill the dough until it is firm, about an hour, or up to several days.

4 When you are ready to bake the cookies, set the racks in the upper and lower thirds of the oven and preheat to 350 degrees.

5 Cut the dough into three parts and refrigerate two of them. Place one third on a floured surface and flour it lightly. Press and pound the dough gently with a rolling pin to soften it, then roll the dough about ¼ inch thick. Use a 2½- to 3-inch heart-shaped cutter (or any round one) to cut the dough. Place the cookies on the prepared pans, leaving about an inch around each in all directions. If you have a tiny heart-shaped cutter, use it to cut

2⅔ cups all-purpose flour

½ teaspoon ground cinnamon

¼ teaspoon ground cloves

16 tablespoons (2 sticks) unsalted butter, softened

⅔ cup granulated sugar

4 ounces (about 1 cup) whole blanched almonds, finely ground in the food processor

1 cup seedless raspberry jam

Confectioners' sugar for sprinkling

2 or 3 cookie sheets or jelly roll pans covered with parchment or foil

the center out of half the cookies, to make a "window" when they are sandwiched. Or use a small round cutter, or a pastry tube, or leave the cookies unpierced. Repeat with the remaining dough. Mass the scraps together and roll them once again to cut more cookies.

6 Bake the cookies for about 15 minutes, or until they are a very pale golden color. Cool them on the pans on racks.

7 While the cookies are baking, prepare the jam for the filling. Bring the jam to a simmer in a small saucepan over low heat, stirring occasionally. Let the jam reduce until it has thickened slightly, about 5 minutes.

8 After the cookies have cooled, dust the pierced cookies lightly with the confectioners' sugar. Invert the nonpierced cookies and spread each with about ½ teaspoon of the reduced jam. Top with the pierced cookies, sugar side up. Use a small paper cone, a tiny spoon, or the snipped corner of a nonpleated plastic bag to fill in the window of the cookies with more reduced jam.

9 Store the finished cookies between sheets of parchment or wax paper in a tin or plastic container with a tight-fitting cover.

MAKES ABOUT 18 COOKIES

CHOCOLATE CHOCOLATE SANDWICH COOKIES

THIS IS A VARIATION ON A FAVORITE cookie of mine—a dough that's made from just flour, chocolate, and butter (plus a pinch of spice) enhanced by a suave milk chocolate filling. It is particularly easy to make and has all the delicacy and sophistication of recipes that require ten times the trouble.

1 To make the dough, combine the flour, salt, and cloves in a bowl; stir well to mix.

2 In another bowl, beat the butter with a rubber spatula until it is soft and creamy. Beat in the cooled chocolate, stirring until the mixture is smooth. Gently fold in the flour mixture, creating a smooth dough. Scrape the dough onto a piece of plastic wrap and shape it into a rectangle about ½ inch thick. Wrap and chill the dough until it is firm, about an hour.

3 For the filling, combine the cream, butter, and corn syrup in a small saucepan. Bring to a simmer over medium heat. Remove from heat and add the chocolate all at once. Shake the pan to make sure all the chocolate

COOKIE DOUGH

2⅓ cups all-purpose flour

¼ teaspoon salt

¼ teaspoon ground cloves

16 tablespoons (2 sticks) unsalted butter, softened

6 ounces semisweet chocolate, melted and cooled

FILLING

⅓ cup heavy cream

1 tablespoon butter

1 tablespoon light corn syrup

6 ounces milk chocolate, cut into ¼-inch pieces

2 cookie sheets or jelly roll pans covered with parchment or foil

is submerged, then let the chocolate melt for about 2 or 3 minutes. Whisk smooth, then scrape into a bowl and cool to room temperature.

4   When you are ready to bake the cookies, set the racks in the upper and lower thirds of the oven and preheat to 350 degrees. Divide the dough into thirds and return two to the refrigerator. Place one third on a floured work surface. If the dough is hard, pound it gently with the rolling pin to soften it slightly, then flour the surface of the dough and roll it out about 3/16 inch thick. Cut out the cookies with a fluted 2- to 3-inch cutter. Place them on the prepared pans, leaving about an inch around each in all directions. Repeat with the remaining dough. Save all the scraps, then reroll them and cut more cookies.

5   Bake the cookies for about 15 minutes, or until they are firm and dull in appearance. Cool the cookies on the pans on racks.

6   To sandwich the cooled cookies, turn half the cookies over, flat bottom side up. Spoon or pipe about ½ teaspoon of the chocolate filling on each. Top with other cookies, right side up so they are bottom to bottom.

7   Store the finished cookies between sheets of parchment or wax paper in a tin or plastic container with a tight-fitting cover.

MAKES ABOUT 24 SANDWICH COOKIES

LACY CHOCOLATE OATMEAL COOKIE SANDWICHES

⌦⌧

THESE ARE SIMILAR TO THE ALMOND Lace Cookies on page 48, except that these are made with oatmeal instead of ground nuts. And sandwiching two of these crisp, candy-like cookies with chocolate makes them even more luscious.

1 Set the racks in the upper and lower thirds of the oven and preheat to 350 degrees.

2 Pour the melted butter into a bowl; one at a time, stir in the remaining ingredients, except the chocolate, stirring smooth after each addition.

3 Use a ½-teaspoon measure to drop the batter on the prepared pans. Space the cookies about 3 inches apart in all directions, to allow room for them to spread.

4 Bake the cookies for about 8 to 10 minutes, or until they have spread and are brown around the edges and lighter toward the center. Slide the paper or foil onto racks to cool the cookies.

5 When the cookies are completely cool, peel them off the foil and arrange half of them bottom side up on a pan. Use a small offset spatula to spread about ½ teaspoon of chocolate on each inverted cookie. Top with another cookie, bottom to bottom.

8 tablespoons (1 stick) unsalted butter, melted

1 cup rolled oats (regular oatmeal) finely chopped, but not ground to a powder, in the food processor

1 cup sugar

½ teaspoon salt

1 large egg

1 teaspoon vanilla extract

1 teaspoon orange juice, strained

6 ounces semisweet or bittersweet chocolate, melted and cooled, for sandwiching the cookies

3 or 4 cookie sheets or jelly roll pans covered with buttered foil

6 Store the finished cookies between sheets of parchment or wax paper in a tin or plastic container with a tight-fitting cover.

MAKES ABOUT 30 SANDWICH COOKIES

WAFERS

Wafers are among the oldest types of cookies still made. In fact, the predecessors of *pâtissiers* or pastry cooks in France were known as *oublayeurs*, the makers of a type of ancient wafer. And delicate wafers of this type survive to this day in France and especially in Scandinavia

These pleasantly old-fashioned cookies are made in an iron, like waffles. Some, like pizzelle, are probably familiar. Though these used to be made in stove-top irons, electric pizzelle makers are fairly common nowadays (some of them actually have reversible plates that allow them to double as standard breakfast-waffle irons).

Other types of wafers require a special iron that makes cookies thinner than the pizzelle iron does. Fortunately, there is a thriving Scandinavian tradition of wafer making in the Midwest, so it's easy to get both electric and stove-top versions of a *Krumkake* iron. *Krumkake* are typical Norwegian and Swedish wafer cookies that are usually curved into a cone shape as soon as they come off the iron.

And finally, if you want to try some wafers first, before you decide if you want to invest in an iron, you may spread the batter very thin on a nonstick cookie sheet or jelly roll pan and bake it in a moderately hot oven (you'll have the advantage of being able to make several at the same time). This works well for all the recipes except the pizzelle, but doesn't make wafers as thin as an iron does.

Hints for Wafers

1 Make sure the iron is perfectly clean before you start heating it. Bits of batter stuck to the iron will make subsequent wafers stick.

2 Don't overheat the iron—wafers will stick if the iron is too hot.

3 Use a little vegetable oil, rather than butter, to grease the iron—it will be easier to apply and will not smoke as much as butter when it is hot.

4 If you are using a stove-top iron, make sure that it reheats slightly between wafers.

5 If you wish to roll the wafers into cones or cylinders, make sure they don't get too dark. The darker the wafers, the more quickly they become brittle.

6 Storage can be a problem. Most wafers, except pizzelle, are so fragile that it isn't practical to store them for a long time. Lay them on a baking pan in one layer and cover them loosely with aluminum foil if you make them a day or two in advance.

PIZZELLE

THESE CRISP COOKIES ARE THICKER than many other types of wafers. They are made in a special iron and are easy to shape into cones or cylinders after they are baked. My favorite way to use these is to remove the cookie from the iron, place it on a cutting board, and quickly cut it into quarters. These smaller pizzelle are more manageable and easier to eat.

By the way, the correct pronunciation is "peet-sellay."

1 In a bowl, combine the flour, salt, and baking powder, stir well to mix.

2 In another bowl, whisk the eggs and yolk, just enough to mix them together. Whisk in the sugar in a stream, then the anisette and melted butter. Use a rubber spatula to fold in the flour mixture.

3 Set the batter aside while you heat the pizzelle iron. After the iron has been heating for a few minutes, open the cover and grease the top and bottom of the imprints with an oiled paper towel. Close the iron and finish heating.

4 Drop a rounded teaspoon of the batter in the center of each imprint, close the cover, and bake the pizzelle. They are usually ready when the steam stops coming out from between the plates of the iron. (You can peek without ruining them—if they are too pale, close the iron and bake longer.)

1¾ cups all-purpose flour
Pinch salt
2 teaspoons baking powder
2 large eggs
1 large egg yolk
¾ cup sugar
2 tablespoons anisette
8 tablespoons (1 stick) unsalted butter, melted
Vegetable oil for greasing the iron

An electric pizzelle iron

5 Use the point of a paring knife to lift one of the pizzelle out of the iron, then with a wide spatula transfer it to a rack to cool. You may also cut it into quarters or roll it into a cone or cylinder shape over a form. Repeat with the other pizzelle in the iron. There is no need to grease the iron again, unless the pizzelle start to stick. Use the remaining batter to make more pizzelle.

6 Store the cooled wafers between sheets of parchment or wax paper in a tin or plastic container with a tight-fitting cover.

MAKES ABOUT 24 PIZZELLE

VANILLA PIZZELLE: Omit the egg yolk and anisette. Substitute another whole egg (for a total of three) and 1 teaspoon vanilla.

ALMOND (OR HAZELNUT) PIZZELLE: Add ½ cup finely ground blanched almonds or unblanched hazelnuts to Vanilla Pizzelle.

CHOCOLATE PIZZELLE: In the Vanilla, Almond, or Hazelnut Pizzelle, reduce the flour to 1⅓ cups and add ¼ cup unsweetened cocoa powder (sifted after measuring).

CRACKERS AND SAVORY COOKIES

WHEN I FIRST STARTED READING COOKBOOKS there was an important chapter in every book on fancy hors d'oeuvres and all sorts of little canapés (tiny open-faced sandwiches). Nowadays, these fussy little morsels are limited to parties in elegant establishments and those elaborately catered.

When I entertain at home, it's usually a tea party in the afternoon so I can get away with serving mostly sweets, but I often include a savory pastry or two. On the rare occasions that I give dinner parties, I like to serve a couple of things to nibble with drinks before dinner. The recipes in this chapter are some of the things I make then. One really good cheese cookie or salty breadstick, a bowl of olives, and perhaps another bowl of thinly sliced fennel or celery stalks and I consider the hors d'oeuvre problem completely solved.

HINTS FOR CRACKERS AND SAVORY COOKIES

1 When the recipe says to roll the dough very thin, please do exactly that. Most crackers will taste quite dry and woolly if they are too thick.

2 Measure seasonings—especially if a hot or strong one—carefully. Many a recipe has been ruined by an overdose of cayenne pepper or dry mustard. Try the recipe first as written. Then if you think it could use more seasoning, add it.

3 As with all cookies, uniformity is important so they will bake evenly. Make sure you cut pieces of dough accurately so crackers will all be the same size.

4 Resting and chilling times are important with the doughs that need to be rolled very thin—don't rush the process.

5 Crackers and most savory cookies keep well—bake a lot when you know you'll be using them.

PEPPERY CHEDDAR COINS

THOUGH YOU MAY FLAVOR THESE WITH any type of hot pepper, including cayenne or hot paprika, I like black pepper best. For the best flavor use an extra-sharp Cheddar, though if you prefer the taste substitute Gruyère, Gouda, or even Emmenthal.

1 Combine the flour, salt, and pepper in a bowl; stir well to mix.

2 In the work bowl of a food processor fitted with the steel blade, combine the cheese and butter and pulse five or six times to mix. Add the flour mixture and pulse about eight or ten more times, or until the mixture just forms a ball.

3 Scrape the dough onto a floured work surface and form it into a square about ½ inch thick. Cover the dough with plastic wrap and refrigerate it until it is firm enough to roll, 30 minutes to an hour.

4 When you are ready to bake the cookies, set the racks in the upper and lower thirds of the oven and preheat to 350 degrees.

5 Divide the dough in half and place one half on a lightly floured work surface, and the other half in the refrigerator until ready to use. Lightly flour the dough and roll it out to less than ¼ inch thick. Use a floured 2-inch plain or fluted round cutter to cut out the cookies. Place them on the prepared pans, leaving about an inch all around each. Repeat with the remaining dough. Press together and reroll the scraps as they are formed to make more cookies.

1 cup all-purpose flour

½ teaspoon salt

1 teaspoon freshly ground black pepper

4 ounces (about 1 cup) sharp Cheddar cheese, coarsely grated (see Headnote)

8 tablespoons (1 stick) cold unsalted butter, cut into 10 pieces

2 cookie sheets or jelly roll pans covered with parchment or foil

6 Bake the cookies for about 20 minutes, or until they are firm and a light golden color.

7 Slide the papers from the pans to racks to cool.

8 Store the cooled cookies between sheets of parchment or wax paper in a tin or plastic container with a tight-fitting cover.

MAKES ABOUT 40 COOKIES

GRUYÈRE AND ALMOND ROSETTES

THIS EASY CHEESE COOKIE IS ELEGANTLY surmounted by a whole blanched almond for an extra bit of crunch. The recipe is loosely adapted from *Les heures et les jours Wittamer* ("*The Hours and Days at Wittamer*") (Editions Lannoo, 1994) by Jean-Pierre Gabriel.

1 To make the dough, in a bowl, combine the flour and salt and stir well to mix.

2 In the bowl of a standing electric mixer fitted with the paddle attachment, beat together on medium speed the butter and cheese for about 2 or 3 minutes, or until soft and well mixed. Scrape down the sides of the bowl and beater and add the flour mixture. Mix on low speed only until a dough forms.

3 Scrape the dough onto a piece of plastic wrap and form it into a square about ½ inch thick. Wrap the dough and refrigerate it until it is firm enough to roll, about 30 minutes to an hour.

4 When you are ready to bake the cookies, set the racks in the upper and lower thirds of the oven and preheat to 350 degrees.

5 Divide the dough in half, refrigerate one piece, and place the other piece on a lightly floured work surface. Lightly flour the dough and roll it out to just less than ¼ inch thick. Use a floured 1½-inch fluted round cutter to cut out the cookies. Place them on the prepared pans, leaving about an inch all around each in all directions. Repeat with the remaining dough, then press together and

1¼ cups all-purpose flour

½ teaspoon salt

8 tablespoons (1 stick) unsalted butter, softened

4 ounces (about 1 cup) finely grated Swiss Gruyère

EGG WASH

1 large egg, well beaten with 1 pinch salt

About 40 whole blanched almonds for finishing

2 cookie sheets or jelly roll pans covered with parchment or foil

reroll the scraps to make more cookies. After all the cookies are on the pans, brush over one cookie with the egg wash, then immediately place an almond on top of it. Repeat until all the cookies are egg washed and topped with almonds.

6 Bake the cookies for about 20 minutes, or until they are firm and a light golden color.

7 Slide the papers from the pans to racks.

8 Store the cooled cookies between sheets of parchment or wax paper in a tin or plastic container with a tight-fitting cover.

MAKES ABOUT 40 COOKIES

ROSEMARY BREAD STICKS

~⦿~

THESE CRUNCHY BREAD STICKS ARE probably my favorite non-sweet cookie. They are excellent on their own, but sometimes I serve them alongside a platter of thinly sliced prosciutto. When I wrap the ham around them, it makes sort of a prosciutto lollipop.

1 Pour the water into a small bowl and whisk in the yeast. Set aside while you prepare the other ingredients.

2 In the work bowl of a food processor fitted with the steel blade, combine the flour, cornmeal, oil, and salt and pulse five times to mix. Add the rosemary and the yeast mixture. Pulse repeatedly, ten or twelve times, until the dough forms a ball.

3 Scrape the dough into an oiled bowl, then turn it over so that the top is oiled. Cover the bowl tightly with plastic wrap and let the dough double in bulk at room temperature, about an hour. Press the dough to deflate it, then return it to the bowl. Re-cover the dough with plastic wrap and refrigerate it for an hour or two or up to 24 hours.

½ cup warm water, about 110 degrees

1½ teaspoons active dry yeast

1¼ cups all-purpose flour

⅓ cup stone-ground yellow cornmeal

2 tablespoons extra-virgin olive oil

1 teaspoon salt

2 tablespoons chopped fresh rosemary

2 jelly roll pans sprinkled with cornmeal

4 When you are ready to bake the bread sticks, scrape the dough onto a lightly floured surface and press it into a rough rectangle. Divide the dough into three equal pieces, then divide each in half to make six pieces. Finally, divide each piece into equal quarters, to make twenty-four.

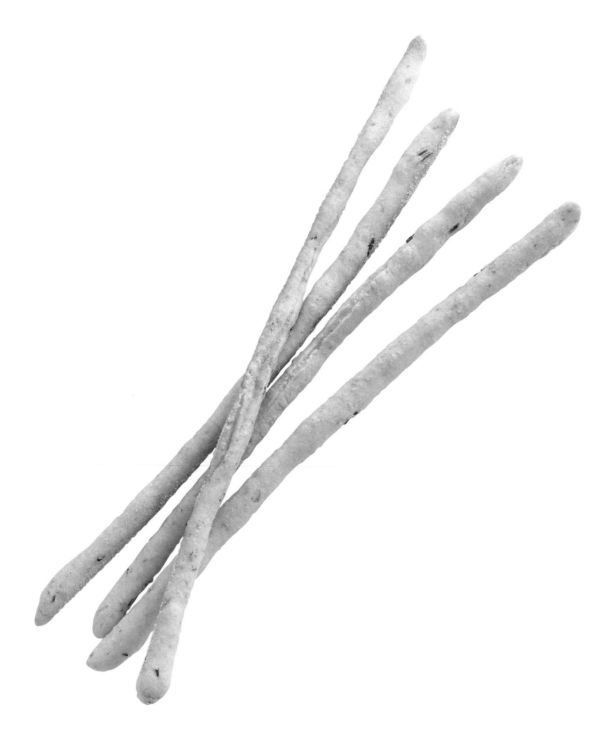

5 One at a time, roll each of the pieces of dough under the palms of your hands to make a thin stick about 12 inches long. Place on one of the prepared pans. Repeat with the remaining pieces of dough. Put twelve on each pan, spacing them about an inch or a little less apart. Set aside for half an hour or until the sticks puff a little.

6 About 20 minutes before you intend to bake the bread sticks, set the racks in the upper and lower thirds of the oven and preheat to 350 degrees. Bake the risen bread sticks about 15 to 20 minutes, or until they are golden and crisp.

7 Cool the bread sticks on the pans on racks.

8 Store the cooled bread sticks between sheets of parchment or wax paper in a tin or plastic container with a tight-fitting cover.

MAKES ABOUT 24 BREADSTICKS

Perfect Cookies, CAKES, and Chocolate

INTRODUCTION TO CAKES

CAKES PLAY AN IMPORTANT PART IN OUR LIVES. The dramas of christenings, birthdays, bar mitzvahs, graduations, and, of course, weddings, always include a cake as part of the festivities. Cakes have only been with us for a few hundred years.

In most countries, a cake is a pound cake or fruitcake. Layer cakes and molded cakes with mousse or other soft fillings are more often referred to as desserts, but we use the term *cake* for all these sweet treats. In this book, I use the term to describe round, rectangular, or loaf-shaped baked desserts that may be filled or not, and that may have only one or several layers—in short, what we Americans generally think of as cakes. Although there are some recipes that straddle the line between cake and pastry, I have used the general rule that if there is a dough that has to be rolled out, then it is a pastry dough, resulting in a pie, not a cake. A pie or pastry is made from a dough, a cake is made from a batter. The one exception is yeast-risen coffee cakes; the mixtures for those are almost always doughs and sometimes need to be rolled.

This introduction will take you through all you need to know about cake ingredients and equipment. Begin with the principle professional bakers use: Get organized. If you are making a simple cake (mix-bake-cool-eat), you need only make sure you have all the ingredients before you start. If the cake is more elaborate, with multiple components (cake layer, moistening syrup, filling, frosting, garnish) consider preparing them over a several-day period before you assemble the cake: you will have a much easier time of it, and the whole process will be a pleasure instead of a chore.

A quick explanation about the recipes: One of my greatest pleasures is sharing recipes with family, friends, students, and acquaintances. Many of the recipes in my books, in turn, are ones people have given me. When I use someone else's recipe, I always test it thoroughly and often make adjustments in the ingredients and/or instructions to ensure good results. When a recipe comes from a book or periodical, it has been subjected to the same process—that is why such a recipe is described as "based on" another.

These cake recipes are the product of a lifetime of collecting and baking. I hope you enjoy them.

INGREDIENTS

USING THE BEST—AND THE CORRECT—ingredients makes all the difference between success and failure in cake baking. It will take you only a few minutes to go over the descriptions of the ingredients below, but doing so will ensure that you use the right ones when you try the recipes.

FLOUR

Flour used for cake baking is milled from wheat of the botanical genus of *Triticum*. Wheat may be "hard" or "soft," terms that refer to the actual hardness or softness of the wheat berries, or kernels, themselves. Hard wheat produces flour rich in gluten-forming proteins—substances that make doughs elastic and springy, desirable in a bread dough or some pastry doughs, but not in a cake batter. This is why cake recipes call for all-purpose flour or cake flour, both of which are made from soft wheat and are weaker than the strong hard wheat flours.

ALL-PURPOSE FLOUR All-purpose flour is used for some cakes, especially ones that don't rise to great heights. All purpose flour may be bleached or unbleached. Although unbleached all-purpose flour has a slightly higher protein content than bleached, the two can be used interchangeably in the recipes here that call for all-purpose flour.

CAKE FLOUR Finely milled and always bleached, making it suitable for very delicate cakes, such as sponge and angel cakes. It is used in many other types of cakes too. If you have to substitute all-purpose flour for cake flour, use 14 tablespoons (1 cup minus 2 tablespoons) all-purpose flour for every cup of cake flour called for.

SELF-RISING CAKE FLOUR This is cake flour with salt and baking powder added. Use it only in recipes that specify it—it can not be substituted for regular cake flour.

CORNSTARCH A pure starch extracted from corn and very finely milled. It is used in combination with wheat flour to produce cakes with an especially fine and delicate texture.

POTATO STARCH Very similar in both appearance and results to cornstarch, it is sometimes used in Passover cakes, for which no grain may be used.

CRUMBS Bread or cake crumbs are sometimes called for in recipes. Make sure they are fresh. Making bread crumbs yourself—a simple matter in the food processor—from either hard or soft bread is always superior to using commercial bread crumbs.

Sugar contributes more than sweetness to cakes. In butter cakes, it helps the batter absorb air through friction between the butter and sugar during mixing. In any cake, it contributes tenderness and crust color and enhances the cake's ability to retain moisture.

GRANULATED SUGAR Regular granulated sugar is called for in all the recipes. I never use superfine sugar, which is very finely ground granulated sugar.

BROWN SUGAR Refined sugar that has molasses added to it for flavor and color, brown sugar may be light or dark, depending on the amount of molasses added. Granulated light brown sugar is also available; it works the same in recipes as the moist kind.

CONFECTIONERS' SUGAR Very finely ground granulated sugar, this always has about 3 percent cornstarch added by weight to prevent clumping. The cornstarch would add a chalky taste if the confectioners' sugar were added to whipped cream so it is best to use granulated for this purpose. It is dusted over some cakes as a garnish and is also a standard ingredient in simple icings made by just adding liquid to confectioners' sugar and heating before applying to a cake.

CORN SYRUP Corn syrup is a liquid sweetener made from corn. Light (colorless) corn syrup may be added to cooked sugar syrups or to other sugar-rich recipes such as boiled icing or seven-minute frosting to make them pliable and easy to spread. Light corn syrup is the moistening added to marzipan. Dark corn syrup functions in the same way, but it is used only when its molasses-y or slightly caramelized flavor is desired.

HONEY Though there are many specialty honeys, I usually buy a fairly dark natural honey, but I have used the plain old supermarket variety too. Dark honey has a deeper flavor and seems to impart more taste and less sweetness than lighter honeys.

MOLASSES Used often in old-fashioned cake recipes, molasses is a by-product of the sugar refining process. Molasses labeled "unsulphured" is milder in flavor than molasses that has been treated with sulphur to purify it. The latter type is not identified as sulphured molasses—the label usually states that it is "robust flavored." I usually buy unsulphured molasses because even a mild molasses flavor is fairly strong. However, most of the recipes in this book that use molasses call for such small amounts that I can't imagine substituting the stronger-flavored one would make any difference.

LEAVENERS

The additives that make cakes rise are called leaveners. Yeast, a natural leavener, is a living plant organism that releases carbon dioxide as part of its life cycle and helps some cake batters to rise. Chemical leaveners such as baking powder and baking soda cause carbon dioxide gas to be formed before and/or during baking so that batters rise. Many older recipes call for both baking powder and baking soda—I tend to use one or the other, because an abundance of chemical leaveners can give a cake a strange soapy taste. Many cakes, of course, rise simply through the expansion of air cells in the eggs or egg whites that are part of the batter.

BAKING POWDER Originally considered a substitute for yeast, baking powder enables mixtures that would otherwise remain dull and leaden to rise into delicate cakes. It was already popular by the last quarter of the nineteenth century, when it was made from a combination of cream of tartar (acid) and baking soda (alkali). This primitive baking powder formed carbon dioxide gas in the batter when the acid-and-alkali combination encountered liquid. Nowadays, double-acting baking powder is a more sophisticated combination of chemicals that cause the batter to leaven first from the presence of liquid and then in the heat of the oven.

BAKING SODA Baking soda or bicarbonate of soda, predated baking powder as the first chemical leavener. Highly alkaline, it reacts with an acid ingredient in a batter. The most common ones of these are: cocoa, chocolate, honey, molasses, brown sugar, sour cream, yogurt, and buttermilk.

YEAST Before baking powder or baking soda, yeast was much used in cake making. Coffee cakes owe their light texture to yeast. Though these cakes have one foot firmly planted in the world of breads, they have been sweetened and enriched to the point that they really are cakes.

FLAVORINGS

Whether it's a spoonful of vanilla extract or a little grated lemon zest, flavoring can transform an ordinary cake into a perfumed delicacy.

VANILLA EXTRACT I use Nielsen-Massey Bourbon vanilla extract. Available in specialty food stores and by mail, it imparts the vanilla flavor that I most enjoy. A few of these recipes call for vanilla beans, the cured seed pods of the vanilla orchid, from which the extract is made.

To use a vanilla bean, split it along the length, then use the point of a paring knife to scrape out the black paste of tiny seeds and add this to the preparation that calls for it. The rest of the bean need not go to waste—if you embed the scraped-out vanilla bean in a sack or canister of sugar, the sugar will absorb the vanilla flavor left in the bean. Some recipes, notably those in which the vanilla is added to liquid that will be heated, just call for the vanilla bean to be split. Heating and whisking the preparation will release the seeds and flavor inside the bean.

OTHER EXTRACTS I regularly use lemon, orange, almond, and anise extracts. Make sure the ones you purchase are pure, natural extracts. Sometimes the tiny print on the label will reveal that the little bottle is filled with artificial extracts.

FLAVORING OILS There are excellent citrus oils available. Use them just as you would extracts, but in smaller quantities.

LIQUORS AND LIQUEURS I sometimes use spirits (distilled alcohol) and liqueurs (alcohol mixed with flavoring and sugar) to enhance cakes and/or fillings. Follow these simple rules to use liquor in a recipe: Use more if the liquor is to be baked in the batter, because the alcohol will evaporate substantially and so will some of the flavor. If the liquor is to be added to a cooled cake, make sure it is diluted with sugar syrup, or the cake may take on a strong, even bitter, alcohol flavor. When flavoring icings and buttercreams, add liquors and liqueurs slowly and sparingly. Too much liquid, or liquid added too quickly, can make glazes too thin and cause delicate buttercreams to separate. By the way, cheap brands of liquors and liqueurs tend to have a pretty cheap taste. Just as with most foods, the best quality is often more expensive, but worth it for its superior flavor.

COFFEE

It's easy to use instant coffee or instant espresso for flavoring a cake, mousse, or buttercream, but nothing beats the flavor of fresh-brewed coffee. When I can, I steep 3 Illy coffee pods—pre-measured doses of coffee wrapped in paper, a little like a tea bag—in ¾ cup boiling water until the coffee has cooled completely. Then I squeeze out the pods and keep the resulting triple-strength espresso in the refrigerator in a covered jar. It adds such an excellent coffee flavor that you don't need to use very much. You can do the same thing with ground Illy coffee: Steep 3 heaping tablespoons of the coffee in ¾ cup boiling water. When it has cooled, strain first through a fine strainer to remove most of the grounds, then again through a coffee filter or paper towel set inside a strainer to remove all the grounds. Store as above.

FRUIT

Ripe fresh fruit may be difficult to find in this era of plastic-wrapped trays and sticky-labeled fruit. Below is a list of good staple fruits to use in the recipes here. Locally grown height-of-the-season produce can always be substituted with excellent results.

APPLES Golden Delicious is a good all-purpose apple, but if you like a tarter flavor, Granny Smith works well. McIntosh is the best for applesauce, and tiny lady apples make a pretty platter decoration when they are in season in the fall.

PEARS The all-around best pear for use in fillings, poaching, and cakes is a Bartlett. When a Bartlett pear is ripe, its buttery, melting flesh is exquisitely perfumed and although it is sweet, a good Bartlett always retains a slight undertone of acidity in its flavor. If you can find only underripe pears, place them in a closed paper bag at room temperature, and they will ripen perfectly in a day or two.

CITRUS FRUIT

LEMONS I usually buy supermarket lemons, mainly the Eureka variety that is available all over the United States. When I can find them, I like to use sweeter Meyer lemons for frostings and fillings. Meyer lemons are not necessarily a one-for-one substitute for more acidic lemons—you'll probably need about half again as many for a good lemon flavor. Meyer lemons make fine lemon curd, but I find them weak for flavoring buttercream.

ORANGES California Valencia oranges, which are most easily available where I live, are a perfect all-purpose orange for juice, zest, and for segmenting or slicing. I also use Florida juice oranges for their juice; their zest is a little bitter. Florida Honeybells are good for everything during their short midwinter season.

TANGERINES A good tangerine is usually fairly loose skinned. Aside from the American-grown ones available in fall and winter, I use the tiny, sweet clementines imported from Israel, Morocco, and Spain.

LIMES Persian limes, available in supermarkets, are fine for lime-flavored cakes. I tend not to use the zest, which is bitter. Key limes from Florida, in season in the late fall, have a more tart flavor than Persian limes and can be a good substitute, but you have to be careful that they do not make the cake or filling too tart. Never use the zest of Key limes—it is extremely bitter.

PEACHES They must be ripe to have any flavor at all. Although there is a snobbish preference for white-fleshed peaches in some circles, they aren't any good if they aren't perfectly ripe. Locally grown peaches will always be best for any purpose; if the season is short, use them as often as possible, then wait until next year for good ones again.

APRICOTS One of the most elusively flavored of all fruits, apricots are seldom found ripe. Even my local farmers' market has taken to selling underripe apricots that are more sour than any lemon you can imagine. Although they will soften if left at room temperature, they really won't develop more sugar. So always taste if possible before purchasing apricots. A little acidity is fine to balance the sweetness, but too much will annihilate all flavor.

PLUMS The plums I use the most for baking are the prune plums, sometimes called Italian plums, that come at summer's end. I always think of them as "back to school" plums, because they were always a component of my school lunch in early September when I was a child. Although there are several varieties of this type of plum, they are fairly similar in flavor and texture. They work best in a crumb cake or other coffee cake–type presentation with enough sweet ingredients to offset their tartness.

CHERRIES Sweet or Bing cherries are an excellent dessert in themselves, but they are a little bland and too sweet for making cakes. For baking, I prefer a Montmorency or any one of several other varieties of sour cherries. Sour cherries have a fairly short season compared to their sweet counterparts, but they are well worth waiting for. Where I live in New York City, sour cherries from southern New Jersey and upstate New York are available for a couple of weeks only between mid-June and mid-July. The exact season changes every year and may be longer or shorter depending on weather conditions during both the blossoming and fruiting of the trees. If I can't get sour cherries for a pie or crumb cake, I'll make a blueberry pie or cake, rather than substituting sweet cherries—they just don't have the right taste.

Berries

This category encompasses strawberries, raspberries, blueberries, blackberries, currants (red, black, and white), and gooseberries.

Strawberries Most of the United States gets good California-grown berries throughout the year. But if you live in an area where you can get locally grown strawberries, these are the ones to use for shortcakes (or just serve with a bowl of whipped cream and a shaker of sugar). A ripe local strawberry is hard to beat—it has the color, flavor, and perfume that hothouse berries lack.

Raspberries Although raspberries are now available throughout most of the year, local berries have only a short season where I live, occasionally there are sweet and virtually seedless black raspberries and beautiful golden ones in the fall. As a result, raspberries are one fruit I often use in frozen form. I prefer IQF (individually quick frozen) raspberries when I can get them. These are bags of individual berries that have nothing added to them. When I use the frozen berries for a puree, I add sugar and a drop of water and cook them down, then puree and strain them. Cooking them down concentrates the flavor, and the puree can be used to make a great Bavarian cream, sauce, or glaze.

Blueberries I'm actually lucky that fresh blueberries are available only for part of the year, because I would make cakes and pies with them weekly if I could. I love the way they melt to that jam-like consistency after baking—they are my favorite berry. Most of the blueberries I buy in New York come from southern New Jersey. At the end of August and beginning of September, we sometimes get tiny, very spicy-flavored wild blueberries from Maine. If you can get some, by all means use them. Unfortunately, most of the wild Maine blueberries are bought up by industrial bakers for muffin mixes and canned pie fillings.

Blackberries Aside from wild ones that I pick on walks in the country, I don't often use blackberries. They are available during a short season in my local farmers' market, and they are also to be found in IQF form. They are a berry that I more often associate with pies and cobblers, or serving with sugar and cream, than I do with cakes.

Currants Usually used to make jelly or jam, fresh currants are a rarity. The beautiful clusters of fruit, like diminutive bunches of grapes, make a great decoration for a simple cake, though they are a bit tart to eat uncooked and unsweetened. Black currants are called *cassis* in French.

Gooseberries The tart green globes of gooseberries can be great in a crumb cake, though I have to admit I seldom use them.

CHOCOLATE

Good chocolate tastes good before you add it to other ingredients. With the exception of unsweetened chocolate, which is found in the baking aisle of most grocery stores, I usually tell people to buy their chocolate for baking in the candy aisle—bars of imported or domestic bittersweet, semisweet, milk, and white chocolate sold to eat out of hand usually have a better flavor and perform better than "baking chocolate." Nowadays there are more than a dozen brands to choose from, including the brands available at specialty food stores. For recipes that center on chocolate (such as Ganache, page 285, or Chocolate Glaze, page 299), it is especially important to choose a chocolate that tastes good on its own. If the recipe mixes chocolate with butter, eggs, sugar, flour, and flavoring, the taste of the chocolate isn't quite as clear as it is in simpler recipes. Of course you should use the best chocolate possible for this type of recipe too, but the flavor of the most delicate chocolates may be somewhat overwhelmed by the other ingredients.

COCOA I always use alkalized (Dutch-process) cocoa for cakes. It has a superior flavor and performs better than nonalkalized cocoa. The alkalizing process (treating the cocoa with a chemical like baking soda) reduces bitterness and improves the color of the cocoa.

NUTS AND NUT PRODUCTS

Besides being an essential ingredient in many cake batters, nuts and nut products are also often used to garnish and decorate.

ALMONDS Most of these come from California, with some arriving from Spain and a very few from Sicily. I usually use blanched almonds, whole or sliced, for cake baking. Store almonds, like all nuts, in a tightly sealed plastic bag in the freezer. If you can't find blanched whole almonds, place unblanched almonds in a saucepan, cover them with water, and bring to a boil. Drain the almonds in a strainer and pop them out of their skins while they are still warm. (If the skin is still on the sliced almonds you buy, you can't remove it.) If you need to grind the almonds, or plan to keep them before using them, place them on a jelly-roll pan and dry them in a 300-degree oven for about 10 minutes. Cool before using or storing in the freezer.

To enable you to grind almonds, or any nutmeats successfully, they must be at room temperature. Bring nuts stored in the freezer to room temperature for an hour or so before grinding them, or warm them on a jelly-roll pan at 300 degrees for 10 minutes, then cool them before you grind. Grind the almonds in the food processor fitted with the metal blade, pulsing the machine on and off at 1-second intervals and occasionally scraping the inside bottom edges of the bowl with a table knife or metal spatula between pulses. Use the same technique for grinding all nuts.

Bitter almonds are not eaten in the United States, but they are used with sweet almonds to make almond extract. That essential bitter almond perfume is their contribution.

Almond paste This is made from equal quantities of blanched almonds and sugar and is used as an ingredient in cake batters and in marzipan. The best almond paste comes in a can, not in a sausage shape in a cellophane wrapping. There are several good national brands of almond paste available in supermarkets or specialty stores.

Hazelnuts These are grown in Oregon, but many come from the Piemonte in northwestern Italy and from Turkey. Hazelnuts are usually used chopped or ground. I find chopping them with a knife difficult, so I usually wrap them in a towel and crush them with the bottom of a heavy saucepan. Nuts first broken that way won't roll all over your cutting board, and you can then chop them finer with a knife. To grind hazelnuts, see Almonds, opposite.

To blanch hazelnuts, place them in a jelly-roll pan and toast them in a 350-degree oven for about 10 to 15 minutes. To test whether or not they are ready, remove a hazelnut from the pan, let it cool for a few seconds, and then rub it to see if the skin flakes off easily. If it doesn't, toast a few seconds longer. Pour the toasted hazelnuts onto a damp towel and gather the towel around them. Rub the hazelnuts in the towel to loosen the skins, then go over them one by one to separate them from the skin; it doesn't matter if every speck of skin doesn't come off.

Praline Paste A delicious flavoring made from hazelnuts and sugar, praline paste is available in specialty stores. One of my favorite buttercreams is made with praline paste, and it is a natural and luxuriously smooth and rich partner with chocolate of all kinds.

Walnuts For decorating, I use walnut halves, or walnut pieces if the recipe calls for them to be chopped or ground. Walnuts can become very pasty when they are ground. To avoid this, add a few tablespoons of the sugar from the recipe to the walnuts in the food processor. Otherwise, follow exactly the same rules as for almonds, above, but scrape the bottom of the bowl every few pulses to prevent caking.

Pecans A close cousin to that all-American nut, the hickory nut, pecans come from the Southern states. They are also very popular in Mexico and more recently, in Australia. I always have to restrain myself from eating more pecans than I'm putting into the recipe. Their sweet and buttery flavor is difficult to resist. When grinding pecans, follow the directions above for walnuts; they are less likely to get pasty than walnuts.

PISTACHIOS These delicious green gems come from California and the Middle East. A small quantity of Sicilian pistachios are imported, and they are worth seeking out for their exotic bitter almond flavor and incredibly bright green color. In general, California pistachios are not as green as the Middle Eastern and Sicilian varieties. To blanch pistachios, start the same way as for almonds, above, but after you drain the pistachios, rub them in a towel and go over them one by one to separate them from the skins. Dry them in the oven afterwards as with almonds, but be careful that they don't start to toast, or they will lose their color.

PINE NUTS Nineteenth-century French baking author Pierre Lacam recommended substituting pine nuts for almonds because they were so much cheaper. Today the opposite is true, but pine nuts can still contribute a very delicate flavor to cakes. I like them especially in light fruit cakes or combined with a crumb topping on a delicately flavored cake with fresh fruit.

EGGS

Eggs are the most essential ingredient in cake baking, responsible for the structure, lightness, and richness of cakes, fillings, and frostings. I always use large eggs (24 ounces per dozen). Remember that the weight is by the dozen and the weight of individual eggs may vary. This doesn't much affect recipes that use whole eggs or yolks, but sometimes if I'm preparing meringues, I like to measure the egg whites by volume, using a liquid-measure cup. In this book, recipes calling for egg whites include a measure such as ½ cup. If I have leftover egg whites, I store them in a covered glass jar in the refrigerator for a few days or freeze them for up to a month. Plastic snack bags and half-pint plastic containers are ideal for a few egg whites—just be sure to mark the bag or container with indelible pen to indicate the number of egg whites in it. To use the whites, thaw them in the refrigerator overnight, or at room temperature. If you have thawed them at room temperature, use them right away.

Leftover yolks will keep well for up to a day or two if stored like this: Place the unbroken yolks in a small bowl, sprinkle with a teaspoon of water, and press plastic wrap directly against the yolks, without breaking them. Keep refrigerated for no more than 48 hours, and use right from the refrigerator. Egg yolks can be frozen by stirring a teaspoon of light corn syrup into every 3 or 4 yolks and pressing plastic wrap directly against the surface, before sealing the container.

DAIRY PRODUCTS

BUTTER My personal favorite baking ingredient, butter has to be of good quality to make an outstanding cake or buttercream. Always use unsalted butter, and make sure it is fresh by using this simple test: Unwrap a stick of butter and scrape the surface with a dull knife, removing a strip about ¼ inch wide. If the butter below the surface is lighter in color, the butter has oxidized—it has been exposed to air and the outside has begun to turn rancid. Never accept oxidized butter from a store; if you have taken it home, return it immediately. Sometimes butter that has begun to oxidize is put on sale so the store can get rid of it. Unfortunately, it is no bargain at any price.

Recipe testing has proven it dozens of times—a cake batter made with butter that has been allowed to soften is lighter and has a better texture than one made with cold butter beaten until it is soft. When a recipe calls for softened butter, make sure you leave the butter, still in its wrapper or covered with plastic wrap, outside the refrigerator for at least an hour. Don't place the butter in the sun or put it on a hot stove to hasten the process—that will melt the butter, not soften it. If you're very careful, you can place the butter in a microwave-safe bowl and microwave it for a few seconds at a time to soften it.

MILK The recipes in this book use whole milk. Honestly, though, if you are making a yeast-risen cake that requires only a small amount of milk, it doesn't really matter if you use a low-fat milk. However, I always use whole milk when making anything custardy. I don't think lower-fat milks make a good pastry cream or crème anglaise.

CREAM I use heavy whipping cream that is 36 percent butterfat. Although richer cream is available to chefs (40 percent butterfat), we tested all the recipes in this book with the ultrapasteurized cream that you can buy in the supermarket. Remember, for whipped cream, have the bowl, beater, and cream cold.

SOUR CREAM I never use reduced-fat sour creams in recipes, though I suppose they are okay on a baked potato.

CHEESES

Among the richest ingredients for baking, cheese is made by slightly curdling milk, cream, or a combination and draining off the resulting liquid.

CREAM CHEESE I used to think it was important to use cream cheese without vegetable gum additives, but I discovered that cheesecakes, notably, are less smooth when made with the drier and rougher-textured cheeses. Now I use regular full-fat cream cheese from the supermarket for baking.

MASCARPONE A luscious Italian cream cheese, mascarpone has a softer texture than our cream cheese. It is an essential ingredient in Tiramisù (page 358) and in some of the cheesecake recipes.

RICOTTA Another Italian cheese, ricotta is a deliciously milky curd cheese. Though it has a somewhat rough texture, when eggs and other ingredients are added, ricotta smooths out very well. If I use it uncooked for a mousse recipe, I usually process the ricotta in the food processor to make it smoother. The best-tasting and firmest ricotta is the freshly made kind you can find in an Italian deli. If you don't have one near you, try to find a local commercially made brand.

In the course of my travels to teach at cooking schools around the United States, I have encountered supermarket ricotta that has been frozen and defrosted before it was sold: the resulting ricotta has a dry, chalky texture and has completely lost its milky flavor and rich texture.

EQUIPMENT

HAVING THE RIGHT EQUIPMENT makes baking even more of a pleasure. The good news is that you don't have to buy it all at once. I've been collecting baking equipment for thirty-five years and I still can't visit a kitchenware store, no matter what state or country I'm in, without emerging with a few cookie cutters or an implement (and recipe) necessary to the preparation of a local specialty. Although the best things are not always the most expensive, buying high-quality pans, tools, and small appliances means that they will last a lifetime. I still have my first KitchenAid mixer, which I bought when I was in high school—close to forty years later, it whips up egg whites and everything else to perfect peaks.

ELECTRICAL APPLIANCES

HEAVY-DUTY STAND MIXER This makes quick work of mixing, beating, and whipping. Use the flat paddle for all general mixing purposes such as preparing butter and pound cake batters, cheesecake batters, and any firm mixture, such as marzipan. Use the whisk attachment only for incorporating air, as in whipping egg whites or cream. It's nice to have an extra mixer bowl and whisk for those batters that require whipping whites and yolks separately.

HAND MIXER If you're just starting out baking and have a limited budget, a hand mixer will do all but the most heavy-duty jobs, such as beating marzipan or mixing bread doughs. Having an extra set of beaters is handy for batters that require separately beaten egg whites.

FOOD PROCESSOR Back in the dark ages, before there were food processors, we used hand grinders, graters, and knives to—slowly and laboriously—do everything the food processor now does in seconds. A food processor can be used to mix some simple batters, though I usually rely on my stand mixer for that. The processor mixes ingredients very efficiently, but it doesn't incorporate air in the process, which is why I always prefer the mixer for batters. A processor, though, can't be beat for grinding nuts.

BLENDER I think a blender makes better purees—and does so more quickly—than a food processor.

A good assortment of whisks, rubber spatulas, and wooden spoons is essential for all cooking and baking. If you have not done a lot of baking, you may need to purchase the following few specialty items before you begin using this book.

SPATULAS I like small and large offset (the smooth blade steps down from the handle) spatulas for finishing cakes. A wide griddle spatula—whether or not it has a perforated blade—can be useful for transferring cake layers to cooling racks and onto platters.

THERMOMETERS A thermometer can be a great help in getting consistent results with recipes. Excellent battery-operated digital thermometers are available as close as your local hardware store. These are perfect for tempering chocolate or monitoring the heat of delicate mixtures such as crème anglaise.

KNIVES This is definitely an area where you want to get the very best you can afford. The three essential knives for cake baking are a paring knife, a chef's chopping knife, and a serrated bread knife, for slicing through cake layers. The latter should have as long a blade as you can find. For the paring and chef's knives, buy whatever size feels comfortable in your hand. I also like a long thin narrow-bladed slicing knife for cutting cakes into portions.

CHOCOLATE CHOPPER A four-pronged ice pick does a great job of breaking chocolate into ½- to ¼-inch pieces. Be careful: the ends of the picks are sharp and can ruin a countertop or wooden cutting board. I use a less expensive nylon board for chopping chocolate; then the board makes a quick trip through the dishwasher to remove the chocolate stains—difficult to do by hand.

BAKING PANS Most of the baking pans I own are aluminum. I have nested sets of 2-inch-deep round cake pans in 8-, 9-, 10-, and 12-inch diameters—all of these are used in the recipes here. Both 9 × 5 × 3-inch and 8½ × 4½ × 2¾-inch loaf pans are called for, as are both 10 × 15-inch and 12 × 18-inch jelly-roll pans. To round out the assortment, you'll need a 12-cup Bundt pan and a 10-inch tube pan with a removable bottom for angel cakes. Add a couple of springform pans—9- and 10-inch—for molded cakes and cheesecakes, and you've got all the pans you'll need to make the recipes in this book.

A *Bundt pan* is a fluted tube pan with a rounded bottom, so that when the cake is unmolded, it has a curved, gently rounded, ridged top. The most common size is 10 inches in diameter and holds 12 cups, and that's the one you'll need for all the recipes that call for Bundt pans.

Angel food cake pans come in two pieces: the bottom and tube are one part and the pan sides another. I keep a separate one just for angel food and sponge cakes that need to be baked in ungreased pans, as any trace of fat in the pan would prevent such cakes from rising properly.

DESSERT RINGS Known as entremet rings in French, these are sturdy round metal rings. For molded cakes, they are placed on a cardboard round, set on a sheet pan or cookie sheet, and filled with layers of cake and filling. The dessert ring is removed after the cake has chilled, leaving it on the cardboard base. They are available in many diameters.

SILPAT This is a silicone mat used to line a baking sheet and provide a perfect nonstick surface. A Silpat is very useful when you are making ladyfingers. They are also excellent for cookies such as tuiles and tulipes that spread and need to be lifted while still hot from the pan and shaped.

FLEXIPAN These flexible silicone baking pans come in a variety of shapes and sizes and provide a nonstick medium for baking cakes and smaller items such as madeleines and financiers. If you use them, always remember to place them on a jelly-roll pan before you fill them, or they could buckle on the way to the oven and spill their contents.

Decorating Equipment

PASTRY BAGS These used to be made from canvas, and were a real pain to clean. Nowadays I often use disposable bags. If you want reusable pastry bags, the nylon or plastic-coated canvas ones are thin, flexible, waterproof (important when you are piping whipped cream), and easy to clean: soak them in soapy water with a little bleach added, then rinse thoroughly under running water. (Sometimes I just rinse these bags and add them to kitchen laundry to be run through the washing machine; I don't think they would survive a trip through the dryer.)

TUBES These tips, which are inserted into the end of the pastry bag, come in many shapes and sizes. Recipes here that require piping always state the Ateco tube number as these are easy to find. Tubes are widely available in kitchenware stores and through mail-order.

Paper Goods

PARCHMENT PAPER Invaluable for lining pans, making cones (instant disposable pastry bags), and transferring dry ingredients to the mixer, parchment paper comes in rolls or in large sheets. The large sheets, designed to be used on commercial sheet pans, are approximately 18 by 24 inches. These are useful because the standard roll of parchment paper isn't wide enough to line both the bottom and sides of some rectangular pans. Lacking parchment paper, I use wax paper or aluminum foil for lining pans.

CARDBOARD ROUNDS I like putting a cardboard round under a layer cake when I'm finishing it. The convenience of having a cake on a base that you can pick up and move around is a real advantage.

MEASURING

Accurate measuring can make the difference between a successful cake and a failure.

LIQUID MEASURES I always use Pyrex measuring cups for liquids. Place the glass (or clear plastic) measuring cup on a level surface and fill it so that the liquid reaches the top of the line for the measurement you need. If you have low countertops, it may be necessary to do a deep knee bend to read the level. Or stand the cup on a shelf at eye level to get a good reading. Measuring cups that hold 2 or more cups are excellent for measuring large amounts, but I never use a large cup measure for measuring less than a cup, because these can be less accurate for smaller amounts.

DRY MEASURES Nested dry-measure cups that come in ¼-, ⅓-, ½-, and 1-cup gradations are used to measure dry ingredients. If you buy a set of dry-measure cups that also has ⅔- and ¾-cup measures, send those immediately to the potting bench or the sandbox—it is too easy to mistake one of those cups for another size and ruin a recipe. To use the cups for powdery dry ingredients such as flour, confectioners' sugar, and cocoa powder, put the correct-size cup on a piece of wax paper and gently spoon in the ingredient until the cup overflows, then level it with the back of a knife or with a metal spatula. Granulated sugar can be scooped up with a cup measure, but it is the only ingredient I measure that way.

MEASURING SPOONS I usually scoop up ingredients with measuring spoons—the quantities being measured are small enough that I don't think it matters if the ingredient is slightly packed in the spoon. To measure spoonfuls of liquid, pour the liquid into the spoon—just don't do the pouring over your bowl of batter, or any excess will overflow into it.

COFFEE CAKES

THESE ARE THE CAKES for when that familiar feeling comes over you: "I want something really good to eat but I don't know what I want." These are cakes that you don't necessarily bake for a special occasion, but because you want to have something in the house in case someone drops by. They're also great to take on picnics or send to school for lunches and to whip up when you want to bake something quick to take to a friend or neighbor who doesn't have time to bake.

A coffee cake should be easy to prepare: no fussy procedures and no fancy, time-consuming touches. One of the cakes in this chapter has a chocolate glaze—it is a more "sitting down for coffee at the dining room table" type of coffee cake. All the others can be prepared quickly, even mixed by hand, in one step.

The name *coffee cake* distinguishes these recipes from dessert cakes, because they are more simple both in preparation and in flavor. Serve them in slices or wedges, and with a favorite beverage.

A few of these recipes call for yeast; they are the only ones in the book that use it. Here are a few hints about working with yeast.

1 Always store dry yeast in the freezer to prolong its life.

2 If you buy dry yeast in bulk, make sure you keep in mind its expiration date.

3 Always use warm, not hot, water to dissolve yeast. Warm water activates the yeast quickly; hot water would kill it.

4 Always allow yeast dough to rise in an area free of drafts. Cool air can chill the yeast and keep the dough from rising.

5 If you prefer to use compressed (fresh) yeast, a 2-ounce yeast cake equals a strip of three dry yeast envelopes. So, if you only need one envelope for the recipe, use a third of the yeast cake. Crumble the yeast and use it the same way you would dry yeast, whisking it into warm liquid.

6 Don't be afraid to try baking with yeast—it's really easy and well worth it for the great things you can make.

IRISH CURRANT AND RAISIN CAKE

〜 ೨ ೯ 〜

RIGHTFULLY THIS CAKE belongs in the chapter with the other cakes that contain dried fruit, but to me it is the quintessential coffee cake. It is a quick and easy version of a cake that I remember from my childhood, made by the mother of my school friend, the late Noel Giles. Noel and I consumed about a ton of this cake per year between the ages of twelve and eighteen–a taste of it still makes me feel like a teenager.

1 Set a rack in the middle of the oven and preheat to 350 degrees.

2 Stir together the 2¼ cups flour, the baking powder, baking soda, and salt in a bowl.

3 In the bowl of a heavy-duty mixer, beat the butter and sugar with the paddle on medium speed until soft and light, about 5 minutes. Add the egg, beating until smooth.

4 Decrease the mixer speed to low and beat in half the flour mixture. Stop and scrape down the bowl and beater with a rubber spatula. Beat in the buttermilk, then the remaining flour mixture.

5 Give the batter a final mix with the rubber spatula.

6 Toss the currants and raisins with the remaining 1 tablespoon flour and fold them into the batter. Scrape the batter into the prepared pan and smooth the top.

7 Bake for about 45–55 minutes, or until the cake is well risen and deep gold and a toothpick inserted in the center emerges clean.

2¼ cups unbleached all-purpose flour (spoon flour into dry-measure cups and level off) plus 1 tablespoon

1 teaspoon baking powder

½ teaspoon baking soda

½ teaspoon salt

8 tablespoons (1 stick) unsalted butter, softened

¾ cup sugar

1 large egg, at room temperature

½ cup currants

½ cup golden raisins

¾ cup buttermilk or milk

One 2-inch-deep 8-inch round cake pan, buttered and bottom lined with parchment or wax paper

8 Cool in the pan on a rack for about 30 minutes, then invert the cake onto a rack and remove the pan and paper. Invert the cake onto another rack and cool completely.

STORAGE: Wrap in plastic and keep at room temperature, or double-wrap and freeze for longer storage.

MAKES ONE 8-INCH CAKE, ABOT 12 SERVINGS

ONTBIJTKOEK
Dutch Breakfast Cake

THIS IS PRETTY MUCH A STAPLE on the Dutch breakfast table, available in every bakery, super-market, and convenience store. This version from my friend cookbook dealer Bonnie Slotnick has an extra fillip of crystallized ginger.

In Holland, this cake is eaten with butter, but I think it's fine on its own.

1 Set a rack in the middle of the oven and preheat to 350 degrees.

2 In a large bowl, stir together the flour, baking powder, and spices.

3 Place the brown sugar in a medium bowl and stir in the milk, adding it slowly so the sugar doesn't lump. Pour the milk mixture all at once into the flour mixture and stir until the batter is smooth. Stir in the crystallized ginger, if using.

4 Pour the batter into the prepared pan.

5 Bake for 1 hour, or until the cake begins to leave the sides of the pan and is nicely browned and a toothpick inserted in the center emerges clean.

6 Cool the cake in the pan on a rack for about 15 minutes, then invert onto the rack and let cool completely.

7 Wrap the cake well in plastic wrap and let age at room temperature or in the refrigerator for at least a day. (Served too soon, it has a rubbery quality that disappears otherwise.)

2 cups all-purpose flour (spoon flour into dry-measure cup and level off)

1 teaspoon baking powder

1 teaspoon ground cinnamon

½ teaspoon freshly grated nutmeg

½ teaspoon ground ginger

½ teaspoon ground allspice

1 cup firmly packed dark brown sugar

1 cup milk

½ cup (about 3 ounces) crystallized ginger, cut into ¼-inch pieces, optional

One 8½ × 4½ × 2¾-inch loaf pan, buttered and bottom lined with buttered aluminum foil

STORAGE: Wrapped well in plastic, this keeps almost indefinitely at room temperature.

MAKES ONE 8½ × 4½-INCH LOAF CAKE, 16 SLICES

ORANGE POPPY SEED CAKE

～⌒⌒～

CRUNCHY POPPY SEEDS and mellow orange flavor complement each other perfectly in this lovely Australian cake.

1 Set a rack in the middle of the oven and preheat to 350 degrees.

2 Combine the flour, baking powder, and baking soda in a bowl and stir to mix.

3 In the bowl of a heavy-duty mixer, beat the butter and sugar with the paddle on medium speed until soft and light, about 5 minutes. Beat in the eggs one at a time, beating until smooth after each addition.

4 Decrease the mixer speed to low and add half the flour mixture. Stop the mixer and scrape down the bowl and beater with a rubber spatula. Beat in the sour cream, then the remaining flour mixture.

5 Use a large rubber spatula to give the batter a final mix. Fold in the poppy seeds. Scrape the batter into the prepared pan.

6 Bake for about 1 hour, or until the cake is well risen and deep gold and a toothpick inserted in the center emerges clean.

7 While the cake is baking, prepare the syrup: Combine all the ingredients in a nonreactive saucepan and bring to a simmer, stirring occasionally to dissolve the sugar. Strain through a fine-mesh strainer into a measuring cup.

CAKE BATTER

1¾ cups all purpose flour (spoon flour into dry-measure cups and level off)

1 teaspoon baking powder

1 teaspoon baking soda

½ pound (2 sticks) unsalted butter, softened

1 cup sugar

3 large eggs

One 8-ounce container sour cream

½ cup poppy seeds

ORANGE SYRUP

2 tablespoons finely grated orange zest

¾ cup strained fresh orange juice

¾ cup sugar

Strips of orange zest for decorating

One 9-inch springform pan, buttered and bottom lined with buttered parchment or wax paper

8 When the cake is baked, place it on a jelly-roll pan. Use a skewer to poke about 20 holes into the cake. Gradually pour the syrup all over the top of the cake until it is all absorbed. If any of the syrup leaks out of the springform pan, spoon it back over the cake. The cake absorbs the syrup rather slowly.

9   Transfer the cake to a rack and cool to room temperature.

10   Remove the pan sides and slide the cake, on the paper, onto a platter. Run a sharp knife between the cake and the paper and pull out the paper.

STORAGE: Keep under a cake dome at room temperature.

MAKES ONE 9-INCH CAKE, ABOUT 12 TO 16 SERVINGS

CHOCOLATE CHIP–
CREAM CHEESE COFFEE CAKE

JUST READING THE NAME OF THIS cake makes me want to get up and bake one. Its rich texture, surprise of the chocolate chips inside, and crisp topping make a memorable cake.

1 Set a rack in the middle of the oven and preheat to 350 degrees.

2 In a medium bowl, stir together the flour, baking powder, baking soda, and salt.

3 In the bowl of a heavy-duty mixer, beat the cream cheese, butter, and sugar with the paddle on medium speed until soft and light, about 5 minutes. Add the eggs one at a time, beating until smooth after each addition.

4 Decrease the mixer speed to low and add half the dry ingredients. Stop the mixer and scrape down the bowl and beater. Beat in the milk, then beat in the remaining dry ingredients.

5 Give the batter a final mix with a large rubber spatula. Fold in the chocolate chips, and spread the batter evenly in the prepared pan.

CAKE BATTER

2 cups cake flour (spoon flour into dry-measure cup and level off)

1 teaspoon baking powder

¼ teaspoon baking soda

¼ teaspoon salt

One 8-ounce package cream cheese, softened

½ pound (2 sticks) unsalted butter, softened

1¼ cups sugar

2 large eggs

¼ cup milk

One 12-ounce bag semisweet chocolate chips

CRUMB TOPPING

½ cup all-purpose flour (spoon flour into dry-measure cup and level off)

½ cup rolled oats

¼ cup firmly packed light brown sugar

1 teaspoon ground cinnamon

4 tablespoons (½ stick) unsalted butter, melted

One 12-cup straight-sided tube pan, buttered and floured

6　To make the crumb topping, stir all the dry ingredients together in a mixing bowl, mixing well. Stir in the butter and continue stirring until the mixture forms large crumbs. Sprinkle the crumb topping evenly over the batter.

7　Bake for about 50 to 55 minutes, or until the cake is well risen, the crumbs are golden, and a toothpick inserted into the center emerges clean.

8　Cool the cake in the pan on a rack for about 15 minutes. Invert the cake to a plate, remove side and bottom of pan, then invert again onto the rack to cool completely.

9　Slide the cake onto a platter.

Storage: Wrap in plastic and keep at room temperature for up to several days, or double-wrap and freeze for longer storage.

Makes one 9-inch cake, about 12 servings

SOUR CREAM COFFEE CAKE

❧

I REMEMBER MAKING THIS coffee cake as a teenager, probably from the same recipe. It comes from my Aunt Virginia. She has always liked to bake, and this is a recipe she makes frequently. Thanks also to Alan Cohen, who shared a similar recipe.

1 Set a rack in the middle of the oven and preheat to 350 degrees.

2 Stir together the flour, baking powder, and baking soda in a bowl, mixing well.

3 In the bowl of a heavy-duty mixer, beat the butter and sugar with the paddle on medium speed until soft and light, about 5 minutes. Beat in the eggs one at a time, beating until smooth after each addition.

4 Decrease the mixer speed to low and beat in one-third of the flour mixture, followed by half the sour cream. Stop the mixer and scrape down the bowl and beater. Beat in another third of the flour mixture, then the remaining sour cream. Stop and scrape again. Beat in the remaining flour mixture.

5 Give the batter a final mix with a large rubber spatula.

6 To make the topping, stir the ingredients together until evenly mixed.

CAKE BATTER

2 cups all-purpose flour (spoon flour into dry-measure cup and level off)

1 teaspoon baking powder

½ teaspoon baking soda

½ pound (2 sticks) unsalted butter, softened

1½ cups sugar

2 large eggs

One 8-ounce container sour cream

WALNUT TOPPING

1 cup (about 4 ounces) walnuts, coarsely chopped

¼ cup sugar

2 teaspoons ground cinnamon

One 12-cup tube pan, buttered and floured

7　Scrape half the batter into the prepared pan and sprinkle with half the topping. Cover with the remaining batter and smooth the top. Sprinkle with the remaining topping.

8　Bake for 50 to 55 minutes, or until the cake is well risen and deep gold and a toothpick inserted midway between the side of the pan and the central tube emerges clean.

9　Cool in the pan on a rack for 30 minutes, then invert onto a plate and lift off the pan. Invert the cake onto a rack to cool completely.

STORAGE: Keep wrapped in plastic or under a cake dome at room temperature, or double-wrap and freeze for longer storage.

MAKES ONE 10-INCH TUBE CAKE, ABOUT 16 SERVINGS

VARIATIONS

Add ½ cup dark raisins or currants to the topping. Bake in two buttered and parchment- or wax paper–lined 9 × 5 × 3-inch loaf pans (especially good if you intend to freeze one or both of the cakes). They will probably be done in around 45 minutes, but check at 35 to 40 minutes.

NOTE: Sometimes the top of the cake is not perfectly flat after baking because of the topping—don't worry, the cake is okay.

CHOCOLATE COFFEE CAKE

⤜᷾◠᷾⤛

WHAT GOES BETTER WITH COFFEE than chocolate? This fancy coffee cake comes from David Grice of Dallas.

1 Set a rack in the middle of the oven and preheat to 325 degrees.

2 Stir together the flour, baking soda, and salt in a bowl.

3 In the bowl of a heavy-duty mixer, beat the butter and sugar with the paddle on medium speed until soft and light, about 5 minutes.

4 Stop the mixer, scrape in the chocolate, and beat it in on medium speed. Beat in the eggs one at a time, beating until smooth after each addition. Stop the mixer and use a rubber spatula to scrape down the bowl and beater.

5 Decrease the mixer speed to low and beat in one-third of the flour, followed by half the sour cream. Stop and scrape again. Repeat with another one-third of the flour and the remaining sour cream, then stop and scrape. Beat in the remaining flour mixture.

6 Give a final mix to the batter with a large rubber spatula. Scrape the batter into the prepared pan and smooth the top.

7 Bake for about 55–60 minutes, or until the cake is well risen and a toothpick inserted halfway between the side of the pan and the central tube emerges clean.

CAKE BATTER

2 cups all-purpose flour (spoon flour into dry-measure cup and level off)

2 teaspoons baking soda

¼ teaspoon salt

½ pound (2 sticks) unsalted butter, softened

1½ cups sugar

8 ounces semisweet or bittersweet chocolate, melted and cooled

4 large eggs

One 8-ounce container sour cream

GANACHE GLAZE

1 cup heavy whipping cream

8 ounces semisweet chocolate, cut into ¼-inch pieces

2 tablespoons triple-strength brewed espresso (see page 190)

One 12-cup tube or Bundt pan, buttered and floured

8 Cool the cake in the pan on a rack for 10 minutes, then invert onto the rack, remove the pan, and let cool completely.

9 When the cake is completely cooled, make the glaze. Bring the cream to a simmer in a saucepan. Remove from the heat, add the chocolate, and allow to stand for 3 minutes to melt the chocolate. Add the espresso to the glaze and whisk until smooth. Let cool to room temperature.

10 Place the cake, on the rack, on a jelly-roll pan to catch drips. Pour the glaze over the cake in a spiral, starting from the center and working outward. Leave the cake on the rack until glaze is set.

11 Use a wide metal spatula to slide the cake onto a platter. (Chill the pan the glaze dripped onto, then scrape the glaze off and save it—you can freeze it, then melt and cool it and use it to flavor a chocolate buttercream.)

STORAGE: Keep the cake under a dome at cool room temperature—refrigeration will dull the glaze.

MAKES ONE 10-INCH TUBE OR BUNDT CAKE, ABOUT 16 SERVINGS

215

CAKES

PEGGY'S COFFEE CAKE

‿◞ ◟‿

THIS UNIQUE RECIPE comes from my friend Peggy Tagliarino. She says her mother, Blanche Levine, still makes it for her when she visits her in Florida.

You will need to plan ahead for this recipe: The dough has to chill for at least 8 hours, or overnight, before filling and rolling it. Then, the chilled dough takes quite a while to rise, about 2 hours or so.

1 To make the dough, warm the milk slightly in a small saucepan over low heat. Pour the milk into a bowl and whisk in the yeast. Set aside while you prepare the other ingredients.

2 In the bowl of a heavy-duty mixer, beat the butter and sugar with the paddle on medium speed until soft and light, about 3 minutes. Beat in the egg yolks one at a time, through the vanilla.

3 Decrease the mixer speed to low and beat in one-third of the flour. Beat in the yeast mixture, then stop and scrape down the bowl and beater with a rubber spatula. Beat in another third of the flour, then the sour cream. Stop and scrape again. Beat in the remaining flour and continue beating for 2 to 3 minutes longer, or until the dough is fairly smooth.

4 Scrape the dough into a large bowl, cover it tightly with plastic wrap, and refrigerate it for at least 8 hours, or overnight.

5 Scrape the dough out onto a floured surface and flour it lightly. Press the dough into an even rectangle with your hands, then roll it out to a rectangle about 12 × 18 inches.

DOUGH

½ cup milk

2 envelopes (5 teaspoons) active dry yeast

½ pound (2 sticks) unsalted butter, softened

¼ cup sugar

3 large egg yolks

½ teaspoon vanilla extract

4 cups all-purpose flour (spoon flour into dry-measure cup and level off)

½ cup sour cream

FILLING

3 large egg whites

1 cup sugar

2 tablespoons ground cinnamon

½ cup dark raisins

½ cup (about 2 ounces) chopped walnuts

One 10-inch tube pan, buttered

6   To make the filling, in the clean, dry mixer bowl, whip the egg whites with the whisk attachment on medium speed until very white and opaque. Increase the speed to medium-high, and add the sugar in a slow stream (if you go too fast, the egg whites will deflate). Continue to whip the egg whites until they hold a firm peak.

7   Spread the meringue over the dough within one inch of the ledge. Sprinkle evenly with the cinnamon, raisins, and nuts. Roll the dough up from a long side, like a jelly roll. Carefully ease the rolled cake into the prepared pan seam-side up (this will eventually be the bottom of the cake), making sure the two ends join.

8   Cover the pan with plastic wrap or a towel and leave to rise for about 2 hours, or until the pan is about three-quarters full.

9   Meanwhile, set a rack in the middle level of the oven and preheat to 350 degrees.

10   Bake for about 1 hour, or until the cake is firm, well risen, and deep gold (the toothpick test doesn't work here because of the soft filling).

11   Cool the cake in the pan on a rack for about 15 minutes, then invert onto the rack to cool completely.

STORAGE: Keep under a cake dome, or wrap well and freeze; defrost, reheat, to refresh in 350° oven for 10 minutes, and cool before serving.

MAKES ONE 10-INCH TUBE CAKE, ABOUT 16 SERVINGS

POUND CAKES AND BUTTER CAKES

POUND CAKE BECAME POPULAR in both the British Isles and in America in the eighteenth century, when it was called, simply, "a cake." The "pound cake" name originated from the proportions of the ingredients (one pound each of butter, sugar, eggs, and flour). Rich yet delicate, a good pound cake may be perfumed with vanilla, citrus, or spice. Preparation has only one trick, and it is an easy one to master: make sure the butter is soft before you begin to mix. Many pound cakes are baked as loaves, but I find that pound cakes have an excellent texture and superior lightness when they are baked in a tube pan. A tube pan also bakes the cake more quickly because of the heat conducted into the center of the pan through the tube, and this makes for a moister cake. Any of the recipes in this chapter can be baked in a tube pan—use the basic test for doneness and insert a toothpick in the cake midway between the side of the pan and the central tube: when the toothpick emerges clean, the cake is done.

HINTS FOR PERFECT POUND AND BUTTER CAKES

1 Always start with very soft butter.

2 Don't rush the mixing—many of these batters are leavened only by the air beaten into them during mixing.

3 Always have eggs and any liquids as close to room temperature as possible, and add them to the batter gradually. Adding liquid too quickly, or adding too much at a time can make a cake batter separate, resulting in a heavy, greasy texture instead of a light one.

4 For a loaf cake, line the pan or at least the bottom with parchment paper.

5 If the top of a cake baked for a long time seems to be coloring too deeply, cover the cake loosely with aluminum foil. Placing the cake pan on a heavy cookie sheet or jelly-roll pan will protect the bottom of the cake from coloring too deeply.

6 Cool pound cakes in the pan for a few minutes, then invert onto a rack or board. Invert again so that the cake cools completely right side up.

7   To store pound cakes, keep tightly wrapped in plastic and foil at room temperature for up to a couple of days, or freeze for longer.

8   Although finer than coffee cakes, pound cakes are served in the same way—with a favorite beverage. If the last few slices of a pound cake seem dry, lightly toast them and serve with butter or jam.

ALTERNATING LIQUID AND DRY INGREDIENTS

Many of the recipes that follow call for alternating liquid and dry ingredients when you add them to the batter. For pound cakes or any butter cake, always begin and end with the flour. Here's why: The buttery base of these batters does not absorb a lot of liquid easily. If the butter is forced to absorb too much liquid (usually eggs), the butter will reach its saturation point, and the result will be a separated batter with unabsorbed liquid in it. If this happens, the cake will be heavy. So it's far better to start by adding just some of the liquid to the butter and sugar mixture, then add the rest alternating it with the flour. The flour brings the batter together and prevents separation. For most recipes, these ingredients are incorporated in five additions: flour, liquid, flour, liquid, flour.

CLASSIC POUND CAKE

THIS ALMOST DOESN'T NEED A RECIPE because it is based on the classic proportions of a pound of each of the four main ingreødients: butter, sugar, eggs, and flour. I have played with the quantities a little bit so that the recipe doesn't make such a large cake. I like to flavor this type of pound cake with just a little vanilla—it keeps the flavor delicate and doesn't mask the lovely flavor of the butter. If you want more vividly flavored pound cake, try any of the milk-based ones or the high-ratio pound cakes later in the chapter.

1 Set a rack in the middle of the oven and preheat to 325 degrees.

2 Place the butter and sugar in the bowl of a heavy-duty mixer and beat on medium speed with the paddle attachment until very light, about 5 minutes. Beat in the vanilla. One at a time, beat in 3 of the eggs, beating until smooth after each addition.

3 Reduce the mixer speed to low and beat in one-third of the flour, then another egg, beating until smooth after each addition. Stop the mixer occasionally to scrape the bottom and sides of the bowl with a rubber spatula. Beat in another third of the flour, then, after the flour has been absorbed, beat in the final egg. Scrape again and beat in the last of the flour.

4 Use the rubber spatula to give a final mix to the batter, then scrape it into the prepared pan and smooth the top.

5 Bake for about 1¼ to 1½ hours, or until the cake is well risen, cracked on top, and well-colored and a toothpick inserted into the center emerges dry.

½ pound (2 sticks) unsalted butter, softened

1 cup sugar

2 teaspoons vanilla extract

5 large eggs, at room temperature

2 cups cake flour (spoon flour into dry-measure cup and level off), sifted after measuring

One 9 × 5 × 3-inch loaf pan, buttered and bottom lined with parchment or foil

6 Cool the cake in the pan for a few minutes, then unmold it onto a rack and turn right side up to finish cooling.

STORAGE: Wrap the cake in plastic wrap and then foil so it doesn't dry out, and serve within a few days. For longer storage, wrap and freeze; defrost, loosely covered, at room temperature.

MAKES ONE 9 × 5-INCH LOAF CAKE, ABOUT 12 SERVINGS

VARIATIONS

VANILLA BEAN POUND CAKE: Omit the vanilla extract. Split a vanilla bean lengthwise and scrape out the seeds with the point of a paring knife. Add the vanilla seeds to the butter and sugar mixture. The vanilla flavor will be stronger than a cake made with extract, and the visible vanilla seeds make a strong "vanilla statement."

MACE POUND CAKE: Add ¼ teaspoon ground mace to the flour.

HINT OF LEMON POUND CAKE: Add the finely grated zest of a large lemon to Classic Pound Cake or Vanilla Bean Pound Cake.

MRS. LINCOLN'S POUND CAKE

~⁊ ᥱ~

THIS RECIPE WAS GIVEN TO ME by my friend and associate Andrea Tutunjian. It comes from a typewritten collection of recipes amassed by her maternal grandmother, Antoinette Bianco. The famous mid-century food writer Clementine Paddleford wrote about receiving a recipe for this cake from Mrs. Weibert Scott of Bridgeton, New Jersey, who said it came from President Lincoln's family via her cousins the Yorks and the Huckebys.

Regardless of its real or imaginary presidential pedigree, this is an excellent old-fashioned pound cake.

1 Set a rack in the middle of the oven and preheat to 325 degrees.

2 Stir together the flour and mace in a bowl, mixing well.

3 Place the butter and sugar in the bowl of a heavy-duty mixer fitted with the paddle attachment and beat on medium speed until the mixture is very light, about 5 minutes. Beat in the vanilla. One at a time, beat in 3 of the eggs, beating until smooth after each addition.

4 Reduce the mixer speed to low and beat in one-third of the flour, then another egg, beating until smooth after each addition and stopping the mixer occasionally to scrape the bottom and sides of the bowl with a rubber spatula. Beat in another third of the flour, then, after the flour has been absorbed, the remaining egg. Scrape again and beat in the last of the flour.

2 cups bleached all-purpose flour (spoon flour into dry-measure cup and level off)

½ teaspoon ground mace

½ pound (2 sticks) unsalted butter, softened

1⅔ cups sugar

1 teaspoon vanilla extract

5 large eggs, at room temperature

Two 8½ × 4½ × 2¾-inch loaf pans, buttered and bottoms lined with parchment

5 Use the rubber spatula to give a final mix to the batter, then scrape it into the prepared pan and smooth the top.

6 Bake for about 1 hour, or until the cake is well risen, cracked on top, and well colored and a toothpick inserted into the center emerges dry.

7 Cool the cake in the pan for a few minutes, then unmold it onto a rack and turn right side up to finish cooling.

STORAGE: Wrap the cake in plastic wrap and then foil to ensure that it doesn't dry out, and serve within a few days. Or wrap and freeze for longer storage; defrost loosely covered at room temperature.

MAKES TWO 8½ × 4½-INCH LOAF CAKES, ABOUT 12 TO 16 SERVINGS

223

CAKES

CREAM CHEESE POUND CAKE

C REAM CHEESE GIVES this pound cake its richness and density. Many thanks to my dear friend Sheri Portwood of Dallas for the recipe.

1 Set a rack in the lower third of the oven and preheat to 325 degrees.

2 Stir the flour and baking powder together in a bowl, mixing well.

3 Place the butter, cream cheese, and sugar in the bowl of a heavy-duty mixer and beat on medium speed with the paddle attachment until very light, about 5 minutes. Beat in the vanilla. One at a time, beat in 4 of the eggs, beating until smooth after each addition.

4 Reduce the mixer speed to low and beat in one-third of the flour, then another egg, beating until smooth after each addition. Stop the mixer occasionally to scrape the bottom and sides of the bowl with a rubber spatula. Beat in another third of the flour, then, after the flour has been absorbed, the last egg. Scrape again and beat in the last of the flour.

5 Use the rubber spatula to give a final mix to the batter, then scrape it into the prepared pan and smooth the top.

6 Bake for about 65 to 75 minutes, or until cake is well risen, cracked on top, and well-colored and a toothpick inserted into the center emerges dry.

CAKE BATTER

2 cups bleached all-purpose flour (spoon flour into dry-measure cup and level off)

1 teaspoon baking powder

½ pound (2 sticks) unsalted butter, softened

One 8-ounce package cream cheese (I use Philadelphia), softened

2 cups sugar

2 teaspoons vanilla extract

6 large eggs, at room temperature

RUM GLAZE

3 cups confectioners' sugar

2 tablespoons white rum

2 tablespoons water

One 12-cup tube or Bundt pan, buttered and floured

7 Cool the cake in the pan for a few minutes, then unmold it onto a rack and turn right side up to finish cooling.

8 To make the glaze, combine the sugar, rum, and water in a medium saucepan and stir until smooth, then heat over very low heat just until lukewarm. Drizzle over the cake with a spoon, or use a parchment paper cone, or pour the glaze over to cover the entire cake.

STORAGE: Wrap cake in plastic wrap and then foil to ensure it doesn't dry out, and serve within a few days. For longer storage, wrap and freeze; defrost, loosely covered, at room temperature. If you intend to freeze or otherwise keep the cake for more than a day, don't glaze it until the day you intend to serve it.

MAKES ONE 10-INCH TUBE OR BUNDT CAKE, ABOUT 10 SERVINGS

225

CAKES

NEWARK CAKE

୨ ୦ ୧

I WAS BORN IN NEWARK, NEW JERSEY, and I am completely crazy for anything from, by, or about Newark. So when I found this recipe in Marian Harland's *Breakfast, Luncheon, and Tea* (Scribner, Armstrong, and Company, 1875) I had to try it. Harland was one of the nineteenth-century's most prolific cookbook authors and novelists. Her husband, William Terhune, was a Dutch Reform clergyman and pastor of various churches in the New Jersey–Pennsylvania area, including one in Newark; hence the name of the cake.

1 Position a rack in the lower third of the oven and preheat to 325 degrees.

2 Place the flour, sugar, baking powder, and salt in the bowl of a heavy-duty mixer fitted with the paddle attachment. Add the butter and beat on the lowest speed for about 2 minutes, or until the ingredients are well combined.

3 Meanwhile, whisk together the remaining batter ingredients in a mixing bowl.

4 Increase the mixer speed to medium and add one-third of the liquid ingredients. Beat for 2 minutes, then stop the mixer and scrape down the bowl and beater. Add another third of the liquid, beat for 2 minutes, and scrape. Finally, add the remaining liquid and beat and scrape as before.

5 Use a large rubber spatula to give the batter a final vigorous stir, then scrape it into the prepared pan and smooth the top.

4 cups all-purpose flour (spoon flour into dry-measure cup and level off)

2 cups sugar

1 tablespoon baking powder

1 teaspoon salt

½ pound (2 sticks) unsalted butter, softened

6 large eggs

1 cup milk

1 teaspoon freshly grated nutmeg

1 teaspoon almond extract

Confectioners' sugar for finishing

One 12-cup tube or Bundt pan, buttered and floured

6 Bake for about 1¼ to 1½ hours, or until a toothpick inserted into the cake halfway between the side of the pan and the central tube emerges clean.

7 Cool the cake in the pan on a rack for 10 minutes, then invert onto the rack to finish cooling.

8 Just before serving, dust the cake generously with confectioners' sugar.

STORAGE: Wrap the cake in plastic wrap and then foil to ensure it doesn't dry out, and serve within a few days. For longer storage, wrap and freeze. Defrost loosely covered at room temperature.

MAKES ONE 10-INCH TUBE OR BUNDT CAKE, ABOUT 16 SERVINGS

MORRIS CAKE

~ ∞ ~

THIS IS ANOTHER NINETEENTH-CENTURY CAKE from Marian Harland's *Breakfast, Luncheon, and Tea* (see page 226). I updated the recipe so as to mix the batter in the high-ratio manner (see page 229), but aside from that, it is the same wonderful cake it was about 125 years ago.

1   Position a rack in the lower third of the oven and preheat to 325 degrees.

2   Place the flour, sugar, baking soda, and nutmeg in the bowl of a heavy-duty mixer fitted with the paddle attachment. Add the butter and beat on the lowest speed for about 2 minutes, or until the ingredients are well combined.

3   Meanwhile, whisk all the remaining batter ingredients in a mixing bowl until well combined.

4   Increase the mixer speed to medium and add one-third of the liquid ingredients. Mix for 2 minutes, then stop the mixer and scrape down the bowl and beater. Add another third of the liquid, beat for 2 minutes, and scrape again. Finally, add the remaining liquid and beat and scrape as before.

5   Use a large rubber spatula to give the batter a final vigorous stir, then scrape the batter into the prepared pan and smooth the top.

6   Bake for about 1¼ to 1½ hours, or until a toothpick inserted into the cake halfway between the side of the pan and the central tube emerges clean.

4 cups all-purpose flour (spoon flour into dry-measure cup and level off)

2 cups sugar

1 teaspoon baking soda

½ teaspoon freshly grated nutmeg

½ pound (2 sticks) unsalted butter, softened

5 large eggs

One 8-ounce container sour cream

1 teaspoon vanilla extract

Confectioners' sugar for finishing

One 12-cup tube or Bundt pan, buttered and floured

7   Cool the cake in the pan on a rack for 10 minutes, then invert onto the rack to finish cooling.

8   Just before serving, dust the cake generously with confectioners' sugar.

STORAGE: Wrap the cake in plastic wrap and then foil to ensure it doesn't dry out, and serve within a few days. For longer storage, wrap and freeze; defrost loosely covered at room temperature.

MAKES ONE 10-INCH TUBE OR BUNDT CAKE, ABOUT 16 SERVINGS

HIGH-RATIO CAKES

A high-ratio cake is one in which the weight of the sugar equals or exceeds the weight of the flour. (This applies to many pound and butter cakes, but not all.) The high proportion of sugar can make the batter separate, resulting in a coarse texture in the baked cake. The "high ratio" mixing method, developed in the 1940s by Procter and Gamble, prevents the batter from separating and yields a particularly fine textured cake.

Basically, you first mix all the dry ingredients with the softened butter. Then the liquids, including the eggs, are combined and added in three parts. The resulting baked cake has a great texture and moist crumb. To convert a recipe to the high-ratio method of mixing, first check to see if the sugar equals or exceeds the flour: calculate 8 ounces for a cup of sugar and 4 ounces for a cup of all-purpose flour. If and only if the recipe passes this test, you can combine all the dry ingredients in the mixer bowl, add the softened butter, and beat for 2 minutes on low speed. Then add the liquids, mixed together, one-third at a time, beating for 2 minutes on medium speed between each addition.

HIGH-RATIO POUND CAKE

THIS RECIPE WAS LITERALLY A FIND. When I sat down to write this chapter, it was in the folder of pound cake recipes I had been collecting. It was handwritten on a recipe card stapled to a typed version of the recipe.

1 Set a rack in the lower third of the oven and preheat to 350 degrees.

2 Place the flour, sugar, baking powder, and salt in the bowl of a heavy-duty mixer fitted with the paddle attachment, add the butter, and beat on the lowest speed for about 2 minutes, or until the ingredients are well combined.

3 Meanwhile, whisk all the remaining ingredients together in a mixing bowl until well combined.

4 Increase the mixer speed to medium, add one-third of the liquid ingredients, and mix for 2 minutes. Stop the mixer and scrape down the bowl and beater. Add another third of the liquid, beat for 2 minutes, and scrape again. Finally, add the remaining liquid and beat and scrape as before.

5 Use a large rubber spatula to give the batter a final vigorous stir, then scrape it into the prepared pan and smooth the top.

2½ cups bleached all-purpose flour (spoon flour into dry-measure cup and level off)

1¾ cups sugar

2 teaspoons baking powder

1 teaspoon salt

½ pound (2 sticks) unsalted butter, softened

¾ cup milk

3 large eggs, at room temperature

1 large egg yolk

2 teaspoons vanilla extract

One 12-cup tube or Bundt pan, buttered and floured

6 Bake for about 1 hour and 15 minutes, or until a toothpick inserted into the cake halfway between the side of the pan and the central tube emerges clean.

7 Cool the cake in the pan on a rack for 10 minutes, then invert onto the rack to finish cooling.

STORAGE: Wrap the cake in plastic wrap and then foil to ensure it doesn't dry out, and serve within a few days. For longer storage, wrap and freeze; defrost loosely covered at room temperature.

MAKES ONE 10-INCH TUBE OR BUNDT CAKE, ABOUT 16 SERVINGS

VARIATIONS

LEMON POUND CAKE: Substitute lemon extract for the vanilla.

PECAN, WALNUT, OR HAZELNUT POUND CAKE: Fold 1 cup coarsely chopped pecans, walnuts, or hazelnuts, tossed with 1 tablespoon flour, into the batter when you are giving it the last mix with the spatula.

HIGH-RATIO LEMON-BUTTERMILK POUND CAKE

～つ ᦂ ᧉ～

AFTER YOU BAKE THIS CAKE, you soak it with a lemon and vanilla syrup that adds just the right note of tartness and moisture. See the variations at the end of the recipe for a sprightly orange or lemon-lime version. Many thanks to my friend Gary Peese of Austin, Texas, for this recipe.

1   Position a rack in the lower third of the oven and preheat to 325 degrees.

2   Place the flour, sugar, baking powder, and salt in the bowl of a heavy-duty mixer fitted with the paddle attachment, add the butter, and beat on the lowest speed for about 2 minutes, or until the ingredients are well combined.

3   Meanwhile, whisk all the remaining batter ingredients together in a mixing bowl until well combined.

4   Increase the mixer speed to medium and add one-third of the liquid, and mix for 2 minutes. Stop the mixer and scrape down the bowl and beater. Add another third of the liquid, beat for 2 minutes, and scrape again. Finally, add the remaining liquid and beat and scrape as before.

5   Use a large rubber spatula to give the batter a final vigorous stir, then scrape it into the prepared pan and smooth the top.

CAKE BATTER

2½ cups bleached all-purpose flour (spoon flour into dry-measure cup and level off)

2 cups sugar

2 teaspoons baking powder

½ teaspoon salt

½ pound (2 sticks) unsalted butter, softened

4 large eggs, at room temperature

3 large egg yolks

½ cup buttermilk

1 tablespoon grated lemon zest

1 tablespoon strained fresh lemon juice

1 teaspoon vanilla extract

LEMON SYRUP

½ cup water

½ cup sugar

⅓ cup fresh lemon juice, strained

2 teaspoons vanilla extract

One 12-cup Bundt pan, buttered and floured

6   Bake for about 1 hour, or until a toothpick inserted into the cake halfway between the side of the pan and the central tube emerges clean.

7   Cool the cake in the pan on a rack for 10 minutes, then invert onto the rack to finish cooling.

8   To make the syrup, bring the water and sugar to a boil in a small saucepan. Remove from the heat and stir in the lemon juice and vanilla. Brush the hot syrup evenly all over the cake. Gradually brush until it is all absorbed.

STORAGE: Wrap the cake in plastic wrap and then foil to ensure it doesn't dry out, and serve within a few days. For longer storage, wrap and freeze; defrost loosely covered at room temperature.

MAKES ONE 10-INCH BUNDT CAKE, ABOUT 16 SERVINGS

VARIATIONS

LEMON SOUR CREAM OR YOGURT POUND CAKE: Substitute sour cream or plain yogurt for the buttermilk.

ORANGE BUTTERMILK POUND CAKE: Substitute orange zest and juice for the lemon and orange extract for the vanilla extract in the batter. Make the syrup with $1/3$ cup strained fresh orange juice and 2 tablespoons lemon juice. This cake can also be made with sour cream or yogurt as above.

LEMON-LIME BUTTERMILK POUND CAKE: Substitute lime juice for the lemon juice in the batter. Use half lemon and half lime juice for the syrup. This cake can be made with sour cream or yogurt as above.

233

HIGH-RATIO FRESH GINGER POUND CAKE WITH LEMON GLAZE

~୭ ୨ ୦~

IF YOU LOVE THE PUNGENT FLAVOR of fresh ginger, this is the cake to go with your cup of tea. The bit of lemon zest in the batter complements the ginger flavor. I like the cake very gingery, but if you just want a hint of ginger, you can use less. This moist, spicy cake is perfect for a brunch or picnic.

1 Set a rack in the lower third of the oven and preheat to 325 degrees.

2 Place the flour, sugar, baking powder, and salt in the bowl of a heavy-duty mixer fitted with the paddle attachment and add the butter. Beat on the lowest speed for about 2 minutes, or until the ingredients are well combined.

3 Meanwhile, combine all the remaining batter ingredients in a mixing bowl.

4 Increase the mixer speed to medium and add one-third of the liquid ingredients. Mix for 2 minutes, then stop the mixer and scrape down the bowl and beater. Add another third of the liquid, beat for 2 minutes, and scrape again. Finally, add the remaining liquid and beat and scrape as before.

5 Use a large rubber spatula to give the batter a final vigorous stir, then scrape it into the prepared pan and smooth the top.

CAKE BATTER

2½ cups bleached all-purpose flour (spoon flour into dry-measure cup and level off)

2 cups sugar

2 teaspoons baking powder

½ teaspoon salt

½ pound (2 sticks) unsalted butter, softened

4 large eggs

3 large egg yolks

½ cup milk

⅓ cup grated fresh ginger (see Note)

1 tablespoon finely grated lemon zest

1 teaspoon vanilla extract

LEMON GLAZE

3 cups confectioners' sugar

2 tablespoons strained fresh lemon juice

2 tablespoons white rum or water

One 12-cup Bundt or tube pan, buttered and floured

6 Bake for about 1 hour, or until a toothpick inserted into the cake halfway between the side of the pan and the central tube emerges clean.

7 Cool the cake in the pan on a rack for 10 minutes, then invert onto the rack to finish cooling.

8 To make the glaze, stir the sugar, lemon juice, and rum together in a medium saucepan until smooth, adding a teaspoon or two of water, if necessary, to make a smooth glaze. Then heat over very low heat just until lukewarm. Drizzle over the cake with a spoon or use a parchment paper cone.

STORAGE: Wrap the cake in plastic wrap and then foil to ensure it doesn't dry out, and serve within a few days. For longer storage, wrap and freeze; defrost loosely covered at room temperature. If you intend to freeze or otherwise keep the cake for more than a day before serving, don't glaze it until the day you will serve it.

MAKES ONE 10-INCH BUNDT CAKE, ABOUT 16 SERVINGS

NOTE: To get ⅓ cup of grated ginger, you'll need to start with about 3 ounces fresh ginger. Peel the ginger and grate it on a grater with ¼-inch oval holes—if you try to grate it on a finer grater, you'll only get juice. You can also chop the ginger very fine with an extremely sharp stainless steel knife, or coarsely chop it and then whir it in the food processor to mince it.

BOURBON PECAN POUND CAKE

⁓ ୨ ୧ ⁓

BOURBON AND PECANS, both products of the South, are a natural combination. Because of the bourbon, the cake keeps well and stays moist.

1 Position a rack in the lower third of the oven and preheat to 325 degrees.

2 Place the flour, sugar, baking powder, and salt in the bowl of a heavy-duty mixer fitted with the paddle attachment and add the butter. Beat on the lowest speed for about 2 minutes, or until the ingredients are well combined.

3 Meanwhile, combine the remaining batter ingredients except the pecans in a mixing bowl, mixing well.

4 Increase the mixer speed to medium and add one-third of the liquid ingredients. Mix for 2 minutes, then stop the mixer and scrape down the bowl and beater. Add another third of the liquid, beat for 2 minutes, and scrape again. Finally, add the remaining liquid and beat and scrape as before.

5 Use a large rubber spatula to give the batter a final vigorous stir. Fold in the floured pecans, then scrape the batter into the prepared pan and smooth the top.

2½ cups bleached all-purpose flour (spoon flour into dry-measure cup and level off) plus 1 tablespoon

1 cup packed light brown sugar

1 cup granulated sugar

2 teaspoons baking powder

½ teaspoon salt

½ pound (2 sticks) unsalted butter, softened

4 large eggs

3 large egg yolks

½ cup best Kentucky bourbon

2 teaspoons vanilla extract

1½ cups finely chopped (not ground) pecans, tossed with 1 tablespoon flour

Confectioners' sugar for finishing

One 12-cup tube or Bundt pan, buttered and floured

CAKES

6 Bake for about 65 to 75 minutes, or until a toothpick inserted into the cake halfway between the side of the pan and the central tube emerges clean.

7 Cool the cake in the pan on a rack for 10 minutes, then invert onto the rack to finish cooling.

8 Just before serving, dust the cake generously with confectioners' sugar.

STORAGE: Wrap the cake in plastic wrap and then foil to ensure it doesn't dry out, and serve within a few days. For longer storage, wrap and freeze; defrost loosely covered at room temperature.

MAKES ONE 10-INCH TUBE OR BUNDT CAKE, ABOUT 16 SERVINGS

VARIATIONS

ALMOND RUM POUND CAKE: Substitute chopped blanched whole almonds for the pecans and white rum for the bourbon. Add 1 teaspoon almond extract along with the vanilla extract.

HAZELNUT DARK RUM POUND CAKE: Substitute coarsely ground unblanched hazelnuts for the pecans and dark rum for the bourbon.

CAKES MADE WITH FRESH
OR DRIED FRUIT

SIMPLE CAKES TAKE BEAUTIFULLY TO FRESH FRUIT. I could possibly live on blueberry crumb cake, pausing only occasionally to vary it with a plum or apricot version. Apple cakes almost received their own chapter—I had literally dozens of them in my folder for this chapter. I combined the best recipes into new versions.

Also included in this chapter are those poor fruitcakes that everyone loves to hate. I'm so tired of the lame attempts at insipid humor at the expense of the fruitcake. People who don't like fruitcake dislike it for one of the following reasons:

1   The fruitcake was probably large and baked at too high a temperature, making it very dark on the outside, with a bitter flavor.

2   The candied fruit used was of dubious quality. Good candied fruit is expensive, there's no way around it. To make it properly, each piece of citrus rind must be treated many times. First it has to be blanched: the rinds repeatedly brought to a boil and drained to remove bitterness. Then the fruit or rind is cooked in small batches in sugar syrup repeatedly over the course of several weeks. The candied fruit in the little plastic containers in the supermarket is not made this way.

A last word about candied fruit—if you do buy the mixed kind sold in the supermarket, read the label: if the first ingredient is grapefruit rind, don't buy it—that's a guarantee it will be very bitter. If you buy candied fruit sold in bulk, taste a piece before purchasing. You'll be able to tell if it's the right kind very easily.

This chapter also contains recipes for cakes made with vegetables. Don't get scared—there are none that contain beets, sauerkraut, or rutabagas, though I like all of those things perfectly well as vegetables. But I've included a few really good carrot and pumpkin recipes. Their purpose in a cake batter is to contribute moisture, and in the case of carrots, there is an extra bonus of sweetness.

FRESH BANANA LOAF CAKE

⚬⚬⚬

THIS WELL-PERFUMED BANANA CAKE comes from my dear friend and second mother, Ann Amedolara Nurse. Besides being a terrific cook, Ann loves to bake. This banana loaf is one of her specialties. By the way, the secret to getting the most vivid banana flavor is to mash the bananas with a fork, not to puree them in the food processor.

1   Position a rack in the middle of the oven and preheat to 350 degrees.

2   Stir together the 3½ cups flour, the baking powder, baking soda, and cinnamon in a large bowl, mixing well. In a medium bowl, toss the nuts and raisins with the remaining 1 tablespoon flour.

3   Place the brown sugar in a large mixing bowl and add the eggs one at a time, stirring with a rubber spatula. (Adding the eggs gradually to the sugar makes them incorporate more smoothly than the standard way of adding the sugar to the eggs, preventing lumps of brown sugar from forming.) Switch to a whisk and whisk the mixture for a few seconds to lighten it. Whisk in the oil in a stream, then whisk in the sour cream and vanilla.

4   Use a rubber spatula to fold half the flour mixture into the egg mixture. Stir in the mashed bananas. Fold in the remaining flour mixture, then fold in the nuts and raisins. Scrape the batter into the prepared pans and smooth the tops.

3½ cups all-purpose flour (spoon flour into dry-measure cup and level off) plus 1 tablespoon

2 teaspoons baking powder

2 teaspoons baking soda

1 teaspoon ground cinnamon

2 cups (about 8 ounces) walnuts or pecans, coarsely chopped

1 cup dark raisins

2 cups firmly packed light brown sugar

4 large eggs

1¼ cups vegetable oil, such as corn or canola

One 8-ounce container sour cream

1 tablespoon vanilla extract

3 cups mashed very ripe bananas (about 8 large)

Two 9 × 5 × 3-inch loaf pans, buttered and bottoms lined with buttered parchment or wax paper

5 Bake for about 70 to 80 minutes, or until the cakes are well risen and a toothpick inserted into the center emerges clean.

6 Cool the cakes in the pans for 5 minutes, then unmold onto a rack and turn right side up to cool. Remove the paper after cooling.

SERVING: This is a good plain cake, but it can also be served with lightly sweetened vanilla- or rum-flavored whipped cream.

STORAGE: Wrap the cooled cake in plastic and keep at room temperature for up to several days, or double-wrap and freeze for longer storage.

MAKES TWO 9 × 5-INCH LOAF CAKES, ABOUT 16 SERVINGS

BLUEBERRY CRUMB CAKE

I MAKE THIS, ONE OF MY VERY FAVORITES, at least half a dozen times every summer. See the variations at the end of the recipe for crumb cakes made with other fruit.

CAKE BATTER

1½ cups all-purpose flour (spoon flour into dry-measure cup and level off)

1 teaspoon baking powder

¼ teaspoon salt

8 tablespoons (1 stick) unsalted butter, softened

¾ cup sugar

2 large eggs

2 large egg yolks

1 teaspoon vanilla extract

3 cups (1½ pint baskets) blueberries, rinsed, picked over, and dried

CRUMB TOPPING

1 cup all-purpose flour

⅓ cup firmly packed light or dark brown sugar

½ teaspoon ground cinnamon

¼ teaspoon freshly grated nutmeg

6 tablespoons (¾ stick) unsalted butter, melted

One 9 × 13 × 2-inch baking pan, lined with buttered foil

1 Position a rack in the middle of the oven and preheat to 350 degrees.

2 Stir together the flour, baking powder, and salt in a bowl, mixing well.

3 In the bowl of a heavy-duty mixer, beat the butter and sugar with the paddle attachment on medium speed for about 5 minutes, or until soft and light. One at a time, beat the eggs, beating until smooth after each addition. Beat in the vanilla.

4 Decrease the mixer speed to low. Add half the flour mixture, then scrape down the bowl and beater with a rubber spatula. Add the

yolks and mix well. Finally, add the remaining flour mixture.

5 Use a large rubber spatula to give a final stir to the batter, then scrape it into the prepared pan and smooth the top. Scatter the blueberries evenly over the batter (don't press them in).

6 To make the crumb topping, combine the flour, sugar, cinnamon, and nutmeg in a bowl. Stir in the melted butter and rub to coarse crumbs with your fingers. Scatter the crumbs as evenly as possible over the berries.

7 Bake for about 40 minutes, until the cake is firm and crumbs are well colored.

8 Cool the cake in the pan on a rack, then cut cake into 2-inch squares.

SERVING: This is casual food—it can be served on a plate or eaten out of hand.

STORAGE: Keep at room temperature, covered with plastic wrap.

MAKES ONE 9 × 13-INCH CAKE, ABOUT 24 SERVINGS

VARIATIONS

CHERRY CRUMB CAKE: Substitute 3 cups (1½ pounds) pitted sour cherries for the blueberries.

APRICOT CRUMB CAKE: Substitute about 16 medium apricots, rinsed, pitted, and quartered, for the blueberries. Arrange the quarters in rows, cut side up, on the batter.

PEACH CRUMB CAKE: Substitute 3 cups peeled, pitted, and diced peaches for the blueberries.

243

FRESH APPLE CAKE FROM MRS. APPENZELLER (5D)

～⤳ ⤴～

ANA RAMBALDI, A GREAT BAKER of Ukranian-Argentine descent, is also the superintendent of a Greenwich Village apartment building. The recipe came from a tenant with whom Ana traded recipes.

1   Position a rack in the middle of the oven and preheat to 350 degrees.

2   Stir together the flour, baking soda, and spices in a bowl, mixing well.

3   In a large bowl, whisk the eggs just to break them up. Whisk in the sugar in a stream. Continue to whisk for a minute or so to lighten the mixture, then whisk in the oil in a slow stream and vanilla.

4   Use a rubber spatula to fold in the flour mixture. Fold in the apples, raisins, and nuts. Scrape the batter into the prepared pan and smooth the top.

5   Bake for about an hour, or until the cake is well risen and well colored and a toothpick inserted into the center emerges clean.

6   Cool the cake in the pan on a rack for 5 minutes, then turn it out onto another rack, turn it right side up again onto a rack to cool completely.

SERVING: Serve this cake plain or with vanilla or cinnamon ice cream.

2 cups all-purpose flour (spoon flour into dry-measure cup and level off)

1 teaspoon baking soda

1 teaspoon freshly grated nutmeg

½ teaspoon ground cinnamon

3 large eggs

1 cup sugar

1 cup vegetable oil, such as corn or canola

2 teaspoons vanilla extract

3 cups peeled, cored, and chopped Golden Delicious apples (2 to 3 large apples)

½ cup dark raisins, coarsely chopped

½ cup (about 2 ounces) walnuts, coarsely chopped

One 12-cup tube pan, buttered and floured

STORAGE: Wrap the cooled cake in plastic and keep at room temperature for up to several days, or double-wrap and freeze for longer storage.

MAKES ONE 10-INCH CAKE, ABOUT 12 SERVINGS

WALNUT APPLESAUCE CAKE WITH HONEY–CREAM CHEESE FROSTING

~⤻ ⤸~

THIS CAKE IS BASED ON A RECIPE I FOUND inside a cookbook I bought at a used book store. It was on a fine fold-over note, written in a cultivated hand and dated July 21, 1952; the note is addressed to Louise and is signed Mary. This is a perfect cake for the early fall, when the first McIntosh apples come into season.

CAKE BATTER

3 cups all-purpose flour (spoon flour into dry-measure cup and level off)

1½ teaspoons baking soda

½ teaspoon salt

1 teaspoon ground cinnamon

½ teaspoon ground cloves

½ teaspoon freshly grated nutmeg

1½ cups dark raisins or currants

1½ cups (about 6 ounces) walnut pieces

½ pound (2 sticks) unsalted butter, softened

1 cup granulated sugar

1 cup firmly packed dark brown sugar

4 large eggs

1½ cups unsweetened applesauce (see Note)

CREAM CHEESE FROSTING

8 tablespoons (1 stick) unsalted butter, softened

One 8-ounce package cream cheese, softened

⅓ cup mild honey

1 teaspoon vanilla extract

½ cup (about 2 ounces) chopped toasted walnuts

One 9 × 13 × 2-inch baking pan, buttered and lined with buttered parchment or foil

1   Position a rack in the middle of the oven and preheat to 350 degrees.

2   Stir together the flour, soda, salt, and spices in a bowl, mixing well. In a small bowl, combine the raisins and walnuts. Add 2 tablespoons of the flour mixture, tossing to coat; set aside.

3   In the bowl of a heavy-duty mixer fitted with the paddle attachment, beat together the butter and sugars on medium speed until soft and light. Beat in the eggs one at a time, beating until smooth after each addition.

4   Beat in one-third of the flour mixture, then beat in half the applesauce. Scrape down the bowl and beater. Beat in another third of the flour mixture, then the remaining applesauce, and scrape again. Beat in the remaining flour mixture. Fold in the raisins and walnuts.

5   Scrape the batter into the prepared pan and smooth the top.

6   Bake for about 45 minutes, or until a toothpick inserted in the center of the cake emerges clean. Cool in the pan on a rack.

7   To make the frosting, combine the butter, cream cheese, honey, and vanilla in the bowl of a heavy-duty mixer fitted with the paddle and beat on medium speed until soft and light, about 3 minutes.

8   Invert the cake onto a cardboard rectangle or a platter and remove the paper. Run knife around the sides to release the cake. Spread the frosting on the top of the cake, then sprinkle with the chopped walnuts.

STORAGE: Store under a cake dome. Unfrosted, this cake keeps well for a few days at room temperature if well wrapped in plastic, or double-wrap and freeze for longer storage; defrost before frosting.

MAKES ONE 9 × 13-INCH CAKE, ABOUT 24 SERVINGS

NOTE: To make applesauce, peel, core, and slice 4 medium McIntosh apples. Combine them with ¼ cup water in a nonreactive pan and cook until the apples are very soft and falling apart. Puree in a food processor or blender if desired (for a very smooth puree), then measure out 1½ cups for the recipe.

PHYLLIS VACARELLI'S PUMPKIN PECAN LOAF CAKE

~⊙ ⊙~

THIS IS A SPECIALTY of Los Angeles cooking school owner and teacher Phyllis Vacarelli. It is an easy cake to prepare—all the ingredients are just stirred together.

1 Position a rack in the middle of the oven and preheat to 350 degrees.

2 Combine 3 cups of the flour and all the remaining ingredients except the pecans and raisins in the bowl of a heavy-duty mixer fitted with the paddle attachment. Beat for 2 minutes on low speed.

3 Toss the pecans and raisins with the remaining 2 tablespoons flour and fold them into the batter. Scrape the batter into the prepared pans and smooth the tops.

4 Bake for about 1 hour, or until a toothpick inserted in the center emerges clean.

5 Cool for 10 minutes, then invert onto a rack and turn right side up to cool completely.

SERVING: This is a perfect breakfast or brunch cake.

STORAGE: Wrap and keep at room temperature, or freeze for longer storage.

MAKES TWO 9 × 5-INCH LOAF CAKES, ABOUT 16 TO 18 SERVINGS

3 cups all-purpose flour (spoon flour into dry-measure cup and level off) plus 2 tablespoons

1 cup firmly packed dark brown sugar

1 cup granulated sugar

1 teaspoon freshly grated nutmeg

1 teaspoon ground cinnamon

1 teaspoon baking soda

1 teaspoon baking powder

½ teaspoon salt

One 16-ounce can unsweetened pumpkin

⅓ cup water

1 cup vegetable oil, such as corn or canola

2 teaspoons vanilla extract

6 large eggs

2 cups (about 8 ounces) pecans, coarsely chopped

½ cup (about 3 ounces) dark or golden raisins

Two 9 × 5 × 3-inch loaf pans, buttered and floured

MARTHA TURNER'S CARROT CAKE

~⟋ 𝒢 ⟍~

THE QUINTESSENTIAL CARROT CAKE. This is one of the few cakes in which I ever use canned fruit. The pineapple makes it moist and tart. Thanks to Martha Turner of Greensboro, North Carolina, for the recipe.

CAKE BATTER

2 cups all-purpose flour (spoon flour into
    dry-measure cup and level off)

2 teaspoons baking powder

1½ teaspoons baking soda

2 teaspoons ground cinnamon

4 large eggs

2 cups sugar

1½ cups vegetable oil, such as corn
    or canola

2 cups peeled and finely grated carrots
    (about 4 large carrots)

One 8-ounce can crushed pineapple in juice

¾ cup (about 3 ounces) pecans,
    coarsely chopped

CREAM CHEESE ICING

12 ounces cream cheese, softened

12 tablespoons (1½ sticks) unsalted butter,
    softened

1 tablespoon vanilla extract

1 cup (about 4 ounces) pecans, coarsely
    chopped and lightly toasted

6 cups confectioners' sugar, sifted after
    measuring

Three 2-inch deep 9-inch round cake pans, buttered and bottoms lined with buttered parchment or wax paper

1 Set the racks in the upper and lower thirds of the oven and preheat to 325 degrees.

2 Stir together the flour, baking powder, baking soda, and cinnamon in a bowl, mixing well.

3 Whisk the eggs in a large mixing bowl. Whisk in the sugar and continue whisking briefly until light, about 1 minute. Whisk in the oil in a slow stream.

4 Stir in the carrots, the pineapple with its juice, and the pecans, then fold in the dry ingredients. Scrape the batter into the prepared pans and smooth the tops.

5 Bake for about 45 minutes, switching the position of the pans top and bottom and back to front, once during baking, until the cake layers are firm and golden and a toothpick inserted in the center emerges clean.

6 Cool the cake in the pans for 10 minutes, then invert onto racks to finish cooling. Remove the paper before icing.

7 To make the icing, in the bowl of a heavy-duty mixer fitted with the paddle, beat the cream cheese, butter, and vanilla on medium speed until very soft and light, about 5 minutes. Decrease the mixer speed to low and gradually beat in the confectioners' sugar. Once all the sugar is incorporated, increase the speed to medium and beat for 5 minutes longer.

8 To assemble the cake, place one layer on a platter or cardboard round and spread with one-third of the icing. Top with another layer and spread with another third of the icing.

Place the last layer on top, bottom side up, and, using a large offset spatula, frost the top and sides of the cake with the remaining icing. Sprinkle the toasted pecan pieces on top of the cake, and press into sides.

STORAGE: Keep under a cake dome at room temperature.

MAKES ONE 9-INCH THREE-LAYER CAKE, ABOUT 16 SERVINGS

FRUIT CAKES

The cakes in the following recipe contains preserved fruits. The simplest cakes are merely enriched with raisins or candied peel, the more complex are the all-out, whole-bottle-of-rum type of fruitcake that's aged for a few months before serving. If you have been wary of fruitcake in the past, try a simple one first, then work your way up to the extravaganzas.

Aging Fruitcake

Some fruitcakes benefit from a long rest before they are served. The cake becomes tender and less likely to crumble when sliced, and the flavor mellows. To age a cake, sprinkle it liberally with dark rum or other strong spirits of your choice. Not only does the rum flavor the cake, it also acts as a preservative. Cut off about a foot of new cheesecloth (more for larger cakes) and soak it with the same spirits. Wrap the fruitcake in the soaked cheesecloth, then wrap in several layers of plastic wrap and finish with a double layer of aluminum foil. As a further precaution, place the cake in a plastic container or tin with a tightly fitting cover. Store the cake in the coolest place you can find, but not the refrigerator or kitchen. Check the cake occasionally and sprinkle with a little more rum if it seems to be drying out.

Storing Fruitcake

To store fruitcake for any length of time, follow the directions for aging above. Or, if you don't want to use alcohol, wrap it well and store in the freezer.

MACAO CHRISTMAS CAKE

〜❡ ❡〜

THIS RECIPE COMES FROM A DEAR FRIEND, chef and cookbook author Rosa Ross. Rosa's mother, Edris de Carvalho, made this cake every holiday season at their family home in Macao, the former Portuguese colony near Hong Kong. The food of Macao is mainly Chinese and Portuguese, but there is also a broad vein of English influence (from the British presence in Hong Kong), evident in food like this fruitcake. Don't be put off by the quantity of nutmeg, or be tempted to reduce it or leave it out—the spice gives the cake a delicate and pleasant perfume.

1 Set a rack in the lower third of the oven and preheat to 275 degrees.

2 In a large bowl, stir together the dried and candied fruit and the almonds, mixing well. Toss with ¼ cup of the flour.

3 In a medium bowl, combine the remaining 2¾ cups flour, the nutmeg, and baking powder, mixing well.

4 In the bowl of a heavy-duty mixer fitted with the paddle, beat the butter and sugar on medium speed for about 5 minutes, or until light and fluffy. Beat in the eggs one at a time, beating until smooth after each addition. Beat in one-third of the flour, then the brandy. Scrape down the bowl and beater with a rubber spatula. Beat in another third of the flour, then beat in the crème de cacao. Scrape again. Beat in the remaining flour.

8 ounces dark raisins

8 ounces golden raisins

8 ounces dried currants

4 ounces candied orange peel,
    cut into ¼-inch dice

4 ounces candied lemon peel,
    cut into ¼-inch dice

½ cup (about 2 ounces) slivered blanched
    almonds

3 cups all-purpose flour (spoon flour into
    dry-measure cup and level off)

2½ whole nutmegs, finely grated

1½ teaspoons baking powder

½ pound (2 sticks) unsalted butter,
    softened

1 cup sugar

6 large eggs, at room temperature

½ cup Cognac or other brandy

¼ cup crème de cacao

One 12-cup tube or Bundt pan,
buttered and floured

5 Use the rubber spatula to give a final mix to the batter. Fold in the floured fruit.

6 Scrape the batter into the prepared pan and smooth the top. Bake for about 2 to 2½ hours, or until a toothpick inserted into the cake halfway between the side of the pan and the central tube emerges clean.

7 Cool the cake in the pan on a rack for about 20 minutes, then invert onto a rack, remove the paper, and cool completely.

SERVING: Serve thin slices of this cake with coffee or tea. Around the holidays, it is always on my table at teatime.

STORAGE: See Aging Fruitcake and Storing Fruitcake, page 251. Wrap in Cognac- or brandy-soaked cheesecloth, but do not moisten the cake itself—it is too delicately flavored and would take on a harsh alcohol taste—or keep at room temperature for up to a week.

MAKES ONE 10-INCH TUBE OR BUNDT CAKE, ABOUT 24 SERVINGS

CHEESECAKES

ALMOST ALL OF THE WORLD'S DESSERT CUISINES have their own version of cheesecake. Creamy, smooth, rich, and with just a tiny sour tinge to temper the sweetness, cheesecake heads the list of the richest and most requested of all cakes.

Though I too love cheesecake, I have always been mystified that it appears on steak-house menus—who could eat a piece of such a rich cake after such a rich main course? With that thinking in mind, I usually serve only the lightest cheesecakes for dessert. The richer ones I reserve for midafternoon tea or coffee—or if I do serve one as a dessert, it is only after a very light lunch or supper. In my childhood, cheesecake always appeared as one of the dozen or so desserts after Thanksgiving dinner. I could never resist it, but even as a child I always regretted indulging in it.

The cheesecakes in this chapter fall into two different categories.

1 Cream-Cheese Cakes: Plain, or with the addition of sour cream, these are the classic New York–style cheesecakes. They probably entered the American baking repertoire with immigrants from Eastern Europe, as this type of cheesecake is eminently a Russian or Polish-style dessert.

2 Curd-Cheese Cakes: These are the ones made from ricotta, cottage cheese, or farmer cheese and hail primarily from Italy, in the case of ricotta, or from Germany and Eastern Europe, in the case of the other curd cheeses.

CHEESECAKE RULES

Cheesecakes aren't difficult to make, but you have to follow these very simple rules:

1 When a recipe says have the ingredients at room temperature, it means it. Room-temperature cream cheese, sugar, and eggs will combine to make a smooth lump-free batter.

2 Don't overmix the batter. If the ingredients are at room temperature, the batter will smooth out with almost no effort. If the ingredients are cold and firm, no amount of beating will smooth them—you're just beating unwanted air into the batter, which will make the cheesecake rise too much while it is baking, only to sink dismally in the center as it cools.

3 Bake most cheesecakes in a pan of water. This helps reduce bottom heat so that the cheesecake sets without rising and developing a soufflé-like texture.

4 Don't overbake the cheesecake. If it looks as though it has puffed a little and it has taken on a tiny bit of color, and the baking time stated in the recipe has elapsed, take the cheesecake out of the oven. Yes, it will still look a little wobbly in the center—it's supposed to.

PREVENTING CRACKS

Following the three rules above will also help prevent the top of the cheesecake from cracking. Before baking, loosening the top of the cheesecake from the side of the pan by running the point of a sharp paring knife between the cheesecake and the side of the pan (just about ½ inch down) all around—press the knife against the pan, not the cake—will also help prevent cracks. If despite all your precautions there is a tiny crack or two, then it's time for that strawberry topping—see page 260.

CHEESECAKE CRUSTS

I decided not to have any pastry doughs that need to be rolled out in a book about cakes, but there are quite a few alternatives for the bottom of a cheesecake.

1   Nothing: Butter the bottom of the pan, cut a disk of parchment paper the same size as the bottom of the pan, place it in the pan, and butter it, too.

2   Crumb base: Line the pan with buttered paper as above, then scatter a ⅛-inch layer of graham cracker, cookie, or cake crumbs evenly over the bottom of the pan and press them down firmly. Some of these recipes call for a mixture of butter and cookie crumbs.

3   Crisp crust: This is like a crumb topping mixture that you press onto the buttered paper; see page 258.

4   Cake: Place a thin slice of a sponge or butter cake on the buttered paper before pouring in the batter. Ideally, a cake layer to be used as a cheesecake base should be baked in a pan larger than the cheesecake pan and then cut to size. If you bake it in a pan of the same size, the base will be too small because the cake will shrink a little as it cools.

SPRINGFORM OR OTHER PANS

All the recipes here call for springform pans, but you can also use a 3-inch-deep round cake pan of the same diameter. Such pans are actually called cheesecake pans and are available from several equipment suppliers. If you use a pan that doesn't have removable sides, you'll have to invert the cheesecake to unmold it. Don't worry—it's easy.

UNMOLDING CHEESECAKES

To unmold a baked cheesecake successfully, follow the instructions below as though your life depended on it:

1 Wrap the cooled-to-room-temperature cheesecake very well in plastic wrap and chill it overnight. No, two hours in the refrigerator isn't a replacement for twelve; several hours in the freezer can be, though.

2 Remove the cheesecake from the refrigerator and unwrap it. Save the plastic wrap. If there is a little condensation on the chilled cheesecake, leave it there. If not, dribble or spray about 1 teaspoon water evenly over the top of the cheesecake.

3 Loosen the cheesecake from the sides of the pan with a thin sharp knife: insert it between the pan and the cheesecake and run it around the entire inside of the pan, scraping against the pan, not the cake.

4 Turn on a burner on your stove to a moderate flame, or halfway between low and high if electric. Place the cheesecake pan on the burner and rotate it so that the entire bottom of the pan becomes slightly heated—the whole process should take only 5 seconds.

5 Place the plastic wrap over the pan—you don't need to press it against the top of the cheesecake.

6 Cover the plastic wrap with a perfectly flat plate, platter, cutting board, or piece of stiff cardboard—a cake circle is ideal.

7 Invert the pan onto the plate or other surface. The cheesecake should drop right out. If it doesn't, give the bottom of the pan a bit of a swat. If that doesn't work, invert the whole package, remove the plate or cardboard and plastic wrap, and reheat the pan bottom.

8 Once you succeed in getting the cheesecake to drop out of the pan, remove the paper from the bottom of the cheesecake.

9 Place a flat platter or cardboard over the bottom of the cheesecake and invert the whole package again. Remove the top platter or cardboard and the plastic wrap (which will not have stuck to the cheesecake because of the little bit of moisture on the cheesecake top). Gently pat the top of the cake dry with a paper towel, without pressing too hard.

For cheesecakes in springform pans: If you have a wide metal spatula, you may be able simply to loosen the cheesecake base from the pan bottom and slide it onto a platter, without inverting it—it really depends on how firm the cheesecake is when you do it. This works best with a very well chilled baked cheesecake. I have tried this with chilled cheesecakes that have sponge cake bases though, and sometimes they buckle.

You can also invert a cheesecake baked in a springform pan to unmold it, following the instructions above. It's easier to do because you'll only need to remove the pan bottom and paper. I strongly suggest doing this, especially if you like to take cheesecakes to friends—you'll never lose another springform bottom again.

CHEESECAKE BASES

The following recipes for cheesecake bases are all interchangeable, though I like the crumb-type bases best with baked cheesecakes. The more delicate sponge base is better with unbaked cheese-cakes.

PLAIN CHEESECAKE BASE

THIS IS AN EASY WAY to make a pastry-like base for a cheesecake without the bother of rolling out dough. The crumbly flour and butter mass is pressed into the bottom of the buttered and paper-lined pan. Not only does having a base under the cheesecake make it easier to cut and serve, but it makes the cake easier to unmold after it is baked and chilled.

1   Position a rack in the middle of the oven and preheat to 350 degrees.

2   Using a heavy-duty mixer fitted with the paddle, or a wooden spoon, beat together the butter and sugar until light and fluffy. Beat in the yolk until smooth. Combine the flour, baking powder, and salt and gently fold into the butter mixture with a rubber spatula. The mixture will be crumbly.

3   Place the mixture in the pan and use your hands to pat it down evenly and firmly over the bottom. Pierce the surface at 1-inch intervals with a fork.

4   Bake for 15 to 20 minutes, or until the crust is golden and firm. Transfer to a rack to cool slightly before covering with the cheesecake batter.

MAKES A BASE FOR ONE 9- OR 10-INCH CHEESECAKE

3 tablespoons unsalted butter, softened

3 tablespoons sugar

1 large egg yolk

1 cup all-purpose flour (spoon flour into dry-measure cup and level off)

½ teaspoon baking powder

⅛ teaspoon salt

One 9-inch springform pan, bottom buttered and lined with buttered parchment paper

VARIATION

COCOA CHEESECAKE BASE: Reduce the 1 cup flour to ¾ cup and add 3 tablespoons alkalized (Dutch-process) cocoa powder, sifted after measuring, to the dry ingredients.

SOUR CREAM CHEESECAKE

❧ ❧

WHEN PEOPLE TALK ABOUT REAL NEW YORK cheesecake, this is the recipe they mean. Rich and creamy, this cheesecake has just a hint of acidity from the sour cream.

1 Position a rack in the middle of the oven and preheat to 350 degrees.

2 To make the base, beat together the butter and sugar by hand until light and fluffy. Beat in the yolk until smooth. Combine the flour, baking powder, and salt and, with a rubber spatula, gently fold into the butter mixture. The mixture will be crumbly.

3 Place the dough in the pan and use your hands to pat it down evenly and firmly over the bottom.

4 Bake for about 25 minutes, until the crust is golden and baked through. Transfer to a rack and reduce the oven temperature to 325 degrees.

5 To make the batter, in the bowl of a heavy-duty mixer fitted with the paddle attachment, beat the cream cheese on the lowest speed just until smooth, no more than 30 seconds. Stop the mixer and scrape down the bowl and beater. Add the sugar in a stream, mixing for no more than 30 seconds. Stop and scrape again. Add 1 cup of the sour cream and mix only until it is absorbed, no more than 30 seconds. Repeat with the remaining sour cream. Add the eggs one at a time, mixing only until each is absorbed; stop and scrape after each addition. Beat in the vanilla extract.

CHEESECAKE BASE

3 tablespoons unsalted butter, softened

3 tablespoons sugar

1 large egg yolk

1 cup bleached all-purpose flour (spoon flour into dry-measure cup and level off)

¼ teaspoon baking powder

⅛ teaspoon salt

CHEESECAKE BATTER

1 pound cream cheese

1 cup sugar

One 16-ounce container sour cream

3 large eggs

2 teaspoons vanilla extract

One 3-inch-deep 9-inch springform pan, bottom buttered and lined with parchment or wax paper; one 10 × 15-inch jelly-roll pan or roasting pan

6 Wrap heavy-duty aluminum foil around the bottom of the springform pan so it comes at least 1 inch up the sides. Pour the batter into the pan. Place the pan in a jelly-roll pan or roasting pan and pour warm water into the pan to a depth of ½ inch.

7 Bake the cheesecake for about 55 minutes, or until it is lightly colored and firm except for the very center. Remove from the oven and lift the cheesecake out of the hot water. Remove the foil and let cool completely on a rack. Wrap the cheesecake and chill overnight.

8 To unmold the cheesecake, run a knife or thin spatula around the inside of the pan, pressing the knife against the pan, not the cake. Unbuckle the pan side and lift off. Leave the cake on the base, or run a spatula under the cake base and slide the cake onto a platter.

MAKES ONE 9-INCH CHEESECAKE,
ABOUT 12 SERVINGS

VARIATION

STRAWBERRY CHEESECAKE: Rinse, hull, and slice 2 pints of strawberries. Starting at the outer edge of the baked and chilled cheesecake, arrange the strawberry slices in concentric circles, points outward, like the petals of a flower. Heat ½ cup currant jelly and reduce until slightly thickened, then glaze the berries, using a pastry brush.

PAUL'S CHEESECAKE

⌁

THIS EXCELLENT CHEESECAKE comes from my friend Paul Kinberg of Dallas.

1 Position a rack in the middle of the oven and preheat the oven to midway between 300 and 325 degrees.

2 In the bowl of a heavy-duty mixer fitted with the paddle, beat the cream cheese on low speed until smooth. Beat in the sugar in a stream. Beat in the eggs one at a time, stopping to scrape the bowl and beater with a rubber spatula each time and beating until smooth after each addition. Beat in the vanilla, then beat in the sour cream.

3 Pour the batter into the prepared pan.

4 Bake for exactly 1 hour. Turn off the oven, without opening the door, and leave the cheesecake in the oven for exactly 1 hour more.

5 Cool the cheesecake in the pan on a rack, then wrap in plastic and refrigerate until firm. Unmold according to the instructions on page 256.

CHEESECAKE BATTER

1½ pounds cream cheese

1½ cups sugar

6 large eggs

1½ teaspoons vanilla extract

One 16-ounce container sour cream

1 Cheesecake Base, page 258, baked and cooled

One 9- or 10-inch springform pan, buttered

SERVING: Serve thin wedges of this rich cake.

STORAGE: Wrap leftovers in plastic and refrigerate. Bring to room temperature before serving.

MAKES ONE 9- OR 10-INCH CHEESECAKE, ABOUT 12 SERVINGS

LESLIE'S LAYERED CHEESECAKE

THIS IS A GREAT CHOCOLATE-AND-VANILLA cheesecake that won first prize for Leslie Sutton, a very talented baker and artist, at a Connecticut cheesecake baking contest.

CHOCOLATE COOKIE CRUST

1¾ cups chocolate wafer crumbs

5 tablespoons unsalted butter, melted

CHEESECAKE BATTER

1½ pounds cream cheese, softened

1 cup sugar

Pinch salt

3 large eggs

One 8-ounce container sour cream

1 teaspoon vanilla extract

7 ounces semisweet chocolate, melted

TOPPING

One 16-ounce container sour cream

¼ cup sugar

One 3-inch-deep 9-inch springform pan, bottom buttered and lined with parchment or wax paper

1 Position a rack in the middle of the oven and preheat to 350 degrees.

2 To make the crust, put the cookie crumbs in a bowl and stir in the butter with a fork. Press the mixture evenly and firmly over the bottom and most of the way up the sides of the pan.

3 To make the batter, in the bowl of a heavy-duty mixer fitted with the paddle attachment, beat the cream cheese, sugar, and salt on low speed until smooth. Beat in the eggs one at a time, stopping often to scrape down the bowl and beater. Beat in the sour cream and vanilla.

4 Pour half the batter into prepared pan.

5 Stir the melted chocolate into the remaining batter and carefully pour it over the plain batter.

6 Bake the cheesecake for 40 minutes.

7 While the cheesecake is baking, prepare the topping. Stir the sour cream and sugar together until smooth.

8 Pour the topping over cheesecake and smooth it with a spatula. Increase the oven temperature to 450 degrees and bake for 10 minutes.

9 Cool the cheesecake in the pan on a rack, then wrap in plastic and refrigerate until firm. Unmold according to the instructions on page 260.

SERVING: Serve thin wedges of this rich cake.

STORAGE: Wrap leftovers in plastic and refrigerate. Bring to room temperature before serving.

MAKE ONE 9-INCH CHEESECAKE, ABOUT 16 SERVINGS

SHARI'S INDIVIDUAL MASCARPONE CHEESECAKES

⤳ ৩ ⤳

THE RECIPE FOR THIS DELICIOUS CHEESECAKE was given to me by Shari Lepore, an old friend who is also a cooking teacher.

1 Position a rack in the middle of the oven and preheat to 300 degrees.

2 In the bowl of a heavy-duty mixer fitted with the paddle attachment, beat the cream cheese and sugar on medium speed until smooth. Add the mascarpone and beat until smooth. Beat in eggs one at a time, scraping down the bowl and beater often. Beat in the vanilla.

3 Place the prepared molds in the roasting pan and fill the molds to within ½ inch of the top. Pour about an inch of warm water into the pan.

4 Bake for about 30 minutes, or until the cakes are no longer liquid in the center.

5 Turn off the oven and leave door ajar. Cool the cheesecakes in the oven for about 30 minutes, then chill the cheesecakes until firm.

6 To unmold, invert and remove the cups and paper.

2 pounds cream cheese, softened

2¼ cups sugar

One 500-gram (about 18 ounces or 1¾ cups) container imported mascarpone, softened

7 large eggs

1 tablespoon vanilla extract

Twenty-one 4-ounce aluminum foil cups, buttered and bottoms lined with buttered parchment or wax paper; a shallow roasting pan large enough to hold the cups

SERVING: Serve with sliced sugared strawberries or raspberries, or a combination.

STORAGE: Wrap leftovers in plastic and refrigerate. Bring to room temperature before serving.

MAKES 21 INDIVIDUAL CHEESECAKES

DARK AND WHITE CHOCOLATE CHEESECAKE

〜◦ ◦〜

TWO LAYERS OF CHOCOLATE CAKE make this cheesecake complex and elegant.

1 Position a rack in the middle of the oven and preheat to 350 degrees.

2 In the bowl of a heavy-duty mixer fitted with the paddle attachment, beat half the cream cheese on the lowest speed until smooth, no more than 30 seconds. Stop the mixer and scrape down the bowl and beater. Add ½ cup of the sugar in a stream, beating for no more than 30 seconds. Stop and scrape again. Add the melted dark chocolate, beating only until it is absorbed, no more than 30 seconds. Beat in 1 teaspoon of the vanilla. Add 3 of the eggs, one at a time, mixing only until each is absorbed. Stop and scrape after each addition and transfer to another bowl if you only have one mixer bowl.

3 Make the white chocolate batter following the same procedure as for the dark chocolate batter, using the remaining ingredients.

CHEESECAKE BATTER

2 pounds cream cheese

1 cup sugar

5 ounces bittersweet or semisweet chocolate, melted

2 teaspoons vanilla extract

6 large eggs

5 ounces white chocolate, melted

One 9-inch layer 1942 Devil's Food Cake, page 339, sliced into two layers

One 3-inch-deep 9-inch springform pan, bottom buttered and lined with parchment or wax paper; one 10 × 15-inch jelly-roll pan

4 Wrap heavy-duty aluminum foil around the bottom of the springform pan to come at least 1 inch up the sides. Place one of the cake layers in the bottom of the pan. Pour the dark chocolate batter into the pan. Place the other cake layer on the batter and pour in the white chocolate batter.

5 Place the pan in the jelly-roll pan and pour warm water into the pan to a depth of ½ inch. Bake the cheesecake for about 75 minutes, or until it is lightly colored and firm except for the very center. Remove from oven and take the cheesecake pan out of the hot water. Remove the foil and cool completely on a rack.

6 Wrap the cheesecake and chill overnight. Unmold according to the directions on page 260.

MAKES ONE 9-INCH CHEESECAKE, ABOUT 16 SERVINGS

PIZZA DOLCE DI RICOTTA

THIS MOST TYPICAL ITALIAN DESSERT is often served as an Easter specialty in southern Italy. The flavorings vary slightly according to the region, and toasted slivered almonds, chopped chocolate, and grated lemon and orange zest are sometimes included.

1 Position a rack in the middle of the oven and preheat to 350 degrees.

2 Using a wooden spoon, beat the ricotta in a large bowl until smooth. Stir in the sugar, then stir in the eggs one at a time. Being careful not to overmix, stir in the anisette, vanilla, and ½ teaspoon of the cinnamon.

3 Pour the mixture over the crust and sprinkle the top with the remaining ½ teaspoon cinnamon.

4 Bake for about 45 minutes, or until the cheesecake is well colored, slightly puffed, and firm except in the very center.

5 Cool the cake in the pan on a rack, then wrap in plastic and refrigerate until firm. Unmold according to the instructions on page 260.

RICOTTA BATTER

3 pounds whole-milk ricotta

1 cup sugar

8 large eggs

2 tablespoons anisette

2 teaspoons vanilla extract

1 teaspoon ground cinnamon

1 Cheesecake Base with Ground Nuts, made with almonds, baked and cooled

One 2-inch-deep 12-inch round cake pan, bottom buttered and lined with buttered parchment or wax paper

SERVING: Serve thin wedges of this rich cake.

STORAGE: Wrap leftovers in plastic and refrigerate. Bring to room temperature before serving.

MAKES ONE 12-INCH CHEESECAKE, ABOUT 16 SERVINGS

SPONGE AND FOAM CAKES

FROM THE POINT OF VIEW OF BAKING CHEMISTRY, sponge and foam cakes are some of the most interesting. Relatively few of these light cakes contain a leavening such as baking powder or soda. Most rise from the expansion of air cells beaten into the eggs during mixing. Once the batter goes into the oven, the heat makes the air cells expand and cause the cake to rise.

There are four main types of sponge and foam cakes.

1   Angel Food: These are almost always made exclusively with egg whites. I like to serve these extremely light and delicate cakes with sweetened fruit or berries.

2   Génoise: This very delicate French-style sponge cake is made with whole eggs that are combined with sugar and heated over simmering water before being whipped by machine; then the dry ingredients are folded in. Génoise layers form the bases of many layered, rolled, and molded cakes, and they are often moistened with sugar syrup for extra moisture and flavor.

3   Separated-Egg Sponge, called *Biscuit* (bees-kwee) in French: For this type: the yolks are whipped with part of the sugar, the whites are whipped separately, the remaining sugar is incorporated, and then the two foams are combined and the dry ingredients folded in. Many sponge cakes are made in this way, including ladyfingers, sponge bases for mousse and Bavarian cakes, tube cakes, Passover sponge cake, and even the Italian pan di Spagna.

4   Chiffon Cakes: These are barely more than fifty years old—the recipe was supposedly developed by a salesman who then sold it to General Mills. Most chiffon cake recipes descend from the same source, pamphlets and other promotional material circulated by General Mills in the 1940s and '50s. The one I used as the basis for these recipes was published by General Mills in 1948. Chiffon cakes are made by mixing all the ingredients (which include baking powder and vegetable oil) except the egg whites, then whipping the egg whites and folding the rest of the batter into the whites. A cake with a delicate texture and more flavor than an ordinary sponge cake, is the result.

A NOTE ABOUT SIFTING

Though I don't sift flour before measuring it, in these recipes the flour (or a combination of flour and cornstarch and/or cocoa) is sifted over the batter before it is folded in. This makes it easier to incorporate the dry ingredients into the batter and consequently results in less mixing and more air (for leavening) in the batter.

CLASSIC ANGEL FOOD CAKE

UNTIL VERY RECENTLY, I had always made angel food cakes with self-rising cake flour—the baking powder in the flour providing a little "insurance" that the cake would rise no matter what. When I started working on an angel food recipe for this book, I was haunted by a comment made by Marion Cunningham, one of the founders of The Baker's Dozen in San Francisco, author of many cookbooks, and an expert baker. Marion had found, in recent tests, that all-purpose flour also worked for angel food and that the resulting baked cakes had more body and character than those made with cake flour. I experimented, and this is the result—the best angel food cake you'll ever bake or eat. Adding lemon juice to the egg whites not only imparts a pleasant delicate flavor, but it also helps to stabilize the egg whites by slightly toughening the walls of the bubbles formed during whipping. Many other recipes use cream of tartar for this purpose.

1 Set a rack in the middle level of the oven and preheat to 325 degrees.

2 Put ¾ cup of the sugar in a small bowl. In another small bowl, mix the remaining ¾ cup sugar evenly with the flour. Sift the mixture three times to aerate it.

3 In the bowl of a heavy-duty mixer fitted with the whisk attachment, whip the egg whites and salt on medium speed until foamy. Add the lemon juice and vanilla and continue whipping until the whites are very white and opaque and beginning to hold a shape. Increase the speed to medium-high and whip in the sugar from the bowl in a slow stream. Continue to whip until the egg whites hold a soft, glossy peak.

1½ cups sugar

1 cup bleached all-purpose flour
(spoon flour into dry-measure cup and level off)

1½ cups egg whites (from about 12 large eggs)

¼ teaspoon salt

1 tablespoon strained fresh lemon juice

1 teaspoon vanilla extract

One 10-inch tube pan with removable bottom, ungreased; a narrow-necked bottle (such as a wine bottle) to hang the cake on after it is baked (see Note); a strainer or sifter

4 Quickly sift one-third of the flour and sugar mixture over the egg whites. Gently fold in with a rubber spatula, making sure you scrape across the bottom of the bowl as you fold to prevent the flour mixture from accumulating there and possibly causing lumps. Repeat with another third of the flour and sugar mixture, then finally with the remainder.

5 Scrape the batter into the pan and run the spatula through the batter to eliminate any large air pockets.

6 Bake for about 45 to 55 minutes, or until the cake is well risen, well colored, and firm to the touch. Be careful not to overbake, or the cake will fall. Invert the central tube of the pan onto the neck of the bottle and allow the cake to cool completely upside down.

7 To remove the cooled cake from the pan, run a long thin knife all around the sides of the pan, scraping against the pan rather than the cake. Remove the pan sides and run the knife around the central tube under the cake. Invert the cake onto a platter, easing it off the central tube with your fingers.

SERVING: Serve with whipped cream and/or fruit.

STORAGE: Wrap in plastic or keep under a cake dome at room temperature, or wrap well and freeze for longer storage.

MAKES ONE 10-INCH TUBE CAKE, ABOUT 12 SERVINGS

VARIATIONS

CINNAMON ANGEL FOOD CAKE: Add 2½ teaspoons ground cinnamon to the flour and sugar mixture, stirring it in thoroughly. (You can use the same proportions for any other spice, such as ginger.)

FIVE-SPICE ANGEL FOOD CAKE: Chinese five-spice powder has a stronger flavor than any single spice so add just 2 teaspoons of it to the flour mixture.

COCOA ANGEL FOOD CAKE: Add 3 tablespoons alkalized (Dutch-process) cocoa powder to the flour mixture and sift together once to eliminate any lumps in the cocoa.

NOTE: Make sure the cake pan is completely clean, dry, and free of grease of any kind. If you have never baked an angel food cake before, first invert the pan onto the bottle to make sure the pan's central tube will fit over the neck of the bottle. The cake needs to hang to cool after it is baked; it would compress and fall if cooled right side up.

PLAIN GENOISE

〜๑ ๑〜

THIS RICH, DELICATE CAKE forms the basis for many filled, frosted, and glazed cakes. A good plain génoise is hard to beat—it has an elegance that derives from its simplicity, and I even like them un-adorned. Many recipes for génoise add butter as an enrichment. Unfortunately, sometimes the extra manipulation the incorporation of the butter necessitates causes these light batters to fall. So I prefer to add a few extra egg yolks instead—they not only help enrich the cake, they also provide greater stability to the foam, ultimately making the batter easier to prepare.

1 Set a rack in the middle level of the oven and preheat to 350 degrees.

2 Half-fill a medium saucepan with water and bring it to a boil over high heat. Lower the heat so the water is simmering.

3 Whisk the eggs, yolks, salt, and sugar together in the bowl of a heavy-duty mixer. Place over the pan of simmering water and whisk gently until the mixture is just lukewarm, about 100 degrees (test with your finger). Attach the bowl to the mixer and, with the whisk attachment, whip on medium-high speed until the egg mixture is cooled (touch the outside of the bowl to tell) and tripled in volume. The egg foam will be thick and will form a slowly dissolving ribbon falling back onto the bowl of whipped eggs when the whisk is lifted.

4 While the eggs are whipping, stir together the flour and cornstarch.

3 large eggs
3 large egg yolks
Pinch of salt
¾ cup sugar
½ cup cake flour (spoon flour into dry-measure cup and level off)
¼ cup cornstarch

One 9-inch round cake pan or 9-inch springform pan, buttered and bottom lined with buttered parchment or wax paper; a strainer or sifter

5 Sift one-third of the flour mixture over the beaten eggs. Use a rubber spatula to fold in the flour mixture, making sure to scrape all the way to the bottom of the bowl on every pass through the batter to prevent the flour mixture from accumulating there and making lumps. Repeat with another third of the flour mixture and finally with the remainder.

6 Scrape the batter into the prepared pan and smooth the top.

7 Bake the génoise for about 25 minutes, or until well risen, deep gold, and firm to the touch.

8 Immediately use a small paring knife to loosen the cake from the sides of the pan. Invert the cake onto a rack, then reinvert onto another rack and let the cake cool right side up on the paper. Remove the paper when the cake is cool.

STORAGE: Wrap in plastic wrap and refrigerate for several days, or double-wrap and freeze for up to a month.

MAKES ONE 9-INCH ROUND LAYER

VARIATIONS

CHOCOLATE GENOISE: Reduce the cake flour to ⅓ cup, increase the cornstarch to ⅓ cup, and add ¼ cup alkalized (Dutch-process) cocoa powder to the flour and cornstarch mixture, sift.

GENOISE SHEET: Bake either the plain or chocolate batter in a 10 × 15-inch jelly-roll pan that has been buttered and lined with buttered parchment at 400 degrees for about 10 to 12 minutes. Make sure the cake doesn't overbake and become too dry, especially if it is to be rolled. (Makes one 10 × 15-inch layer.)

273

CAKES

BISCUIT BATTER

~ ୬ ୧ ~

THIS IS A CLASSIC FRENCH PREPARATION for making ladyfingers and also for making piped-out thin sponge-cake bases for under mousse-type desserts. If you like, you may also use a thin slice of a piped biscuit disk under a cheesecake, either baked or unbaked. The name, by the way, has nothing to do with baking powder biscuits, and it's pronounced "bee-skwee"—a very old name in French for a cake layer.

To make this easier to prepare, like any sponge cake with separated eggs, it's good to have two bowls and whisks for your mixer. If you don't, either use a hand mixer for the yolks and your heavy-duty mixer for the whites, or use the bowl and whisk for the yolks, scrape them into another bowl, and wash the bowl and whisk in hot soapy water and dry them before proceeding to whip the whites.

1 Set racks in the upper and lower third of the oven and preheat to 350 degrees.

2 Whisk the yolks, half the sugar, and the vanilla in the bowl of a heavy-duty mixer. Place the bowl on the mixer with the whisk attachment and whip on medium speed until very aerated and pale yellow, about 3 minutes.

3 In a clean, dry mixer bowl combine the egg whites and the salt. Whip on medium speed with the whisk attachment until the whites are very white and opaque. Increase speed to medium-high, and whip in the remaining sugar in a stream, continuing to whip the whites until they hold a firm, dull peak.

4 large eggs, separated

½ cup sugar, divided

1 teaspoon vanilla extract

Pinch of salt

1 cup cake flour or bleached all-purpose flour (spoon the flour into dry-measure cup and level off)

Confectioners' sugar for dusting the tops of the ladyfingers

Two cookie sheets or jelly-roll pans lined with parchment (if you are going to make a disk or disks, trace a 9-inch circle on the paper and turn the paper over)

4 Remove the bowl from the mixer and fold the yolks into the whites with a large rubber spatula.

5 Put the flour in a strainer or sifter and sift it over and fold it into the batter in three additions, making sure to scrape the bottom of the bowl with the spatula to keep the flour from accumulating there.

6 Fit a pastry bag with a ½-inch plain tube (Ateco #806). Spoon about a third of the batter into the bag and twist the top of the bag to seal.

7 To pipe fingers, touch the tube to the paper on the pan and squeeze gently while pulling the bag back toward you, making a 3-inch finger. To stop the flow of the batter, stop squeezing and proceed to the next finger, positioning the tube about 2 inches away from the first finger. You can pipe 3 rows of 6 fingers on a typical jelly-roll pan. Immediately after you have piped a full pan of the fingers, generously sift the confectioners' sugar over them and put them right in the oven. Continue with the remaining batter.

8 To pipe a disk, start with the bag perpendicular to the pan in the center of the traced circle. Squeeze gently, keeping the end of the tube about ½-inch above the surface of the pan and allowing the batter to flow out the same diameter as the end of the tube.

Continue gently squeezing until the circle is filled in. Alternatively, take several large spoonfuls of the batter and spread them in the circle with a small offset spatula. It doesn't matter if you don't pipe or spread a perfect circle, you can trim it later. It is important to keep the batter at a fairly even thickness on the pan.

9 The disks don't have to be dusted with confectioners' sugar because they are inside the dessert.

10 Bake the fingers and/or disk(s) for about 15 minutes, until they are well risen, deep golden, and firm when pressed with a fingertip.

11 Slide the papers from the pans to racks to cool. Use the fingers and disks as soon as they are cooled.

STORAGE: The disks may be wrapped and refrigerated or frozen. The fingers don't hold up as well—they tend to bruise on the surface or harden if kept more than a day—they are best used freshly baked.

MAKES ABOUT 3 DOZEN LADYFINGERS OR TWO ROUND DISKS, OR A COMBINATION

PASSOVER SPONGE CAKE

OF COURSE MY RECIPE for Passover sponge cake comes from Kyra Effren, the ultimate *balabusta*. Kyra is the first one up in North Dallas every morning, and by 6 o'clock, the most enticing smells issue from her kitchen. Is it a wonder I look forward to my stays in Dallas?

During Passover, Jews refrain from eating anything made with grain and anything fermented or leavened in any way. The only exceptions are matzoh, a cracker made with wheat flour that is prepared under religious supervision, and kosher wine, fermented under supervision. Passover cakes usually contain matzoh meal (ground matzohs) or potato starch, or a combination. This cake uses special matzoh cake meal, which is more finely ground than regular matzoh meal. Sponge cake is a popular Passover dessert not only because it is parve (it contains neither meat nor dairy and so can be eaten with any meal), but also because, unlike many other cakes, it works well made with matzoh cake meal and potato starch.

1 Set a rack in the middle of the oven and preheat to 325 degrees.

2 Whisk the yolks and 1 cup of the sugar together in the bowl of a heavy-duty mixer, then whip with the whisk attachment on medium speed until very aerated and pale yellow, about 3 minutes. Whip in the water and lemon juice.

3 In a clean, dry mixer bowl, whip the 8 egg whites and the salt with the clean, dry whisk attachment on medium speed until the whites are very white and opaque. Increase the speed to medium-high, and whip in the remaining ½ cup sugar in a stream. Continue to whip until the whites hold a firm, dull peak.

7 large eggs, separated

1½ cups sugar

2 tablespoons water

1 tablespoon strained fresh lemon juice

1 large egg white

¼ teaspoon salt

½ cup matzoh cake meal (see Note)

½ cup potato starch

One 10-inch tube pan with removable bottom, ungreased; a narrow-necked bottle (such as a wine bottle) to hang the cake on after it is baked

4 With a large rubber spatula, fold the yolks into the whites.

5 Put the matzoh meal and potato starch in a strainer or sifter and, in 3 additions, sift the mixture over the batter and fold it in. Make sure to scrape the bottom of the bowl with the spatula to keep the meal and starch from accumulating there and causing lumps.

6 Scrape the batter into the pan and run the spatula through the batter to eliminate any large air pockets.

7 Bake for 35 to 45 minutes, or until the cake is well risen, well colored, and firm to the touch. Be careful not to overbake, or the cake will fall. Invert the central tube of the pan onto the neck of the bottle and allow the cake to cool completely upside down.

8 To remove the cooled cake from the pan, run a long thin knife around the sides of the pan, scraping against the pan rather than the cake. Remove the pan sides and run the knife around the central tube and under the cake. Invert the cake onto a platter, easing it off the central tube with your fingers.

SERVING: Serve with fruit, if you like.

STORAGE: Wrap in plastic or keep under a cake dome at room temperature, or wrap well and freeze for longer storage.

MAKES ON 10-INCH TUBE CAKE, ABOUT 16 SERVINGS

NOTE: Matzoh cake meal is available in the kosher section of the supermarket around Passover. It is also, of course, available at Passover stores in large Jewish neighborhoods.

277

PAN DI SPAGNA

THE JURY IS STILL OUT on whether the name of this Italian sponge cake means "Spanish bread," which would be the literal translation, or whether *spagna* is really a corruption of *spugna,* or sponge. Fortunately it doesn't matter—the cake is delicious.

1 Position a rack in the middle of the oven and preheat to 350 degrees.

2 Whisk together the yolks, 6 tablespoons of the sugar, and the vanilla in the bowl of a heavy-duty mixer, then whip with the whisk attachment on medium speed until very aerated and pale yellow, about 3 minutes.

3 In a clean, dry mixer bowl, whip the egg whites and salt with the whisk attachment on medium speed until the whites are very white and opaque. Increase the speed to medium-high, and whip in the remaining 6 tablespoons sugar in a stream. Continue to whip the whites until they hold a firm, dull peak.

4 Use a large rubber spatula to fold the yolks into the whites.

5 Put the flour and cornstarch in a strainer or sifter and, in 3 additions, sift the mixture over the batter and fold it in. Make sure to keep scraping the bottom of the bowl with the spatula to keep the flour from accumulating there and causing lumps.

6 Scrape the batter into the prepared pan and smooth the top.

4 large eggs, separated

¾ cup sugar

1 teaspoon vanilla extract

Pinch of salt

½ cup all-purpose flour (spoon flour into dry-measure cup and level off)

½ cup cornstarch

One 2-inch-deep 9- or 10-inch round cake pan, buttered and bottom lined with parchment or wax paper

7 Bake the cake for 30 to 40 minutes, until it is well risen and feels firm when pressed gently with the palm of your hand. Immediately run a small knife or spatula around the inside of the pan to loosen the cake. Unmold the layer onto a rack. Leave the paper on it and turn the layer right side up onto a rack to cool. Remove the paper when the cake is cool.

STORAGE: Double-wrap the layer in plastic and keep it in the refrigerator up to 5 days, or freeze it for longer storage.

MAKES ONE 9- OR 10-INCH ROUND LAYER

MARBLE SPONGE CAKE

~ ⌒ ~

THIS WINS MORE FRIENDS FOR SPONGE CAKE than any other recipe I know. It's not difficult to make—in fact, the eggs are prepared exactly the same way as for many other sponge cakes. The only trick is that once you combine the white and yolks and then divide the batter, you must move quickly so that the white batter doesn't deflate while you are folding the dry ingredients into the chocolate batter.

1 Set a rack in the middle of the oven and preheat to 350 degrees.

2 In a small bowl stir together ½ cup of the flour and ¼ cup of the cornstarch, for the white batter. In another small bowl, stir together the remaining ¼ cup flour, ¼ cup cornstarch, and the cocoa, for the chocolate batter. Set aside.

3 Whisk together the yolks, ½ cup plus 2 tablespoons of the sugar, and the vanilla in the bowl of a heavy-duty mixer, then whip with the whisk attachment on medium speed until very aerated and pale yellow, about 3 minutes.

4 In a clean, dry mixer bowl, whip the egg whites and salt with the clean, dry whisk attachment on medium speed until the whites are very white and opaque. Increase the speed to medium-high, and whip in the remaining ½ cup plus 2 tablespoons sugar in a stream. Continue to whip until the whites hold a firm, dull peak. With a large rubber spatula, fold the yolks into the whites.

¾ cup all-purpose flour (spoon flour into dry-measure cups and level off)

½ cup cornstarch

3 tablespoons alkalized (Dutch-process) cocoa powder

6 large eggs, separated

1¼ cups sugar

2 teaspoons vanilla extract

Pinch salt

One 10-inch tube pan with removable bottom, ungreased, a narrow-necked bottle (such as a wine bottle) to hang the cake on after it is baked

5 Pour half the egg mixture into the bowl in which the yolks were whipped. In 2 additions, sift the dry ingredients for the white batter over the egg mixture and fold them in; set the bowl aside. Do the same with the dry ingredients for the chocolate batter and the remaining egg mixture.

6 Spoon half the white batter into the tube pan, leaving the top surface somewhat irregular. Spoon half the chocolate batter over the white batter, then repeat with the layering.

7 Bake for about 45 minutes, or until the cake is well risen and feels firm when pressed gently with the palm of the hand. Invert the central tube of the pan onto the neck of the bottle and allow the cake to cool completely upside down.

8 To remove the cooled cake from the pan, run a long thin knife around the sides of the pan, scraping against the pan rather than the cake. Remove the pan sides and run the knife around the central tube and under the cake. Invert the cake onto a platter, easing it off the central tube with your fingers.

SERVING: Serve with whipped cream and/or fruit.

STORAGE: Wrap in plastic or keep under a cake dome at room temperature, or wrap well and freeze for longer storage.

MAKES ONE 10-INCH TUBE CAKE, ABOUT 16 SERVINGS

KYRA'S HOT MILK SPONGE

〜✑ ✑〜

THIS IS CERTAINLY THE EASIEST of all sponge cakes to prepare, and it has a moist and delicate texture. It makes great cake layers and is also perfect to use in a trifle.

1   Set the rack in the center of the oven and preheat to 375 degrees.

2   Combine the milk and butter in a 1½-quart saucepan and cook over low heat, stirring occasionally, until the butter is completely melted. Remove from the heat.

3   Meanwhile, stir together the flour and baking powder in a bowl, mixing well.

4   In a medium mixing bowl, whisk the eggs to break them up. Whisk in the salt, then whisk in the sugar in a stream and continue to whisk for about 30 seconds, or until the mixture has lightened somewhat. Whisk in the extracts. Gently whisk in the milk and butter mixture, then use the whisk to gently incorporate the flour mixture in about 4 additions, whisking until smooth after each addition.

5   Divide the batter between the prepared pans. Bake for 15 to 20 minutes, or until the cakes are well risen, smooth, deep gold, and firm when touched in the center with a fingertip.

8 tablespoons (1 stick) unsalted butter, cut into 8 pieces

½ cup milk

1½ cups all-purpose flour (spoon flour into dry-measure cup and level off)

2 teaspoons baking powder

3 large eggs

¼ teaspoon salt

1 cup sugar

¾ teaspoon almond extract

¼ teaspoon vanilla extract

Two 2-inch-deep 9-inch round cake pans buttered and bottoms lined with parchment or wax paper

6   Run a small paring knife around the sides of the pans to loosen the cake. Invert each layer onto a rack, then immediately invert to another rack, leaving the paper on the cake, and let cool. Remove the paper when the layers are cool.

STORAGE: Wrap the layers in plastic wrap and refrigerate for several days, or freeze for up to a month.

MAKES TWO 9-INCH ROUND LAYERS

CAKES

DELICATE VANILLA CHIFFON CAKE

❧ ❧

I ALWAYS THINK OF A CHIFFON CAKE as an angel food cake that has decided to put on the dog. Their appearance—since they are both baked in large tube pans—is similar and so is their characteristic lightness. But chiffon cakes are moister and more tender than angel foods because of the presence of both egg yolks and oil in the batter. A good chiffon cake depends a great deal on getting the egg whites just right, so read Whipping Egg Whites (page 291) before preparing the cake.

1 Set a rack in the middle of the oven and preheat to 350 degrees.

2 Sift the cake flour into the bowl of a heavy-duty mixer. Add 1¼ cups of the sugar and the baking powder and stir well to mix.

3 In a medium bowl, stir together the oil, egg yolks, water, and vanilla. Stir the liquid ingredients into the dry ingredients, then beat with the paddle on medium speed for about a minute, or until smooth.

4 In a clean, dry mixer bowl, whip the egg whites and salt with the whisk attachment on medium speed until very white and opaque and beginning to hold a shape. Increase the speed to medium-high, and whisk in the remaining ¼ cup sugar in a stream. Continue to whip the egg whites until they hold a firm peak.

5 With a large rubber spatula, fold the yolk mixture into the whipped whites, making sure you scrape the bottom of the bowl each time the spatula passes through so the batter is thoroughly mixed. Pour the batter into the prepared pan and smooth the top.

2¼ cups cake flour (spoon flour into dry-measure cup and level off)

1½ cups sugar

1 tablespoon baking powder

½ cup vegetable oil, such as corn or canola

4 large egg yolks

¾ cup cold water

2 teaspoons vanilla extract

1 cup egg whites (from 7 or 8 large eggs)

Pinch of salt

One 10-inch tube pan with removable bottom, ungreased; a narrow-necked bottle (such as a wine bottle) to hang the cake on after it is baked

6   Bake for about 55 to 60 minutes, or until the cake is deep gold and firm; a toothpick inserted halfway between the side of the pan and the central tube should emerge clean. Invert the central tube onto the neck of the bottle and let the cake cool completely upside down.

7   To remove the cooled cake from the pan, run a long thin knife around the sides of the pan, scraping against the pan rather than the cake. Remove the pan sides and run the knife around the tube and under the cake. Invert the cake onto a platter, easing it off the central tube with your fingers.

SERVING: Use a sharp serrated knife to cut the cake. Serve with whipped cream and/or fruit.

STORAGE: Wrap in plastic or keep under a cake dome at room temperature, or wrap well and freeze for longer storage.

MAKES ONE 10-INCH TUBE CAKE, ABOUT 16 SERVINGS

VARIATIONS

ORANGE CHIFFON CAKE: Substitute strained fresh orange juice for the water and orange extract for the vanilla.

LEMON CHIFFON CAKE: Substitute ⅓ cup strained fresh lemon juice plus enough water to make ¾ cup for the water. Substitute lemon extract for the vanilla.

BROWN SUGAR CHIFFON CAKE: Substitute 1¼ cups firmly packed dark brown sugar for the first sugar added to the batter. Use ¼ cup granulated sugar for the egg whites, as in the recipe above. Brown Sugar Chiffon cake is pictured on page 284.

CHOCOLATE CHIFFON CAKE

❧ ❧

I THINK MOST CHIFFON, angel food, and tube-pan sponge cakes are best left unadorned, but this rather lean chocolate chiffon cake turns into something spectacular with a little chocolate ganache frosting. The ganache is easy to make and complements the lightness of the cake perfectly.

CAKE BATTER

½ cup alkalized (Dutch-process) cocoa powder

¾ cup boiling water

1¾ cups cake flour (spoon flour into dry-measure cup and level off)

1 tablespoon baking powder

1¾ cups sugar

½ cup vegetable oil, such as corn or canola

6 large egg yolks

1 teaspoon vanilla extract

1 cup egg whites (from 7 or 8 large eggs)

½ teaspoon salt

GANACHE

¾ cup heavy whipping cream

1 tablespoon light corn syrup

2 tablespoons butter

10 ounces semisweet or bittersweet chocolate, cut into ¼-inch pieces

One 10-inch tube pan with removable bottom, ungreased; a narrow-necked bottle (such as a wine bottle) to hang the cake on after it is baked

1 Set a rack in the middle of the oven and preheat to 350 degrees.

2 Sift the cocoa into a small mixing bowl. Stir in the boiling water until smooth. Set aside to cool.

3 Sift the cake flour into the bowl of a heavy-duty mixer. Add the baking powder and 1¼ cups of the sugar and stir well to mix.

4 In a medium bowl, stir together the oil, egg yolks, and vanilla. Stir the liquid ingredients and the cooled cocoa mixture into the dry ingredients, then beat with the paddle on

medium speed for about a minute, or until smooth.

5 In a clean, dry mixer bowl, whip the egg whites and salt with the whisk attachment on medium speed until very white and opaque and beginning to hold a shape. Increase the speed to medium-high, and whisk in the remaining ½ cup sugar in a stream. Continue to whip the egg whites until they hold a firm peak.

6 With a large rubber spatula, fold the yolk mixture into the whipped egg whites, making sure you scrape the bottom of the bowl each time the spatula passes through so the batter is thoroughly mixed. Pour the batter into the prepared pan and smooth the top.

7 Bake for about 55 to 60 minutes, or until the cake is deep gold and firm; a toothpick inserted halfway between the side of the pan and the central tube should emerge clean.

8 While the cake is baking, prepare the ganache. Bring the cream, corn syrup, and butter to a boil in a medium saucepan. Off the heat, add the chocolate and swirl the pan to make sure all the chocolate is submerged. Allow to stand for 3 minutes, then whisk until smooth. Pour into a bowl and refrigerate until the ganache reaches spreading consistency; check it often to make sure it doesn't harden, or it will be impossible to frost the cake.

9 Remove the cake from the oven, invert the central tube onto the neck of the bottle, and let the cake cool completely.

10 To remove the cooled cake from the pan, run a long thin knife around the sides of the pan, scraping against the pan rather than the cake. Remove the pan sides and run the knife around the central tube and under the cake. Invert the cake onto a cardboard cake round or a platter, easing it off the central tube with your fingers.

11 To finish, spread the top and sides of the cake with the cooled ganache, swirling it on with the tip of an offset metal spatula. Chill the cake briefly to set the ganache.

Serving: Use a sharp serrated knife to cut the cake.

Storage: Keep under a cake dome at room temperature, or wrap loosely and refrigerate; remove from the refrigerator an hour before you serve the cake so that the ganache isn't hard. Or, for longer storage, wrap the unfrosted cake well and freeze; frost the cake after it is defrosted.

Makes one 10-inch tube cake, about 16 servings

WALNUT CHIFFON CAKE

∼୨ ଓ∼

THIS DELICATE CHIFFON CAKE is enlivened with chopped walnuts and a bit of walnut oil. Sometimes I also add a bit of some spice to brighten the flavor—see the pecan variation at the end of the recipe.

1 Set a rack in the middle of the oven and preheat to 350 degrees.

2 Sift the cake flour into the bowl of a heavy-duty mixer. Add the brown sugar and the baking powder and stir well to mix.

3 In a medium bowl, stir together the oil, egg yolks, water, and vanilla. Stir the liquid ingredients into the dry ingredients, then beat with the paddle on medium speed for about a minute, or until smooth.

4 In a clean, dry mixer bowl, whip the egg whites and salt with the whisk attachment on medium speed until very white and opaque and beginning to hold a shape. Increase the speed to medium-high, and whisk in the remaining ½ cup sugar in a stream. Continue to whip the egg whites until they hold a firm peak.

5 Use a large rubber spatula to fold the yolk mixture and walnuts into the whipped egg whites. Make sure you scrape the bottom of the bowl each time the spatula passes through to mix the batter thoroughly. Pour the batter into the prepared pan and smooth the top.

6 Bake for about 55 to 60 minutes, until the cake is deep gold and firm; a toothpick inserted halfway between the side of the pan

2¼ cups cake flour (spoon flour into dry-measure cup and level off)

1 cup granulated light brown sugar

½ cup granulated sugar

1 tablespoon baking powder

½ cup walnut oil, or a combination of half walnut and half vegetable oil, such as corn or canola

4 large egg yolks

¾ cup cold water

2 teaspoons vanilla extract

1 cup egg whites (from 7 or 8 large eggs)

1 cup walnuts (about 4 ounces), finely chopped by hand (not ground)

One 10-inch tube pan with removable bottom, ungreased; a narrow-necked bottle to hang the cake on after it is baked

and the central tube should emerge clean. Invert the central tube of the pan onto the neck of the bottle and allow the cake to cool completely.

7 To remove the cooled cake from the pan, run a long thin knife around the sides of the pan, scraping against the pan rather than the cake. Remove the pan sides and run the knife around the central tube and under the cake. Invert the cake onto a platter, easing it off the central tube with your fingers.

SERVING: Use a sharp serrated knife to cut the cake. Serve with whipped cream and/or fruit.

STORAGE: Wrap in plastic or keep under a cake dome at room temperature, or wrap well and freeze for longer storage.

MAKES ONE 10-INCH TUBE CAKE, ABOUT 16 SERVINGS

VARIATIONS

HAZELNUT CHIFFON CAKE: Substitute chopped blanched hazelnuts (see page 195 for instructions on how to remove the skin) and hazelnut oil for the walnuts and walnut oil.

PECAN CHIFFON CAKE: Substitute chopped pecans for the walnuts. Use vegetable oil instead of walnut oil and add ½ teaspoon ground cinnamon to the dry ingredients.

MERINGUE CAKES

ALL OF THE CAKES IN THIS CHAPTER have at least one meringue layer. The Swiss Zuger Kirschtorte combines meringue layers and sponge layers. Whenever I begin to make one of these cakes in a class, someone will invariably say, "I don't like meringue." But later on, when we serve the desserts and the meringue hater tastes the delicate, nutty dacquoise, he or she just as invariably exclaims, "I didn't know meringue tasted like this." The meringue cakes and layers here have nothing to do with Aunt Betty's lemon meringue pie that you were forced to eat as a child. I love the way baked meringue layers provide textural interest in an otherwise soft dessert and the way the crispness of meringue layers shows off a rich, creamy filling such as the buttercream in a dacquoise.

And, not only are meringues fun to make and good to eat, they are also the ultimate bake-ahead cake layer; just keep them in a plastic bag at room temperature. If they absorb some humidity and soften, simply unwrap and bake them on a cookie sheet at your oven's lowest setting for half an hour, and they'll be perfectly crisp again.

MERINGUE TERMINOLOGY

The type of meringue that's piped out and baked into layers is usually referred to as ordinary meringue or French meringue. Raw egg whites are beaten with sugar until stiff, then more sugar (granulated or confectioners') is folded in. The technique of incorporating some of the sugar gently at the end makes meringues that are tender rather than cement-like. Some recipes may call for the addition of an acidic ingredient such as lemon juice, vinegar, or cream of tartar. Acid makes the walls of the bubbles that form in the egg whites firmer so that they don't burst as easily and consequently have better stability during mixing. Sometimes cocoa or ground nuts are added with the second part of the sugar to make a chocolate or nut meringue. Nut meringues have a lot of confusing names: Dacquoise (see page 294), Succès, Progrès, Japonais, Grillage. *Succès* is the most common French term for a nut meringue, and I use it occasionally in a recipe. *Japonais* is the Swiss name for the same thing. But to confuse things further, there is also a Swiss meringue.

Unlike the Japonais, a Swiss meringue is a heated meringue. To make one, you combine the egg white(s) and all the sugar in the mixer bowl and whisk the mixture over a pan of simmering water until it is hot and the sugar is dissolved, then you whip it with the mixer. I like to use this type when the meringue is going to be spread or piped on a cake as an icing or used as a base for a mousse or buttercream. There is another type, called Italian meringue, which is not used in this book. For this, a hot sugar syrup is poured over the egg whites as they are whipping. Italian meringue works very well if made in large quantities, but I don't consider it practical in small ones. Too much of the sugar syrup sticks to the bowl and the whisk, and it's also very difficult to take an accurate temperature reading on a small quantity of syrup.

PIPING MERINGUE DISKS

The most efficient way to make meringue layers is to pipe the meringue. This is really a lot easier than the following directions make it sound. When you pipe the meringue mixture, you want it to fall onto the baking sheet in a cylindrical coil with the same diameter as the tube you're using to pipe it. As long as you use a steady pressure and keep the bag moving, piping these layers is easy and fun.

1 Place the tube in the pastry bag and push it firmly into the narrow opening from the inside. There's no need to try to seal off the tube of the bag, because meringue is too thick to flow out on its own while you are filling the bag. Fold over the top third of the bag to make a cuff. Hold the bag with your non-writing hand, sliding your hand under the cuff and gripping the bag with your open hand, as though you were holding a fat jar.

2 Use a large kitchen spoon or rubber spatula to fill the bag almost to the top fold. Unfold the cuff and twist it to seal the top of the bag.

3 Grip the top of the bag with your writing hand, with the twisted area between your thumb and first finger. This will make it easy to keep the bag closed as you squeeze out the meringue.

4 Squeeze the top of the bag as you would an orange half. It's not really necessary to use your other hand (how many hands do you use to write?), but some people like to guide the bag with the first finger of this hand. DO NOT wrap your hand around the bottom of the bag—you won't be able to see what you are piping, and you will inevitably start squeezing with both hands so your pressure will be uneven.

5 start in the center of the area you have traced on the parchment paper, usually a circle. Position the bag perpendicular to the pan and touch the tip of the tube to the pan. Squeezing slowly, lift the tube about an inch above the pan and begin to make a clockwise spiral with the end of the tube, making sure it is always perpendicular to the pan. Don't worry if the lines are a little wavy—it takes

a few tries to get used to this. Move from the waist rather than your shoulders—this motion seems to make the flow from the bag more even and less choppy.

6 When you get to the end of the spiral, stop squeezing and lower the tube to the surface again to stop the flow. (If you need to refill the bag during the process, stop the flow in the same way, then just resume at that spot.)

7 Or, to pipe an oval, start with a straight line several inches long down the center, then spiral clockwise around that first straight line.

WHIPPING EGG WHITES

Sponge cakes (see page 268) and meringue cakes depend on perfectly whipped egg whites for success. Though it isn't difficult to whip egg whites, here are a few suggestions that will make the process easier.

1 Always separate eggs when they are cold—the whites are more viscous and the white flows out in pretty much one glob.

2 Avoid passing the yolk repeatedly back and forth from one half of the shell to the other—once or twice should do it. Going back and forth too often can break the yolk and mix some yolk into the whites, which would prevent the whites from whipping up well.

3 Always make sure that your mixer bowl and beater are perfectly clean, dry, and free of any grease, which would also prevent the whites from whipping well.

4 Whip egg whites on medium speed—fairly slow whipping builds up a good structure of air cells in the whites and allows them to whip to the highest volume.

5 When adding sugar to whipped egg whites, always wait to add it until the whites can hold a very soft peak. Adding sugar before the egg whites have built up a good volume of air will make it difficult for them to absorb more air.

6 Always use whipped egg whites immediately—if they stand, they will separate and lose the air so carefully whipped into them.

CHOCOLATE MERINGUE CAKE

MOST CHOCOLATE MERINGUE CAKES are versions of Gaston LeNotre's famous Concorde cake. The Concorde consists of oval layers of chocolate meringue sandwiched with ganache and covered with broken cylinders of meringue, made by piping straight lines of meringue onto the baking sheet. This version uses the chocolate meringue layers, but fills and frosts them with a light chocolate buttercream and finishes the outside with crushed chocolate meringue—easier to do and just as good.

1 Set the racks to divide the oven in thirds and preheat to 300 degrees.

2 To make the meringue, in the bowl of a heavy-duty mixer, whip the egg whites and salt with the whisk attachment on medium speed until white and opaque, about 3 to 4 minutes. Increase the speed to medium-high, and whip in the granulated sugar in a stream. Continue to whip until the egg whites hold a very stiff peak.

3 Sift the confectioners' sugar and cocoa powder together several times. With a rubber spatula, fold the cocoa mixture into the beaten egg whites.

4 Using a pastry bag filled with a ½-inch plain tube (Ateco 806), pipe four 9-inch disks of meringue on the prepared pans (see page 290 for complete instructions).

5 Bake for about 30 to 35 minutes, or until the meringues are firm on the outside and almost baked through. Bake in 2 batches, if necessary. Cool the meringue layers on the pans.

CHOCOLATE MERINGUE LAYERS

1¼ cups egg whites (from 9 or 10 large eggs)

Pinch salt

1¼ cups sugar

2 cups confectioners' sugar

⅓ cup alkalized (Dutch-process) cocoa powder

CHOCOLATE BUTTERCREAM

½ cup egg whites (from about 3 to 4 large eggs)

1 cup sugar

¾ pound (3 sticks) unsalted butter, softened

4 ounces bittersweet chocolate, melted with ¼ cup water

Confectioners' sugar for finishing

Four cookie sheets or jelly-roll pans, lined with parchment

6 To make the buttercream, combine the egg whites and sugar in the bowl of a heavy-duty mixer and whisk over a pan of simmering water until the mixture is hot and the sugar is dissolved, about 3 minutes. Attach the bowl to the mixer and whip with the whisk on medium speed until the mixture is cooled. Switch to the paddle attachment and beat in the butter about 3 tablespoons at a time. Continue to beat until the buttercream is smooth and thick. Beat in the cooled chocolate.

7 To assemble, trim the 3 best meringue disks to an even 9-inch diameter. Crush the trimmings and the remaining layer. Place one layer on a platter or cardboard round and spread it with one-third of the buttercream. Repeat with another disk and another third of the buttercream. Place the last layer on top and spread the top and sides of the dessert with the rest of the frosting. Press the crushed meringue onto the top and sides of the dessert. Chill to set the frosting.

8 Just before serving, dust the cake with confectioners' sugar.

SERVING: Cut this rich cake into small portions with a very sharp serrated knife.

STORAGE: Wrap and refrigerate. Bring to room temperature before serving.

MAKES ONE 9-INCH CAKE, ABOUT 12 SERVINGS

VARIATIONS

RASPBERRY MERINGUE CAKE: Make a raspberry buttercream by adding ⅓ cup cooled, strained, and reduced raspberry puree (cook 1 cup of frozen raspberries until thick, then puree and strain) to the buttercream instead of the chocolate.

WHIPPED CREAM MERINGUE CAKE: Substitute 3 cups heavy whipping cream, whipped with ⅓ cup sugar and 2 teaspoons vanilla extract, for the buttercream.

HAZELNUT DACQUOISE

⁓ᓚ ᓂ⁓

A CRISP AND CHEWY COMBINATION of hazelnut meringue layers and a rich coffee cream, a dacquoise is the ultimate elegant dessert. This recipe is an adaptation of Gino Coffaci's classic, incorporating the additions to the original dacquoise we made for the opening of Windows on the World in 1976—making it all hazelnut and leaving the top bare. The top of the dacquoise is not covered with buttercream but lightly dusted with confectioners' sugar.

1 Position the racks in the upper and lower thirds of the oven and preheat to 300 degrees.

2 To make the layers, combine the nuts, 1 cup of the sugar, and cornstarch in a food processor and coarsely grind the nuts.

3 In the bowl of a heavy-duty mixer, whip the egg whites and salt with the whisk on medium speed until white and opaque. Increase the speed to high and gradually whip in the remaining 1 cup sugar. Continue to whip until the whites hold a firm peak.

4 Use a large rubber spatula to fold the extract and the nut mixture into the meringue.

5 Using a pastry bag fitted with a ½-inch plain tube (Ateco 806), pipe three 10-inch disks of meringue onto the prepared pans (see page 290).

6 Bake for about 30 minutes, until the meringues are firm. Bake in two batches if necessary. Leave on the pans to cool.

HAZELNUT MERINGUE LAYERS

3 cups (about 12 ounces) hazelnuts, toasted and skinned

2 cups sugar

3 tablespoons cornstarch

1¼ cups egg whites (from 9 or 10 large eggs)

Pinch salt

2 teaspoons vanilla extract

MOCHA BUTTERCREAM

½ cup egg whites (from 3 or 4 large eggs)

1 cup sugar

¾ pound (3 sticks) unsalted butter, softened

3 tablespoons triple-strength brewed coffee or 2 to 3 tablespoons instant espresso mixed with 2 tablespoons hot water, cooled

½ cup (about 2 ounces) chopped, toasted hazelnuts for finishing

Three cookie sheets or jelly-roll pans, lined with parchment; trace a 10-inch circle on each piece of paper, then turn it over

7 To make the buttercream, combine the egg whites and sugar in the bowl of a heavy-duty mixer and whisk over a pan of simmering water until the mixture is hot and the sugar is dissolved, about 3 minutes. Attach the bowl to the mixer and whip the whites with the whisk on medium speed until cooled. Switch to the paddle attachment and beat in the butter about 3 tablespoons at a time. Continue to beat until the buttercream is smooth and thick. Beat in the cooled coffee mixture.

8 To assemble, trim each meringue layer to an even 10-inch circle. Place one on a cardboard round or platter and spread with one-third of the buttercream. Top with a second layer and spread with another third of the buttercream. Place the third layer on top and press gently to level. Cover the sides of the dessert with the remaining buttercream. Press the chopped hazelnuts into the buttercream. Chill to set.

SERVING: Cut this rich cake into small portions with a very sharp serrated knife.

STORAGE: Wrap and refrigerate. Bring to room temperature before serving.

MAKES ONE 10-INCH CAKE, ABOUT 12 TO 16 SERVINGS

VARIATIONS

DACQUOISE PRALINEE: For an all-hazelnut dacquoise, flavor the buttercream with ⅓ cup praline paste instead of the coffee. (This cake is sometimes called Gâteau Succès.)

ALMOND DACQUOISE: Substitute toasted blanched almonds for the hazelnuts in the meringue layers. Fill and finish with a coffee or lemon buttercream in Chapter 13.

GATEAU PROGRES: Prepare almond meringue layers as for Almond Dacquoise, above. Fill the layers and cover the top and sides of the dessert with Ganache Pralinée (page 282). Press toasted sliced almonds all over the outside of cake.

SANS RIVAL: This is the most popular cake in the Philippines. Substitute lightly toasted cashews for the hazelnuts in the meringue and the garnish. Omit the coffee from the filling and add 2 teaspoons vanilla extract.

ZUGER KIRSCHTORTE

Kirsch Cake from Zug in Switzerland

THE SWEETNESS OF THE ALMOND MERINGUE LAYERS contrasts very successfully with the strong kirsch flavor in the cake and buttercream.

1 Position the racks to divide the oven into thirds and preheat to 325 degrees.

2 To make the Japonais, combine the almonds and confectioners' sugar in the bowl of a food processor and process until the almonds are ground very fine.

3 In the bowl of a heavy-duty mixer, whisk the egg whites with the whip at medium speed until white and opaque. Increase the speed and beat in the sugar in a stream. Continue to beat until the egg whites hold a firm peak.

4 Use a rubber spatula to fold in the almond mixture.

5 Spread the meringue to make two thin 9½-inch disks on the paper-lined pans. Bake for about 30 minutes.

6 To make the syrup, bring the sugar and water to a boil. Cool, then add the kirsch.

7 To make the buttercream, combine the egg whites and sugar in the bowl of a heavy-duty mixer, set it over simmering water, and whisk gently until the mixture is hot and sugar is dissolved. Attach the bowl to the mixer and whip with the whisk on medium speed until completely cooled. Switch to the paddle attachment and gradually beat in the butter.

JAPONAIS

¾ cup (about 3 ounces) whole blanched almonds

1 cup confectioners' sugar

½ cup egg whites (from 3 or 4 large eggs)

½ cup sugar

KIRSCH SYRUP

⅓ cup sugar

¼ cup water

¼ cup kirsch

KIRSCH BUTTERCREAM

½ cup egg whites (from 3 or 4 large eggs)

1 cup sugar

¾ pound (3 sticks) unsalted butter, softened

⅓ cup kirsch

Pink food coloring

One 9-inch layer Plain Genoise, page 272

Confectioners' sugar and toasted sliced almonds for finishing

Two cookie sheets or jelly-roll pans, lined with parchment; trace a 9½-inch circle on each sheet, then turn it over

Continue beating until the buttercream is smooth. Beat in the kirsch a little at a time, beating until smooth after each addition. Beat in just enough food coloring to tint the buttercream a pale pink.

8 To assemble, trim the crust from the top and sides of the génoise. Using a 9-inch cardboard cake round as a guide, trim the Japonais layers to even 9-inch circles. Place a dab of the buttercream on the cardboard and place one of the Japonais layers on it. Spread it with one-third of the buttercream. Moisten the génoise layer with half the syrup and invert it onto the buttercream. Moisten with the remaining syrup. Spread the génoise with another third of the buttercream and place the second Japonais layer on top. Spread the remaining buttercream around the sides of the cake. Press the toasted, sliced almonds into the buttercream and dust the top of the cake with confectioners' sugar. Use a serrated knife to trace a diagonal lattice pattern across the top of the cake.

SERVING: Cut this rich cake into small portions with a very sharp serrated knife.

STORAGE: Wrap and refrigerate. Bring to room temperature before serving.

MAKES ONE 9-INCH CAKE, ABOUT 12 SERVINGS

VARIATION

ZUGER RAHMKIRSCHTORTE: The whipped cream version of this cake is a popular specialty at Confiserie Heini in Lucerne, Switzerland. Whip 2 cups heavy whipping cream with ¼ cup sugar and ¼ cup kirsch until the cream holds a firm peak. Use the whipped cream in place of the buttercream, and cover both the top and outsides of the cake with whipped cream. Press white chocolate shavings into the whipped cream.

RATHAUSTORTE

Town Hall Cake

THIS IS A SPECIALTY OF CONFISERIE SCHIESSER in Basel, Switzerland. The pastry shop is right next to the famous medieval town hall and the cake is decorated with an outline of the building silhouetted with confectioners' sugar. It's a slightly complicated cake, but the various elements can be prepared over several days.

ALMOND SPONGE LAYER

4 large eggs, separated

Pinch salt

¾ cup sugar

¾ cup cake flour

1 cup (about 4 ounces) blanched almonds, finely ground

JAPONAIS

¾ cup (about 3 ounces) whole unblanched almonds

1 cup confectioners' sugar

4 large egg whites

½ cup sugar

RUM SYRUP

⅓ cup sugar

¼ cup water

¼ cup dark rum

HAZELNUT-RUM BUTTERCREAM

4 large egg yolks

⅓ cup dark rum

½ cup sugar

¾ pound (3 sticks) unsalted butter

1 cup (about 4 ounces) skinned toasted hazelnuts or ½ cup praline paste

3 tablespoons water

CHOCOLATE GLAZE

½ cup heavy whipping cream

4 ounces bittersweet chocolate, cut into ¼-inch pieces

FOR FINISHING

½ cup chopped toasted hazelnuts

Confectioners' sugar

One 2-inch-deep 9-inch round cake pan, buttered and bottom lined with parchment or wax paper; two cookie sheets or jelly-roll pans, lined with parchment paper–trace a 9-inch circle on each sheet, then turn it over

1   Position the racks to divide the oven into thirds and preheat to 350 degrees.

2   To make the sponge layer, whisk the yolks with 6 tablespoons of the sugar until light and thickened.

3   In the bowl of a heavy-duty mixer, whip the egg whites and salt with the whisk attachment on medium speed until very white and increased in volume. Increase the speed to medium-high and add the remaining 6 tablespoons sugar in a stream. Continue to beat until the whites hold a firm peak. Fold in the yolks, then fold in the flour and ground nuts.

4   Pour the batter into prepared cake pan and bake for about 25 minutes. Remove the cake from the oven and lower the oven temperature to 325 degrees. Immediately unmold the cake layer onto a rack, leave paper on, then invert it onto another rack to cool.

5   To make the Japonais, combine the almonds and confectioners' sugar in the bowl of a food processor and process until the nuts are finely ground.

6   In the bowl of a heavy-duty mixer, whip the egg whites with the whisk attachment on medium speed until white and opaque. Increase the speed to medium-high and beat in the sugar in a stream. Continue to beat until the whites hold a firm peak. Use a rubber spatula to fold in the almond mixture.

7   Spread the meringue Japonais thinly in patters to make two thin 9½-inch disks on the paper-lined pans. Bake for about 30 minutes.

8   To make the syrup, bring the sugar and water to a boil. Cool, then add the rum.

9   To make the buttercream, whisk the yolks in the bowl of an electric mixer, then whisk in the rum and sugar. Place the bowl over a pan of simmering water and whisk continuously until the mixture thickens. Attach the bowl to the mixer and whip with the whisk attachment on medium speed until cooled. Switch to the paddle attachment and gradually beat in the butter. Continue beating until the buttercream is smooth.

10   Place the hazelnuts in the food processor with the water and process until very smooth. Beat into the buttercream. (If you use praline paste, omit the water.)

11   To assemble, trim the crust from the top of the almond sponge. Using a 9-inch cardboard cake round as a guide, trim the Japonais layers to even 9-inch circles. Place a dab of the buttercream on the cardboard and place one of the Japonais layers on it. Spread it with one-quarter of the buttercream.

Slice the almond cake into two layers and place one over the buttercream. Moisten it with half of the syrup and spread with another quarter of the frosting. Place the other almond layer on top and moisten with the rest of the syrup. Spread the layer with another quarter of the buttercream and place the second Japonais layer over it. Spread the remaining buttercream over the top and sides of the cake. Chill the cake while you prepare the glaze.

12 Bring the cream to a simmer in a small saucepan over low heat. Remove from the heat and add the chocolate. Let stand for 2 minutes, then whisk until smooth. Pour into a small bowl and allow to cool to room temperature.

13 When the glaze has cooled, remove the cake from the refrigerator and pour the glaze onto the center of the top. Use an offset spatula to spread the glaze to the edges—if some drips down the sides, just smooth it away with the spatula. Press the chopped hazelnuts into the buttercream on the sides of the cake.

14 Just before serving dust the top edges of the cake with confectioners' sugar.

SERVING: Cut this rich cake into small portions with a very sharp serrated knife.

STORAGE: Wrap and refrigerate. Bring to room temperature before serving.

MAKES ONE 9-INCH CAKE, ABOUT 12 SERVINGS

NUT CAKES

IF ASKED FOR THEIR FAVORITE CAKE, most people will come up with something replete with pecans or coconut, perhaps remembered from childhood, perhaps from a great bakery or restaurant. Such memories are testimony to the richness and flavor nuts impart.

Before you begin to prepare any of these recipes, review the instructions for toasting, blanching, and grinding nuts on pages 194 to 196—the cakes will turn out much better if you do.

NUT CAKE LAYER

❧ ❧

THIS EASY RECIPE makes a moist and flavorful layer, which can be served as is with a sprinkling of confectioners' sugar, or used for some of the more elaborate cakes in the chapter on layer cakes.

1 Position a rack in the middle of the oven and preheat to 350 degrees.

2 Pulse the nuts repeatedly in a food processor to finely grind them; make sure they do not become pasty. Transfer the nuts to a bowl and stir with a small whisk to aerate. Sift the flour over the nuts, but do not mix them together.

3 In the bowl of a heavy-duty mixer fitted with the whisk, whip the yolks with 6 tablespoons of the sugar on medium speed until light, about 3 to 4 minutes.

4 In a clean, dry mixer bowl, beat the egg whites and salt with the whisk on medium speed until the whites hold a very soft peak. Increase the speed to high and beat in the remaining 6 tablespoons sugar in a stream. Continue to beat until the whites hold a soft peak.

1 cup (about 4 ounces) whole unblanched almonds, pistachios, or skinned hazelnuts or 1¼ cups (about 4 ounces) walnut or pecan pieces

¾ cup cake flour

4 large eggs, separated

¾ cup sugar

Pinch salt

One 2-inch-deep 9- or 10-inch round cake pan, buttered and bottom lined with buttered parchment or wax paper

5 Using a rubber spatula, fold in the yolks, then fold in the ground nuts and cake flour.

6 Scrape the batter into the prepared pan and smooth the top with a metal spatula. Bake the cake for about 30 minutes, until well colored and firm.

7 Unmold the cake onto a rack, then invert onto another rack to cool right side up. Remove the paper when the cake is cool.

SERVING: Serve this cake as a tea cake, or use it in layer cakes

STORING: Wrap in plastic and keep at room temperature for up to a week, or double-wrap and freeze for longer storage.

MAKES ONE 9- OR 10-INCH CAKE

CHOCOLATE NUT CAKE: Substitute ½ cup cake flour and 3 tablespoons alkalized (Dutch-process) cocoa powder, sifted together, for the ¾ cup cake flour.

BROWN BUTTER–HAZELNUT
FINANCIER

THIS TRADITIONAL FRENCH DESSERT probably got the name *financier* because of its richness. It is made with an unusual batter in which ground hazelnuts, sugar, and flour and a large quantity of melted butter are folded into egg whites that have been beaten with sugar. The egg whites fall and liquefy as the butter is folded in, but the cake rises well nonetheless.

1 Position a rack in the middle of the oven and preheat to 350 degrees.

2 Pulse the hazelnuts and ¾ cup of the sugar in a food processor until the nuts are finely ground. Pour into a bowl and stir in the flour.

3 Melt the butter over low heat and continue to cook for a minute or so, until it turns a light golden color. Remove from the heat and let cool, then add the rum and vanilla.

4 In the clean, dry bowl of a heavy-duty mixer fitted with the whisk, beat the egg whites with the salt until they form a very soft peak. Beat in the remaining ¾ cup sugar in a very slow stream, and continue beating until the egg whites hold a soft peak again.

5 Beginning with the hazelnut mixture, alternately fold in the hazelnut and butter mixtures, one-third at a time. Pour the batter into the prepared pan and smooth the top.

6 Bake for about 50 minutes, until the cake is well risen and golden. The center should feel firm when pressed with the palm of your hand.

1 cup (about 4 ounces) blanched whole
    hazelnuts, lightly toasted and skinned
1½ cups sugar
1 cup all-purpose flour (spoon flour into
    dry-measure cup and level off)
10 tablespoons (1¼ sticks) unsalted butter
2 tablespoons dark rum
2 teaspoons vanilla extract
1 cup egg whites (from 7 or 8 large eggs)
Pinch salt
Confectioners' sugar for finishing

One 2-inch-deep 10-inch round cake pan,
buttered and bottom lined with buttered
parchment or wax paper

7 Cool the financier briefly on a rack, then unmold and remove the paper. Turn the cake right side up to finish cooling.

BALOIS

Almond Cake from Basel

～◦♋◦～

THIS RICH, MOIST ALMOND CAKE is a specialty of Confiserie Schiesser in Basel, Switzerland. I've organized the ingredients list a little differently from the usual form, because I think having each step in the assembly process identified simplifies the preparation. It makes the recipe look more complicated than it is—basically this is just a very rich almond sponge cake.

½ cup (about 2 ounces) sliced blanched almonds

ALMOND PASTE

2 cups (about 8 ounces) sliced blanched almonds

1 cup sugar

2 tablespoons light corn syrup

1 teaspoon vanilla extract

2 large egg whites

EGGS AND YOLKS

3 large eggs

3 large yolks

EGG WHITES

⅓ cup egg whites (from 2 or 3 large eggs)

¼ cup sugar

FLOUR AND BUTTER

1 cup all-purpose flour (spoon flour into dry-measure cup and level off)

8 tablespoons (1 stick) unsalted butter, melted and still hot

Confectioners' sugar for finishing

One 12-cup Bundt or tube pan, generously buttered

1 Set a rack in the lower third of the oven and preheat to 350 degrees. Coat the buttered pan with the ½ cup blanched sliced almonds.

2 To make the almond paste, pulse the almonds and sugar in a food processor until the nuts are finely ground, then let the machine run until the mixture starts to become somewhat pasty. Add the corn syrup and vanilla and process for 1 minute. Then add the egg whites and let process for another minute. Scrape the almond mixture into a medium bowl.

3 In the bowl of a heavy-duty mixer fitted with the whisk attachment, beat the eggs and yolks on medium speed until very aerated, about 5 minutes. One-third at a time, fold the egg mixture into the almond mixture.

4 In a clean, dry mixer bowl, whip the egg whites with the clean, dry whisk attachment on medium speed until they are very white and opaque and just beginning to hold a shape. Increase the speed to medium-high and add the sugar in a stream. Continue to whip until the whites hold a soft peak.

5 Fold one-third of the egg whites into the batter. Fold in all the flour, then another third of the egg whites. Fold in the butter and, finally, the remaining egg whites.

6 Pour the batter into the prepared pan and bake for about 45 to 50 minutes, or until the cake is well risen and colored and a toothpick inserted midway between the side of the pan and the central tube emerges dry.

7 Cool the cake in the pan on a rack for 5 minutes, then unmold onto a rack to cool.

SERVING: Serve with fruit or a fruit sauce.

STORAGE: Keep wrapped in plastic at room temperature, or double-wrap and freeze for longer storage.

MAKES ONE 10-INCH BUNDT OR TUBE CAKE

FARINA GARGANTAG

Almond and Farina Cake

THIS RECIPE IS FROM one of my oldest and dearest friends, Sandy Leonard. He recently moved into an Armenian neighborhood and has learned to prepare many wonderful ethnic dishes, among them this excellent cake.

1 Position a rack in the middle of the oven and preheat to 350 degrees.

2 In the bowl of an electric mixer fitted with the whisk, beat the eggs and sugar at medium speed until light. Beat in the melted butter, nuts, lemon zest, vanilla, and cinnamon until smooth. Stir in the farina (or Cream of Wheat) and baking powder.

3 Pour the batter into the prepared pan. Bake for 45 minutes, or until the cake is firm to the touch and a toothpick inserted in the center comes out clean. Transfer to a rack to cool in the pan.

4 To make the syrup, bring the sugar, water, and lemon juice to a boil in a small pan over medium heat. Continue to boil for 5 minutes without stirring, then remove from the heat and let cool to lukewarm.

5 To finish, cut the cooled cake into diamonds or rectangles in the pan, and pour the warm syrup over it. Top each piece with an almond.

MAKES ONE 9 × 13-INCH CAKE, ABOUT 24 SERVINGS

CAKE BATTER

5 large eggs

1 cup sugar

½ pound (2 sticks) unsalted butter, melted

1 cup (about 4 ounces) coarsely chopped blanched or unblanched almonds

Grated zest of 1 lemon

1 teaspoon vanilla extract

½ teaspoon ground cinnamon

2 cups farina or Cream of Wheat

1 tablespoon baking powder

LEMON SYRUP

2 cups sugar

1 cup water

1 tablespoon fresh lemon juice

24 blanched whole almonds for finishing

One 9 × 13-inch baking pan, bottom lined with parchment or wax paper

VARIATIONS

This cake can also be baked in a 10-inch round cake pan. Cut it into 24 slim slices, with an almond on each.

Some recipes use semolina instead of farina. Some add ½ teaspoon rose water to the syrup after it has cooled to lukewarm.

NOTE: Grate the zest of the lemon before squeezing the juice—it is much easier than trying to do it the other way around.

BRAUNE LINZERTORTE
Dark Linzertorte

THIS TRADITIONAL VIENNESE SWEET has a texture more like cake than pastry. It's a perfect make-ahead dessert because it freezes and defrosts perfectly.

1 Position a rack in the middle of the oven and preheat to 350 degrees.

2 To make the dough, mix all the dry ingredients together in a bowl. Rub in the butter until the mixture looks like fine sand. Beat the egg and yolk together and use a fork to stir them into the dough, stirring only until the dough is smooth. It will be very soft.

3 Spread half the dough over the bottom of the springform pan. Cover the dough with the raspberry preserves, leaving a 1-inch border of pastry all around. Using a pastry bag fitted with a ⅜-inch plain tube (Ateco 804), pipe a diagonal lattice of dough over the preserves, then pipe a border of large dots around the outer rim. Gently paint the lattice and border with the beaten egg white and strew with the sliced almonds.

4 Bake the torte for about 40 minutes. Cool in the pan on a rack.

5 Remove the sides of the pan and loosen the bottom of the torte with the point of a small knife. Slide the torte onto a platter and dust with confectioners' sugar.

DOUGH

1½ cups all-purpose flour (spoon flour into dry-measure cup and level off)

1 cup (about 5 ounces) ground hazelnuts

¾ cup sugar

1 teaspoon ground cinnamon

¼ teaspoon ground cloves

1 teaspoon baking powder

12 tablespoons (1½ sticks) butter

1 large egg

1 large egg yolk

FOR FINISHING

⅔ cup raspberry preserves

1 large egg white, lightly beaten

¼ cup (about 1 ounce) sliced blanched almonds

Confectioners' sugar

One 9-inch springform pan, buttered

SERVING: This is good as either a dessert or a tea cake.

STORAGE: Store loosely covered at room temperature for up to 2 days, or wrap tightly and freeze.

MAKES ONE 9-INCH CAKE, ABOUT 12 SERVINGS

VARIATION

WEISSE LINZERTORTE (WHITE LINZERTORTE): Substitute ground blanched almonds for the hazelnuts. Omit the cinnamon and add the grated zest of 1 lemon and 1 teaspoon vanilla to the egg and yolk before stirring them into the dough.

TORTA DI NOCCIOLE
ALLA VERONESE
Hazelnut Cake from Verona

THIS RICH AND VIRTUALLY FLOURLESS CAKE is popular in the hazelnut-growing areas outside Verona. Although the original does not demand it, the torta would be wonderful with a little lightly whipped unsweetened cream.

1 Set a rack in the middle of the oven and preheat to 350 degrees.

2 Put the hazelnuts in a food processor and pulse until finely ground but not oily. Transfer them to a bowl and pour the bread crumbs over them, but don't mix them together.

3 With a heavy-duty mixer fitted with the whip, beat the yolks. Beat in the Marsala, then beat in ⅓ cup of the sugar. Continue beating until the mixture is very light.

4 In a clean, dry bowl (and clean beaters), or in a heavy-duty mixer fitted with the clean, dry whip, beat the egg whites with the salt. Continue beating until the whites hold a very soft peak. Increase the speed to medium-high and beat in the remaining ⅓ cup sugar in a slow stream. Continue to beat until the egg whites hold a soft, shiny peak.

5 Fold in the yolk mixture, then fold in the hazelnut and bread crumb mixture just until it is half incorporated. Pour the melted butter down the side of the bowl and continue to fold until the batter is smooth, making sure that the tip of the spatula reaches the bottom of the

2 cups (about 10 ounces) unblanched hazelnuts

½ cup fine dry bread crumbs

4 large eggs, separated

3 tablespoons sweet Marsala or dark rum

⅔ cup sugar

Pinch salt

8 tablespoons (1 stick) unsalted butter, melted

Confectioners' sugar for finishing

One 2-inch-deep 10-inch round cake pan, buttered and bottom lined with parchment

bowl on every pass through the batter so that none of the ingredients will remain unmixed at the bottom of the bowl. Be careful not to overmix, or the batter will deflate.

6 Pour the batter into the prepared pan. Bake for about 30 minutes, or until the top is well colored and the center is firm when pressed with a fingertip.

7 Cool the torta in the pan for a minute, then loosen it from the sides of the pan with the point of a small paring knife and invert onto a rack. Invert again onto another rack so the cake cools right side up on the paper.

8 Just before serving, lightly dust the torta with confectioners' sugar.

STORAGE: Keep tightly covered with plastic at room temperature, or refrigerate; bring to room temperature before serving.

MAKES ONE 10-INCH CAKE,
ABOUT 12 SERVINGS

CAKES

CHOCOLATE CAKES

ALTHOUGH THERE ARE CHOCOLATE CAKES throughout this book, the ones here are so specifically and unabashedly chocolate with a capital C they need a section of their own.

Many of these recipes call for melted chocolate. There are two ways to melt chocolate. For either method, begin by cutting the chocolate into ¼-inch pieces.

1 Place the chocolate in a heatproof bowl. Bring a small pan of water to a boil, then take it off the heat. Set the bowl of chocolate over the pan of water and stir occasionally until the chocolate melts.

2 Or, place the cut-up chocolate in a microwave-safe bowl. Microwave the chocolate for 20 seconds at a time, removing it and stirring between blasts.

Using either method, up to a pound of chocolate will melt in 3 to 4 minutes.

PERFECT CHOCOLATE CAKE

THIS ELEGANT AND EASY CAKE is adapted from a recipe in *Sweet Times* (Morrow, 1991), the first book of many by my friend baker and writer Dorie Greenspan, prizewinning author of *Baking with Julia* (Morrow, 1996).

1 Position a rack in the middle of the oven and preheat to 350 degrees.

2 In a bowl, stir together the flour, cocoa, baking powder, and baking soda. Sift the ingredients onto a piece of parchment or wax paper and set aside.

3 In a large bowl with an electric mixer, beat the butter and sugar together at medium speed. Beat in the eggs one at a time, beating until smooth after each addition. Reduce the mixer speed to low and beat in half the dry ingredients. Scrape down the bowl and beater well. Beat in the sour cream, scrape again, and then beat in the remainder of the dry ingredients.

4 Scrape the batter into the prepared pan. Bake for 40 to 45 minutes, or until well risen and a toothpick inserted into the center of the cake emerges clean.

5 Cool the cake in the pan on a rack for 5 minutes, then invert onto a rack and remove the paper. Invert the cake onto a rack again to finish cooling right side up.

6 Just before serving, sift a light dusting of confectioners' sugar over the cake.

1½ cups all-purpose flour (spoon flour into dry-measure cup and level off)

½ cup alkalized (Dutch-process) cocoa powder

1 teaspoon baking powder

¼ teaspoon baking soda

½ pound (2 sticks) unsalted butter, softened

1⅓ cups sugar

2 large eggs, at room temperature

One 8-ounce container sour cream

Confectioners' sugar for finishing

One 9 × 13 × 2-inch baking pan, buttered and bottom lined with parchment or buttered parchment

SERVING: Cut the cake into 3-inch squares.

STORAGE: Store covered at cool room temperature.

MAKES ONE 9 × 13-INCH CAKE, ABOUT 12 SERVINGS

MILK CHOCOLATE MOUSSE CAKE

☙ ❧

THIS RICH CAKE is easy to whip up at the last minute.

1   Position a rack in the middle of the oven and preheat to 325 degrees.

2   In a medium saucepan, bring the water and sugar to a simmer over medium heat, stirring occasionally to dissolve the sugar. Add the butter and cook, stirring occasionally, until the butter is melted. Remove the pan from the heat, add the chocolate, and swirl the pan until chocolate is entirely submerged. Let stand for 2 minutes to melt the chocolate.

3   Meanwhile, in a large mixing bowl, whisk the eggs with the rum and orange zest.

4   Whisk the chocolate mixture until smooth, then whisk it into the egg mixture.

5   Pour the batter into the prepared pan and place the cake pan into the larger one. Pour about 1 inch warm water into that larger pan. Bake for about 1 hour, or until the cake is well risen and firm in the center.

6   Remove the pans from the oven and carefully, using a wide spatula, lift the cake pan out of the larger pan. Cool the cake in the pan on a rack, then wrap the cake, in the pan, and refrigerate.

¾ cup water

¼ cup sugar

8 tablespoons (1 stick) unsalted butter, cut into 8 pieces

18 ounces milk chocolate, cut into ¼-inch pieces

7 large eggs

2 tablespoons dark rum or other liqueur

1 tablespoon grated orange zest

Thinned cream and raspberries for finishing

One 2-inch-deep 8-inch round cake pan, buttered and bottom lined with buttered parchment or wax paper; a larger baking pan or roasting pan to hold the cake pan

7   To unmold the cake, set the pan over low heat for a few seconds to melt the butter between the pan and paper lining. Run a small sharp paring knife around the sides of the pan to loosen the cake. Invert the cake onto a platter and pull off the paper if stuck to cake.

8   Sprinkle the cake lightly with chocolate shavings.

SERVING: Cut into thin wedges to serve.

STORAGE: Store loosely covered at cool room temperature for up to 6 hours; wrap and refrigerate leftovers. For longer storage, leave the cake in the pan, wrap, and refrigerate for up to 1 week or freeze for up to 1 month.

MAKES ONE 8-INCH CAKE, ABOUT 12 SERVINGS

CHOCOLATE PECAN CARAMEL CAKE

⁓ ৩ ৫⁓

THIS IS A GREAT MAKE-AHEAD CAKE for the holiday season. The smooth chocolate of the cake contrasts beautifully with the crunchy pecan caramel topping.

1 Position a rack in the lower third of the oven and preheat to 325 degrees.

2 Stir together the sugar and ¼ cup water in a small saucepan to mix, then bring to a boil over medium heat and cook, without stirring, until the sugar has melted and turned a deep amber. While the sugar is cooking, bring the remaining ¾ cup water to a simmer.

3 Use the water to dilute the caramel to a syrup, adding it a little at a time; make sure to avert your face and to wrap a towel around the hand holding the water pan so you won't be burned by any splattering boiling syrup. Bring the syrup to a good boil to make sure all the caramel is dissolved, and remove from heat. Add the butter and both chocolates and let stand for 2 minutes to melt. Whisk until smooth, then whisk in the eggs two at a time.

4 Pour the batter into the prepared pan, put it into the larger pan, and pour about an inch of hot water into that pan. Bake for about 45 minutes, or until the cake is firm to the touch. Cool on a rack, then refrigerate.

5 To make the pecan caramel, stir the sugar and lemon juice together in a small heavy pan to mix, refrigerate until chilled, place over medium heat, and cook, stirring occasionally, until the mixture becomes a deep amber

CAKE BATTER

¾ cup sugar

1 cup water

6 tablespoons (¾ stick) unsalted butter cut into 6 pieces

8 ounces milk chocolate, cut into ¼-inch pieces

6 ounces bittersweet chocolate, cut into ¼-inch pieces

8 large eggs

PECAN CARAMEL

1 cup (about 4 ounces) pecan pieces, toasted

½ cup sugar

½ teaspoon fresh lemon juice

WHIPPED CREAM

¾ cup heavy whipping cream

1 tablespoon sugar

One 9-inch round cake pan, buttered and bottom lined with buttered parchment; a larger baking pan or roasting pan to hold the cake pan; a jelly-roll pan, buttered for the caramelized pecans

caramel. Stir in the pecans, then pour out onto the buttered pan to cool and harden.

6   When the pecan caramel is cool, finely chop or grind it.

7   To finish the cake, whip the cream with the sugar. Pipe or spread it over the cake. Just before serving, sprinkle the cake with the chopped pecan caramel.

SERVING: Cut into thin wedges to serve.

STORAGE: Store at cool room temperature for up to 6 hours, or, for longer storage, wrap well and freeze up to 1 month.

MAKES ONE 9-INCH CAKE,
ABOUT 10 SERVINGS

CHOCOLATE EMINENCE

Milk Chocolate–Filled Cake with Crunchy Caramelized Hazelnuts

THIS IS A GREAT COMBINATION of flavors and textures. The slightly bitter, crunchy caramelized hazelnuts contrast perfectly with the smooth, rich milk chocolate filling.

1   Position a rack in the middle of the oven and preheat to 350 degrees.

2   Combine the chocolate and water in a heatproof bowl, place the bowl over a pan of hot, but not simmering, water, and stir occasionally until the chocolate is melted and the mixture is smooth. Remove from the heat.

3   In the bowl of a heavy-duty mixer fitted with the whip, beat the yolks with ¼ cup of the sugar until very light.

4   In a clean, dry mixer bowl, with the clean, dry whip, beat the egg whites with the salt until they begin to hold a very soft peak. Raise the speed to medium-high and beat in the remaining ¼ cup sugar in a slow stream.

5   Mix the chocolate mixture into the yolk mixture, then fold in the egg whites.

6   Pour the batter into the prepared pan and smooth the top. Bake for about 15 to 20 minutes, until the top is firm to the touch. Remove the pan from the oven and loosen the sides of the cake with a small sharp knife. Use the paper to help you slide the layer onto a work surface to cool.

CAKE BATTER

6 ounces bittersweet chocolate, cut into ¼-inch pieces

3 tablespoons water

5 large eggs, separated

½ cup sugar

Pinch salt

MILK CHOCOLATE GANACHE

1½ cups heavy cream

4 tablespoons (½ stick) unsalted butter

12 ounces milk chocolate, cut into ¼-inch pieces

HAZELNUT PRALINE

½ cup sugar

½ teaspoon fresh lemon juice

½ cup (about 3 ounces) skinned toasted hazelnuts

Cocoa powder for finishing

One 12 × 18-inch jelly-roll pan, buttered and lined with buttered parchment paper; another jelly-roll pan, buttered, for the praline

7 To make the ganache, bring the cream and butter to a boil. Remove from the heat and add the chocolate. Let chocolate melt, then stir. Whisk until smooth, and refrigerate until thickened, about 1 hour.

8 Meanwhile, prepare the praline. In a medium saucepan, stir the sugar and lemon juice together to mix well. Place over low heat and stir occasionally until sugar is melted and caramelized. Stir in the hazelnuts and scrape the mixture out onto the buttered pan. Allow to cool and harden.

9 Break up the praline and grind to a coarse powder in the food processor.

10 To assemble the cake, using a cake pan as a guide, cut two 9-inch disks out of the cake layer. Dice the scraps and reserve them.

11 In the bowl of a heavy-duty mixer fitted with the whip attachment, whip the ganache to lighten it. Place one cake layer on a cardboard round and spread with one-third of the ganache. Sprinkle with half the praline, and all of the diced cake scraps. Spread another third of the ganache over the cake scraps and top with the other layer. Cover the top and sides of the cake with the rest of the ganache. Press the remaining praline into the sides of the cake.

12 Just before serving, dust the top of the cake with cocoa powder and mark a lattice pattern in the cocoa with a serrated knife.

SERVING: Serve at cool room temperature.

STORAGE: Cover cake lightly and refrigerate for up to two days. Bring to room temperature before serving.

MAKES ONE 9-INCH CAKE,
ABOUT 12 SERVINGS

TUNNEL OF FUDGE CAKE

❧

THIS IS THE RECIPE with which Ella Rita Helfrich of Houston, Texas, won the 1966 Pillsbury Bake-Off. It's still a winner. While baking, the cake develops a creamy, fudgy core, like a tunnel, hence the name.

1 Position a rack in the middle of the oven and preheat to 350 degrees.

2 In a large bowl, with an electric mixer, beat the sugar and butter together on medium speed until light and fluffy. Add the eggs one at a time, beating well after each addition. Gradually beat in the confectioners' sugar. Stir in the flour, cocoa, and nuts until well blended.

3 Spoon the batter into the prepared pan and smooth the top. Bake for 45 to 50 minutes, or until the top is set and the edges are beginning to pull away from the sides of the pan (this cake has a soft center, so the ordinary doneness test of inserting a toothpick does not work).

4 Cool the cake (upright) in the pan on a wire rack for 1½ hours, then invert onto a serving plate and let cool for at least 2 hours.

5 To make the glaze, in a small bowl, stir together all the ingredients, adding enough milk to achieve a drizzling consistency. Spoon over top of the cake, allowing some to run down the sides.

SERVING: This is really a dessert cake—it's great with some whipped cream.

CAKE BATTER

1¾ cups sugar

28 tablespoons (3½ sticks) unsalted butter, softened

6 large eggs

2 cups confectioners' sugar

2¼ cups all-purpose flour (spoon flour into dry-measure cup and level off)

¾ cup alkalized (Dutch-process) cocoa powder

2 cups (about 8 ounces) chopped walnuts

CHOCOLATE GLAZE

¾ cup confectioners' sugar

¼ cup alkalized (Dutch-process) cocoa powder

6 to 8 teaspoons milk

One 10-inch Bundt or tube pan, buttered

STORAGE: Store under a cake dome at room temperature; press plastic wrap against the cut surfaces of the cake to prevent excessive ooze.

MAKES ONE 10-INCH BUNDT OR TUBE CAKE, ABOUT 16 SERVINGS

LAYER CAKES

THESE CLASSIC "GOOEY" CAKES, rich with filling and frosting surrounding moist, flavorful cake layers, are among the most popular of all baked sweets.

To ensure success with layer cakes, keep in mind the following points.

1   Use a long very sharp serrated knife to trim or cut through layers. This is a case of the right tool making all the difference between success and failure.

2   After cutting through or trimming cake layer(s), brush the work surface free of crumbs, which otherwise have a way of getting mixed into the frosting when you put your spatula down.

3   Use an offset spatula to spread on fillings and frostings. The side of the blade is best for making flat, even layers of filling.

4   Don't fuss endlessly over the outside of the cake—if it isn't perfect, you can always use some chocolate shavings or chopped nuts to mask any flaws.

RASPBERRY CREAM CAKE

∽૭ ૯∼

THIS CAKE IS A SORT OF RASPBERRY VERSION of the famous Black Forest cherry cake.

1 To make the whipped cream, combine the cream, sugar, and vanilla in a large bowl and whip until soft peaks form.

2 To assemble, place one of the cake layers on a cardboard cake round and spread with a thin layer of whipped cream. Cover with most of the raspberries, reserving a few for garnish, then cover the berries with more cream. Add the second layer and cover the top and sides of the cake with the remaining whipped cream. Press chocolate shavings into the sides of the cake and decorate the top with the reserved raspberries.

3 Just before serving, dust the cake lightly with confectioners' sugar.

SERVING: This cake is best served as soon as it is assembled. It is delicious with additional fresh raspberries on the side.

STORAGE: Store in the refrigerator, covered, for up to 2 days.

MAKES ONE 9-INCH CAKE,
ABOUT 12 SERVINGS

WHIPPED CREAM

2 cups heavy whipping cream

¼ cup sugar

1 teaspoon vanilla extract

Two 9-inch layers 1942 Devil's Food Cake, page 339

Two ½-pint baskets raspberries

FOR FINISHING

Chocolate shavings

Confectioners' sugar

GATEAU DES ILES

⦾ ᧿ ᧿

THIS "ISLAND CAKE" COMBINES the flavors of the Caribbean in a sweet, delicate tribute.

1 To make the syrup, bring the water and sugar to a boil in a small saucepan. Let cool, and stir in the rum.

2 To make the filling, combine the cream, coconut cream, and vanilla in a bowl and whip to form soft peaks.

3 To assemble the cake, split the génoise horizontally into 3 layers. Place the bottom layer on a cardboard cake round and moisten with some of the syrup. Spread with one-third of the whipped cream and top with half the pineapple. Repeat with the next layer, more syrup, another third of the cream, and most of the remaining pineapple. Top with the last layer and moisten with the remaining syrup.

4 Cover the top and sides of the cake with the remaining whipped cream and press the coconut into it. Decorate with the pineapple wedges.

NOTE: Coconut cream is a sweetened coconut product usually used for making drinks. The most common brand is Coco Lopez.

RUM SYRUP

1/3 cup water

1/3 cup sugar

1/3 cup white rum

COCONUT FILLING

2 cups heavy whipping cream

1/2 cup coconut cream (see Note)

1 teaspoon vanilla extract

1 cup chopped fresh pineapple

One 9-inch layer Plain Génoise, page 272

2 cups (about 3½ ounces) sweetened shredded coconut for finishing

6 or 8 pineapple wedges

SERVING: This cake is best served as soon as it is assembled.

STORAGE: Store loosely covered in the refrigerator for up to 2 days.

MAKES ONE 9-INCH CAKE, ABOUT 12 SERVINGS

CHOCOLATE-PISTACHIO-RASPBERRY CAKE

～◎ ◎～

THIS STRIKING AND UNUSUAL DESSERT combines three flavors that harmonize beautifully in both taste and appearance.

CAKE BATTER

1 cup (about 4 ounces) blanched pistachios

½ cup all-purpose flour (spoon flour into dry-measure cup and level off)

4 large eggs, separated

¾ cup sugar

Pinch salt

GANACHE FILLING

8 ounces bittersweet chocolate, cut into ¼-inch pieces

2 ounces milk chocolate, cut into ¼-inch pieces

1 cup heavy whipping cream

FRAMBOISE SYRUP

⅓ cup water

⅓ cup sugar

⅓ cup framboise (raspberry eau-de-vie)

WHIPPED CREAM

1½ cups heavy whipping cream

2 tablespoons sugar

2 tablespoons framboise

FOR FINISHING

Two ½-pint baskets raspberries

Milk chocolate shavings

Blanched pistachios

One 2-inch-deep 10-inch round cake pan, buttered and bottom lined with parchment or wax paper

1 Position a rack in the middle of the oven and preheat to 350 degrees.

2 Grind the pistachios until fine in the food processor; make sure they don't become pasty. Combine with the flour.

3 In the bowl of a heavy-duty mixer fitted with the whisk, beat the egg yolks with 6 tablespoons of the sugar until light.

4 In a clean, dry mixer bowl, with a clean, dry whisk, beat the egg whites with the salt on medium speed until they become white and opaque. Increase the speed to medium-high and beat in the remaining 6 tablespoons sugar. Continue to beat until the whites hold a firm peak. Fold in the yolks, then fold in the pistachio mixture.

5 Pour the batter into prepared pan and bake for about 30 minutes. Unmold the layer onto a rack, then invert onto another rack to cool.

6 To make the ganache, combine the chocolates in a bowl. Bring the cream to a boil and pour over the chocolate. Let stand for 2 minutes, then whisk until smooth. Refrigerate the ganache, whisking often, until cool but not set.

7 To make the syrup, combine the water and sugar in a small pan and bring to a boil. Let cool, and stir in the framboise.

8 To make the whipped cream, combine the cream, sugar, and framboise in a large bowl and whip until light but not firm.

9 To assemble the dessert, split the pistachio cake horizontally into 2 layers. Place one on a cardboard cake round. Moisten with half the syrup and spread wwith most of the ganache, reserving some for decoration. Distribute most of the raspberries over the ganache, again

saving some for decorating. Cover with a layer of whipped cream. Place the second layer on the cream and moisten it with the remaining syrup. Cover the top and sides of the cake with the remaining whipped cream and press the chocolate shavings into the sides of the cake.

10 Pipe a border of rosettes around the top edge of the cake with the remaining ganache and decorate the rosettes with the reserved raspberries and some pistachios. Place some chopped pistachios in the center and dust them lightly with confectioners' sugar.

SERVING: Serve chilled.

STORAGE: Store covered in the refrigerator for up to 2 days.

MAKES ONE 10-INCH CAKE, ABOUT 12 SERVINGS

STRAWBERRY MERINGUE CAKE

~~ ୨ ୧ ~~

THIS IS AN IDEAL CAKE for June and July, when strawberries are at their peak. The fruit filling and the meringue are light, and because the recipe calls for neither whipped cream nor buttercream, there is nothing to melt in hot weather.

1 To make the filling, rinse, hull, and slice the berries. Place one-quarter of the berries in a saucepan with the sugar and bring to a boil.

2 Meanwhile, combine the lemon juice, kirsch, and cornstarch. Off the heat, stir the cornstarch mixture into the strawberry mixture. Return to a boil, stirring, and cook for 2 minutes. Remove from the heat and cool, then stir in the remaining sliced berries.

3 To make the syrup, combine the water and sugar in a small pan and bring to a boil; cool. Stir in the lemon juice and kirsch.

4 Use a sharp serrated knife to slice each of the génoise layers into 2 layers. Only 3 layers will be used to assemble the cake. Place one layer on a cardboard round or platter and brush with one-third of the syrup. Spread with half the filling. Top with the second layer and, brush with syrup, and spread with the remaining filling. Place the last layer on top and moisten with the remaining syrup.

5 Meanwhile, preheat the oven to 400°F.

6 To make the meringue, combine the egg whites and sugar in the bowl of an electric mixer. Whisk over simmering water until the egg whites are hot and the sugar is dissolved.

STRAWBERRY FILLING

2 pints strawberries

½ cup sugar

1 tablespoon fresh lemon juice

1 tablespoon kirsch

2 tablespoons cornstarch

LEMON-KIRSCH SYRUP

⅓ cup water

⅓ cup sugar

2 tablespoons fresh lemon juice

2 tablespoons kirsch

COVERING MERINGUE

¾ cup egg whites (from 6 or 7 large eggs)

1 cup sugar

Two 10-inch layers Classic Génoise, page 272

Attach the bowl to the mixer and beat with the whisk at medium speed until the meringue has increased in volume and is cool.

7 Frost the top and sides of the cake with the meringue.

8 Place the cake on a cookie sheet and put in the oven for just 3 to 4 minutes to color the meringue. Remove the cake from the oven

and cool, then decorate with the reserved strawberries and the sliced almonds.

SERVING: Serve the cake as soon as it has cooled.

STORAGE: Refrigerate leftovers.

MAKES ONE 9-INCH CAKE, ABOUT 12 SERVINGS

APRICOT MARZIPAN CAKE

〜◜◞◟〜

THIS IS A VARIATION OF A FAMOUS Viennese sponge cake called a Punschtorte, which is soaked with a flavorful rum syrup and covered with marzipan. It is a perfect summer cake because there is no filling or frosting to melt in the heat.

1   To make the syrup, bring the sugar and water to a boil in a small saucepan. Cool, and stir in the rum, orange juice, lemon juice, and vanilla.

2   To make the glaze, bring the preserves and water to a boil in a small saucepan over medium heat, stirring occasionally. Strain into another pan and simmer until the glaze becomes sticky. Set aside.

3   To make the marzipan, in the bowl of a heavy-duty mixer, beat the almond paste and 1 cup of the sugar with the paddle attachment on low speed until the sugar is almost absorbed. Add the remaining 1 cup sugar and beat slowly until the mixture resembles fine crumbs. Add the corn syrup a little at a time, stopping frequently and checking to see if you can knead the marzipan smooth; the marzipan will still appear crumbly, and you may not need all the syrup. Remove to a work surface and knead until smooth. Pull off a small piece of the marzipan and wrap in plastic. Add

PUNCH SYRUP

¼ cup water

⅓ cup sugar

¼ cup dark rum

¼ cup fresh orange juice

2 tablespoons fresh lemon juice

1 teaspoon vanilla extract

APRICOT GLAZE

1½ cups apricot preserves

¼ cup water

MARZIPAN

4 ounces almond paste

2 cups confectioners' sugar

About ⅓ cup light corn syrup

Red food coloring

Cornstarch for rolling out the marzipan

One 9-inch layer Classic Génoise,
    page 272

DECORATION

1 ounce semisweet chocolate, melted

enough coloring to the remaining marzipan to tint it a pale pink, then wrap it in plastic.

4 Slice the cake horizontally into 3 layers and place one on a platter or cardboard round. Moisten with syrup and brush with glaze. Top with the second layer, moisten it, and brush with glaze. Place the remaining layer on top and brush the top and sides of the cake with the glaze.

5 Dust a work surface with cornstarch. Roll out the pink marzipan to a thin round about 14 inches in diameter. Drape it over the cake and trim away the excess. Gather the scraps together, and roll into a rope under your palms. Use the rope to finish the bottom of the cake. Use a paper cone to pipe a chocolate design on the cake with the melted chocolate. Finally, make a flower or other decoration from the reserved white marzipan for the center of the cake.

SERVING: Cut into thin slices to serve.

STORAGE: Store at a cool room temperature for up to 2 days.

MAKES ONE 9-INCH CAKE, ABOUT 16 SERVINGS

COCONUT-RASPBERRY LAYER CAKE

～୭ ౿～

THIS IS A GREAT COMBINATION of colors, tastes, and textures—raspberry preserves, white cake layers, lemon buttercream, and fluffy white coconut. A perfect old-fashioned layer cake.

CAKE BATTER

2¼ cups cake flour (spoon flour into dry-measure cup and level off)

1 tablespoon baking powder

½ teaspoon salt

8 tablespoons (1 stick) unsalted butter, softened

1½ cups sugar

2 teaspoons finely grated lemon zest

½ teaspoon lemon extract

1¼ cups milk

½ cup egg whites (from about 3 to 4 large eggs)

LEMON BUTTERCREAM

½ cup egg whites (from about 4 large eggs)

1 cup sugar

20 tablespoons (2½ sticks) unsalted butter, softened

¼ cup strained fresh lemon juice

1 teaspoon vanilla extract

FOR FINISHING

½ cup seedless raspberry preserves

One 7-ounce bag sweetened shredded coconut

Two 9-inch round cake pans, buttered and bottoms lined with buttered parchment or wax paper

1 Position a rack in the middle of the oven and preheat to 350 degrees.

2 Sift the cake flour, baking powder, and salt onto a piece of parchment or wax paper.

3 In the bowl of a heavy-duty mixer, beat the butter and sugar with the paddle attachment at medium speed until light, about 3 minutes. Beat in the lemon zest and extract.

4 In a bowl, whisk together the milk and egg whites. Add one-third of the flour mixture to the butter mixture and beat until smooth. Scrape down the bowl and beaters. Beat in half the egg white mixture until incorporated, then beat in another third of the flour mixture. Scrape down the bowl and beaters. Beat in the remaining liquid until absorbed, followed by the remaining flour mixture; scrape well after each addition.

5 Divide the batter between the prepared pans and smooth the tops. Bake for about 30 to 35 minutes, until well risen and a toothpick inserted in the center emerges clean. Cool the layers in pans for 5 minutes, then invert onto racks to cool. Peel off the paper.

6 To make the buttercream, whisk together the egg whites and sugar in the bowl of an

electric mixer. Whisk over a pan of simmering water until the egg whites are hot and the sugar is dissolved. Attach the bowl to the mixer and whip with the whisk until cool and increased in volume. Switch to the paddle attachment and beat in the butter until smooth. Beat in the lemon juice and vanilla.

7 To assemble the cake, slice each layer horizontally in half. Place one layer on a cardboard round or a platter and spread with one-third of the jam and one-quarter of the buttercream. Top with another layer and repeat. Repeat with the third layer. Place the last layer on top and spread the top and sides of the cake with the remaining buttercream.

Press the coconut all over the outside of the cake.

SERVING: Serve at cool room temperature.

STORAGE: Cover loosely and refrigerate for up to 2 days; bring to room temperature before serving.

MAKES ONE 9-INCH CAKE,
ABOUT 12 SERVINGS

BUTTER CAKE LAYERS

MOST OF THE FOLLOWING RECIPES, which are used for the layer cakes in this chapter, are mixed according to traditional methods, but none of them includes whipped egg whites as a component—I think they make the cake layers more complicated to prepare and don't really contribute much to the lightness of the finished cake.

If the sugar weighs the same as the flour or more, you can use the high-ratio method (see page 229) to mix the batter. Mix and match these layers with the recipes in this chapter and with fillings, frostings, and glazes.

1942 DEVIL'S FOOD CAKE LAYERS

THIS RECIPE COMES FROM Virginia Lo Biondo, my aunt Virginia's sister-in-law. Mrs. Lo Biondo told me she got the recipe from a neighbor during World War II and that it was already an old recipe at the time. It's her family's favorite cake. Frost with fluffy white icing or whipped ganache.

3 ounces unsweetened chocolate

1 Position a rack in the middle of the oven and preheat to 350 degrees.

2 Melt the chocolate in a large heatproof bowl set over hot, but not simmering, water. Let cool.

3 Stir together the flour, baking soda, and salt in a bowl, mixing well.

4 Add the butter to the chocolate, then pour in the boiling water and stir well to mix. Whisk in the sugar and sour cream. Stir in the flour mixture. Whisk in the eggs.

5 Pour the batter into the prepared pans and smooth the tops.

6 Bake for about 25 to 30 minutes, or until the layers are well risen and firm to the touch; and a toothpick inserted emerges clean. Cool the layers in the pans on racks for 5 minutes, then unmold onto racks to finish cooling.

1⅓ cups bleached all-purpose flour (spoon flour into dry-measure cup and level off)

¾ teaspoon baking soda

½ teaspoon salt

6 tablespoons (¾ stick) unsalted butter, cut into 6 pieces

¾ cup boiling water

1½ cups sugar

6 tablespoons sour cream or buttermilk

2 large eggs

Two 9-inch round cake pans, buttered and bottoms lined with parchment or wax paper

CAKES

STORAGE: If you are going to use the layers the day you bake them, wrap in plastic and keep at room temperature. Double-wrap and freeze for longer storage.

MAKES TWO 9-INCH ROUND LAYERS

ROLLED CAKES

ROLLED CAKES FALL INTO THE CATEGORY of baked things that are as much fun and as interesting to make as they are to eat! Most rolled cakes are really easy to prepare. To make sure they turn out perfectly, just bear in mind a few tricks.

1   Be sure not to overbake the cake—a dry cake is impossible to roll.

2   To help conserve moisture after the cake is baked, cool it, on the paper it was baked on, on a countertop rather than a rack.

3   Spread the filling over the top of the cake, so that the surface that was against the bottom of the pan becomes the outside of the roll.

4   Don't be afraid of rolling the cake: once you have positioned the cake on its paper as directed, give a fold and just lift the paper—the paper will push the cake and make it roll itself up.

5   To tighten the cake around the filling, holding the bottom of the paper, press on the top of the roll, through the paper, with the side of a clipboard or cookie sheet.

6   Chill the roll to set the filling in a nice cylindrical shape. Then finish the cake after it has chilled. Bring it back to room temperature to serve unless it is filled and finished with whipped cream, in which case, keep it refrigerated until serving.

7   When serving, two thinner slices of a rolled cake look better to serve than one thick one.

BUCHE DE NOEL

∽ 𝒞 ∼

THERE ARE MANY FLAVOR and presentation variations for the traditional French Christmas log. I like this one because chocolate cake and coffee buttercream are not an excessively sweet combination. The marzipan decorations can be prepared well in advance and kept loosely covered until needed.

1 To make the buttercream, whisk the egg whites and sugar together in the bowl of an electric mixer. Set the bowl over simmering water and whisk gently until the sugar is dissolved and the egg whites are hot. Attach the bowl to the mixer and whip with the whisk on medium speed until cooled. Switch to the paddle and beat in the softened butter and continue beating until the buttercream is smooth. Dissolve the instant coffee in the liquor and beat into the buttercream.

2 Turn the génoise layer over and peel away the paper. Invert onto a fresh piece of paper. Spread the layer with half the buttercream. Use the paper to help you roll the cake into a tight cylinder. Transfer to baking sheet and refrigerate. Reserve the remaining buttercream for the outside of the bûche.

3 To make the marzipan, combine the almond paste and 1 cup of the sugar in the bowl of an electric mixer and beat with the paddle attachment on low speed until the sugar is almost absorbed. Add the remaining 1 cup sugar and mix until the mixture resembles fine crumbs. Add half the corn syrup, then continue mixing until a bit of the marzipan holds together when squeezed, adding

COFFEE BUTTERCREAM

4 large egg whites

1 cup sugar

24 tablespoons (3 sticks) unsalted butter, softened

2 tablespoons instant espresso powder

2 tablespoons rum or brandy

1 Chocolate Génoise Sheet, page 273

MARZIPAN

8 ounces almond paste

2 cups confectioners' sugar

3 to 5 tablespoons light corn syrup

FOR FINISHING

Cocoa powder

Red and green food coloring

Confectioners' sugar

additional corn syrup a little at a time, as necessary; the marzipan in the bowl will still appear crumbly. Transfer the marzipan to a work surface and knead until smooth.

4 To make marzipan mushrooms, roll one-third of the marzipan into a 6 inches long cylinder and cut into 1-inch lengths. Roll half the lengths into balls. Press the remaining cylindrical lengths (stems) into the balls (caps) to make mushrooms. Smudge with cocoa powder.

5 To make holly leaves, knead green color into half the remaining marzipan and roll it into a long cylinder. Flatten with the back of a spoon, then loosen it from the surface with a spatula. Cut into diamonds to make leaves, or use a cutter.

6 To make holly berries, knead red color into a tiny piece of marzipan. Roll into tiny balls.

7 To make pinecones, knead cocoa powder into the remaining marzipan. Divide in half and form into 2 cone shapes. Slash the sides of cones with the points of a pair of scissors.

8 Unwrap the cake. Trim the ends on the diagonal, starting the cuts about 2 inches away from each end. Position the larger cut piece on the bûche about ⅔ across the top. Cover the bûche with the reserved buttercream, making sure to curve around the protruding stump. Streak the buttercream with a fork or decorating comb to resemble bark. Transfer the bûche to a platter and decorate with the marzipan. Sprinkle the platter and bûche sparingly with confectioners' sugar "snow."

STORAGE: Keep at cool room temperature. Cover leftovers loosely and keep at room temperature.

MAKES ABOUT 12 SERVINGS

CHOCOLATE SOUFFLE ROLL

~⁹ ℃~

LOOSELY BASED ON JAMES BEARD'S chocolate roll, this is a perfect dessert to prepare on short notice.

1 Position a rack in the middle of the oven and preheat to 350 degrees.

2 Combine the chocolate with the liqueur or water and the butter in a heatproof bowl. Place the bowl over a pan of hot, but not simmering, water and stir occasionally with a rubber spatula until the chocolate is melted and the mixture is smooth. Stir in the yolks one at a time, beating well after each addition.

3 In the bowl of a heavy-duty mixer fitted with the whisk, whip the egg whites with the salt at low speed until they are just beginning to hold a very soft peak, then raise the speed and whip in the sugar in a slow stream. Continue whipping until the egg whites hold a firm peak. Stir one-quarter of the egg whites into the chocolate batter to lighten it, then fold the chocolate batter into the remaining egg whites.

4 Pour the batter into the prepared pan and smooth the top. Bake for about 15 minutes, until the layer is firm to the touch.

5 Remove the pan from the oven and loosen the sides of the cake with a small sharp knife. Using the paper to help, slide the layer onto the work surface to cool, about 20 minutes.

CAKE BATTER

6 ounces semisweet chocolate, finely chopped

¼ cup orange or raspberry liqueur or water

2 tablespoons unsalted butter

6 large eggs, separated

Pinch salt

½ cup sugar

FOR FINISHING

1 cup heavy whipping cream

2 tablespoons sugar

1 tablespoon liqueur, optional

One ½-pint basket raspberries

One 10 × 15-inch jelly-roll pan, buttered and lined with parchment or wax paper

6 To assemble the roll, slide a cookie sheet under the layer. Cover the layer with a clean piece of parchment or wax paper and another pan, and turn the cake over. Lift off the top pan and peel off the paper stuck to the layer. Replace with a clean sheet of paper, replace the pan, and invert again. Remove the top pan and paper.

7 In a medium bowl, whip the cream with the sugar and liqueur, if using, until it holds a firm peak. Use a metal spatula to spread the cream over the layer. To roll the cake, pick up one long edge of the paper and use it to help you ease the layer into a curve, then continue lifting the paper to roll the layer and roll it directly onto a platter, seam side down. Trim the ends of the roll and refrigerate, loosely covered until ready to serve.

8 To serve, decorate each slice with some of the raspberries.

STORAGE: Keep refrigerated until serving time, and refrigerate leftovers.

MAKES ABOUT 12 SERVINGS

WALNUT CREAM ROLL

～ ⌒ ～

ONE OF THE BEST HOLIDAY DESSERTS, and one of the easiest to prepare.

1 Position a rack in the middle of the oven and preheat to 375 degrees.

2 Pulse the walnuts in the bowl of a food processor until finely ground but not pasty. In a bowl sift the flour over the walnuts; do not mix.

3 Whip the yolks with the brown sugar until light. In a clean, dry mixer bowl, whip the whites and salt until they are white and opaque. Whip in the sugar in a stream; whip until the whites hold a firm peak. Fold in the yolk mixture, then fold in the walnut mixture.

4 Spread the batter evenly in the prepared pan. Bake for about 15 minutes, or until the cake is well risen and firm in the center. Slide the cake onto a work surface to cool.

5 To assemble, slide a cookie sheet under the cake and cover it with a clean piece of parchment and another cookie sheet. Invert the cake, lift off the pan, and remove the paper. Cover with a clean piece of paper, replace the pan, and then turn the layer over again. Lift off the top pan and paper.

6 In a medium bowl, whip the cream with the sugar, rum, and vanilla until the cream holds a firm peak. Spread the cake with half the whipped cream and roll up tightly. Place the roll seam side down on a platter, and cover with the remaining cream. Sprinkle with

CAKE BATTER

1⅓ cups (about 5 ounces) walnuts

⅓ cup cake flour (spoon flour into dry-measure cup and level off)

4 large eggs, separated

⅓ cup firmly packed brown sugar

Pinch salt

⅓ cup granulated sugar

WHIPPED CREAM

2½ cups heavy whipping cream

⅓ cup sugar

1 tablespoon dark rum

2 teaspoons vanilla extract

1 cup (4 ounces) chopped toasted walnuts

One 10 × 15-inch jelly-roll pan, buttered and lined with buttered parchment or wax paper

the chopped walnuts. Trim the ends on the diagonal and keep the cake chilled.

STORAGE: Keep refrigerated until serving time, and refrigerate leftovers.

MAKES 12 TO 16 SERVINGS

STRAWBERRY ROULADE

THIS STRAWBERRY ROLL IS ELEGANT in appearance but less rich than a roll covered with whipped cream rather than the light meringue.

1 To make the filling, rinse the strawberries. Select 4 or 5 of the best berries to use for decoration and refrigerate them. Hull and slice the remaining berries. Combine the sliced berries with the sugar, kirsch, and lemon juice in a bowl and refrigerate for 1 hour.

2 Drain the berries, reserving the juice. In a medium bowl, whip the cream with the vanilla. Fold in the berries.

3 To assemble, remove the paper from the bottom of the génoise and place the layer right side up on a clean piece of paper. Moisten the layer with the reserved strawberry juices. Spread with the filling and roll it up, wrapping it tightly in the paper. Place the roll in the freezer on a baking sheet while you prepare the meringue.

4 Preheat the oven to 400°F.

5 Whisk the egg whites and sugar in the bowl of an electric mixer, place over a pan of simmering water, and whisk until the egg whites are hot and the sugar is dissolved. Attach to the mixer and beat with the whip attachment on medium speed until cooled.

STRAWBERRY FILLING
1 pint strawberries

2 tablespoons sugar

1 tablespoon kirsch

2 teaspoons fresh lemon juice

1 cup heavy whipping cream

1 teaspoon vanilla extract

1 plain Génoise Sheet, page 272

COVERING MERINGUE
½ cup (about 4 large) egg whites

⅔ cup sugar

Confectioners' sugar for finishing

6 Place the cake roll on a baking sheet and cover with meringue, reserving a little meringue for decoration. Pipe several rosettes of meringue along the top. Dust the meringue with confectioners' sugar.

7 Place the cake on the center rack in the oven to color the meringue, about 1 to 2 minutes; turn the pan several times so the meringue colors evenly. Cool, then chill the roll.

8 Trim the ends of the cake on a diagonal. Slide the roulade onto a platter and decorate with the reserved strawberries.

STORAGE: Keep refrigerated until serving time, and refrigerate leftovers.

MAKES 12 TO 16 SERVINGS

MOST OF THESE CAKES have fillings that are soft or liquid until they set. Such cakes are made in molds to contain the filling so it sets neatly within the cake. Although there are many types of molds for making such cakes, I still prefer to use a springform pan for most of them: they're easy to find and relatively inexpensive, and, of course, they can be used for cheesecakes and other types of cakes as well. Some of the molded cakes here are made in a dome shape. I usually like to use Pyrex mixing bowls for these. Although they have a flattish bottom, which gives a slightly flat top to the dessert, you can compensate by doming the frosting slightly.

ERDBEEROBERSTORTE
Strawberry Whipped Cream Cake

ALTHOUGH VIENNA HISTORICALLY has been famous for desserts with mountains of whipped cream, this dessert is a little less rich. Try it with raspberries or cherries when they are in season.

CAKE BATTER

5 large eggs

1 teaspoon grated lemon zest

½ cup sugar

1 cup cake flour (spoon flour into dry-measure cup and level off)

ORANGE SYRUP

¼ cup water

¼ cup sugar

¼ cup orange liqueur

STRAWBERRY FILLING

2 pints strawberries

¾ cup sugar

2 envelopes gelatin

⅓ cup water

2 cups heavy whipping cream

FOR FINISHING

1½ cups heavy whipping cream

¼ cup sugar

2 teaspoons vanilla extract

1 pint strawberries, rinsed, halved, and patted dry

Chocolate shavings

Confectioners' sugar

One 10-inch springform pan, buttered and bottom lined with parchment or wax paper

1 Position a rack in the middle of the oven and preheat to 350 degrees.

2 Whisk the eggs, lemon zest, and sugar together in the bowl of an electric mixer. Set over simmering water and whisk until lukewarm. Attach the bowl to the mixer and beat with the whisk on medium speed until increased in volume, and cold.

3 Sift the cake flour over the egg mixture in three or four additions, folding it in with a rubber spatula.

4 Pour the batter into the prepared pan and bake for about 30 minutes. Unmold the cake onto a rack, then invert onto a rack to cool right side up.

5 To make the syrup, bring the sugar and water to a boil in a saucepan. Cool, and stir in the orange liqueur.

6 To make the filling, rinse, hull, and halve the strawberries. Puree half of them in the food processor (you should have 1 cup puree). Whisk the sugar into the puree and set it aside. Reserve the remaining strawberries.

7 Sprinkle the gelatin over the water in a small bowl and let stand until softened. Set the bowl over simmering water and stir to melt the gelatin. Stir a little of the puree into the melted gelatin, then whisk the gelatin into the remaining puree.

8 Whip the cream until it holds a shape and fold it into the puree.

9 Slice the cooled cake horizontally into 2 equal layers. Slice one of the layers horizontally in half. Place the thicker layer in the bottom of the springform pan and moisten it with one-third of the syrup. Pour in half the strawberry filling and distribute the reserved strawberries over the filling. Cover with one of the thin layers and moisten it. Pour in the remaining filling and top with the last layer. Moisten it with the remaining syrup. Refrigerate to set the filling, 4 to 6 hours.

10 To finish, whip the cream with the sugar and vanilla until it holds a shape. Run a knife between the side of the springform and the cake, then unbuckle the side of the pan. Unmold the cake. Cover it completely with the whipped cream, reserving some for decoration. Using a pastry bag fitted with a star tip, decorate the top of the cake with rosettes of whipped cream. Decorate the top of the cake with the strawberries. Press chocolate shavings into the sides of the cake and sprinkle some onto the very center of the top. Dust the chocolate shavings on the top very lightly with confectioners' sugar.

SERVING: Serve the cake shortly after finishing.

STORAGE: Store the filled cake in the refrigerator for up to 2 days. Don't finish with whipped cream and shavings until just prior to serving.

MAKES ONE 10-INCH CAKE, ABOUT 12 SERVINGS

NOTE: You may substitute a 9-inch génoise layer, page 272, for the cake layer here.

SHOGGITORTE

֍

THIS IS A TYPICAL SWISS CHOCOLATE CAKE—Swiss bakers like to combine a rich sponge cake with a light chocolate mousse.

1 To make the mousse, whip the cream in a large bowl until it holds a soft peak. Refrigerate while you prepare the other ingredients.

2 Sprinkle the gelatin over the water in a small bowl and allow to soften for 5 minutes.

3 Whisk the egg whites and sugar together in the bowl of an electric mixer. Set the bowl over a saucepan of simmering water and whisk constantly until the egg whites are hot and the sugar is dissolved, about 3 minutes: test a little between your thumb and forefinger—if the mixture is gritty, continue to heat until all the sugar is dissolved. Whisk the softened gelatin into the egg whites. Attach the bowl to the mixer, fitted with the whisk attachment, and beat the whites until increased in volume, somewhat cooled, and soft and creamy. Do not overbeat, or the meringue will become dry or grainy. Allow the meringue to cool to room temperature, stirring occasionally.

CHOCOLATE MOUSSE FILLING

2 cups heavy whipping cream

1 envelope gelatin

¼ cup cold water

1 cup egg whites (from 7 or 8 large eggs)

1 cup sugar

8 ounces bittersweet chocolate, melted

One 9-inch layer Chocolate Génoise,
    page 273

Chocolate shavings for finishing

One 10-inch springform pan

4 When the meringue is cool, whisk about one-third of it into the chocolate, then quickly fold the chocolate mixture back into the remaining meringue. Quickly rewhip the cream if it has separated, and fold the cream into the chocolate mixture.

5   To assemble, using a sharp serrated knife, slice the génoise into 2 layers. Place one of the cake layers in the springform pan and top with half the mousse. Repeat with the remaining layer and remaining mousse. Refrigerate for at least 8 hours, or overnight.

6   To unmold the cake, run a small knife around the inside of the pan. Release the spring and lift off the sides of the pan. Top with chocolate shavings and press more against the side of the cake.

SERVING: Use a thin knife dipped in hot water and wiped clean after each slice to cut the cake.

STORAGE: Store loosely covered in the refrigerator for at least 8 hours before serving.

MAKES ONE 9-INCH CAKE,
ABOUT 12 SERVINGS

DEVIL'S FOOD BOMBE

〜୨ ୧〜

THIS IS A DELICIOUS AND AMUSING WAY to present a chocolate cake filled with whipped cream. You probably won't use all of both layers to assemble the bombe, but you can save the scraps for a trifle.

1 For the filling, whip the cream with the sugar and vanilla to a soft peak.

2 Cut the cake into thin strips no more than ³⁄₁₆-inch thick. Line the bowl with strips of cake, trimming to fit as necessary. Sprinkle with rum. Spread a layer of whipped cream over the bottom, then cover with strips of cake. Sprinkle the cake with rum and spread with more cream. Continue layering in this manner until the bowl is full, ending with a layer of cake. Wrap the bowl and chill for at least several hours, or overnight.

3 Unmold the cake onto a cardboard round or platter. Whip the cream with the sugar and vanilla to a soft peak, and spread all over the outside of the cake.

SERVING: Use a thin knife dipped in hot water and wiped clean after each slice to cut the cake.

STORAGE: Store loosely covered in the refrigerator for up to 8 hours before serving.

MAKES ABOUT 12 SERVINGS

FILLING

3 cups heavy whipping cream

½ cup sugar

2 teaspoons vanilla extract

One 9-inch layer 1942 Devil's Food Cake, page 339

⅓ cup dark rum

FOR FINISHING

1 cup heavy whipping cream

2 tablespoons sugar

½ teaspoon vanilla extract

One 2½-quart bowl, buttered and lined with plastic wrap

CLASSIC CHOCOLATE CHARLOTTE

~⌇ ⌇~

IN A CLASSIC CHARLOTTE SHAPE, this dessert is as elegant in appearance as in flavor.

1 To line the mold, trim the ends of 6 or 8 of the sponge fingers to a V shape and fit them together in the bottom of the mold. Line the sides of the mold with sponge fingers, saving some to cover the top of the mousse after the mold is filled.

2 To make the mousse, put the chocolate in a heatproof bowl and melt it over a saucepan of hot, but not simmering, water. Remove from the water and beat in the butter.

3 Whisk the yolks, liqueur, and sugar together in the bowl of an electric mixer. Place the bowl over a pan of simmering water and whisk until slightly thickened. Attach the bowl to the mixer and beat with the whisk attachment until cool. Fold in the chocolate mixture.

4 Whip the cream into soft peaks. Fold it into the chocolate mixture and pour into the lined mold. Cover with the reserved sponge fingers. Chill to set the mousse, at least 8 hours, or overnight.

5 Unmold the charlotte onto a platter.

Ladyfingers, page 274-275 in sponge cake chapter

CHOCOLATE MOUSSE FILLING

1 pound semisweet chocolate, finely chopped

8 tablespoons (1 stick) unsalted butter cut into 8 pieces

4 large egg yolks

⅓ cup orange liqueur

⅓ cup sugar

1 cup heavy whipping cream

One 2½-quart charlotte mold, buttered and lined with plastic wrap

SERVING: Use a thin knife dipped in hot water and wiped clean after each slice to cut the cake.

STORAGE: Store loosely covered in the refrigerator for up to 8 hours before serving.

MAKES ABOUT 12 SERVINGS

ZUCCOTTO ALLA RICOTTA

THIS ELEGANT FLORENTINE DESSERT uses a layer of pan di Spagna to line a bowl which is then filled with a rich ricotta mousse. The chocolate and pistachios add a bit of crunch to the rich filling.

1 Cut out a disk the size of the top of your bowl from the pan di Spagna and cut the rest of it into 2 large wedges. Cut the wedges into thin slices and line the bowl with them. Sprinkle with the rum. Reserve the disk to cover the filling.

2 To make the filling, combine the ricotta and confectioners' sugar in the food processor and process until smooth, about 2 minutes. Transfer to a large bowl.

3 Combine the rum and anisette in a small bowl and sprinkle the gelatin over the surface. Allow it to soak until softened, about 5 minutes, then place over a saucepan of simmering water and stir to melt. Whisk the dissolved gelatin into the ricotta mixture, then stir in the chocolate and pistachios. Whip the cream to soft peaks, and fold it in.

4 Pour the filling into the prepared mold and cover with the reserved disk of pan di Spagna. Cover with plastic wrap and chill until set, about 6 hours.

One 9-inch layer Pan di Spagna, page 278

¼ cup white rum for sprinkling

FILLING

One 15-ounce container ricotta

1 cup confectioners' sugar

3 tablespoons white rum

1 tablespoon anisette

1 envelope gelatin

3 tablespoons (about 1 ounce) chopped bittersweet chocolate

3 tablespoons (about 1 ounce) chopped pistachios

1 cup heavy whipping cream

FOR FINISHING

1 cup heavy whipping cream

2 tablespoons sugar

½ cup chopped pistachios

One 1½-quart bowl, buttered and lined with plastic wrap

5 Remove the plastic wrap and invert the bowl onto a platter. Remove the bowl and plastic wrap. Whip the cream with the sugar to soft peaks. Cover the Zuccotto with the cream. Sprinkle with the chopped pistachios.

SERVING: Serve the cake shortly after finishing.

STORAGE: Store the cake without the whipped cream, covered, in the refrigerator for up to 2 days. Finish the cake just prior to serving.

MAKES ONE 8- TO 9-INCH CAKE, ABOUT 16 SERVINGS

STRAWBERRY CHARLOTTE
WITH STRAWBERRIES

A CHARLOTTE IS ALWAYS ELEGANT in appearance and it's easy to prepare ahead of time. For the best flavor, use ripe local strawberries for the filling. That makes this a seasonal dessert, but it's worth waiting for.

1 Trim the ladyfingers to height of the sides of the springform pan. Line the bottom of the pan with the scraps. Line the sides of the pan with the trimmed ladyfingers, rounded sides out. Refrigerate until the filling is ready.

2 To make the Bavarian, rinse, hull, and slice the berries. Place in a saucepan with the sugar, bring to a boil over low heat, and simmer gently for about 10 minutes, until slightly thickened. Cool, then puree in a blender or processor. Transfer to a bowl and stir in the kirsch and lemon juice.

3 Place the water in a small heatproof bowl and sprinkle the gelatin over the surface. Allow to stand for 5 minutes, then place over a pan of simmering water and stir to melt. Cool the gelatin slightly.

4 Whip the cream until it holds a shape but is not too stiff. Whisk the dissolved gelatin into the puree, then fold in the cream. Pour the filling into the lined mold and chill for at least 8 hours, or overnight.

5 To unmold the charlotte, run a knife around the inside of the pan, release the sides of the pan, and remove. Decorate with strawberries.

Ladyfingers, page 274-275 in sponge cake chapter

STRAWBERRY BAVARIAN

2 pints strawberries

¾ cup sugar

2 tablespoons kirsch

1 tablespoon fresh lemon juice

1½ envelopes gelatin

¼ cup cold water

2 cups heavy whipping cream

FINISHING

1 pint strawberries, rinsed and halved

One 10-inch springform pan

SERVING: Use a thin knife dipped in hot water and wiped clean after each slice to cut the cake.

STORAGE: Store loosely covered in the refrigerator for up to 8 hours before serving. To prepare in advance, keep the cake covered in the refrigerator, but only glaze strawberries on the day you plan to serve the dessert.

MAKES ONE 10-INCH CAKE, ABOUT 12 SERVINGS

TIRAMISU

I HAVE SERVED THIS WITH GREAT RESULTS for more than 20 years.

1 To make the syrup, combine the water and sugar in a saucepan and bring to a boil. Cool, and stir in the coffee and brandy.

2 To make the filling, whisk the yolks in the bowl of an electric mixer, then whisk in the sugar and Marsala. Set over a pan of simmering water and whisk until thickened. Attach the bowl to the mixer and beat with the whisk attachment until cooled. (This is the zabaione.)

3 Mash the mascarpone in a bowl with a rubber spatula until smooth. Fold in the zabaione. Whip the cream, and fold it in.

4 Cut the pan di Spagna crosswise into thin slices. Place a layer of slices in the bottom of the gratin dish and brush with syrup. Spread with half the filling. Repeat with another layer of syrup and cake filling, ending with a layer of pan di Spagna and the remaining syrup.

5 Whip the cream with the sugar. Spread the whipped cream over the surface of the dessert. Sprinkle with cinnamon and coffee grounds. Refrigerate for several hours.

SERVING: Use a large spoon to serve.

STORAGE: Store covered in the refrigerator for up to 2 days.

MAKES ABOUT 12 SERVINGS

ESPRESSO SYRUP
½ cup water
½ cup sugar
½ cup very strong brewed espresso
¼ cup Italian brandy, such as Stock (*not* grappa)

FILLING
3 large egg yolks
⅓ cup sugar
⅓ cup sweet Marsala
1 cup mascarpone, at room temperature
1 cup heavy whipping cream

One 9- or 10-inch layer Pan di Spagna, page 278

FOR FINISHING
1 cup heavy whipping cream
2 tablespoons sugar
Ground cinnamon
Coffee grounds

One 2-quart gratin dish or glass bowl

INDIVIDUAL CAKES

THE MAIN ATTRACTION OF INDIVIDUAL CAKES lies in the fact that you get your very own whole cake. Seriously, though, these are elegant, and, for the most part, easy, ways to make a great impression when you want to keep things fairly simple. The madeleines and financiers are also perfect accompaniments to a simple dessert like ice cream, or with coffee after dessert.

FRUIT FINANCIERS

❧ ꙮ ❧

THIS FRUIT-FILLED VERSION OF A FINANCIER is made with softened, as opposed to melted, butter for a moist texture that holds the fruit in suspension (rather than having it all fall to the bottom).

¾ cup (about 3 ounces) ground almonds

¾ cup all-purpose flour (spoon flour into dry-measure cup and level off)

¾ cup sugar

Grated zest of 1 lemon

6 tablespoons (¾ stick) unsalted butter, softened

1 tablespoon rum

1 teaspoon vanilla extract

3 large egg whites

1 pint blueberries or raspberries

½ cup sliced almonds for finishing

Nine 3¾-inch tart pans, buttered and floured

1 Position the racks to divide the oven into thirds and preheat to 350 degrees.

2 In the bowl of a heavy-duty mixer, mix the ground almonds, flour, sugar, and lemon zest with paddle until combined. Add the butter and continue beating for 2 minutes.

3 Beat the rum and vanilla into the egg whites, then beat into the butter mixture in two additions, beating for 2 minutes after each addition and scraping down the bowl and beater as necessary.

4 Fill each pan with ¼ cup of batter. Sprinkle with the berries and sliced almonds.

5 Bake for about 35 minutes. Unmold and serve.

SERVING: Serve the cakes alone or with whipped cream and/or a fruit sauce or compote.

STORAGE: Store covered at room temperature, or wrap well and freeze for longer storage.

MAKES ABOUT 9 INDIVIDUAL CAKES, DEPENDING ON THE SIZE OF THE MOLDS

COFFEE-PECAN MERINGUES

༄ ༅ ༄

THE SWEETNESS OF PECANS contrasts perfectly with the slight bitterness of the coffee filling.

PECAN MERINGUES

4 large egg whites

Pinch salt

1 cup sugar

¾ cup (about 3 ounces) ground pecans

¼ teaspoon ground cinnamon

2 tablespoons cornstarch

COFFEE BUTTERCREAM FILLING

4 large egg yolks

½ cup sugar

⅓ cup very strong brewed coffee

½ pound (2 sticks) unsalted butter, softened

2 tablespoons dark rum

FOR FINISHING

Chopped toasted pecans

Confectioners' sugar

Two 12 × 18-inch jelly-roll pans, lined with parchment paper

1 Position the racks to divide the oven into thirds and preheat to 300 degrees.

2 To make the meringues, in the bowl of a heavy-duty mixer, beat the egg whites and salt with the whisk attachment on medium speed until white and opaque. Increase the speed to medium-high and beat in ½ cup of the sugar in a stream. Continue to beat until the egg whites are very firm, but not dry.

3 Combine the remaining ½ cup sugar with the ground pecans, cinnamon, and cornstarch and fold into the egg whites. Spoon the batter into a pastry bag fitted with a ½-inch plain tube (Ateco 806) and pipe 3-inch fingers onto the prepared pans.

4 Bake the meringues for about 25 minutes, until golden and fairly dry. Watch them carefully, as they burn easily.

5 To make the buttercream, whisk the yolks together in the bowl of an electric mixer. Whisk in the coffee, then the sugar. Place the bowl over a pan of simmering water and whisk until the mixture is thickened. Attach to the mixer and beat with the whisk on medium speed until cold. In 5 or 6 additions, beat in the butter, then beat in the rum.

6 Line up half the fingers, rounded side down, on a parchment- or wax paper–lined pan. Pipe a line of the buttercream down each finger, then top with the remaining fingers, flat side facing the filling. Pipe a rosette of buttercream onto the center of each. Sprinkle the rosettes with chopped pecans and dust very lightly with confectioners' sugar.

SERVING: Serve at cool room temperature.

STORAGE: Store the unfilled meringues in the freezer, well wrapped, until 6 hours before serving. Defrost before finishing.

MAKES ABOUT 24 INDIVIDUAL CAKES

NICOLE KAPLAN'S MADELEINES

THIS RECIPE COMES FROM the talented pastry chef of New York's Eleven Madison Park restaurant.

1 In a small pan, melt the butter over medium heat and then continue to cook until it begins to smell nutty and turns brown. Remove from the heat and strain through a fine sieve into a bowl.

2 In the bowl of a heavy-duty mixer fitted with the whisk, beat the eggs and sugar until fluffy. Sift the flour, baking powder, and salt over the eggs and fold in with a rubber spatula. Fold in the butter and lemon zest. Spoon the batter into a pastry bag fitted with a ¼-inch plain tip. Refrigerate for at least 2 hours, or overnight.

3 When you are ready to bake, set the racks to divide the oven into thirds and preheat to 375 degrees.

4 Pipe the batter into the prepared molds, filling them three-quarters full. Bake until the madeleines form humps and are nut brown around the edges, about 12 minutes.

5 Remove the pans from the oven and bang them on a countertop to release the madeleines. Carefully lift out any that stick, using the point of a knife to help you. Wrap in a napkin to keep warm. Repeat with the remaining batter.

7 tablespoons unsalted butter

5 large eggs

½ cup plus 3 tablespoons sugar

1¼ cups unbleached all-purpose flour (spoon flour into dry-measure cup and level off)

1 teaspoon baking powder

Large pinch of fine sea salt

Grated zest of 1 lemon

Madeleine molds, buttered and floured

SERVING: These are great for dessert, exquisite with tea.

STORAGE: Store in an airtight container at room temperature.

MAKES 24 MADELEINES, DEPENDING ON THE SIZE OF THE MOLDS USED

CHOCOLATE-RASPBERRY CUBES

TRY FOLDING A BASKET OF FRESH RASPBERRIES into the raspberry filling before spreading it over the cake layer.

1 To make the syrup, bring the water and sugar to a boil in a small saucepan. Cool, and add the raspberry eau-de-vie.

2 To make the filling, bring the raspberries to a boil in a nonreactive saucepan and reduce slightly. Puree in a food processor or blender and strain to remove the seeds. Set aside to cool.

3 Whisk the egg whites and sugar together in the bowl of an electric mixer. Set over a pan of simmering water and whisk until the egg whites are hot and the sugar has dissolved. Attach the bowl to the mixer and beat with the whisk attachment until the mixture has cooled. Switch to the paddle attachment and beat in the butter gradually. Continue to beat until smooth, then beat in the raspberry puree and eau-de-vie.

4 To make the glaze, bring the cream to a boil in a small saucepan. Remove from the heat, add the chocolate, and allow to stand for five minutes. Whisk until smooth, then strain and cool.

RASPBERRY SYRUP

¼ cup water

⅓ cup sugar

2 tablespoons raspberry Framboise

RASPBERRY FILLING

One 10- or 12-ounce package frozen raspberries

4 large egg whites

¾ cup sugar

½ pound (2 sticks) unsalted butter, softened

2 tablespoons raspberry eau-de-vie

CHOCOLATE GLAZE

1 cup heavy whipping cream

8 ounces semisweet chocolate, cut into ¼-inch pieces

1 Chocolate Génoise Sheet, page 273

FOR FINISHING

20 raspberries

Gold leaf

5 Cut the génoise in half to make two 9 × 12-inch layers. Place one on a cardboard rectangle and moisten with half the syrup. Spread with three-quarters of the raspberry filling. Top with the remaining layer and moisten with the remaining syrup. Spread the top with the remaining filling, and chill to set.

6 Spread the cooled glaze over the top of cake, and chill to set.

7 Using a sharp knife dipped into hot water and wiped clean between each cut, cut the cake into 2-inch cubes. Decorate with the raspberries and gold leaf.

SERVING: Serve these delicate but rich cakes as dessert.

STORAGE: Store at cool room temperature for up to 6 hours. For longer storage, cover loosely and refrigerate or freeze.

MAKES ABOUT 20 INDIVIDUAL CAKES

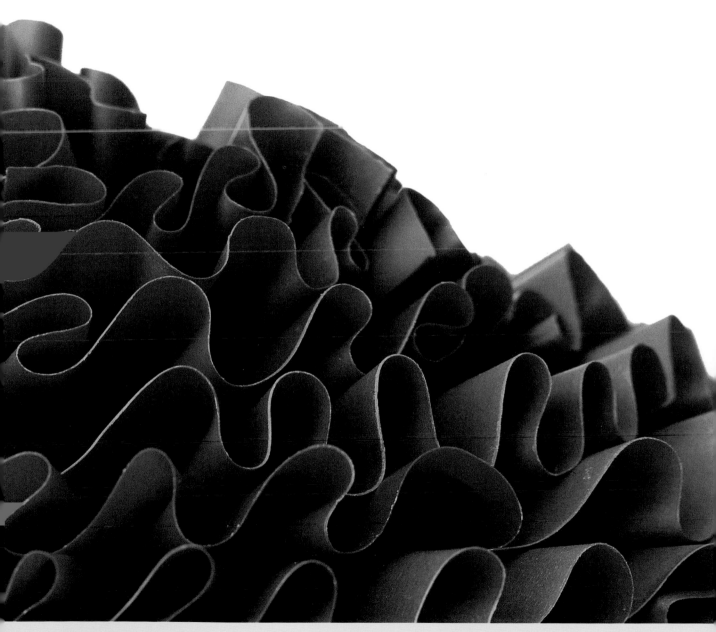

Perfect Cookies, Cakes, and CHOCOLATE

INTRODUCTION TO CHOCOLATE

THOUGH MY FATHER, NUFRE MALGIERI, was not particularly fond of sweets, he did like chocolate. The selection of chocolate candy available in our 1950s inner-city neighborhood was nothing compared to what is available nowadays; nevertheless, there still were many to choose among besides the ubiquitous Hershey bars, both plain and with almonds. My father once brought me a surprise when I was about five or six years old. He unwrapped a small, thin candy bar about four inches square and said, "Guess what this is." I looked—it was an off-white color and was marked in squares like a chocolate bar. I sniffed—it had a scent of orange. I tasted—it was like sweet chocolate perfumed with a delicate orange flavor. The bar was a then common Dutch brand of orange-flavored white chocolate (yes, I know white chocolate isn't really chocolate). I was delighted.

Thus my obsession with chocolate began.

Another of my early chocolate memories is of going with my grandfather to his club on a Saturday afternoon. The bartender kept chocolate bars in the refrigerator behind the bar and I always got a cold, firm milk chocolate bar to break apart square by square and eat while my grandfather greeted his friends.

And every Easter was a time when my cousins and I received enormous baskets of chocolates and other confections from parents, grandparents, godparents, aunts, and uncles. Every basket had as its centerpiece a large milk chocolate bunny or egg, richly decorated with dark chocolate and piped flowers made of hard sugar icing, probably royal icing. There were also little eggs, hollow or filled with chocolate or sometimes nut pastes or gianduja, and of course the inevitable jelly beans and marshmallow chicks.

I think the first chocolate dessert I remember enjoying was my grandmother's pizza di crema, a kind of pie with a sweet crust filled with chocolate pastry cream scented with vanilla and cinnamon and studded with candied citron. It was a typical Easter dessert (a wonder we could eat dessert after all the chocolate in the Easter baskets) and was always part of the selection of sweet and savory ricotta and cream pies that my maternal grandmother, Clotilda Lo Conte, made for the holiday.

My grandmother made lots of delicate cakes and pastries, and although I never learned a recipe from her, watching her and observing the pleasure that her baking brought everyone inspired a love of baking in me.

I started experimenting on my own in my late teens. One of the first things I tried was a fancy chocolate dessert involving ladyfingers and a rich chocolate filling. I found the recipe in a not very precisely translated cookbook by a French countess. The imposing-sounding recipe called for soaking the ladyfingers in ½ cup of kirsch diluted with an equal amount of water, and then adding another half cup of kirsch to the chocolate filling.

Unfortunately the resulting strong, alcoholic flavor made the dessert inedible. Undaunted, I tried the recipe again (this time with about a tenth of the kirsch) and began my lifelong passion for collecting recipes for chocolate desserts and confections.

My quest for additions to my collection has taken me from southern France to British Columbia—it's never too long a trip if there is chocolate at the end of it.

Before I knew it I had finished college—still experimenting with cooking and baking at every chance—and decided to attend culinary school instead of graduate school.

My first great chocolate mentor was my teacher Albert Kumin. In his classes at the Culinary Institute of America, Albert created beautiful, decorative, and edible confections with chocolate and sugar. Before, I had only seen art like his made in porcelain.

His ability with chocolate was and is unsurpassed. It was he who convinced me that I should go to Switzerland for an apprenticeship after graduation. In the early 1970s there was no better place for a chocolate lover. I was fascinated with the beautiful chocolate cakes and the precisely uniform and perfect pralinés—the Swiss name for dipped chocolate candies—in the windows of elegant and expensive pastry shops in Zurich, where I worked, and in the other cities and towns I visited. The air in Switzerland seemed chocolate-scented and in some places it actually was, as I discovered when I first visited Kilchberg on Lake Zurich, the site of the Lindt chocolate factory. My recipe collection increased as I traded school recipes with fellow apprentices and assistant pastry chefs and made weekly rounds of the city's pastry shops. I sketched and made notes on the contents of window displays and occasionally scraped a few extra francs together from my meager pay to buy a few chocolate truffles or some intricately decorated little pastries.

Visits in Switzerland and France to stores that sold professional equipment started my collection of chocolate molds, cutters, dipping forks, and thermometers. Fortunately, nowadays all these pieces of equipment are easily available from importers in the United States.

After working in Switzerland, Monaco, and France for about five years, I returned to New York to work with Albert Kumin at Windows on the World when it opened in 1976. We made one chocolate extravaganza after another. Another of my great chocolate inspirations has been Robert Linxe, of La Maison du Chocolat in Paris and New York. The first time Monsieur Linxe came to Peter Kump's Cooking School in New York, I assisted him in preparing for his class—a great experience. His knowledge of chocolate is unsurpassed. He is equally at home preparing sumptuous chocolate desserts or beautiful confections. He is, in fact, the only person I have ever known who can judge the temper of chocolate by just looking at it: one stir and he knows if the chocolate is at the right degree of viscosity and temperature.

His skill fanned the flames of my passion for chocolate and I decided to return to France to learn more. Thanks to the kind efforts of my friend Rachel Akselrod I spent a whirlwind week working in the Valrhona factory, at Tain-l'Hermitage, near Valence in France. Under the able tutelage of Valrhona's head of research and development, Paul Bernard-Bret, I spent that week molding, dipping, and preparing confections of every type imaginable. It was like a short stay at a chocolate Harvard!

Since then I have taught innumerable classes in making chocolates and chocolate desserts, and although my previous books have all had a goodly amount of chocolate desserts in them, this is my first all-chocolate book. I hope you enjoy using it as much as I have enjoyed writing it.

A Short History of Chocolate

Throughout most of its three-thousand-year history, chocolate has been exclusively used as a beverage. After its introduction to Europe in the sixteenth and seventeenth centuries, various other uses were found, bringing chocolate into use as an ingredient in desserts and cakes, up to the point in the nineteenth century when eating chocolate of the type we know today came into common use.

For a fascinating read, look at Sophie D. Coe and Michael D. Coe's *The True History of Chocolate* (Thames and Hudson, 1996). The Coes have traced the history of chocolate from its beginnings in the lowlands of Mexico to its present-day use as one of the most popular food products in the world. Because they are scholars in the true sense of the word (Mrs. Coe is deceased, and her husband is a professor at Yale University) they have no axes to grind and, aside from a few swipes at food writers, have traced the origin and development of chocolate throughout its history with great objectivity and impartiality.

The main milestones in the history of chocolate are:

Cocoa beans were discovered, processed, and first made into a beverage by the Olmec, an ancient Mexican civilization that flourished during the last millennium B.C.E.

Use of chocolate as a beverage passed from the Olmec to the Maya, the Toltec, and finally the Aztecs. The Aztecs incorporated chocolate beverages of different types even into their religious rites and began to use cocoa beans as currency. They used a *metate*, or grinding stone to crush the roasted cocoa beans into a paste.

When the first Spanish Conquistadores came to Mexico early in the sixteenth century, they tasted chocolate beverages and began to adapt them to their own use, finally exporting cocoa beans to Spain toward the end of the sixteenth century.

During the seventeenth century, use of chocolate as a beverage spread to both Italy and France, mainly by religious who had been to Mexico and returned to their convents and monasteries in those countries. By the middle of the sixteenth century chocolate was also introduced into Britain, perhaps by pirates who had preyed on ships headed for Spain. The chocolate used at this time would resemble a coarse version of present-day unsweetened chocolate, though it was sometimes sold in a sweetened form, resembling the disks of chocolate available from Mexican chocolate companies to this day, used for making hot chocolate.

During the eighteenth century, the use of chocolate as a beverage became more widespread throughout Europe and the first efforts at using chocolate as an ingredient in dessert recipes began. It has a prominent entry in Diderot's *Encyclopedia*, where the roasting and grinding processes are well illustrated.

The nineteenth century saw the development of the types of chocolates that we know today. Treating cocoa powder with alkali occurred in Holland when Conrad van Houten invented the process in 1828. This gave the cocoa a darker color and a somewhat milder flavor and the use of this type of cocoa powder persists to this day.

Candy bars first appeared in England in the middle of the nineteenth century, though it wasn't until the last quarter of the century that the Swiss chocolatier Rudolphe Lindt invented the process of conching (see page 376), making the resulting chocolate smoother and creamier.

Jean Tobler, another Swiss chocolate technician, is said to have discovered the need for and the process of tempering at the very end of the nineteenth century, when he realized that the addition of extra cocoa butter to the mixture for eating chocolate made it more palatable. Milk chocolate had been invented by another Swiss, Daniel Peter, when he used some of Henri Nestlé's dry milk in a formula for chocolate years before.

American chocolate pioneers include James Baker, who opened a chocolate factory in Massachusetts in 1765 to manufacture chocolate for beverages. His grandson, Walter Baker, took over the business, which still exists, supplying baking chocolate to this day. Milton Hershey discovered a process of using actual milk, rather than milk powder, in the manufacture of milk chocolate and that process is still used to this day to manufacture the many tons of Hershey's chocolate produced.

Today's fancy chocolate cakes and candies are a far cry from the Aztec beverage that the Conquistadores discovered a little more than 450 years ago. We are fortunate to live in a world where the use of chocolate has become so developed and refined so that there are chocolates and chocolate recipes available for almost every mood. The history of chocolate will continue to unfold for many centuries to come.

Where Chocolate Comes From
The Chocolate Tree

All chocolate comes from the tree that is botanically identified as *Theobroma cacao*—one of about 20 species of the genus *Theobroma*, from the Greek meaning "food of the gods." Only one other species is edible—*Theobroma bicolor*—and it is used to make a beverage in Mexico and part of Latin America.

The tree, which originated in the lowlands of southern Mexico, grows in a belt around the world delineated by 20 degrees north and south of the equator in Africa, the Caribbean, Hawaii, South America, and the South Seas.

There are three varieties of *Theobroma cacao*: Criollo (creole), a frail plant which produces very high-quality chocolate; Forastero (foreigner), a more robust plant which makes a less delicate chocolate; and Trinitario (trinitarian), a natural cross between the two other varieties, which occurred in Trinidad.

High temperatures, high humidity, and an abundance of the little insects known as midges, which pollinate the flowers as they bloom, are necessary to the growth of the Theobroma tree. It produces flowers constantly in tufts of bark all over its trunk and branches. Though only a small percentage of flowers actually produce fruit, they bloom throughout the year, without a particular flowering season, unlike fruit trees that grow in temperate climates. If the flowers do produce fruit, the result is large pods that may range from bright orange to brown in color, surrounding a white, acidic flesh and a center of about 20 to 40 almond-shaped beans. The beans are the part that becomes chocolate. Both the tree and its fruit are referred to as *cacao*, although the chocolate-producing beans are referred to as cocoa beans.

After the pods are harvested, they are broken open—usually with a machete—and the beans are removed. Though I have heard that a beverage similar to lemonade is made from the flesh, I know of no commercial use for it.

The beans, which are covered with a white skin, are first piled on the ground, covered, and allowed to ferment. During fermentation, when the beans germinate—at a temperature of about 120 degrees—the first sign of chocolate flavor develops.

After the beans have fermented, they are uncovered and exposed to the sun to dry and arrest the fermentation.

The next step is to roast them. Though beans are often roasted where they are grown, it is just as common for fermented and dried beans to be roasted far from the growing site in the factory where the beans will be made into chocolate.

After roasting, the husks, which have become dry and papery, are removed. This is usually done by crushing the beans slightly until they break into smaller pieces known as nibs. Then the skin is easy to remove. Often a chocolate factory will purchase fully processed nibs to use for making chocolate.

How Chocolate Is Manufactured

At the chocolate factory, the process of making chocolate may begin with either nibs or beans. Chocolates made from a blend of different beans usually start with dried, unroasted beans, whereas chocolates made from one type of bean usually start with nibs that were roasted and skinned where they were grown. Of course there are exceptions to both cases.

The first step is to crush the skinned nibs into chocolate liquor—a misleading term because it is only liquid when it is heated and it contains no alcohol. Chocolate liquor, also confusingly known as cocoa solid or solids, is the pure essence of the roasted and skinned cocoa bean, and is commonly available as unsweetened chocolate.

Chocolate liquor may also be pressed to extract its natural fat, cocoa butter, which is used in both the confectionery and cosmetic industries. What remains of chocolate liquor after most (about 85 percent) of the cocoa butter has been pressed out is called a "cake." Cakes are sometimes further defatted and ground to become cocoa powder. Cocoa treated with an alkali during processing is referred to as alkalized or Dutch process cocoa.

For the manufacture of other types of chocolate, finely pulverized sugar and flavoring (usually artificial vanilla) are added to the paste of crushed nibs. Lecithin, an emulsifying agent derived from soybeans, is also added to keep the chocolate mixture from separating during manufacture or when the chocolate is melted. Often extra cocoa butter is added at this point, especially if the end product is to be high-quality chocolate.

After all the ingredients are mixed together they are conched. Conching refers to the process of beating the chocolate mixture constantly for a period of sometimes several days. This decreases bitterness and diminishes the particle size, giving the chocolate a smoother "mouth feel."

After conching, the chocolate is tempered (for a full explanation of tempering, see pages 384–385) and molded into large or small bars, depending on its destination. After this, all that remains is the wrapping and shipping.

If the chocolate is to be made into candies, after tempering it usually goes by pipeline directly to be mixed with other ingredients or molded into candies.

CHOCOLATE TYPES

The many different brands and flavors of chocolate may be easily grouped into several types.

COCOA POWDER: Available as both nonalkalized and alkalized (Dutch process) cocoa. Cocoa is used in baking and in making candies as well as in beverages. When used as an ingredient in recipes in this book, alkalized or nonalkalized cocoa is always specified. If you have no alkalized cocoa powder and must substitute nonalkalized cocoa, add a pinch of baking soda to the cocoa.

POWDERED CHOCOLATE OR GROUND CHOCOLATE: More available in Europe than North America, ground chocolate is a sweet powder made from semisweet chocolate that does not have a very high cocoa butter content. It is best used as a flavoring for whipped cream or as a beverage mix. I don't usually use it for baking.

BAKING CHOCOLATE: These are the 1-ounce squares of chocolate commonly available in the supermarket. They usually come in semisweet and unsweetened varieties, and are best used in recipes in which chocolate is one of many ingredients. With the possible exception of high-quality unsweetened chocolate used in some confections, this type of chocolate is almost always used only in baking

COUVERTURE CHOCOLATE: The name means "covering" and it derives from the fact that this type of chocolate may be tempered and used for molding and dipping. But confusingly there are also many eating or "candy bar" type chocolates that qualify as couverture. Basically, the chocolate has to have enough added cocoa butter to make it fluid when it melts because otherwise it would be impossible to pour into molds or use for dipping. Couverture may also be used for almost any other purpose—its high cocoa butter content does not make it unsuitable for use in candies or in baking, although the most costly couvertures would be wasted if combined with other ingredients and baked.

WHAT'S THE BEST CHOCOLATE?

Chocolate must adhere to strict laws governing its content, as you can easily see from the FDA's chart of obligatory percentages of ingredients opposite. Even so, wide differences exist in the flavor and performance of chocolate. How can you tell which is the best?

First of all, use chocolate for the purpose for which it was intended. Don't try to make a truffle center with baking chocolate or to coat a mold with chocolate that isn't fluid enough. Once you know the right type of chocolate for your recipe, the best chocolate is the one that tastes best to you. Remember, texture and smoothness matter a lot with chocolate, especially when the chocolate is used with few or no other ingredients. Chocolate should be smooth, not grainy on the tongue and palate, and should melt easily. So taste a few different brands before you invest in a lot of any one particular chocolate.

EATING CHOCOLATE: Though many chocolates sold for eating are enhanced with additives that contribute flavor or texture, plain bars—especially the 3- or 4-ounce bars of imported eating chocolate—are ideal for tempering. To test this, melt an ounce or two of chocolate in a heatproof bowl placed in another bowl of hot tap water. If the melted chocolate flows freely when you lift some of it with a spoon it will be good for tempering.

COMPOUND COATING: Though this is not really chocolate, the best coatings are chocolate products, which contain some pure chocolate. Compounds are chocolate-flavored products in which the cocoa butter is enhanced or replaced by hard vegetable fat, a practice that occurs in the preparation of some confections and the manufacture of "candy melts" or other types of nonchocolate coatings. Compounds are used because they require no tempering, though the best compounds are merely an inferior substitute for chocolate. Some of these are manufactured to be used for glazing cakes and pastries, as the French name *pâte à glacer* (icing or glazing paste) would suggest. The best compounds taste good—though never as good as pure chocolate. Beware of little disks called candy melts, sold in candy-molding hobby stores: Taste one and you'll know why. Compound coatings come in many different colors (in fact, they used to be referred to as summer coatings, because they are harder and therefore less likely to melt in hot weather) and are sometimes used in the preparations of certain chocolate decorations.

Chocolate Flavors

Although describing chocolate flavors really has to do with semantics and percentages of cocoa solid, here are the norms used for defining the different types of chocolate according to the minimum percentages of chocolate liquor, sugar, and other ingredients used by the FDA:

	CHOCOLATE LIQUOR	SUGAR	EMULSIFIER	FLAVOR ADDITIVES
Unsweetened	100%	—	1%	Variable
Bittersweet	35%	Variable	1%	Variable
Semisweet	35%	Variable	1%	Variable
Sweet	15%	Variable	1%	Variable
Milk	10%	Variable	1%	12% whole milk

NOTE: White confectionery bars, not to say white "chocolate," contain no chocolate liquor; therefore, they may not strictly be called chocolate.

Nonchocolate Ingredients

To prepare the recipes in this book you will need ingredients other than chocolate. What follows are descriptions and specifications for the nonchocolate ingredients used in the recipes.

FLOUR: Both all-purpose flour and cake flour are called for. Although you may not substitute one for the other (all-purpose flour contains a higher percentage of gluten-forming proteins and is better used for pastry doughs), I don't think it matters if you use bleached or unbleached all-purpose flour. All cake flour is bleached. In the cake chapter, some recipes use all-purpose flour for cakes. I use self-rising cake flour for angel food cake, but not for any other recipe. And remember: Always measure flour or any other dry ingredient by gently spooning it into a dry measuring cup, then leveling the cup with the back of a knife or with a spatula.

Other starches used in the recipes that follow are cornstarch and bread crumbs. If you purchase dry bread crumbs instead of preparing your own by pulverizing stale bread in the food processor, make sure you buy the unflavored kind. Occasionally a recipe may call specifically for fresh bread crumbs. To make them, reduce fresh white bread, crust removed, to fine, moist crumbs in the food processor. A variation on a recipe to make a Passover cake may suggest substituting potato starch, matzoh meal, or a combination.

SUGARS: I always use plain granulated, not superfine, sugar. When a recipe calls for dark or light brown sugar, use that exact type for best results. The only difference between them is the strength of the molasses flavor, which is more pronounced in dark brown sugar. Don't hesitate to substitute granulated light brown sugar for the moist type. For accurate measuring always remember to pack and press moist brown sugar into a dry-measure cup. Confectioners' sugar is called for in some recipes, often for dusting a finished cake or pastry—do not use it as a substitute for granulated sugar.

LIQUID SUGARS: Light and dark corn syrup, honey, molasses, and maple syrup are called for in some recipes. Corn syrup contributes smoothness to preparations from candy centers to ices. Honey, molasses, and maple syrup are only used when their flavor is desired.

DAIRY PRODUCTS: When milk is specified in recipes it refers to whole milk. Cream is always heavy whipping cream, though I like to use half and half for crème anglaise and some ice cream mixtures, but in those cases I specify it in the recipe. Butter is always unsalted and eggs are always graded large.

Other dairy products found in the recipes include cream cheese and sour cream. Be careful not to purchase the "light" or fat-free versions, which will not perform the same way as the full-fat version. Mascarpone, the Italian cream cheese, is called for in a recipe or two as is crème fraîche, the slightly fermented French cream.

LEAVENERS: Double-acting baking powder, baking soda, active dry yeast, and compressed yeast are called for in recipes. Do not substitute instant or rapid-rise yeast for dry yeast. If you buy dry yeast in bulk, use 2½ teaspoons of dry yeast for one envelope.

NUTS: Many nut products are used in the preparation of chocolate candies and desserts. Always be sure nuts are fresh. If possible, taste them where you buy them—if nuts have become rancid, they taste bitter. Rancid nuts will render any recipe inedible. Store all nuts in heavy-duty plastic bags in the freezer. If you will be keeping them only a short time before using them, store dry and airtight at a cool room temperature.

ALMOND PRODUCTS: Whole almonds are available as natural almonds, with the skins on, or blanched, with the skins removed. To blanch almonds, place them in a saucepan and cover with water. Bring to a boil over medium heat and drain in a strainer or colander. Place the hot, wet almonds on a clean kitchen towel, then fold the towel over them and rub—most of the almonds will separate from the skins and the ones that have not will pop out easily if you squeeze them.

Sliced almonds are flat slices of whole almonds, either blanched or natural. Slivered almonds are cut into matchstick shapes and granulated almonds are slivered almonds that have been cut across into little cubes. If you can't find granulated almonds, hand-chopped slivered almonds are a good substitute. Almond flour is the commercial form of ground almonds—great if you can find it because it's finer than you can grind it yourself. To make your own, pulse room-temperature almonds repeatedly in the food processor, stopping occasionally to scrape down the inside bottom of the bowl with a metal spatula. Stop pulsing the machine before the almonds become sticky. If you want to grind almonds that have been stored in the freezer, let them come to room temperature first or the condensation will make them pasty—or warm them slightly on a jelly-roll pan in a 350-degree oven, then cool them to room temperature before grinding. Always buy almond paste that comes in a can. The type that comes in a cellophane-wrapped cylinder has little almond flavor and is usually dried out.

HAZELNUT PRODUCTS: Hazelnuts or filberts come in all the above forms except slivered and granulated. Sliced hazelnuts are rare, though they exist. To blanch hazelnuts, toast them at 350 degrees on a jelly-roll pan for 10 or 15 minutes, or until the skins crack and shatter off easily. Then rub the nuts in a towel—damp terry cloth works best—and separate the nuts from the skins.

Praline paste, a rich mixture of hazelnuts and sugar the consistency of peanut butter, is called for in some recipes. It is also made from almonds or a combination of almonds and hazelnuts.

PECANS: Pecans are sold shelled as halves or pieces or a combination—the latter is an economical choice for pies, tarts, and candies.

WALNUTS: Walnuts are available like pecans; neither needs to be blanched. They may both be ground in the food processor, but be careful, they turn to paste easily. I find that hand-chopping pecans and walnuts works better.

PISTACHIOS: The best come from Sicily and are all but unavailable outside Europe. Always buy pistachios in a Middle Eastern grocery store and try to get Turkish or other imported varieties, which are greener and more flavorful than the California ones. Blanch pistachios—an essential step when cooking with them—like almonds.

MACADAMIAS: These expensive nuts usually come salted. Most of the time, all traces of salt can be removed by bringing the nuts to a boil in fresh water and rinsing in running cold water after draining. Place on a jelly-roll pan and dry out at 300 degrees in the oven for 5 minutes. Cool before using.

PINE NUTS: Buy these in bulk at an import store—the tiny jars in the supermarket are ridiculously high in price. Always taste pine nuts before using. They are highly subject to turning rancid.

PEANUTS: I like to use the honey-roasted type for the occasional cookie or candy. For peanut butter, grind warm, skinned, toasted peanuts in a food processor. They will turn into a slightly chunky butter much better than the salt- and oil-laden supermarket varieties.

OILS: I always use a mild oil, such as canola or corn.

HERBS AND SPICES: Keep these tightly covered in a cool, dark place—I don't even keep mine in the kitchen anymore. Don't buy large quantities—it is much better to buy herbs and spices often than to use inferior-tasting ones.

LIQUORS AND LIQUEURS: Don't skimp here. The best available are often the most expensive, but by using the best, you will avoid adding an off flavor to your dessert or candy. Fine liquors and liqueurs (sweetened liquors) should enhance the flavor of chocolate and good desserts—they should never dominate the flavor or taste bitter.

INSTANT ESPRESSO: This comes in a 1-ounce jar; if you can't find instant espresso, use 1½ times the quantity in regular instant coffee.

GENERAL BAKING EQUIPMENT

ELECTRIC MIXER: Although you may use a hand mixer for most of the recipes here, I use a Kitchen-Aid 5-quart mixer for all general mixing and whipping.

FOOD PROCESSOR: This is no longer an optional piece of equipment. I use a seven-cup food processor for many purposes such as grinding nuts and mixing pastry doughs.

PANS AND MOLDS: Buy the best, heavy-duty aluminum baking pans you can afford. Though they may be easy to find in kitchenware stores, be sure to check local restaurant supply stores for the best quality at more reasonable prices. Recipes in this book will call for 8-, 9-, or 10-inch-diameter pans that are 2 inches deep.

PIE PANS: I always use a plain 9-inch Pyrex pie pan. This is not the one with a fluted edge and two handles, which is deeper and holds almost twice as much as the plain one.

TART PANS: I use the fluted-sided, removable-bottom type, which are usually available in tinned metal. I prefer these to the black steel ones, which are prone to rust and sometimes make baked goods turn out too dark.

ALUMINUM FOIL BAKING PANS: If you are going to try a recipe and don't have a particular size pan, it can be practical to pick up a foil pan in the supermarket. One caveat: Be sure to place the aluminum foil pan on a cookie sheet or jelly-roll pan before filling it. This will prevent it from buckling when full of batter and insulate it a little better during baking. I especially like the 4-ounce pleated foil cups for individual cakes.

CAKE CIRCLES OR CARDBOARDS: These come in a variety of sizes from a cake-decorating or specialty store. See Sources at the end of the book.

Primary Lessons in Working with Chocolate

Storage

The best chocolate in the world can't survive improper storage and handling. Though a little bloom (cocoa butter or sugar rising to the surface of chocolate blocks that have warmed up and cooled down again) won't necessarily hurt what you are preparing, it's better to keep your chocolate at a uniform 65 degrees with about 50 percent humidity to avoid having this happen.

If you live in a warm climate, store in an air-conditioned room; failing that, refrigerate or freeze, but if you do, be on the lookout for condensation. This can be a problem, especially on chocolate that is to be melted—then the little beads of moisture can cause the chocolate to become grainy while it is melting.

If chocolate becomes dry and grainy and hardens (the process is called seizing) while it is melting, add a teaspoon of vegetable oil and stir until the chocolate is smooth again. Adding the oil will not affect your recipe if you are going to bake the resulting dough or batter. Chocolate that has seized cannot be tempered (see pages 384–385). Adding oil to smooth out seized chocolate makes it no longer pure chocolate and only pure chocolate can be tempered.

Chopping

To chop small pieces of chocolate such as 1-ounce squares, a sharp chef's knife or even a serrated knife (makes the job easy but is bad for the blade) works well. If you want chocolate very finely chopped, cut it into ¼-inch pieces by hand, then pulse pieces in the food processor with metal blade until finely chopped.

A four-tined ice pick makes quick work of chopping large blocks of chocolate—you will likely find one at the hardware store.

For all the recipes in this book, chocolate should be cut into ¼-inch pieces.

Melting

To melt large quantities of chocolate, put it in a roasting pan and place in an oven with a pilot light—in several hours the chocolate will melt slowly and perfectly.

In a microwave oven, place the chocolate in a microwave-safe bowl and set oven at half power. Microwave for 30 seconds at a time, stirring chocolate between zaps.

On the stove, bring a saucepan half filled with water to a boil; turn off heat. Put chocolate in a heatproof bowl and place the bowl over the hot water. Stir occasionally as chocolate melts.

When melting chocolate with hot ingredients, add cut-up chocolate to hot ingredients in the bowl or pan, then wait a minute or two so that the heat of the cream, melted butter, or sugar syrup can penetrate the chocolate. Then, after you are sure the chocolate has melted, whisk the mixture smooth.

Though there are entire books written about tempering, what follows is a fast, simple description of how to accomplish this process with a minimum of laboratory talk and incomprehensible statistics.

Why temper? When you raise the temperature of chocolate above 91.5 degrees and melt it, the crystals of cocoa butter (all hard saturated fats form crystals) melt and lose their shape. When the chocolate cools back to about 80 degrees it will harden again, but the crystals, having been rendered unstable by the rise in temperature during melting, will not automatically resume their previous shape. The resulting chocolate will look dull and streaky rather than shiny and its texture will be grainy rather than smooth. Tempering is a process of manipulating the temperature of melted chocolate to make the cocoa butter crystals resume their previous shape so that the chocolate returns to the stable condition it was in before you melted it.

Tempering is necessary if the chocolate is to be used for molding, dipping, or coating. It is not necessary if the melted chocolate is to be used in a baked item or in a candy center that contains other ingredients. Tempering is only for when the chocolate is unadulterated. The exception to this rule is when preparing simple candies such as clusters or bark, where nuts and/or broken candy are added to the chocolate. If the chocolate is not tempered, the clusters will not have the right consistency or appearance. To temper accurately you must have a chocolate thermometer.

How to temper: Melt, cool, reheat—three simple steps, but you need to monitor the temperature of the chocolate exactly.

1 MELT THE CHOCOLATE. You may use any method you choose, but make sure the temperature of the chocolate rises to between 115 and 120 degrees. If the chocolate melts but doesn't get hot enough, the crystals of cocoa butter will not melt completely and it will be impossible to temper the chocolate—even if you accomplish the other two steps perfectly. This is the single greatest cause of failure in tempering chocolate. Warm, untempered, melted chocolate is referred to as virgin chocolate.

2 COOL THE CHOCOLATE. My favorite way is to do nothing—leave the chocolate at a cool room temperature, stirring it occasionally, until the temperature drops into the low eighties. You can tell this is happening when the chocolate starts to set around the top edge in the bowl.

Other ways of cooling the chocolate are tabling and seeding.

Tabling: Pour about half the melted chocolate out onto a smooth non-porous surface, such as a marble slab. Spread the chocolate back and forth with a metal spatula until it starts to cool and to thicken slightly. Keeping it moving constantly, scrape it back into the bowl of virgin chocolate. Pitfall to avoid: Leaving the chocolate on the marble too long and having it solidify. This is to be avoided, but if it happens, just scrape the hardened chocolate into a clean, dry bowl and remelt it by whatever method you used.

Seeding: Add some large chunks of unmelted chocolate to the virgin chocolate to bring down the temperature—this is the same principle as using ice cubes in a drink. The unmelted chocolate not only cools, it also seeds the virgin chocolate with stable crystals, encouraging the chocolate to be in good temper. Pitfalls to avoid: Adding too much seed and having the chocolate solidify in the bowl. The right amount to add is about 20 percent of the weight of the virgin chocolate.

3 **Reheat the chocolate:** After you have cooled the chocolate into the low eighties, the last step is to raise the temperature of the chocolate into the tempered range. This is 88 to 91 for dark chocolate and 86 to 88 for milk chocolate and white chocolate. The best way to do this is to lower the bowl with the chocolate over a pan of hot, not simmering, water for a few seconds at a time. Use your thermometer to gauge the temperature of the chocolate accurately. Pitfall to avoid: If you heat the chocolate above the high end of the tempered range, you must start all over again, and re-melt the chocolate to between 115 and 120 degrees, or the chocolate will not be in good temper.

When you really need to temper: For anything molded or coated or dipped, the chocolate must be in good temper. For truffles, I do a quick temper when I am going to roll the truffles in cocoa, confectioners' sugar, grated chocolate, or ground nuts—in this case I just melt the chocolate and cool it to about 90 degrees, and it works well all the time.

Keeping chocolate in temper: There are many ways to keep chocolate in temper once you have gotten it to the correct temperature. One way is to add small amounts of virgin chocolate to the tempered chocolate as the tempered chocolate cools. But, if you add too much and the temperature goes above the tempered range, you must start all over again. Other ways to keep chocolate in good temper: place the bowl of chocolate on a heating pad wrapped in a thick towel and safely placed inside a plastic bag, with the heating pad set at low. I have done this successfully on many occasions. Still another way is to keep the bowl of tempered chocolate half in the aura of a 250-watt heat lamp set about a foot from the top of the bowl. This method has to be monitored the chocolate may overheat.

BASIC CAKE LAYERS FOR CHOCOLATE CAKES

The following recipes are for cake layers used later in this chapter. Though each recipe makes a cake that stands alone, each is really best suited to being finished in one way or another.

CHOCOLATE GENOISE

This versatile French sponge cake may be used in any number of ways—usually it is filled and frosted or rolled.

1 Set a rack at the middle level of the oven and preheat to 350 degrees.

2 Sift together the cake flour, cornstarch, and cocoa through a fine-meshed strainer over a piece of wax paper to break up any small lumps in the cocoa. Set sifted ingredients aside with the strainer.

3 Whisk together the eggs, yolks, sugar, and salt in the bowl of an electric mixer. Place the bowl over a pan of simmering water and continue whisking gently until the mixture is lukewarm, about 100 degrees. This should take only a minute or two.

4 Whip with the electric mixer on high speed until the mixture is cooled and increased in volume, about 3 to 4 minutes.

5 Remove bowl from mixer and sift in dry ingredients, in three additions, gently folding each third in with a rubber spatula. Pour the batter into the prepared pan and spread the top even with a spatula.

⅓ cup cake flour

⅓ cup cornstarch

¼ cup alkalized (Dutch process) cocoa powder

3 large eggs plus 3 large egg yolks

¾ cup sugar

Pinch salt

One 9 or 10 × 2-inch round layer pan, or a 9-inch springform pan, buttered and the bottom lined with a disk of parchment or wax paper

6 Bake the layer about 30 minutes, until it is well risen and the center is firm to the touch.

7 If necessary, loosen the layer from the side of the pan with a small knife or spatula and invert the cake onto a rack. Place another rack on the cake and invert again. Remove the top rack, so that the layer cools right side up, still on the paper.

MAKES 1 ROUND LAYER, 9 OR 10 INCHES IN DIAMETER BY 2 INCHES DEEP

PLAIN CAKES

ALTHOUGH THESE CAKES ARE ANYTHING but plain in flavor and texture, they are so called because they are served unadorned by filling or frosting. These are all great cakes to take on picnics or pack in lunches. Serve them for tea or for those odd hours of the day when you "just want something."

TORTA CAPRESE

Neapolitan Chocolate Walnut Cake

THIS RICH CAKE, WHICH CONTAINS very little flour, derives its intense flavor from walnuts and chocolate. It is not difficult to prepare and also keeps well.

1 Set a rack at the middle level of the oven and preheat to 350 degrees.

2 In a large mixer bowl, beat the butter with half the sugar until soft and light. Beat in the melted chocolate, then the yolks, one at a time, scraping bowl and beater(s) often. Continue beating until the mixture is smooth and light.

3 Place the walnuts in the bowl of a food processor and grind them finely, pulsing the machine on and off at 1-second intervals. Be careful that the walnuts do not become gummy. Stir the walnuts into the batter, then the flour.

4 In a clean, dry bowl, beat the egg whites until they hold a very soft peak, then beat in the remaining sugar in a slow stream. Continue to beat until the whites hold a soft, glossy peak. Stir ¼ of the whites into the batter,

10 tablespoons (1¼ sticks) unsalted butter, softened

¾ cup sugar, divided

8 ounces semisweet chocolate, melted and cooled

7 large eggs, separated

1½ cups walnut pieces, about 6 ounces

⅓ cup all-purpose flour

Confectioners' sugar for finishing

One 10-inch round cake pan, 2 inches deep, buttered and the bottom lined with parchment or wax paperparchment or wax paper

then with a rubber spatula fold in the rest so that no streaks remain.

5 Pour the batter into the prepared pan and smooth the top. Bake about 40 minutes, until the center is firm when pressed with a fingertip.

6 Cool the cake in the pan for 10 minutes. The cake may sink slightly, though this does not affect its texture. Trim off any loose crust and invert the cake on a rack, remove the pan and paper, and allow to cool completely.

SERVING: Dust the cake with confectioners' sugar and slide onto a platter.

STORAGE: Keep cake under a cake dome at room temperature.

MAKES ONE 10-INCH ROUND CAKE, ABOUT 10 SERVINGS

COCOA BANANA COFFEE CAKE

～◦◦～

THE RECIPE FOR THIS EXCELLENT and easy cake comes from my friend Jennifer Migliorelli.

1 Set a rack at the middle level of the oven and preheat to 350 degrees.

2 In a mixing bowl, mix together the bananas and sour cream; set aside.

3 Sift together the flour, cocoa, baking soda, and salt onto a piece of wax paper and set aside.

4 Use an electric mixer set at medium speed to beat the butter and sugar until well combined, then beat in the eggs, one at a time, beating until smooth after each addition.

5 Beat in half the flour mixture. Scrape bowl and beater(s) well. Beat in the banana mixture, scrape bowl again, then beat in the remaining flour mixture and scrape well again.

6 Bake 55 to 65 minutes until well risen and a toothpick inserted halfway between the side of the pan and the tube emerges clean.

1½ cups mashed very ripe bananas (about 4)

One 8-ounce container sour cream

1¼ cups all-purpose flour

¾ cup alkalized (Dutch process) cocoa powder

1½ teaspoons baking soda

¾ teaspoon salt

12 tablespoons (1½ sticks) unsalted butter, softened

1½ cups sugar

3 large eggs

One 10-cup Bundt pan, buttered and floured, tapped to remove excess flour

SERVING: This is great with chocolate ice cream.

STORAGE: Keep cake under a cake dome at room temperature

MAKES 1 BUNDT CAKE, ABOUT 12 LARGE SERVINGS

COCOA ANGEL FOOD CAKE WITH RASPBERRY COMPOTE

⁓ ⁐

SERVING AN ANGEL CAKE with a compote always dresses it up.

1   Set a rack at the middle level of the oven and preheat to 325 degrees.

2   Combine the self-rising cake flour, cocoa, and ½ cup of the sugar in a small mixing bowl and stir well with a small whisk to combine. Set aside.

3   In a clean, dry bowl, use an electric mixer on medium speed to whip the egg whites with the salt until they are frothy. Continue beating the egg whites until they are white and opaque, and are beginning to hold their shape when the beaters are lifted. Increase the speed to high and gradually whip in the remaining ¾ cup sugar, continuing to whip the egg whites until they hold a soft, glossy peak. Beat in the vanilla extract.

4   Remove bowl from mixer and sift a third of the cocoa mixture over the whites. Use a rubber spatula to fold gently. Repeat with another third of the cocoa mixture, then fold in the remaining cocoa mixture. Fold slowly and deliberately, scraping across the bottom of the bowl with the spatula often. This will prevent the cocoa mixture from accumulating there and forming lumps. Scrape the batter into the pan, then cut into the batter with a series of

CAKE BATTER

1 cup self-rising cake flour

⅓ cup alkalized (Dutch process) cocoa powder, sifted before measuring

1¼ cups sugar, divided

1½ cups egg whites (about 12 or 13 from large eggs)

¼ teaspoon salt

2 teaspoons vanilla extract

RASPBERRY COMPOTE

Two ½-pint baskets fresh raspberries

¼ cup sugar

1 tablespoon raspberry liqueur

1 teaspoon lemon juice

1 ungreased 10-inch tube pan with removable bottom, *not nonstick*

side-by-side vertical chops, to break up any large air bubbles in the batter. Smooth the top.

5   Bake the cake for about 40 to 45 minutes, until it is well risen and firm when pressed with a fingertip.

6   Immediately after removing the cake from the oven, invert the pan and hang it with the center tube over the neck of a bottle (don't worry, the cake won't fall out). Cool the cake completely.

7   After it is cool, take the pan off the bottle. Insert a thin knife between cake and pan and scrape against the pan, all the way around to loosen the cake. To remove the cake from the pan lift the central tube, then slide knife all around between pan bottom and cake, then around central tube. Invert the cake to a platter or cake stand.

8   For the compote, crush one quarter of the berries and combine with the sugar, liqueur, and lemon juice. Gently fold in the remaining raspberries.

SERVING: To cut an angel food cake, use a sharp serrated knife and cut back and forth with a sawing motion, rather than cutting straight down, which would only compress the cake. Serve each slice with some of the compote on the side.

STORAGE: Keep under a cake dome at room temperature or wrap well and freeze. Defrost and bring to room temperature before serving. Store the compote tightly covered and in the refrigerator.

MAKES ONE 10-INCH CAKE, 10 TO 12 SERVINGS

CHOCOLATE CHIP POUND CAKE

⤙ ℰ ℰ ⤚

DON'T NEGLECT TO TRY THIS ONE—it's easy and delicious and one of those cakes to make when you just want to have something terrific in the house, although it's also perfect for special occasions.

The recipe comes from my cousin, Karen Ludwig. It originally came from Karen's stepmother, Julie Rocco

1 Set a rack at the middle level of the oven and preheat to 350 degrees.

2 Stir the flour, baking powder, and salt together in a bowl. Combine the chocolate chips and chopped nuts in another bowl and toss them with a tablespoon of the flour mixture.

3 In a large mixer bowl beat the butter and sugar at medium speed until the mixture is light in color and fluffy, about 5 minutes. Add the egg yolks, one at a time, beating smooth between each addition. Beat in the vanilla.

4 On lowest speed, beat in a third of the flour mixture, scrape bowl and beater(s), then beat in half the milk, scrape bowl and beaters again and do so after each addition. Continue to alternate adding another third of the flour, the remaining milk, and the remaining flour, scraping well after each addition.

5 In a clean, dry mixer bowl, beat the egg whites with a pinch of salt. Continue beating until the egg whites hold a soft peak. Stir about a third of the egg whites into the batter to lighten it, then fold in the remaining egg whites with a rubber spatula. Stir in the

3 cups all-purpose flour

2 teaspoons baking powder

½ teaspoon salt, plus a pinch for the egg whites

One 12-ounce bag semisweet chocolate chips

1 cup coarsely chopped walnuts or pecans, about 4 ounces

16 tablespoons (2 sticks) unsalted butter, softened

2 cups sugar

4 large eggs, separated

1 teaspoon vanilla extract

1 cup whole milk

Confectioners' sugar for finishing

One 10-cup (10-inch) Bundt or tube pan, buttered and floured

chocolate chips and nuts. Pour the batter into the prepared pan and smooth the top with the spatula.

6 Bake the cake for 65 to 75 minutes, or until it is well risen and a thin knife inserted midway between the side of the pan and the central tube emerges clean.

MAKES ONE 10-INCH CAKE

CHOCOLATE MAYONNAISE CAKE

~⦿ ⦿~

CHOCOLATE MAYONNAISE CAKE WAS invented in the thirties by the wife of a grocery salesman, to boost his mayonnaise sales. The mayonnaise adds a richness and moistness to the cake. This recipe was shared by biochemist Liza Davies, a friend and colleague from the King's Supermarket cooking schools in New Jersey.

Chocolate mayonnaise cake will always have a special place in my heart. On September 30, 1987 (also my fortieth birthday), I prepared the presentation cake (shaped like a 5-foot-tall jar of mayonnaise, complete with gold-leaf label) for Hellman's mayonnaise's seventy-fifth anniversary celebration.

1 Set a rack at the middle level of the oven and preheat to 350 degrees.

2 In a large mixing bowl, combine the flour, sugar, cocoa, and baking soda and stir well to mix.

3 In another bowl, whisk together the buttermilk, mayonnaise, and vanilla; stir into the dry ingredients to form a smooth batter.

4 Pour the batter into the prepared pan and bake for 45 to 50 minutes, or until risen and a small knife or toothpick inserted in the center of the cake emerges clean.

5 Cool the cake in the pan for 5 minutes, then invert onto a rack and peel off the paper. Cool completely.

6 To serve, dust lightly with confectioners' sugar.

SERVING: Serve unadorned, accompanied by fruit, or cover the cake with Old-Fashioned Boiled Frosting, page 396.

2 cups all-purpose flour

1 cup sugar

½ cup alkalized (Dutch process) cocoa powder, sifted after measuring

1½ teaspoons baking soda

1 cup buttermilk (or whole milk plus 1 tablespoon distilled white vinegar or lemon juice)

1 cup bottled mayonnaise (I always use Hellman's)

1 teaspoon vanilla extract

Confectioners' sugar for finishing

One 9-inch round cake pan, 2 inches deep, or a 9 × 9 × 2-inch square pan, buttered and the bottom lined with parchment or wax paper

STORAGE: Keep the cake at room temperature under a cake dome, or double-wrap in plastic and freeze. Defrost and bring to room temperature before serving.

MAKES ONE 9-INCH ROUND OR SQUARE CAKE

GERMAN CHOCOLATE MARBLE CAKE

❧ ∂ ❧

I'VE BEEN LISTENING TO MY FRIEND Ceri Hadda go on about this cake for the past fifteen years. It's a specialty of her mother, Anne-Marie Hadda, who brought the recipe with her from Germany. This version is adapted from Ceri's book, *Coffeecakes* (Simon & Schuster, 1992).

1 Set a rack at the middle level of the oven and preheat to 350 degrees.

2 Put the chocolate in a heatproof bowl and place the bowl over a pan of hot, not simmering, water to melt. Remove the bowl from the pan when the chocolate has melted, stir, then allow the chocolate to cool while preparing the rest of the ingredients.

3 Combine the flour, baking powder, and salt in a bowl and stir well to mix. Set aside.

4 Use an electric mixer set at medium speed to beat the butter and sugar until light, about 3 minutes. Beat in the eggs, one or two at a time, beating well between each addition. (After all the eggs are added, the mixture may seem separated–this does not matter.)

5 Beat in the lemon zest, juice, and 2 tablespoons of the rum.

6 Gradually beat the flour mixture into the butter mixture.

7 Remove 3 cups of the batter to a bowl. Stir the remaining 3 tablespoons rum, the milk, and the baking soda into the melted chocolate and immediately beat the chocolate mixture into the 3 cups batter.

9 ounces bittersweet chocolate, cut into 1/4-inch pieces

2½ cups all-purpose flour

2 teaspoons baking powder

Pinch salt

24 tablespoons (3 sticks) unsalted butter, softened

1¾ cups sugar

7 large eggs, at room temperature

Grated zest and strained juice of 1 large lemon (about 1 tablespoon zest and 4 tablespoons juice)

5 tablespoons dark rum, divided

3 tablespoons milk

½ teaspoon baking soda

One 10-inch tube or Bundt pan, or two 9 × 5 × 3-inch loaf pans, buttered and then dusted with flour or dry bread crumbs

8 Spread the chocolate or white batter evenly in the prepared pan(s), then top with the other batter. Plunge a knife or spatula into the cake batter and cut up and down through the batter. Repeat every inch around the cake to marbleize the two batters. Or place alternating spoonfuls of the two batters into the pan(s), then gently stir through once.

9　Bake the tube cake about 1 hour, or until a knife inserted halfway between the edge of the pan and the tube emerges clean. Bake the loaves about 45 minutes, testing them the same way.

10　Cool the cake(s) in the pan(s) on a rack for 15 minutes, then invert to a rack to cool completely.

SERVING: Cut thick slices. This cake needs no accompaniment.

STORAGE: Store under a cake dome or wrap well and freeze.

MAKES ONE 10-INCH TUBE CAKE OR TWO LOAVES

ONE-LAYER CAKES

THESE SINGLE-LAYER CAKES WITH frosting are a little more elaborate than plain cakes. Although still quick and easy to put together for a birthday or special occasion, the addition of frosting or whipped cream dresses them up.

VERMONT FARMHOUSE DEVIL'S FOOD CAKE

 ～

THIS RECIPE WAS GIVEN to me by Copeland Marks, the famous teacher of Asian and Latin American cooking.

CAKE BATTER

2½ cups cake flour

1 teaspoon baking soda

½ teaspoon salt

8 tablespoons (1 stick) unsalted butter, softened

2½ cups dark brown sugar

3½ ounces unsweetened chocolate, melted and cooled

3 large eggs

½ cup sour cream

2 teaspoons vanilla extract

1 cup boiling water

OLD-FASHIONED BOILED FROSTING

3 egg whites, about 6 tablespoons

1 cup granulated sugar

⅓ cup light corn syrup

Pinch salt

One 10-inch springform pan, buttered and the bottom lined with parchment or wax paper

1 Set a rack at the middle level of the oven and preheat to 350 degrees.

2 Sift flour, baking soda, and salt once, then set aside. With an electric mixer set at medium speed, beat butter until soft and light. Add sugar and continue beating until very light, about 5 minutes. Beat in chocolate, then eggs, one at a time. Continue beating until light and smooth.

3 Beat in half the sour cream, then half the flour mixture, scraping bowl and beater(s). Repeat with remaining sour cream and flour mixture, scraping again. Combine vanilla and boiling water and gently beat into batter. Pour

batter into prepared pan and bake for about 45 minutes, until firm and well risen. Cool in pan on rack for 5 minutes, then unmold and cool on a rack.

4 For the frosting, combine all ingredients in bowl of mixer. Whisk to combine, then place over a pan of simmering water, gently whisking until mixture is hot and sugar is dissolved. Use electric mixer on medium speed to beat until cooled, but not dry.

5 To finish, cover top and sides of cake with frosting, swirling it from the center outward.

SERVING: Cut the cake with a moist knife, wiping the blade with a wet cloth between each cut.

STORAGE: Keep cake under a cake dome at room temperature.

MAKES ONE 10-INCH CAKE, ABOUT 12 SERVINGS

TORTA DIVINA

Chocolate Mousse Cake with Liqueur

THIS UNUSUAL CAKE MAY be made in advance. Just make sure to bring it to room temperature before serving.

1 Set a rack at the middle level of the oven and preheat to 325 degrees.

2 Combine the sugar and water in a saucepan and bring to a boil over low heat, stirring occasionally to make sure all the sugar crystals dissolve.

3 Remove the syrup from the heat and stir in the butter and chocolate; allow to stand 5 minutes. Whisk smooth.

4 Whisk liqueur, then the eggs, one at a time, into the chocolate mixture. Be careful not to overmix.

5 Pour the batter into the pan and place in a small roasting pan. Pour 1 inch of warm water into the roasting pan. Bake about 45 minutes, until dessert is set and slightly dry on the surface. Remove cake pan from roasting pan. Cool to room temperature, then cover with plastic wrap. Refrigerate dessert in pan several hours or until chilled. To unmold, run a knife between the dessert and the pan and pass the bottom of the pan over heat for no more than 10 seconds. Invert onto a platter.

6 To finish, whip the cream with the sugar until it holds a soft peak. Spread the whipped

BATTER

½ cup granulated sugar

½ cup water

8 tablespoons (1 stick) unsalted butter, softened

12 ounces semisweet or bittersweet chocolate, cut into ¼-inch pieces

⅓ cup sweet liqueur, such as Cointreau or Chambord

6 eggs

FINISHING

1 cup heavy whipping cream

2 tablespoons sugar

One ½-pint basket fresh raspberries, optional

One 8-inch round pan, buttered and the bottom lined with buttered parchment or buttered wax paper, cut to fit

cream over the top of the dessert. If you wish, decorate the top with the raspberries.

STORAGE: Cover and refrigerate leftovers; bring to room temperature before serving.

MAKES ONE VERY RICH 8-INCH CAKE, ABOUT 8 TO 10 SERVINGS

TEXAS SHEET CAKE

❧ ☙

THERE ARE MANY VERSIONS of this popular cake. This one comes from a combination of recipes from two friends from Texas, Allen Smith and Dorothy Perkins, mother of my friend David Perkins.

1   Set a rack at the middle level of the oven and preheat to 350 degrees.

2   In a large mixing bowl combine the flour, sugar, cinnamon, and baking soda. Stir well to mix.

3   Combine the butter, cocoa, water, and buttermilk in a saucepan and place over low heat. Stir occasionally until the mixture comes to a simmer and the butter is completely melted.

4   Add the contents of the saucepan to the dry ingredients and quickly stir them together. Stir in the eggs and vanilla extract, but stop mixing when the batter is smooth.

5   Scrape the batter into the prepared pan and smooth the top. Bake for about 30 minutes, or until cake is well risen and springs back slightly in the center when touched with a fingertip. Place the pan on a rack to cool for about 15 minutes before spreading on the frosting, which should be applied to the warm cake.

CAKE LAYER

2 cups all-purpose flour

2 cups sugar

1 teaspoon ground cinnamon

1 teaspoon baking soda

16 tablespoons (2 sticks) unsalted butter

¼ cup alkalized (Dutch process) cocoa powder

1 cup water

½ cup buttermilk or milk

2 large eggs

1 teaspoon vanilla extract

FROSTING

8 tablespoons (1 stick) unsalted butter

⅓ cup heavy whipping cream

¼ cup alkalized (Dutch process) cocoa powder

1 teaspoon vanilla extract

4 cups (one 1-pound box) confectioners' sugar

1 cup chopped pecans

1½ cups sweetened shredded coconut

One 13 × 9 × 2-inch pan, buttered and floured

6 To make the frosting, combine the butter, cream, and cocoa in a saucepan and bring to a boil over low heat, stirring occasionally. Remove from heat and add remaining frosting ingredients. Mix well and spread over the top of the still-warm cake. Allow the cake to cool, then cover with plastic wrap.

SERVING: This cake is usually served alone, on the day after it is made. Cut into squares right in the pan and use a wide spatula to lift the squares of cake onto plates. Great with ice cream.

STORAGE: Cover the pan with plastic wrap to keep the cake fresh and moist.

MAKES ONE 13 × 9 × 2-INCH CAKE, ABOUT TWENTY-FOUR 2-INCH SQUARES

TOTAL HEAVEN CHOCOLATE ALMOND CAKE

∽⦾⦿

Although this dessert tastes heavenly, that isn't the whole reason for its name. It was one of our best-selling items at the Total Heaven Baking Company when I owned it with Peter Fresulone and Bill Liederman in the early 1980s.

1 Set a rack at the middle level of the oven and preheat to 350 degrees.

2 Place the almonds in the bowl of a food processor and pulse until finely ground. Combine with the crumbs and cinnamon in a bowl and set aside.

3 Use an electric mixer on medium speed to beat the butter and half the sugar together for about 2 minutes. Then beat in chocolate.

4 Beat in the egg yolks, one a time, beating well after each addition, and scraping down the bowl and beater(s) occasionally with a rubber spatula. Beat in the almond extract.

5 Remove bowl from mixer and stir in almond and crumb mixture.

6 In a clean dry mixer bowl, whip egg whites and salt on medium speed until they are white and opaque and beginning to hold a very soft peak. Increase the speed to high and whip in the remaining sugar 1 tablespoon at a time. Continue to whip the egg whites until they hold a soft peak.

CAKE BATTER

1 cup whole almonds, about 4 ounces

1½ cups fresh white bread or cake crumbs, see Note

1 teaspoon ground cinnamon

12 tablespoons (1½ sticks) unsalted butter, softened

¾ cup sugar, divided

4 ounces bittersweet chocolate, melted and cooled

8 large eggs, separated

½ teaspoon almond extract

Pinch salt

1 batch Ganache Glaze, page 408

¼ cup toasted sliced almonds for finishing

One 10-inch round cake pan, buttered and the bottom lined with parchment or buttered wax paper, cut to fit

7   Stir a quarter of the whipped egg whites into the chocolate batter to lighten it, then fold in the remaining egg whites with a rubber spatula.

8   Scrape the batter into the prepared pan and smooth the top. Bake the cake for 45 minutes, or until it is well risen and a knife or toothpick inserted in the center emerges with only a small amount of batter clinging to it.

9   Cool the cake in the pan on a rack for 5 minutes, then unmold the cake onto the rack to cool. The center of the cake will sink slightly in as it cools. Turn the cooled cake over again so that what was the top while the cake was baking is on top. Use a sharp serrated knife to cut away any high edges and to trim the top of the cake even.

10   Before you glaze the cake, chill it for an hour. Prepare the glaze and let it cool. Invert the cake (so that what was the bottom is now uppermost) onto a piece of cardboard or a springform base and use a small metal offset icing spatula to spread some of the glaze over the entire outside of the cake to seal it. Use no more than a few tablespoons of the glaze. Refrigerate the cake 15 minutes to set the glaze.

11   Set the chilled and masked cake on a rack in a jelly-roll pan and pour the rest of the glaze over the cake starting in the center and pouring outward in larger and larger circles to the edge. Let the glaze run down and cover the sides of the cake. Scatter the almonds around the rim of the cake before the glaze sets.

SERVING: Serve wedges of the cake with whipped cream.

STORAGE: Keep the cake at a cool room temperature until time to serve it. Wrap and refrigerate leftovers but bring them to room temperature before serving.

NOTE: To make fresh, white bread crumbs, trim crusts from firm white or French bread and pulse the bread in the food processor to make fine crumbs. When we made this cake for the baking company, we saved all the scraps from trimming cakes and used those as the bread crumbs. If you want to do this, make your first cake with bread crumbs, then freeze the scraps you trim away until the next time you make it. Use the scraps plus enough bread to make up the quantity of crumbs needed.

MAKES ONE 10-INCH CAKE, ABOUT 12 SERVINGS

ROLLED CAKES

NEAT AND EASY TO SERVE, rolled cakes deserve to be more popular than they are. The one here is a classic—you can serve it as a dessert for the most elegant occasion.

SWISS ROLL

THIS IS THE BRITISH NAME for a cocoa sponge sheet rolled around a whipped cream filling. This one dresses up the plain sponge roll with a little splash of vanilla syrup—more for moisture than flavor—and some chocolate shavings to finish the outside. This is an ideal recipe to prepare in advance—you can make the cake and syrup one day, then whip the cream and finish the cake early on the day you plan to serve it. Thanks to Paul Kinberg and Vicki Russell for sharing their recipes for Swiss rolls.

1 To make the syrup, combine the water and sugar in a small saucepan and bring to a boil over low heat. Cool and add the vanilla.

2 For the whipped cream, combine all ingredients in the bowl of an electric mixer and whip on medium speed until firm but not grainy.

3 To assemble the roll, turn the cooled genoise layer over onto a cookie sheet or cutting board and peel off the paper. Replace with a clean sheet of paper over the layer, then cover paper with another cookie sheet or board and turn the whole stack over again, so that the genoise is right side up on the clean paper. Remove both cookie sheets or boards and leave the genoise on the paper on your work surface.

VANILLA SYRUP

¼ cup water

¼ cup sugar

2 teaspoons vanilla extract

WHIPPED CREAM

3 cups heavy whipping cream

⅓ cup sugar

2 teaspoons vanilla extract

1 batch Genoise Sheet, page 386, baked in
    an 11 × 17-inch jelly-roll pan

FINISHING

1 cup dark or milk chocolate shavings,
    page 525

4 Use a brush to paint the layer with the syrup. Apply it evenly over the whole surface of the layer and use it all.

5 Spread the layer with half of the whipped cream. Arrange the paper so that one of the long sides of the cake is parallel with the edge of the work surface nearest you. Fold ½ inch of that long side of the cake over onto the cream, then, holding the paper to help guide you, let the cake roll up on itself. To tighten the cake and make it a perfect cylinder, position it in the center of the paper and wrap one end of the paper around the cake the long way so that the edges of the paper meet. Hold the bottom paper and use a piece of stiff cardboard or a cookie sheet, held at a 45-degree angle to the cake, to tighten the top piece around the cake.

6 Trim the ends of the roll on a diagonal and roll it off the paper onto a platter. Spread the outside of the cake with the remaining whipped cream and sprinkle the cream evenly with the chocolate shavings.

SERVING: Cut the cake into 1-inch-thick slices. A few raspberries or sliced sweetened strawberries would be a good accompaniment.

STORAGE: Loosely cover the roll with plastic wrap and refrigerate it until you plan to serve it. Cover and refrigerate leftovers.

MAKES ONE 16-INCH-LONG ROLL, ABOUT 12 GENEROUS SERVINGS

LAYER CAKES

PERHAPS THE MOST POPULAR of all cakes, layer cakes are the mainstay of the cake repertoire. Since they require the extra work of assembly after the layer or layers and filling are made, why not divide the work among several sessions, as professional bakers do? If you prepare the cake layers one day, wrap and chill them. Then prepare the frosting and finish the cake early in the day you plan to serve it. Unless the cake is finished with whipped cream—you'll need to refrigerate it—you may leave the cake in a cool place until you plan to serve.

OLD-FASHIONED CHOCOLATE LAYER CAKE

~ ⤳ ⤶ ~

IT WAS TYPICAL IN THE PAST to use a white or yellow cake for the layers with a rich chocolate frosting instead of all-chocolate layers and frosting. This particular version uses tender yellow cake and a fudgy frosting.

CAKE BATTER

2 cups cake flour

2 teaspoons baking powder

¼ teaspoon salt

8 tablespoons (1 stick) unsalted butter, softened

1 cup sugar

6 large egg yolks

1 teaspoon vanilla extract

½ cup milk

CHOCOLATE CREAM FROSTING

1½ cups heavy whipping cream

4 tablespoons (½ stick) unsalted butter

¼ cup light corn syrup

16 ounces semisweet chocolate, cut into ¼-inch pieces

FINISHING

Chocolate shavings, page 525, optional

Two 8-inch round cake pans, 2 inches deep, buttered and the bottoms lined with parchment or wax paper

1 Set a rack at the middle level of the oven and preheat to 350 degrees.

2 In a small bowl, stir together the flour, baking powder, and salt.

3 Use an electric mixer set at medium speed to beat the butter and sugar together. Continue beating until light, about 5 minutes. Beat in the egg yolks, two at a time, beating smooth between each addition. Beat in the vanilla.

4 By hand, using a rubber spatula, stir half the flour mixture into the batter, making sure to scrape the sides of the bowl well. Stir in the milk, then the remaining flour mixture. Scrape well after each addition.

5 Divide the batter between the prepared pans and smooth the top. Bake the layers for about 35 to 45 minutes, or until well risen and a toothpick or a thin knife inserted in the center emerges clean. Cool in the pans for 5 minutes, then unmold and finish cooling the layers on racks. Peel off papers.

6 To make the chocolate cream frosting, combine the cream, butter, and corn syrup in a saucepan. Place over medium heat and bring to a boil, stirring occasionally. Remove from heat, add chocolate, and shake pan gently so that all the chocolate is covered by the hot liquid. Let stand 5 minutes, then whisk smooth. Scrape the frosting into a bowl and let cool to spreading consistency, either in the refrigerator or at room temperature.

7 To assemble the cake, place one of the cooled layers on a cardboard or platter. Spread about half the frosting over the first layer. Top with the second cake layer, flat bottom side up, and spread the top and sides of the cake with the remaining frosting. If you wish, using a spatula, press some chocolate shavings into the frosting on the sides of the cake. (If you try to use your hands, the chocolate will melt from the heat of your hands).

SERVING: Serve the cake in wedges—it needs no accompaniment.

STORAGE: If the cake is made early on the day it is to be served, keep it under a cake dome at a cool room temperature. If you prepare the layers in advance, wrap and freeze them until you are ready to finish the cake. If you prepare the frosting in advance, wrap and refrigerate it, then bring it back to room temperature for several hours so that it turns to spreading consistency.

MAKES ONE 8-INCH 2-LAYER CAKE, ABOUT 10 SERVINGS

CHOCOLATE CHESTNUT CAKE

THIS IS A REALLY GREAT dessert for the holiday season. You can make this cake entirely the day before and chill it. Just bring it to room temperature before serving.

KIRSCH SYRUP
⅓ cup water

⅓ cup sugar

¼ cup kirsch

2 teaspoons vanilla extract

CHESTNUT BUTTER CREAM
24 tablespoons (3 sticks) unsalted butter, softened

1½ cups sweetened chestnut spread, see Note

2 tablespoons kirsch

GANACHE GLAZE
1 cup heavy whipping cream

8 ounces semisweet chocolate, cut into ¼-inch pieces

One 9-inch round Chocolate Genoise, page 386, baked and cooled

FINISHING
Chocolate shavings, page 525

Crystallized violets

A jelly-roll pan and rack for glazing the cake

1 To make the syrup, combine water and sugar in a small saucepan and bring to a boil over low heat. Cool, then stir in the kirsch and vanilla.

2 To make the butter cream, use an electric mixer on medium speed to beat the butter until it is soft and light. Add the chestnut spread, scrape down bowl and beater(s), and continue beating until the butter cream is smooth and light, about 5 minutes. Beat in the kirsch a little at a time, so the butter cream doesn't separate.

3 To make the glaze, bring the cream to a simmer in a saucepan over low heat. Remove from heat and add chocolate all at once. Shake the pan to make sure all the chocolate is submerged in the hot liquid. Let stand 5 minutes, then whisk smooth. Strain into another pan and leave to cool while you assemble the cake.

4 Use a sharp serrated knife to cut the cake into three horizontal layers. Place the layer that was the top of the cake bottom up on a cardboard or springform base. Brush a third of the syrup onto the layer to moisten it. Use an offset icing spatula to spread the layer with a quarter of the butter cream. Cover with the middle layer and moisten it with another third of the syrup and spread it with another quarter of the butter cream. Place the last layer on the cake, so that what was the flat bottom of the cake is now the top surface. Moisten the layer with the remaining syrup.

5 Cover the top and sides of the cake with another quarter of the butter cream, thinly applied. Chill the cake for an hour. Leave the last quarter of the butter cream at room temperature.

6 Place the chilled cake on the rack in the jelly-roll pan and glaze the cake according to the instructions on page 402.

7 Let the cake stand on the rack for a few minutes until the glaze sets, then use a wide spatula to lift the cake from the rack. Use a spatula to press chocolate shavings into the frosting around the bottom edge of the cake.

8 Place the remaining butter cream in a pastry bag fitted with a small star tube and pipe 12 rosettes, equidistant from each other, around the rim of the cake. Top each rosette with a small piece of crystallized violet.

SERVING: Cut the cake into wedges with a knife warmed in hot water and wiped dry between each slice. This rich cake needs no accompaniment.

STORAGE: Keep the cake at a cool room temperature on the day it is made or refrigerate it until the next day. Bring the cake to room temperature before serving. Wrap and refrigerate leftovers.

NOTE: The correct chestnut product for this cake is sweetened chestnut cream, sometimes also called chestnut spread. If you only have unsweetened chestnut puree, use 1¼ cups chestnut puree beaten with ½ cup light corn syrup.

MAKES ONE 9-INCH 3-LAYER CAKE, ABOUT 12 SERVINGS

VARIATION

Omit the chocolate glaze and cover the entire outside of the cake with chocolate shavings. To pipe the rosettes on the shavings, use the tip of a spoon to push the shavings away from the place where you wish to pipe a rosette and make sure the butter cream you are piping touches the butter cream on the cake.

LEMON-SCENTED WHITE CAKE WITH MILK CHOCOLATE FROSTING

THE UNUSUAL FLAVORING for this cake is lemon zest. It is used in both the light, moist cake and the milk chocolate ganache and it delicately perfumes and complements both. It works because the lemon zest, which is rich in the essential oil of lemon, transmits a lemon perfume without any of the acidity of lemon juice, which would mar the chocolate flavor.

1 Set a rack at the middle level of the oven and preheat to 350 degrees.

2 Sift the cake flour, baking powder, and salt onto a piece of parchment or wax paper and set aside.

3 Use an electric mixer set at medium speed to beat the butter and sugar until light, about 3 minutes. Beat in the lemon zest and extract.

4 In a bowl, whisk together the egg whites and milk.

5 Add a third of the flour mixture to the butter and sugar mixture and beat until smooth. Scrape down bowl and beater(s). Beat in half the milk and egg white mixture until incorporated, then beat in another third of the flour mixture. Scrape bowl and beater(s). Beat in remaining liquid until absorbed, followed by remaining flour mixture. Scrape well after each addition.

LEMONY WHITE CAKE

2¼ cups cake flour

3 teaspoons baking powder

½ teaspoon salt

8 tablespoons (1 stick) unsalted butter, softened

1½ cups sugar

2 teaspoons finely grated lemon zest

½ teaspoon lemon extract

½ cup egg whites (from about 4 large eggs)

1¼ cups milk

MILK CHOCOLATE GANACHE

Zest of 2 lemons removed in long strips with a vegetable peeler

2 cups heavy whipping cream

4 tablespoons (½ stick) unsalted butter, softened

20 ounces milk chocolate, cut into ¼-inch pieces

4 ounces bittersweet chocolate, cut into ¼-inch pieces

Two 9-inch round pans, 1½ to 2 inches deep, buttered and lined with buttered parchment or wax paper

6 Divide batter between prepared pans and smooth tops evenly. Bake for about 30 to 35 minutes, until well risen and a toothpick inserted in the center emerges clean. Cool layers in pans for 5 minutes, then invert to racks to cool. Peel off paper. If prepared in advance, double-wrap layers in plastic wrap and chill for up to several days or freeze.

7 To make the ganache, place the pieces of zest in a saucepan and add the cream. Place over low heat and bring to a simmer. Remove from heat and allow to steep about 5 minutes. Remove zests from cream with a slotted spoon and discard them. Add butter to the cream and bring to a boil over low heat. Remove from heat and add chocolates. Shake pan to submerge chocolate and allow to stand 5 minutes. Whisk smooth, then cool to room temperature. Ganache will thicken to spreading consistency.

8 To finish, put one layer right side up on a platter or cardboard. Place ganache in mixer bowl and beat until light, about 20 seconds. Using an offset spatula, spread the layer with a little more than a third of the ganache. Place the other cake layer upside down on the ganache, so that the smooth bottom of the cake layer is uppermost. Spread the top and sides of the cake evenly with most of the remaining ganache.

Serving: This rich cake needs no accompaniment.

Storage: Keep the cake at a cool room temperature before serving. Keep leftovers under a cake dome at a cool room temperature or covered with plastic wrap in the refrigerator.

Makes one 9-inch 2-layer cake, about 12 servings

411

CHOCOLATE

BROWNIES AND BAR COOKIES

I'M A BROWNIE FANATIC and love all sorts of brownies. I even once ran home and baked a brownie recipe that was written on an index card I found on the sidewalk a few blocks from my apartment in New York! Brownies are great because they're practical, like all bar cookies. With just a little effort you can easily make enough for a crowd. I always bake the Supernatural Brownies in this section for Christmas—the holiday wouldn't be the same anymore without them.

BROWNIE HINTS

- Don't overmix—this produces a cakey, dry brownie.

- Watch baking time carefully. Test brownies with a fingertip—they should be soft, but not liquid. An overbaked brownie is dry and uninteresting.

- Let brownies cool completely before attempting to cut. In fact, a few minutes in the refrigerator or freezer makes cutting the brownies much easier. For very moist, fudgy brownies, rinse knife in hot water and wipe between each cut.

- If you are going to store brownies for any length of time, wrap them individually in cellophane or plastic wrap.

BLONDIE SQUARES

~⦿~

THIS IS A GREAT VARIATION on a classic chocolate chip cookie. The batter is not dropped and baked as separate cookies, but is spread in a pan and baked, then cut into chewy, luscious squares, like blond brownies.

1 Set a rack at the middle level of the oven and preheat to 350 degrees.

2 In a mixing bowl stir together the flour, salt, and baking soda to mix.

3 Beat the butter with the sugars until combined. Beat in the eggs, one at a time, and finally the vanilla extract.

4 Stir the flour mixture into the butter mixture, then the nuts and chips.

5 Spread the batter in the prepared pan and bake for about 30 minutes, until well risen and firm to the touch. Cool in the pan on a rack.

6 After cake is cool, invert onto a cutting board and peel away the paper. Cut into 2-inch squares.

STORAGE: Keep the blondies in a tin or plastic container with a tight-fitting lid. Or wrap individually and freeze in a tightly closed plastic container.

MAKES ABOUT THIRTY-SIX 2-INCH SQUARES

2½ cups all-purpose flour

½ teaspoon salt

1 teaspoon baking soda

16 tablespoons (2 sticks) unsalted butter, softened

1¼ cups granulated sugar

¾ cup firmly packed dark brown sugar

2 large eggs

1 teaspoon vanilla extract

½ cup coarsely chopped walnuts or pecans

2 cups (12 ounces) semisweet chocolate chips

One 10 × 15 × 1-inch jelly-roll pan, buttered and lined with buttered parchment or foil

SUPERNATURAL BROWNIES

❧

THOUGH THE NAME sounds an exaggeration, you'll agree that these brownies are absolutely out of this world.

1 Set a rack at the middle level of the oven and preheat to 350 degrees.

2 Bring a saucepan of water to a boil and turn off heat. Combine butter and chocolate in a heatproof bowl and set over pan of water. Stir occasionally until melted.

3 Whisk eggs together in a large bowl, then whisk in salt, sugars, and vanilla. Stir in chocolate and butter mixture, then fold in flour.

4 Pour batter into prepared pan and spread evenly. Bake for about 45 minutes, until top has formed a shiny crust and batter is moderately firm. Cool in pan on a rack. Wrap pan in plastic wrap and keep at room temperature or refrigerated until next day.

5 To cut brownies, unmold onto a cutting board, remove paper, and replace with another cutting board. Turn cake right side up and trim away edges. Cut brownies into 2-inch squares.

SERVING: Serve the brownies on their own or with ice cream and Hot Fudge Sauce, page 512.

STORAGE: The best way to store brownies is to wrap them individually and keep them at room temperature in a tin or plastic container with a tight-fitting cover. Or freeze them.

16 tablespoons (2 sticks) unsalted butter

8 ounces bittersweet or semisweet chocolate, cut into ¼-inch pieces

4 large eggs

½ teaspoon salt

1 cup granulated sugar

1 cup firmly packed dark brown sugar

2 teaspoons vanilla extract

1 cup all-purpose flour

One 13 × 9 × 2-inch pan, buttered and lined with buttered parchment or foil

NOTE: If you have a 12 × 18-inch commercial half-sheet pan, you may double this recipe easily.

MAKES, ABOUT TWENTY-FOUR 2-INCH-SQUARE BROWNIES

VARIATION

Add 2 cups (½ pound) walnut or pecan pieces to the batter.

HARDLY-ANY-FAT FUDGE BROWNIES

〜 ૭ ૯ 〜

THIS IS A GREAT RECIPE if you want to make a dessert for someone on a severely fat-restricted diet. Though these brownies don't have the same richness that full-fat ones do, they have a great taste and texture of their own.

1 Set a rack at the middle level of the oven and preheat to 350 degrees.

2 In a medium bowl, sift together cocoa, flour, baking powder, and salt.

3 In a separate bowl, beat together butter and sugar. Whisk in egg whites, applesauce, and vanilla.

4 Stir flour mixture into applesauce mixture until combined.

5 Pour batter into prepared pan and bake for 35 to 40 minutes or until firm. Cool in pan before cutting into squares.

SERVING: To dress these up, serve with a raspberry or other fat-free berry sherbet.

STORAGE: Keep covered at room temperature, or wrap and freeze.

MAKES SIXTEEN 2-INCH-SQUARE BROWNIES

½ cup alkalized (Dutch process) cocoa powder

1 cup all-purpose flour

1 teaspoon baking powder

½ teaspoon salt

2 tablespoons (¼ stick) unsalted butter, softened

1½ cups sugar

2 large egg whites (¼ cup)

½ cup unsweetened applesauce

1 teaspoon vanilla extract

One 8 × 8 × 2-inch pan, buttered and the bottom lined with a square of parchment or wax paper

DROP COOKIES

QUICK TO MIX AND EASY to shape, the dough for most drop cookies may be scooped up with a spoon and, as the name indicates, plopped onto the pan.

FOR BEST DROP COOKIES

- Don't overmix the batter—it makes the cookies fill up with air, then puff and flatten out while they are baking.

- Try to make cookies uniform so that they will be similar sizes—they will bake more evenly.

- Remember to alternate racks in the oven during baking—reverse the cookies back to front after 8 or 10 minutes and place cookies from upper rack on the lower one and vice versa. Consider doubling the pan—baking on two pans stacked together—or using an insulated cookie sheet for the lower third of the oven, where there is strong bottom heat that can burn delicate cookies.

SPICY CHOCOLATE CHUNK PECAN MERINGUES

❧ ❧

THESE DELICIOUS COOKIES WERE partly inspired by Maida Heatter's Hot and Sweet Meringues flavored with crystallized ginger and macadamia nuts. My recipe gets its bite from ground ginger and white pepper.

1 Set racks in the upper and lower thirds of the oven and preheat to 300 degrees.

2 In the bowl of an electric mixer, combine the egg whites and salt. Whip on medium speed until the egg whites are white and foamy and beginning to hold their shape. Increase speed to high and beat in granulated sugar, 1 tablespoon at a time, until egg whites are stiff, but not dry.

3 Remove bowl from mixer and sift confectioners' sugar over it. Fold in. Before the sugar is completely absorbed, sprinkle on the ginger, pepper, nuts, and chocolate and continue folding until the ingredients are all incorporated.

4 Use a tablespoon to drop meringue onto the prepared pans. Keep the cookies about 1½ inches from one another and from the sides of the pan.

5 Place the pans in the oven and immediately lower the temperature to 275 degrees. Bake about 30 to 35 minutes, until cookies are golden and firm, but not dry all the way through. Cool the meringues on the pans on racks.

4 large egg whites

Pinch salt

½ cup granulated sugar

1 cup confectioners' sugar

1 teaspoon ground ginger

¼ teaspoon freshly ground white pepper

1 cup pecan pieces, lightly toasted and chopped into ¼-inch pieces, about 4 ounces

6 ounces semisweet or bittersweet chocolate, cut into ¼-inch pieces

2 cookie sheets or jelly-roll pans lined with parchment or foil

STORAGE: Keep the meringues between sheets of wax paper in a tin or plastic container with a tight-fitting cover.

MAKES ABOUT 25 TO 35 COOKIES, DEPENDING ON SIZE

OLD-FASHIONED CHOCOLATE CHIP COOKIES

~⊙ ℃~

No book of chocolate desserts would be complete without a recipe for this best and most beloved of all cookies.

1 Set racks in the upper and lower thirds of the oven and preheat to 375 degrees.

2 In a mixing bowl, stir together the flour, salt, and baking soda. Sift the dry ingredients onto a piece of parchment or wax paper.

3 By hand or with an electric mixer, beat together the butter and sugars. Beat in the egg and the vanilla extract until smooth. Stir in the dry ingredients, then the nuts and chocolate chips.

4 Drop the batter by heaping teaspoons onto the prepared pans, keeping the cookies about 3 inches apart on all sides.

5 Bake the cookies for about 12 to 15 minutes, until deep golden and firm. Slide parchment or foil from pans to racks to cool.

STORAGE: Keep the cookies between sheets of wax paper in a tin or other container with a tight fitting cover.

MAKES ABOUT 30 COOKIES

1 cup all-purpose flour

½ teaspoon salt

½ teaspoon baking soda

8 tablespoons (1 stick) unsalted butter, softened

½ cup granulated sugar

¼ cup firmly packed dark brown sugar

1 large egg

1 teaspoon vanilla extract

½ cup walnut or pecan pieces, coarsely chopped

One 6-ounce bag semisweet chocolate chips

2 cookie sheets or jelly-roll pans lined with parchment or foil

REFRIGERATOR COOKIES

WHEN I WAS A CHILD, these were still called "icebox cookies." I guess in the early fifties there were still a few old-fashioned iceboxes persisting where people didn't have electric refrigerators. In any case, these are practical cookies to prepare. The ancestors of industrially made "slice and bake" cookies, these may be made up and shaped days in advance and then cut and baked when it's convenient—or when you just want some freshly baked cookies.

To shape refrigerator cookies, flour the work surface and gently roll the dough into a cylinder. Divide it into the amount of separate pieces the recipe states, then place each on a piece of parchment or wax paper. Roll the cookie dough to the length stated in the recipe, then wrap the paper around it, making a tight cylinder. Chill the logs of dough until ready to slice and bake the cookies.

Give the paper-wrapped logs a second wrapping in plastic if you intend to freeze them—just remember to defrost the cookies in the refrigerator for half a day before trying to slice and bake them.

A hint about slicing the cookies: After you unwrap the log of chilled dough, place it on a cutting board and cut it with a sharp knife. Roll the log of dough a few degrees around every time you slice through it to avoid crushing the log by cutting repeatedly with the log in the same position.

PEPPERY CHOCOLATE SABLÉS

❧

THESE ARE BASED ON a delicious cookie made by my friend and former student Stephen Hoffman.

1 Use an electric mixer to beat butter with sugar, cinnamon, and peppers until very light, about 5 minutes on medium speed.

2 Beat in egg, then egg white. Continue beating until smooth.

3 Sift flour, cocoa, and baking soda over batter, then stir in.

4 Divide dough in half, place each half on a sheet of parchment paper, and shape each into an 8-inch long cylinder. Wrap parchment around dough and chill until firm.

5 Set racks in the upper and lower thirds of the oven and preheat to 325 degrees.

6 Slice dough every ¼ inch and arrange cookies on prepared pans. Bake 15 to 20 minutes. Cool on pans on a rack.

SERVING: These are great on their own or with a creamy dessert.

STORAGE: Keep the cookies between sheets of parchment or wax paper in a tin or plastic container that has a tight-fitting cover.

MAKES ABOUT 60 COOKIES

10 tablespoons (1¼ sticks) unsalted butter, softened
¾ cup sugar
1 teaspoon ground cinnamon
¼ teaspoon cayenne pepper
¼ teaspoon freshly ground black pepper
1 egg
1 large egg white
2 cups all-purpose flour
½ cup alkalized (Dutch process) cocoa powder
½ teaspoon baking soda

2 cookie sheets or jelly-roll pans lined with parchment or foil

VARIATIONS

CHOCOLATE SABLÉS: Omit the cinnamon, cayenne, and black pepper for a plain, but delicious, chocolate cookie.

TRIPLE CHOCOLATE SABLÉS: Add ⅓ cup each dark, milk, and white chocolate chips to the batter for Chocolate Sablés. Not easy to slice after chilling, but a great chocolaty cookie.

PIPED COOKIES

THESE ARE REALLY DROP COOKIES that we use a pastry bag and tube to shape. For this reason, they are some of the most tailored-looking cookies. Piping makes them have a uniform size and appearance that dropping the dough or batter from a spoon would never achieve.

For success in preparing piped cookies, always use the size tube specified in the recipe, unless you are very experienced at piping.

Remember, most piped cookies puff or spread, so leave at least the size of one of the piped cookies as a space before piping the next one.

Pipe cookies onto parchment or foil—though I prefer parchment.

SWISS CHOCOLATE S'S

A SWISS CLASSIC, THESE chocolate meringue S's are fairly easy to prepare. The method in this recipe is simplified—usually the egg whites are whipped and a hot sugar syrup is poured over them, a process I find unnecessarily complicated. The easier technique of heating the egg whites and sugar provides similar—and excellent—results. My thanks to Stephan Schiesser of the Confiserie Schiesser in Basel for this recipe.

1 Set racks in the lower and upper thirds of the oven and preheat to 300 degrees.

2 Bring a pan of water to a boil and lower heat to a simmer. Combine egg whites and sugar in bowl of electric mixer and whip to combine. Place over pan of simmering water and use a wire whisk to stir gently and steadily, until egg white is hot and sugar is dissolved, about 4 or 5 minutes.

3 Place meringue in mixer and whip at medium speed until risen in volume and substantially cooled, but not dry.

4 Pour chocolate over meringue and fold it in with a rubber spatula.

5 Transfer the meringue to a pastry bag fitted with a ½-inch star tube (Ateco #4) and pipe S shapes, about 1½ inches apart, on the prepared pans. Bake the S's about 10 to 12 minutes, until crisp on the outside but still somewhat soft within.

3 large egg whites

14 tablespoons sugar
(measure 1 cup sugar, then remove 2 level tablespoons)

3 ounces unsweetened chocolate, melted and cooled

2 cookie sheets or jelly-roll pans lined with parchment

SERVING: These are great as dessert with a simple ice cream or all alone.

STORAGE: Keep between sheets of wax paper in a tin or plastic container with a tight-fitting cover. They keep well, but are really best on the day they are made.

MAKES ABOUT THIRTY-SIX 2-INCH S'S

CHOCOLATE ORANGE MACAROONS

❧

THE BEST MACAROONS are made with canned almond paste—accept no substitute.

1 Set a rack at the middle level of the oven and preheat to 375 degrees.

2 With an electric mixer, mix almond paste, sugar, and cocoa on low speed. When crumbly, add extract, zest, and 1 egg white; mix until smooth. Add remaining egg whites and continue mixing until the macaroon paste is extremely smooth.

3 Use a ½-inch plain tube (Ateco #6 or #806) to pipe the macaroons on a paper-lined pan. Hold the bag perpendicular to the pan and about ½ inch above it and squeeze out a macaroon about ¾ inch in diameter. Stop squeezing and pull away sideways to avoid leaving a point. Wet a non-terry-cloth towel with warm water. Fold it into a narrow rectangle. Holding one end of the towel in each hand so that the towel hangs fairly loosely, let the towel touch the surface of the macaroons repeatedly to smooth them out.

4 Bake for about 10 to 12 minutes, or until the macaroons are well puffed and slightly firm—do not let them dry out.

8 ounces canned almond paste

¾ cup sugar

¼ cup alkalized (Dutch process) cocoa powder

1 teaspoon orange extract

Grated zest of 1 orange

3 egg whites

1 cookie sheet or jelly-roll pan lined with parchment

STORAGE: Keep the cookies between sheets of wax paper in a tin or other container with a tight-fitting cover.

MAKES 60 COOKIES

CHOCOLATE ALMOND FINGERS

❧ ☙

THESE CRISP, RICH COOKIES are just as good plain as sandwiched with the white chocolate filling in the variation that follows the recipe.

1 Set racks in the upper and lower thirds of the oven and preheat to 350 degrees.

2 Use an electric mixer to beat the butter on medium speed until light. Beat in the sugar in a stream and continue to beat until the mixture whitens.

3 Add the egg whites, one at a time, and continue beating until very creamy. Sift the flour and cocoa powder together several times, stir in the ground almonds, and stir into the batter.

4 Scrape the batter into a pastry bag fitted with a ½-inch plain tube (Ateco #6). Pipe dough out in fingers about 2 inches long by positioning the bag at a 45-degree angle to the pan and letting the bottom of the tube touch the paper. Squeeze and pull the tube about 2 inches toward you, then release pressure and pull the tube away and up to avoid leaving a tail on the cookie. Pipe the cookies about 2 inches apart.

5 Bake for about 10 to 12 minutes, or until cookies have spread and become matte-Serving: These make a great accompaniment for any creamy dessert.

8 tablespoons (1 stick) unsalted butter, softened

½ cup sugar

2 egg whites

½ cup all-purpose flour

2 tablespoons alkalized (Dutch Process) cocoa powder

1 cup ground almonds, about 3½ ounces

2 cookie sheets or jelly-roll pans lined with parchment or foil

STORAGE: Keep in a tin or plastic container with a tight-fitting lid.

MAKES ABOUT 40 COOKIES (20 IF SANDWICHED)

VARIATION

CHOCOLATE ALMOND FINGERS WITH CHOCOLATE FILLING: Stir together ½ cup cold heavy whipping cream and ½ pound dark chocolate, melted and cooled. It should thicken immediately to spreading consistency. Spread or pipe the filling on the flat sides of half the cookies. Top with other cookies, flat sides against the filling.

ROLLED COOKIES

THIN AND DELICATE, ROLLED COOKIES can be as easy or as difficult to prepare as you choose to make them. Follow these simple steps for a pleasurable experience.

When instructed to chill dough before rolling it, press the dough out into a rectangle about ¼-inch thick on plastic wrap. Cover with more plastic wrap and chill until firm—the thin dough will chill quickly.

When you roll the chilled dough, divide it into several small pieces. Don't roll the whole batch at once or the dough will soften before you finish rolling it out and the process will become a nightmare. If you roll small pieces at a time, they will stay firm and easy to manage.

Save the scraps of dough, gently press them together, and chill again before rolling, for the most tender cookies.

Roll cookie dough between ⅛ and ¼ inch thick for best results, unless otherwise specified. Cookies that are too thin may burn easily while baking.

CHOCOLATE THUMBPRINTS

~⊙ ⊙~

THIS IS A GREAT OLD-FASHIONED cookie usually filled with jelly or jam. These are filled with a chocolaty syrup that sets firm in the cookies.

1 Set racks in the upper and lower thirds of the oven and preheat to 325 degrees.

2 For the cookie dough, place butter in a mixing bowl and beat in sugar by hand with a rubber spatula. Beat in the salt, vanilla, and milk. Finally, fold in the flour to make a soft dough.

3 Divide the dough into three parts, then divide each part into twelve pieces. Roll each piece into a sphere and place on prepared pans about 2 inches apart.

4 Using the index finger of one hand, press a deep fingerprint into each cookie.

5 Bake the cookies for about 15 minutes, or until they are golden. Cool on pans on racks.

6 After the cookies have cooled, make the filling. In a small bowl, beat the butter, corn syrup, water, and vanilla. Stir in the chocolate. Using a small spoon, fill the indentation in each cooled cookie with the chocolate mixture. Leave the cookies on the pans until the chocolate filling has set.

COOKIE DOUGH

8 tablespoons (1 stick) unsalted butter, softened

½ cup firmly packed light brown sugar

½ teaspoon salt

1 teaspoon vanilla extract

2 tablespoons milk

1½ cups all-purpose flour

FILLING

1 tablespoon butter, softened

2 tablespoons light corn syrup

1 tablespoon water

1 teaspoon vanilla extract

4 ounces semisweet chocolate, melted

2 cookie sheets or jelly-roll pans lined with parchment or foil

STORAGE: Keep the cookies between sheets of wax paper in a tin or other container with a tight-fitting cover.

MAKES ABOUT 36 COOKIES

CHOCOLATE-DIPPED STARS

THESE ARE EASY TO MAKE, with a base similar to shortbread. A quick dip in chocolate is the finishing touch for these simple, but exquisitely delicate cookies.

1 Use an electric mixer to beat the butter on medium speed until very soft. Beat in the sugar in a stream, then the vanilla, and continue beating until very light. Beat in the yolks, one at a time, beating until very smooth after each addition. After the yolks are beaten in, the mixture should look like butter cream.

2 Sift the cake flour and add it to the butter mixture. Pulse the mixer on and off on lowest speed only until the cake flour is absorbed. Mix no more than necessary to avoid toughening the dough.

3 Scrape the dough from the bowl onto a piece of plastic wrap. Wrap the dough tightly and refrigerate it until firm.

4 Set racks at the upper and lower thirds of the oven and preheat to 325 degrees.

5 Flour a work surface and the dough and roll it to slightly less than ¼-inch thickness. Paint the dough with the egg wash and score it with a fork, or roll over it with a grooved rolling pin or score the dough with a fork and paint it with the egg wash. Cut the dough with a star- or heart-shaped cutter and place the cookies on the prepared pans.

6 Bake for about 15 minutes, until lightly browned—they should still be quite pale. Cool on the pans.

COOKIE DOUGH

16 tablespoons (2 sticks)
    unsalted butter, softened
½ cup sugar
2 teaspoons vanilla
3 egg yolks
2½ cups cake flour
Egg wash: 1 egg beaten with
    a pinch of salt

DIPPING

About 1 pound of good-quality bittersweet
    or semisweet couverture chocolate,
    tempered, see pages 384–385

2 cookie sheets or jelly-roll pans lined
    with parchment, plus extra parchment for
    dipping

7 Melt and temper the chocolate. Dip half of each cookie into the chocolate, so that the pattern on the surface still shows. Place the cookies on parchment paper to dry.

STORAGE: Store the cookies in a cool place in a tin or plastic container with a tight-fitting cover.

MAKES 50 COOKIES

SANDWICH COOKIES

THESE ARE ALL ROLLED OR drop cookies with a filling—usually a bit of jam or ganache. Maybe it's because you get to eat two cookies at the same time, but sandwich cookies always seem more fun and festive to me.

For best results, don't overdo the filling or cookies will become uncontrollably messy. For most cookies between ¼ and ½ teaspoon of filling is enough.

SWISS CHOCOLATE SANDWICH COOKIES

This recipe is adapted from that great work Swiss Baking and Confectionery by Walter Bachmann, a Swiss pastry chef who lived in London after the Second World War.

CHOCOLATE COOKIE DOUGH

12 tablespoons (1½ sticks) unsalted butter, softened

4 ounces semisweet chocolate, melted and cooled

1¾ cups all-purpose flour

GANACHE FILLING

⅓ cup heavy whipping cream

1 tablespoon unsalted butter

1 tablespoon light corn syrup

2 ounces bittersweet chocolate, cut into ¼-inch pieces

2 ounces milk chocolate, cut into ¼-inch pieces

FINISHING

Confectioners' sugar

2 cookie sheets or jelly-roll pans lined with parchment or foil

1 To make the dough, beat the butter by hand in a medium bowl just until it is evenly softened. Quickly beat in the melted chocolate, then the flour. Continue to mix until dough is smooth.

2 Scrape the dough out onto a piece of plastic wrap and press it into a rectangle about ½ inch thick. Wrap and chill the dough until it is firm—about an hour.

3 While the dough is chilling, make the filling. Combine the cream, butter, and corn syrup in a saucepan and bring to a boil over low heat. Remove from heat and add both chocolates.

Shake the pan gently to submerge chocolate in the hot liquid. Let stand 5 minutes, then whisk smooth and scrape filling into a bowl. Let stand at room temperature or in the refrigerator until of spreading consistency.

4 To bake the cookie bases, set racks in the upper and lower thirds of the oven and preheat to 350 degrees.

5 If the dough is very hard, pound it gently with the rolling pin to soften it so that it rolls out more easily. Divide dough in half and, on a floured surface, roll one half about ³/₁₆ inch thick. Use a fluted, round 2-inch cutter to cut the dough into cookies. Place them on prepared pans as they are cut, leaving about an inch between the cookies. Repeat with remaining dough. Save all the scraps. Reroll scraps and cut more cookies.

6 Bake the cookies 12 to 15 minutes, until they are firm and slightly colored. Cool the cookies in the pans on racks.

7 When cookies and filling have cooled, arrange half the cookies, flat side up. Place a dab of filling on them and cover with the remaining cookies, flat sides together. Dust cookies very lightly with confectioners' sugar before serving.

MAKES ABOUT 18 SANDWICH COOKIES

BISCOTTI

NAMED FOR THE ITALIAN for "twice baked," these have recently become one of the most popular cookies in the United States. They all follow the same system: Divide the dough into several pieces and shape it into cylinders. Then place them on pans and bake until risen and firm. Cool and slice, rebaking the slices until crisp. Be careful about the following points in biscotti recipes:

- Make sure the first baking makes the logs of dough firm enough or they will have a heavy core after slicing and rebaking.

- Cool the baked logs completely or they may crumble when you try to slice them. Use a sharp knife and cut thin slices or the biscotti may be hard and not crisp.

- Store the biscotti airtight or they may soften. If they do, place them on a cookie sheet in one layer and bake again at 325 degrees for a few minutes to crisp them.

CRISP CHOCOLATE BISCOTTI

❧ ❧

This is based on a recipe by Ellen Baumwoll, proprietor of Bijoux Doux in New York City.

1 Set a rack at the middle level of the oven and preheat to 325 degrees.

2 Mix together the flour, cocoa, baking powder, and salt and sift into a mixing bowl. Stir in the sugar and nuts.

3 Whisk the eggs and vanilla together and stir into the flour mixture to form a dough.

4 On a lightly floured surface, press dough together. Divide dough in half and roll each half into a log the length of the pan (14 to 18 inches). Place each log on a pan and flatten slightly. Bake for about 30 minutes, until well risen and firm. Cool the logs in the pans.

5 After the logs have cooled, lift them from the parchment and cut each into ½-inch-thick slices with a sharp serrated knife. Replace, cut side down, on paper-lined pans and bake again for about 20 minutes, until dry and crisp. Cool in pans.

Serving: Serve the biscotti with coffee or ice cream.

Storage: Keep in a tin or plastic container with a tight-fitting lid.

Makes about 4 dozen biscotti

1¾ cups all-purpose flour

⅔ cup alkalized (Dutch process) cocoa powder

2 teaspoons baking powder

Pinch salt

1¼ cups sugar

1½ cups chopped skinned hazelnuts or walnuts

4 large eggs

1 teaspoon vanilla extract

2 cookie sheets or jelly-roll pans lined with parchment or foil

VARIATION

Chocolate Espresso Biscotti: Add 3 tablespoons instant espresso powder to the flour mixture.

DRIED CHERRY, CHOCOLATE CHIP, AND PISTACHIO BISCOTTI

This great, easy recipe comes from Andrea Tutunjian, who teaches the career baking course at Peter Kump's New York Cooking School.

1 Set a rack at the middle level of the oven and preheat to 350 degrees.

2 In a mixing bowl, combine the flour, sugar, baking powder, and salt and stir well to mix.

3 Cut the butter into six or eight pieces and toss with the dry ingredients. Rub in the butter, as for a pastry dough. Squeeze the butter and dry ingredients with fingertips and rub the mixture between the palms of the hands. Keep bringing up the dry bits from the bottom of the bowl, and continue rubbing, until all the butter has been absorbed but the mixture remains cool and powdery. Stir in the cherries, chips, and pistachios.

4 Whisk the eggs and vanilla together and use a fork to stir them into the dry ingredients. Continue stirring until the dough masses together. Turn the dough out on a lightly floured surface and press it together. Flour your hands and form the dough into a 12-inch-long cylinder. Cut the cylinder in half, then roll and pull each half until it is 12 inches long. Place the two cylinders on the baking pan, spacing them so they are equidistant from the edges of the pan and each other.

1¾ cups all-purpose flour

¾ cup sugar

1 teaspoon baking powder

¼ teaspoon salt

8 tablespoons (1 stick) unsalted butter

I cup dried cherries

1 cup semisweet chocolate chips, 6 ounces

1 cup unsalted pistachios, about 4 ounces

2 large eggs

2 teaspoons vanilla extract

1 cookie sheet or jelly-roll pan lined with parchment or foil

5 Bake about 25 to 30 minutes, until the dough is well-colored and firm to the touch. Slide the parchment or foil off the pan onto a cutting board to cool the logs. For advance preparation wrap the logs in foil and use them within several days. Or, freeze the baked logs and use them within a month.

6   When the baked logs are cool, peel away the paper and place one log on the cutting board. Use a sharp, serrated knife to slice the log diagonally every ⅓ inch. As they are cut, line up the slices, cut side down, on a paper- or foil-lined cookie sheet (you may need a second pan). Bake the biscotti at 325 degrees about 15 to 20 minutes longer, until they are very light golden in color. Cool the biscotti on the pans on a rack.

SERVING: These are great as an accompaniment to ice cream or a fruit dessert.

STORAGE: Store in a tin or plastic container with a tight-fitting cover at room temperature.

MAKES 60 TO 70 BISCOTTI

MOLDED COOKIES

THE RECIPE FOR MOLDED COOKIES here use a pizzelle maker—a type of waffle iron for shaping.

CHOCOLATE ALMOND PIZZELLE

ALTHOUGH YOU NEED A special type of waffle iron to make these pizzelle (pronounced peet-sellay), it is easy to find and not very expensive. Divide the pizzelle into quarters with a sharp knife after they are baked, or mold them around a cone-shaped form to make delicious, easy ice cream cones. Work quickly; the cookies become crisp as they cool.

1 Whisk the eggs with the sugar and salt until light. Stir in melted butter. Sift together the flour, cocoa, cinnamon, and baking powder and fold into batter. Stir in the almonds.

2 Oil the surface of the imprints and heat pizzelle iron. When hot, place 1 heaping teaspoon of batter on each imprint. Close iron and bake 30 seconds. Cool cookies on racks.

SERVING: These are great as an accompaniment to ice cream.

STORAGE: Keep in a tin or plastic container with a tight-fitting cover. If pizzelle lose their crispness, heat them in a 350-degree oven on a parchment or foil-covered cookie sheet for 5 minutes, then cool on racks.

MAKES ABOUT EIGHTEEN 4-INCH COOKIES

2 large eggs

½ cup sugar

¼ teaspoon salt

4 tablespoons (½ stick) unsalted butter, melted

1 cup all-purpose flour

3 tablespoons alkalized (Dutch process) cocoa powder

½ teaspoon ground cinnamon

1½ teaspoons baking powder

½ cup whole unblanched almonds, finely ground in the food processor

Oil for the iron

A pizzelle waffle iron

TERRINES

A BORROWING FROM ANOTHER KIND of cooking. A terrine is a rectangular mold in which a pâté is baked. When that type of a pâté is unmolded it too is known as a terrine. Because rich chocolate mixtures may be formed in the same types of molds, we now have chocolate terrines. For the recipes that follow a traditional terrine mold isn't necessary. These mixtures are molded in loaf pans and cut into slices for serving. They are convenient to serve and easy to prepare in advance.

TRIPLE CHOCOLATE PUDDING

IF YOUR ONLY EXPERIENCE with chocolate pudding is the packaged variety, you'll be surprised at how good—and easy—this homemade version is.

2 cups whole milk, or use a combination of milk and heavy whipping cream, divided

⅓ cup sugar

2 ounces bittersweet chocolate, cut into ¼-inch pieces

2 ounces milk chocolate, cut into ¼-inch pieces

2 tablespoons cornstarch

2 tablespoons alkalized (Dutch process) cocoa powder

3 large eggs

2 teaspoons vanilla extract, rum, or a sweet liqueur

1 Combine 1½ cups milk with the sugar in a nonreactive saucepan. Whisk to mix. Place over medium heat and bring to a simmer. Remove from heat and add chocolates. Let stand 5 minutes, then whisk smooth.

2 Meanwhile, pour remaining ½ cup of milk in a mixing bowl; whisk in cornstarch, sift in cocoa, then whisk in eggs.

3 Return milk and chocolate mixture to a simmer over low heat, whisking often so it doesn't scorch. Whisk a third of the hot liquid into the egg mixture.

4 Return the remaining milk and chocolate mixture to a simmer and then slowly whisk in the egg mixture, whisking constantly until the mixture thickens and just comes to a boil.

5 Off heat, whisk in vanilla. Fill individual cups or glasses with the pudding and press a piece of plastic wrap against the surface of each, to prevent a skin from forming. Chill the puddings and serve cold, with a spoonful of whipped cream, if desired.

MAKES ABOUT 1 1/2 PINTS PUDDING, ABOUT 6 SERVINGS

Variations

Old-Fashioned Chocolate Pudding:

This uses only semisweet chocolate and a sprinkling of walnuts for an old-fashioned flavor. Substitute 6 ounces semisweet chocolate for the bittersweet and milk chocolates. Omit the cocoa powder and increase the cornstarch to 3 tablespoons. Stir in ⅓ cup finely chopped toasted walnuts or pecans after removing cooked pudding from heat.

Old-Fashioned Chocolate Butterscotch Pudding:

Substitute dark brown sugar for the white sugar. Whisk in 2 tablespoons butter after removing cooked pudding from heat.

BITTERSWEET CHOCOLATE
CRÈME BRÛLÉE

~⟳ ⟲ ⟲~

THIS RICH CUSTARD takes on a delicate complex flavor when chocolate is added.

1 Set a rack at the middle level of the oven and preheat to 300 degrees.

2 Bring cream and sugar to a boil in a nonreactive pan. Remove from heat, add chocolate, and allow to stand 3 minutes to melt. Whisk smooth.

3 Whisk yolks in a bowl, then whisk in chocolate mixture. Strain into gratin dish.

4 Place pans on oven rack. Add warm water to the bottom pan to about half the depth of the gratin dish. Bake about 1 hour, or until set. To test for doneness, insert a thin knife or toothpick in the center of the custard; it should emerge clean. Remove baking dish from roasting pan (leave the pan of water in the oven to cool) and chill custard.

5 To caramelize top, blot any moisture from top of chilled custard. Sprinkle evenly with sugar. Place under preheated broiler, or use blow torch or salamander to caramelize. Refrigerate until serving within several hours of caramelizing.

MAKES ABOUT 8 GENEROUS SERVINGS

CUSTARD CREAM

4 cups heavy whipping cream
½ cup sugar
12 ounces bittersweet chocolate
8 egg yolks

CARAMELIZING THE TOP

½ cup sugar

One 2-quart gratin or other flat baking dish set inside a roasting pan

NOTE: If you use a blow torch for caramelizing the sugar, be careful. Strike a match first, then turn on the torch. Light the torch, then adjust the flame to medium. To caramelize the sugar, move the torch around in small circles, with the nozzle about an inch away from the top of the crème brûlée.

VARIATION

INDIVIDUAL CHOCOLATE CRÈMES BRÛLÉES
Use shallow individual gratin dishes or even ramekins for individual versions of this dessert. Set individual molds in a shallow roasting pan and fill them. Carefully place the pan in the oven, then add hot water to the pan around them.

FLAN DE TRES LECHES Y CHOCOLATE

Mexican Chocolate Flan

THE USE OF CANNED MILK IN different forms is common in recipes from the tropics, where there wasn't much refrigeration until recently. Although this version of baked custard uses fresh milk as one of the leches, that could be replaced by more evaporated milk, or even evaporated cream.

1 Set a rack at the middle level of the oven and preheat to 300 degrees.

2 To make the flan mixture, combine milks, cinnamon stick, and lemon zest in a saucepan. Bring the mixture to a boil, then turn off heat and allow to steep for 15 minutes. Add chocolate, and whisk until melted and smooth. In a large mixing bowl, whisk eggs with vanilla until liquid. Slowly whisk the milk into the eggs.

3 To make the caramel, combine sugar and ½ teaspoon water in a small saucepan. Stir well and place over low heat, stirring occasionally, until the mixture becomes amber in color. Add 3 tablespoons water, allow to return to a boil, then remove from heat.

4 Pour the caramel into the ring mold. Tilt to coat the inside completely, then invert the mold to drain off excess. Pour the flan mixture through a fine strainer into the mold in the roasting pan. Place on oven rack. Add warm water to the bottom pan to a depth of 1 inch. Bake for about 1 hour, or until the custard is set in the center and firm when gently pressed with a fingertip. Remove the ring mold from the roasting pan. (Leave the pan of water in the oven to cool.)

1 can evaporated milk, 12 ounces

1 can sweetened condensed milk, 14 ounces

1 cup fresh milk

1 cinnamon stick

4 strips lemon zest

8 ounces bittersweet chocolate, cut into ¼-inch pieces

8 eggs

1 tablespoon vanilla extract

CARAMEL

½ cup sugar

½ teaspoon plus 3 tablespoons water

One 6-cup ring mold, set inside a small roasting pan

5 Cover the mold with plastic wrap and chill the custard. To unmold, run the point of a small paring knife around the custard to about ¼ inch down from the top of the mold to loosen. Invert a platter over the mold, then invert, hold platter and mold together, and shake several times to loosen custard from mold. Lift off mold and cover custard loosely with plastic wrap. Refrigerate until serving time.

SERVING: Serve thick slice of the custard. Accompany with a spoonful of whipped cream and/or a crisp cookie.

STORAGE: Cover leftovers with plastic wrap and refrigerate.

MAKES ABOUT 8 GENEROUS SERVINGS

VARIATIONS

CHOCOLATE CARAMEL CUSTARD: In the flan mixture, substitute 2 cups milk, 2 cups heavy whipping cream, and ⅓ cup sugar for the three milks; substitute 4 eggs and 4 egg yolks for the 8 eggs.

CARIBBEAN CHOCOLATE CUSTARD: Add ¼ cup dark rum to either the basic recipe or its custard variation above.

FLOURLESS CHOCOLATE SOUFFLÉ

～ ⁊ ⌒ ～

THIS A WONDERFUL AND EASY WAY to make a chocolate soufflé. I always use 4- or 5-ounce individual ramekins. This is adapted from a recipe created by my late friend and associate Peter Kump, a real connoisseur of all things chocolate.

1 Set a rack at the lower third of the oven and preheat to 400 degrees.

2 Combine the chocolate with the coffee in a heatproof bowl. Place bowl over a pan of hot water and allow to melt, stirring occasionally. Stir smooth, remove from the heat, and stir in the butter. Cool to room temperature.

3 Stir in the yolks.

4 Use an electric mixer to whip egg whites with salt until they hold a very light peak. Add sugar gradually and continue to beat until whites form a soft peak.

5 Stir a quarter of the whites into the base. Using a rubber spatula, fold in the remaining whites.

6 Pour batter in buttered and sugared molds, filling molds to the top. Bake for approximately 12 to 15 minutes, or until the soufflés are well risen and baked through, except for the very center, which should remain soft and liquid. (Check one of the soufflés by taking the point of a spoon and using it to lift the top off on one side—it will fall right back into place.)

7 ounces semisweet chocolate

¼ cup strong brewed coffee

4 tablespoons (½ stick) unsalted butter, softened

4 egg yolks

8 egg whites

Pinch salt

¼ cup sugar

Eight 4- to 5-ounce ramekins buttered and sugared, set on a jelly-roll pan

SERVING: Serve the soufflés immediately, on dessert plates. Pass Chocolate Sauce, page 513, and/or whipped cream if you wish.

MAKES 8 SERVINGS

VARIATIONS

CHOCOLATE RASPBERRY SOUFFLÉ: Substitute ¼ cup raspberry liqueur or 2 tablespoons raspberry eau de vie and 2 tablespoons water for the coffee. Serve the soufflé with Raspberry Sauce.

CHOCOLATE ORANGE SOUFFLÉ: Substitute ¼ cup orange liqueur for the coffee.

MILK CHOCOLATE SOUFFLÉ: Substitute 12 ounces milk chocolate for the semisweet chocolate. Reduce the sugar to 1 tablespoon.

CHOCOLATE AND COFFEE POTS DE CRÈME

⌒ ♊ ⌒

THIS RICH AND elegant dessert is perfect after a light dinner.

1 Bring the cream and sugar to a boil with the vanilla bean in a saucepan.

2 Whisk yolks in a bowl. Whisk about a third of the boiling cream into the yolks. Return remaining cream to a boil and whisk in yolk mixture. Continue to cook, whisking constantly, another 15 or 20 seconds, until slightly thickened.

3 Strain cream into a bowl and add chocolate. Whisk smooth, whisk in coffee, and pour into molds. Refrigerate until cooled.

Serving: Serve the pots de crème alone, or with a crisp cookie, such as Chocolate Almond Fingers, page 425.

STORAGE: For advance preparation, cover the pots de crème with plastic wrap and refrigerate. Uncover and leave at room temperature for an hour before serving.

MAKES ABOUT 8 SERVINGS

CUSTARD MIXTURE

2 cups heavy whipping cream

⅓ cup sugar

1 vanilla bean, split

6 egg yolks

12 ounces bittersweet chocolate, cut into ¼-inch pieces

½ cup very strong prepared espresso coffee

Eight 4- to 5-ounce pot de crème cups or ramekins

RICH CHOCOLATE MOUSSE

∽ ᴑ ᴒ ∾

The method used to cook the eggs in this recipe—making them into a sabayon—involves whisking the eggs with sugar and liquid over simmering water until they are hot and cooked. Cooking the eggs this way eliminates most of the danger of salmonella poisoning associated with mousses made from raw eggs.

1   Bring a saucepan of water to a boil and remove from heat. Put cut chocolate and milk in a heatproof bowl and place over the pan of hot water. Stir occasionally to melt chocolate evenly. Once chocolate has melted remove bowl from pan and whisk smooth.

2   While chocolate is melting, whip cream until it holds a soft peak. If it is warm in the room, cover and refrigerate the cream while preparing the sabayon.

3   Return the pan of water to a boil. In a heatproof bowl or the bowl of an electric mixer, whisk the yolks together by hand. Whisk in the sugar and the liquid flavoring. Replace the bowl over the pan of simmering water and beat constantly until the mixture thickens slightly. Remove from heat and use an electric mixer on medium speed to beat sabayon until cool and risen in volume. To finish, by hand whisk the bowl of hot sabayon over a bowl of cold water with a few ice cubes in it until cool and thickened. Do not let the sabayon become ice cold.

12 ounces bittersweet or semisweet chocolate, cut into ¼-inch pieces

½ cup milk

2 cups heavy whipping cream

4 egg yolks

⅓ cup sugar

⅓ cup coffee, orange juice, or sweet liqueur (if using sweet liqueur, reduce sugar to 3 tablespoons)

Chocolate shavings, page 525, whipped cream, or both to garnish

4   To assemble the mousse, whisk the chocolate mixture into the sabayon, and quickly fold in the whipped cream. Place mousse in a bowl or glasses and garnish with extra whipped cream, if desired, and chocolate shavings. Refrigerate until about an hour before serving.

Makes about 6 to 8 servings

SWISS CHOCOLATE MOUSSE

THIS EXTRA-LIGHT, FOAMY MOUSSE is perfect for a buffet when you are also serving other desserts—it adds just the right chocolate note without being overly rich. It is adapted from a recipe in *Swiss Confectionery*, a publication of the Richemont Pastry School in Lucerne. Because this mousse uses gelatin to help it to set, it is better to prepare it the day before you intend to serve it.

1 Whip the cream until it holds a soft peak and refrigerate while preparing other ingredients.

2 Sprinkle the gelatin over the water and allow to soften for 5 minutes.

3 Bring a saucepan of water to a boil, then lower to a simmer. Combine the egg whites and sugar in the bowl of an electric mixer and place over the simmering water. Whisk constantly by hand until egg whites are hot and the sugar is dissolved—about 3 minutes. Test a little between your thumb and forefinger—if the mixture is gritty, continue to heat until all the sugar is dissolved

4 Whisk the softened gelatin into the hot egg whites, then use an electric mixer fitted with whisk attachment to beat whites until risen in volume, somewhat cooled, and soft and creamy in appearance. Do not overbeat or the meringue will become dry or grainy.

5 Allow meringue to cool to room temperature, stirring occasionally if necessary. When it is cool whisk about a third of the meringue into the chocolate, then quickly fold the chocolate mixture back into the remaining meringue.

2 cups heavy whipping cream

1 envelope unflavored gelatin

¼ cup cold water

1 cup egg whites (from about 8 large eggs)

1 cup sugar

8 ounces bittersweet chocolate, melted and cooled

Chocolate shavings, page 525, for finishing

One 2-quart glass serving bowl

6 Quickly rewhip the cream if it has separated and fold it into the chocolate mixture. Pour the mousse into the waiting bowl, cover with plastic wrap, and refrigerate until set, several hours or overnight.

7 Before serving, decorate with the chocolate shavings.

MAKES ABOUT 11/2 QUARTS MOUSSE

LAYERED PARFAIT OF ORANGE AND CHOCOLATE MOUSSES

⁓୨ ୧⁓

THIS EASY RECIPE may be adapted endlessly by changing the flavor of the liqueur.

1 Whip the cream until it holds a soft peak and set aside in the refrigerator.

2 Sprinkle the gelatin over the water in a heatproof bowl and set aside to soften.

3 Bring a saucepan of water to a boil, then lower to a simmer. Combine the yolks, liqueur, and sugar in the bowl of an electric mixer and whisk to mix. Place over simmering water and whisk constantly until mixture becomes foamy and slightly thickened, about 3 to 4 minutes. Remove the bowl from over the water and replace with bowl of gelatin. Leave gelatin over hot water until it is melted and clear.

4 Use an electric mixer fitted with whip to beat yolk mixture until cooled and increased in volume.

5 Whisk gelatin mixture into cooled yolk mixture, then divide mixture into two bowls. Quickly whisk the chocolate into one bowl.

6 Fold half the cream into the chocolate mixture, and the other half into the other bowl.

7 Spoon some of the chocolate mousse into each glass and top with a spoonful of the orange mousse. You will have more chocolate mousse than orange. Continue alternating the two mousses to form stripes up the glasses. Finish with either mousse.

2 cups heavy whipping cream

1 envelope unflavored gelatin

¼ cup cold water

4 egg yolks

⅓ cup orange liqueur

¼ cup sugar

6 ounces bittersweet chocolate, melted and cooled

3 thin orange slices, quartered for decoration

6 deep stemmed glasses, about 6 or 7 ounces capacity each

8 Loosely cover glasses with plastic wrap and refrigerate to set mousse. Garnish each mousse with a slice or two of orange.

MAKES ABOUT 11/2 QUARTS MOUSSE

LAYERED PARFAIT OF MINT AND CHOCOLATE MOUSSES: Substitute white crème de menthe for the orange liqueur. Garnish the parfaits with sprigs of mint.

LAYERED PARFAIT OF AMARETTO AND CHOCOLATE MOUSSES: Substitute amaretto liqueur for the orange liqueur. Crumble a few amaretti cookies or chocolate macaroons, over the mousse.

449

CHOCOLATE

CHOCOLATE OEUFS À LA NEIGE

This dessert, the name of which means "snow eggs" in French, is often confused with Floating Island or *Île Flottante*, the large-size version, for which the meringue is baked in a mold and unmolded in one piece into a sea of crème anglaise. These delicate meringue eggs are poached in a combination of milk and water flavored with a little vanilla and then served with a rich chocolate sauce.

1 To make the meringue eggs, half fill a saucepan with water and bring it to a boil over medium heat. Lower heat so water simmers. Combine egg whites and sugar in the bowl of an electric mixer and place over the pan of simmering water, whisking constantly, until egg whites are hot and sugar is dissolved. Use an electric mixer fitted with the whisk to beat meringue until cooled and increased in volume. The meringue should remain smooth and creamy and not dry and grainy.

2 Prepare the poaching liquid. Combine the milk, water, and vanilla extract in a nonreactive preferably straight-sided shallow pan, such as a sauté pan. Place the pan on low heat and bring to a full boil. While the liquid is heating, line the jelly-roll pan or cookie sheet with paper toweling. This will be to drain the meringue eggs as they are poached.

3 To poach the meringue eggs, you will need two large tablespoons, a small bowl of water to help you form the eggs, and a slotted spoon to lift them out of the poaching liquid after they are cooked. Turn off heat under poaching

MERINGUE EGGS
½ cup egg whites (from about 4 large eggs)
⅔ cup sugar

POACHING LIQUID
1 cup milk
2 cups water
1 teaspoon vanilla extract

FINISHING
1 batch Chocolate Sauce, page 513, or
    Chocolate Crème Anglaise, page 515
Chocolate shavings, page 525

1 jelly-roll pan or cookie sheet

liquid and skim the skin from surface with the slotted spoon. Dip one of the tablespoons in the bowl of water and scoop up a large spoonful of the meringue. Form it into a shape a little larger than an egg. Use the second spoon to ease it off the first one and into the hot liquid.

4 As quickly as possible form 5 more eggs and scrape them off the spoon and into the hot liquid. Quickly turn each over with the slotted

spoon so that the bottom also cooks. Leave them about 10 seconds on the second side, then remove from liquid with slotted spoon and poach 6 more eggs, forming and cooking them in the same way. If you make more than 12 eggs, skim and reheat the liquid before continuing.

5 Cover the tray of meringue eggs loosely with plastic wrap and refrigerate until time to serve.

6 To prepare a portion of the oeufs à la neige, place some of the sauce in the middle of a dessert plate or a dessert bowl and arrange two or three of the meringue eggs on it. Sprinkle with chocolate shavings. Repeat for each portion to be served. Alternately, place sauce in a glass bowl and float the eggs on the sauce and sprinkle them with the shavings. To serve, scoop up an egg or two and place on a plate, then surround with sauce.

MAKES ABOUT 6 SERVINGS

"INSTANT" CHOCOLATE MOUSSE

THIS DESSERT IS READY in just a few minutes—it only needs time to chill before serving.

1 Bring the cream to a boil in a saucepan and remove from heat. Add chocolate and let stand a few minutes; then whisk smooth and pour into a large bowl. Whisk in the liquor and cool. The mixture should cool to room temperature, but not solidify. (If it does, warm the bowl briefly over some warm tap water and stir smooth with a rubber spatula.)

2 When the chocolate mixture has cooled, combine egg whites and sugar in the bowl of a mixer and place over a pan of simmering water, whisking constantly, until egg whites are hot and sugar is dissolved. Use electric mixer to whip until cooled and inflated in volume— do not overbeat or egg whites will become dry.

3 Fold meringue into chocolate mixture, and spoon into glasses or bowl. Garnish with chocolate shavings just before serving.

MAKES ABOUT 1 QUART MOUSSE,
ABOUT 6 GENEROUS SERVINGS

1 cup heavy whipping cream

16 ounces fine-quality bittersweet chocolate, cut into ¼-inch pieces

2 tablespoons dark rum, other liquor, or strong coffee

4 egg whites

½ cup sugar

Chocolate shavings, page 525, for garnishing

6 stemmed glasses, or one 6-cup capacity bowl

VARIATIONS

INSTANT MILK CHOCOLATE MOUSSE: Substitute milk chocolate for the bittersweet chocolate. Decrease sugar to ¼ cup.

INSTANT WHITE CHOCOLATE MOUSSE: Substitute white chocolate for the bittersweet chocolate. Decrease sugar to ¼ cup.

STRIPED PARFAITS OF CHOCOLATE MOUSSE: Alternate layers of white and milk or white and dark mousse, in deep stemmed glasses. Garnish the mousses with mixed white and milk or white and dark chocolate

MARBLED CHOCOLATE TERRINE

❧ ◦ ◦

THIS STRIKING PRESENTATION IS the result of using two different chocolate mousses, one made with semisweet chocolate and the other with white chocolate. Be sure when you serve this dessert to use a very sharp, thin knife, rinsed in warm water and wiped so you make perfect slices. Try serving with some sugared berries and a bit of whipped cream flavored with the same liqueur you use in the terrine.

1 To make the dark chocolate mousse, cut the chocolate into small pieces and combine in a heatproof bowl with the butter. Place bowl over a pan of hot but not simmering water and stir to melt the chocolate. Remove bowl from water and pour in liquid cream in four additions, stirring to incorporate after each. Stir in the liqueur. Cover the mousse with plastic wrap and cool at room temperature. Proceed the same way to make the white chocolate mousse.

2 To finish, place the dark mousse in the bowl of an electric mixer and beat at medium speed until light. If the mousse does not lighten considerably, it may be too warm. Stir over ice water for a minute or two and whip by machine again. Clean the bowl and beater(s) and repeat the process for the white chocolate mousse.

3 For the meringue, combine the egg whites and sugar in the bowl of an electric mixer. Place over simmering water and whisk gently until the egg whites are hot and the sugar is dissolved. Use an electric mixer on medium speed to whip until cool. Fold a third of the

DARK CHOCOLATE MOUSSE
8 ounces semisweet chocolate
4 tablespoons (½ stick) unsalted butter
½ cup heavy whipping cream
1 tablespoon orange liqueur

WHITE CHOCOLATE MOUSSE
12 ounces white chocolate
6 tablespoons (¾ stick) unsalted butter
⅔ cup heavy whipping cream
1 tablespoon orange liqueur

MERINGUE FOR BOTH MOUSSES
3 large egg whites
⅓ cup sugar

ORANGE COMPOTE
4 large oranges
⅓ cup sugar
¼ cup water
3 tablespoons orange liqueur

One 6-cup Pyrex loaf pan, buttered and lined with plastic wrap

meringue into the dark mousse and two thirds into the white mousse.

4 To assemble the terrine, spoon the dark mousse out in five or six piles onto the white mousse. With a small rubber or metal spatula, cut through the two and swirl six or eight times. Do not overmix or there will not be distinct light and dark streaks. Pour the marbled mousse into the prepared pan and give the pan several raps on a towel-covered surface to settle the contents. Cover the pan with plastic wrap and chill about 8 hours. The terrine may be prepared up to 3 days in advance at this point.

5 To unmold the terrine, wipe the outside of the loaf pan with a cloth dipped in hot water and wrung out. Cover the pan with a platter, invert, and lift off the pan. Peel off the plastic wrap and smooth the outside of the terrine if necessary.

6 For the compote, peel and section the oranges and place in a bowl. Bring sugar and water to a boil and pour over oranges. Cool, drain, and sprinkle with liqueur.

SERVING. Cut the terrine with a thin, sharp knife dipped in hot water and wiped between each slice. Serve some of the compote with each slice.

CHOCOLATE ORANGE SHERBET
IN ORANGE SHELLS

THIS IS A BIT OF TROUBLE, but well worth the effort for a special party. You can put the finished desserts in the freezer a day before your party, and remove them shortly before serving.

1   Cut a thin slice off the stem end of each orange so it sits levelly. Stand the oranges on the cut bases and cut off the top quarter of each. These will be the covers of the dessert. Scrape the orange flesh away from the top quarters and set it aside in a bowl. Reserve the orange tops.

2   Use a pointy spoon—or a grapefruit spoon if you have one—to hollow out the oranges. Put orange flesh with the other reserved flesh and place the empty orange skins and the tops on the prepared pan and freeze them. Place the orange flesh in a fine strainer over a bowl and press to extract juice. Reserve 1 cup of the orange juice. Discard the pulp.

3   To make the sherbet, bring the sugar, water, and corn syrup to a boil. Off heat, add the finely cut chocolate, let stand 2 minutes, then whisk smooth. Sift the cocoa powder through a very fine strainer into a small bowl. Whisk the syrup mixture into the cocoa a little at a time to prevent cocoa from forming lumps. Strain the syrup and whisk in the orange juice and orange liqueur. Cool the sherbet mixture and freeze in an ice cream freezer according to the manufacturer's directions.

6 medium navel oranges

⅓ cup sugar

1 cup water

½ cup light corn syrup

3 ounces unsweetened chocolate, cut into ¼-inch pieces

⅔ cup alkalized (Dutch process) cocoa powder

2 tablespoons orange liqueur

1 small roasting pan lined with aluminum foil to hold the oranges in the freezer

4   When the sherbet is frozen, remove the orange shells one at a time from the freezer and fill each with sherbet, mounding it above the top of the shell. Perch a top on each filled orange, leaving the sherbet visible under it. Return the oranges to the freezer as they are filled.

5   After all the filled oranges have frozen solid, remove pan from freezer and wrap well in plastic wrap.

SERVING: Place the oranges in the refrigerator to soften slightly about an hour before you intend to serve them. Serve on a chilled platter.

MAKES 6 GENEROUS SERVINGS

BITTERSWEET CHOCOLATE SHERBET
WITH COCONUT RUM SAUCE

THIS SMOOTH SHERBET WITH a deep chocolate flavor is not excessively sweet. The coconut rum sauce adds just the right note of richness.

1 To make the sherbet, bring the sugar, water, and corn syrup to a boil. Off heat, add the finely cut chocolate, let stand 2 minutes, then whisk smooth.

2 Sift the cocoa powder through a very fine strainer into a small bowl. Whisk the syrup mixture into the cocoa a little at a time to prevent the cocoa from getting lumps. Strain the mixture.

3 Cool and freeze in an ice cream freezer. When it is frozen, place the sherbet in a covered plastic container and store in the freezer.

4 For the sauce, bring the coconut cream and the milk to a boil in a saucepan. Beat the yolks together in a bowl, then beat in a third of the boiling liquid. Return the remaining liquid to a boil and beat the yolk mixture into it. Continue beating over medium heat until the mixture thickens slightly. Do not allow to boil. Strain the sauce into a bowl and cool it. Stir in the vanilla and rum.

SERVING: Serve the sherbet in chilled glasses with a spoonful of the sauce on it.

STORAGE: To keep the sherbet after it has been frozen, press plastic wrap against the surface and store in the freezer.

SHERBET

½ cup sugar

2 cups water

½ cup light corn syrup

3 ounces unsweetened chocolate, cut into ¼-inch pieces

⅔ cup alkalized (Dutch process) cocoa powder

SAUCE

1 cup canned coconut cream, such as Coco Lopez

1 cup milk

4 egg yolks

1 teaspoon vanilla extract

2 tablespoons white rum

MAKES ABOUT 1 1/2 PINTS SHERBET, ABOUT 6 SERVINGS

VARIATIONS

CHOCOLATE COGNAC SHERBET: Add 2 tablespoons cognac to the mixture. Increase the chocolate to 4 ounces (this will offset the softening effect of the alcohol). For other flavor variations, substitute any other strong, nonsweetened spirits such as bourbon, rum, brandy, or fruit eaux de vie for the cognac.

CHOCOLATE GRANITA: Instead of freezing the mixture in an ice cream freezer, place in a stainless steel or other nonreactive pan in the freezer. When the mixture begins to freeze, remove it from the freezer and stir it up, scraping ice from the bottom and sides of the pan with a stainless steel spatula or pancake turner. Return to the freezer and stir and scrape it several more times during the next few hours until all the liquid has frozen to a slushy consistency. Scrape the granita into a chilled container and store it, covered, in the freezer. If the granita becomes hard, remove it from the freezer, roughly chop into 1- to 2-inch pieces and pulse, in a food processor, to restore the slushy consistency. Serve immediately after processing.

Ice Cream Freezers

As a trip to any kitchenware store will show you, there are many fancy (and expensive) ice cream freezers available for home use. The top-of-the-line automatic models are electrically operated refrigerated machines that do all the work of making about a pint of ice cream at a time. The only inconvenience is emptying and refilling the churn when you want to make more than a small amount of ice cream.

There are a few models that have electrically driven mechanisms that you plug in, but place in the freezer to churn, though I don't have any experience using these.

And there are also small hand-operated freezers that have a container which you freeze, then place the ice cream mixture in, and churn by hand at room temperature to make the ice. These work fairly well, especially if you have the container very well frozen before you start.

Old-fashioned American ice cream freezers are worth looking into if you don't want to invest several hundred dollars. Though the oldest types were operated by a hand crank, the modern versions are electrically driven. These are not refrigerated and you must still surround the churn in which the ice cream will freeze with ice and salt. Department and cookware stores carry ice cream machines, especially in spring and summer.

PEARS WITH CHOCOLATE
SHERBET HÉLÈNE

⁓❡ ❡⁓

THIS IS A VARIATION ON the classic French dessert Poires Belle Hélène, or pears with vanilla ice cream and chocolate sauce. This version uses pears poached and chilled, then served with a pear eau de vie–flavored chocolate sherbet. If you like, serve with cold Chocolate Sauce, page 513

1 The sherbet can be prepared up to several days in advance.

2 To poach the pears, place the 4 cups of water and the cubes from a tray of ice in a large saucepan. Add the lemon juice. Cut a piece of parchment or wax paper to fit the circumference of the saucepan. Cut a hole in the center. Peel the pears and cut them in half from the stem to the base; core the pears (a melon-ball scoop is perfect for coring) and immediately place each pear half in the acidulated ice water. When all the pears have been prepared, skim out any remaining ice and pour away excess water to leave the pears covered by about an inch of ice water. Add the sugar and vanilla bean.

3 Cover the top of the pan with the parchment or wax paper and press the paper down until it is below the surface of the liquid—this will help to keep the pears from bobbing up out of the liquid and becoming discolored. Bring to a boil over medium heat. Allow to boil for about a minute, then remove from heat. Let the pears cool in the liquid—they will be tender by the time they have cooled.

1 batch Bittersweet Chocolate Sherbet,
    page 457, flavored with pear eau de vie
6 ripe fragrant medium Bartlett pears,
    about 1½ to 2 pounds
4 cups water
1 tray of ice cubes
2 tablespoons lemon juice
½ cup sugar
1 vanilla bean
Chocolate shavings, page 525

4 If you want to make this in advance, pack the pear halves in a plastic container and cover with syrup. Keep the rest of the syrup to cook another batch of pears—it will keep well in the freezer.

5 To assemble the dessert, arrange 2 pear halves, cut sides up, on a chilled plate or in a shallow stemmed glass. Place a small scoop of the chocolate sherbet on the wide end of each half. Sprinkle with chocolate shavings and serve immediately.

MAKES 6 SERVINGS

PANERA ALLA GIANDUJA

Italian Chocolate Hazelnut Gelato with Cinnamon and Coffee

THIS IS MY FAVORITE ICE CREAM, bar none. The combination of flavors blends to become a hauntingly delicious new taste, with none of the flavors predominating. This is loosely based on a recipe from *Il Gelato Artigianale Italiano* by G. Preti.

1   Combine the milk, corn syrup, and cream in a saucepan. Put the sugar, gelatin, and milk powder in a bowl and stir well to mix. Whisk the dry mixture into the milk mixture. Bring to a simmer over low heat, whisking occasionally.

2   Remove mixture from heat and whisk in remaining ingredients. Whisk smooth, then cool to room temperature, cover, and chill.

3   Freeze the mixture in an ice cream freezer according to the manufacturer's directions. Scoop the frozen gelato into a chilled container, press plastic wrap against the surface, and cover tightly. Freeze until ready to serve.

MAKES ABOUT 2 QUARTS ICE CREAM

1 quart plus ½ cup milk

3 tablespoons light corn syrup

1½ cups heavy whipping cream

1 cup sugar

1 teaspoon unflavored gelatin

½ cup nonfat dry milk

½ teaspoon ground cinnamon

10 ounces bittersweet chocolate, melted

½ cup strong prepared espresso coffee

½ cup praline paste

ROMAN CHOCOLATE GELATO

This is modeled after the light, slushy gelati found at such classic Roman establishments as Giolitti. The chocolate flavor is richer in this ice because the flavor of eggs doesn't interfere with it.

1 Put the milk, corn syrup, and cream in a saucepan. Combine the sugar, gelatin, and milk powder in a bowl and stir well to mix. Whisk the dry mixture into the milk mixture. Bring to a simmer over low heat, whisking occasionally.

2 Remove mixture from heat and whisk in melted chocolate. Cool to room temperature, cover, and chill.

3 Freeze in an ice cream freezer according to the manufacturer's directions. Place the frozen gelato in a chilled container, press plastic wrap against the surface, and cover tightly. Freeze until ready to serve.

Makes about 2 quarts gelato

5 cups milk

3 tablespoons light corn syrup

1½ cups heavy whipping cream

1 cup sugar

1 teaspoon unflavored gelatin

½ cup nonfat dry milk

12 ounces bittersweet chocolate, melted

RICH MILK CHOCOLATE ICE

THIS INCREDIBLY EASY RECIPE comes my friend and mentor, Maida Heatter. Since it has only two ingredients, use the best chocolate you can find and afford.

1   Bring half the milk to a boil in a saucepan.

2   Remove from heat and add chocolate. Shake pan to make sure all the chocolate is covered, then let stand 5 minutes. Whisk smooth, then whisk in the remaining milk. Cool to room temperature.

3   Chill the mixture. If the chocolate rises to the top while the mixture is chilling, stir to reincorporate.

4   Freeze the mixture in an ice cream machine according to the manufacturer's directions. Place the frozen ice milk in a chilled container, press plastic wrap against the surface and cover tightly. Keep frozen until serving time.

STORAGE: Use the ice milk within a few days or it may become icy.

MAKES ABOUT 1 QUARTS ICE MILK

3 cups whole milk, divided
1 pound best-quality milk chocolate, cut into ¼-inch pieces

OLD-FASHIONED CHOCOLATE
ICE CREAM

My MODEL FOR THIS RECIPE is old-fashioned Philadelphia ice cream, made with nothing but light cream, sugar, and flavoring. You'll find this creamy and chocolaty in the extreme, as well as quick and easy to prepare.

1 Bring half the cream and all the sugar to a simmer in a saucepan, stirring occasionally. Remove from heat and add chocolate, shaking pan to make sure all the chocolate is submerged. Let stand 5 minutes. Whisk the chocolate mixture smooth, then whisk in the vanilla and the remaining cream.

2 Chill, stirring occasionally.

3 Freeze in an ice cream machine according to the manufacturer's directions. Place the frozen ice cream in a chilled container, press plastic wrap against the surface, and cover tightly. Freeze until ready to serve.

MAKES ABOUT 1 1/2 QUARTS ICE CREAM

4 cups light cream, divided
⅓ cup sugar
12 ounces best-quality bittersweet
    chocolate, cut into ¼-inch pieces
2 teaspoons vanilla extract

VARIATION

PHILADELPHIA VANILLA ICE CREAM: Omit chocolate; increase sugar to ½ cup. Heat half the cream with sugar to dissolve it, remove from heat and cool. Whisk in remaining cream and vanilla. Chill; freeze and store as above.

FRENCH CHOCOLATE ICE CREAM

THIS IS THE ULTIMATE RICH ICE CREAM made with a cooked custard base of milk, cream, sugar, and egg yolks—similar to the Crème Anglaise on page 215. This ice cream is creamier, richer, and better than anything you can buy. For best results, chill the ice cream mixture overnight before freezing it in an ice cream maker. This makes for a creamier texture in the finished ice cream. Use this as the master recipe for endless flavor variations.

1   Have ready a strainer set in a nonreactive pot or bowl. Set the pot or bowl in a larger bowl or pot half filled with a mixture of ice and water.

2   Combine the milk, cream, and sugar in a large saucepan and whisk once or twice to mix. Place over low heat and bring to a full boil.

3   Meantime, beat yolks together in a bowl until liquid, then whisk in a third of the boiling liquid. Return remaining liquid to a boil and whisk the yolk mixture into it, beating constantly until the custard thickens, about 20 seconds at the most. Be careful not to overcook the custard or it will scramble. Quickly whisk in the cocoa and chocolate.

4   Remove the pan from the heat, never ceasing to whisk, and pour it through the strainer into the pot or bowl set over the ice water. Whisk the strained custard for a few seconds to begin cooling it slightly, then let it cool, stirring occasionally, over the ice water. Cover and refrigerate the cooled custard overnight.

4 cups milk

1 cup heavy whipping cream

1¼ cups sugar

10 egg yolks

1 cup alkalized (Dutch process) cocoa powder

4 ounces best-quality bittersweet chocolate

5   Freeze in an ice cream machine according to the manufacturer's directions. Place the frozen ice cream in a chilled container, press plastic wrap against the surface, and cover tightly. Freeze until ready to serve.

MAKES ABOUT 2 QUARTS ICE CREAM

VARIATIONS

FRENCH VANILLA ICE CREAM: Omit cocoa and chocolate. Add 2 vanilla beans, split lengthwise, to the milk and cream mixture. Cook as above—the vanilla beans will be removed when you strain the custard.

CHOCOLATE CHIP ICE CREAM: Prepare a batch of chocolate or vanilla ice cream according to the above recipe. Melt 4 ounces chocolate with 2 teaspoons mild vegetable oil such as corn or canola. Drizzle the chocolate mixture into the ice cream as it is turning in the churn. Remember to divide the chocolate mixture proportionately if your machine won't hold all the ice cream at once.

CHOCOLATE RUM RAISIN ICE CREAM: After preparing and chilling the ice cream mixture, place ⅔ cup dark raisins in a saucepan. Cover the raisins with water and bring to a boil. Drain the raisins and place them in a small bowl. Cool to room temperature, then stir in 3 tablespoons dark rum. Cover the raisins and place the bowl in the freezer. As soon as the chocolate ice cream is frozen, drain the raisins and stir them into the just-frozen ice cream. Cover and freeze immediately. Use vanilla ice cream as a base for plain rum raisin ice cream.

BLACK FOREST ICE CREAM: Substitute dried cherries for the raisins, above. Substitute kirsch for the rum. Use chocolate ice cream.

MINT CHIP ICE CREAM: Substitute 2 cups loosely packed fresh mint leaves, rinsed and dried, for the vanilla beans in the French Vanilla Ice Cream above. After you bring the milk, cream, sugar, and mint to a simmer, remove the pan from the heat and allow to stand 20 minutes. Return to a boil and continue with step 3 above, and cook the custard—the mint leaves will be removed when you strain the custard. (Add a tiny drop of green food coloring, if you wish.) Chill and freeze the ice cream. Melt 4 ounces chocolate with 2 teaspoons oil and finish as for Chocolate Chip Ice Cream, above.

CHOCOLATE WALNUT CRUNCH ICE CREAM: Prepare a batch of Walnut Praline Topping. As soon as the ice cream is frozen, stir about half the praline in before you store it in the freezer. Save the rest of the praline to sprinkle over the ice cream when you serve it.

Substitute lightly toasted almonds, hazelnuts, macadamias, or pecans for the walnuts, if you wish.

PIQUANT CHOCOLATE GINGER ICE CREAM: Add 1½ teaspoons ground ginger to the ice cream mixture along with the cocoa powder. When the ice cream is frozen, stir in ⅓ cup finely diced crystallized ginger. This contrast of hot and sweet is fun, but not for everybody.

FROZEN CHOCOLATE
BOURBON SOUFFLÉ

~ᗧ ᗧ ᗧ~

THIS LIGHT MOUSSELIKE MIXTURE MAKES a wonderful frozen soufflé. If you don't feel like doing up a mold with a collar to present this as a frozen soufflé, freeze the mixture in a bowl or plastic container and serve it in scoops as you would ice cream—though it is both richer and lighter.

1 Cut a piece of aluminum foil long enough to go around the dish with a little overlap. Fold the foil in half the long way and wrap it around the dish to form a collar that extends about 4 inches above the rim. Tie or tape foil in place.

2 Set the prepared mold in the freezer while preparing the dessert. Whip 1½ cups of the cream until it holds a soft peak and refrigerate.

3 Bring the remaining ½ cup of cream to a simmer in a small saucepan over low heat. Whisk the cream, then the bourbon, into the chocolate. Set aside to cool.

4 Whisk the eggs, egg yolks, and sugar together in a heatproof bowl or the bowl of an electric mixer. Place over a small pan of simmering water and whisk constantly until the eggs are hot, increased in volume, and thickened. Use an electric mixer to whip until cooled to room temperature.

5 Fold the chocolate mixture into the egg mixture, then fold in the whipped cream.

6 Pour into the prepared dish and place in freezer. Cover with plastic wrap after the outside has frozen, about 2 hours after it is placed in freezer. Freeze overnight or for up to several weeks.

2 cups heavy whipping cream, divided
¼ cup best bourbon, such as
    Jack Daniel's
12 ounces finest-quality bittersweet
    chocolate, melted
2 large eggs
4 large egg yolks
⅓ cup sugar
Cocoa powder for finishing

One 6-cup soufflé dish

7 To serve, unwrap the dessert and remove the collar. Wipe the outside of the dish clean with a damp cloth if necessary and use a metal spatula to straighten the sides and top of the dessert. Return to freezer until serving time. Immediately before serving, dust top lightly with cocoa powder.

SERVING: Use two spoons to serve pieces of the frozen soufflé—don't try to cut it into wedges.

MAKES ONE 11/2-QUART SOUFFLÉ DISH, ABOUT 10 SERVINGS

VARIATIONS

FROZEN CHOCOLATE CHIP SOUFFLÉ:

Use a small paring knife to cut 4 ounces of best-quality semisweet or bittersweet eating chocolate into ⅛-inch chunks. Or break the chocolate into 1-inch pieces and pulse it briefly in the food processor to chop. Fold the chocolate into the soufflé mixture along with the whipped cream.

FROZEN CHOCOLATE RUM SOUFFLÉ:

Substitute dark rum for the bourbon. Cognac or any other strong, nonsweetened spirits may also be substituted.

WHITE CHOCOLATE AND LIME FROZEN SOUFFLÉ:

Substitute white chocolate for the dark chocolate and white rum for the bourbon in the basic recipe. Reduce sugar to ¼ cup. Add 2 tablespoons lime juice to the egg mixture before heating it.

Doughs for Pies, Tarts, and Pastries

THE EMPHASIS IN THE RECIPES that follow is mainly on rich, smooth chocolaty fillings, but the doughs that form shells for these fillings are certainly important. The doughs considered here are standard recipes, except for the fact that they are—unusually—all chocolate. These recipes include a tender cookie dough and a dark chocolate sweet dough.

COCOA COOKIE DOUGH FOR TARTLETS AND SMALL PASTRIES

1   Use an electric mixer to beat the butter, confectioners' sugar, and salt until mixed and somewhat lightened, about 2 minutes. Beat in yolks, one at a time, beating smooth after each addition.

2   Remove bowl from mixer and add flour and cocoa. Use a rubber spatula to stir the dry ingredients into the butter mixture. This will form a very soft dough.

3   Scrape the dough from the bowl and spread it in a rough rectangle on a piece of plastic wrap. Wrap and chill the dough until it is firm or for up to several days before using.

NOTE: If the butter is very soft, it is also possible to mix the dough by hand, beating it in with a rubber spatula in a mixing bowl.

MAKES ENOUGH TO LINE ABOUT
24 SMALL TARTLET SHELLS

12 tablespoons (1½ sticks) unsalted butter, softened

¾ cup confectioners' sugar

¼ teaspoon salt

2 large egg yolks

1½ cups all-purpose flour

⅓ cup alkalized (Dutch process) cocoa powder, sifted after measuring

CHOCOLATE

DARK SWEET CHOCOLATE DOUGH

~⁙~

1 To mix the dough in the food processor, combine the flour, sugar, cocoa, salt, and baking powder in work bowl and pulse several times to mix.

2 Add butter to work bowl. Pulse to mix butter in completely. When the butter is incorporated correctly there should be no visible chunks of butter, but the mixture should remain cool and powdery.

3 Beat egg with a fork and add to work bowl. Pulse until dough forms a ball. If the dough does not easily form a ball, add ½ teaspoon water, repeating if necessary, until it does.

4 Remove dough from processor, press into a disk, and wrap in plastic. Chill dough until firm or for up to several days before using.

5 To mix dough by hand, combine dry ingredients in a mixing bowl and stir several times to mix. Rub butter in, mixing it gently with fingertips, until it becomes a fine crumble. No visible pieces of butter should remain, but mixture should stay cool and powdery. Beat egg with a fork and stir into dough mixture. Continue stirring until dough holds together in a mass. Wrap and chill as above.

1 cup all-purpose flour

3 tablespoons sugar

3 tablespoons alkalized (Dutch process) cocoa powder, sifted after measuring

⅛ teaspoon salt

¼ teaspoon baking powder

5 tablespoons cold unsalted butter, cut into 10 pieces

1 large egg

6 To mix dough in a heavy-duty mixer, combine dry ingredients in mixer bowl with paddle attachment. Beat on lowest speed until combined. Add butter. Beat on low speed until butter is absorbed but mixture is still powdery, about 1 minute. Beat egg in a small bowl and add to mixer bowl. Beat on low speed until dough masses around paddle, about 30 seconds. Wrap and chill as above.

THIS RECIPE MAKES THE RIGHT AMOUNT OF DOUGH FOR ANY ONE-CRUST 9-INCH PIE OR TART IN THIS CHAPTER

VARIATION

PLAIN SWEET DOUGH: Substitute 1¼ cups flour for the flour and cocoa. Proceed with recipe in the same manner.

ROLLING DOUGHS AND FORMING PIE AND TART CRUSTS

Place the dough on a floured surface and flour the dough. Press the dough with a rolling pin to soften it and make it thinner. Roll the dough, being careful not to roll over the ends in the same direction you are rolling (this makes the edges of the dough thinner and likely to stick). While you are rolling, move the dough frequently and add pinches of flour under and on the dough to prevent the bottom of the dough from sticking to the work surface and to prevent the rolling pin from sticking to the dough. When the dough is large enough (place the pie or tart pan on it to compare the size—the dough should be a few inches larger in diameter), fold it in half and transfer it to the pan, lining up the fold with the diameter of the pan.

For a pie crust, place the dough in a 9 inch Pyrex pie pan and unfold the dough to fill the pan. Press the dough well into the bottom and sides of the pan and trim away all but ½ inch of the excess dough at the edge of the pan. Fold the excess dough under, making the edge even with the rim of the pan. Flute the edge of the pie by pinching the dough from the outside with the thumb and index finger of the left hand and pushing the dough into the pinch from the inside with the index finger of the right hand. Chill the crust until you are ready to use it.

For a tart crust, place the dough in a 9- or 10-inch tart pan with fluted sides and removable bottom. Unfold the dough into the pan and press and fit the dough well into the bottom and sides of the pan. Let the excess dough hang over the top edge of the pan and roll over the pan with the rolling pin to sever the excess dough. Using the thumb and index finger of your right hand, press down with your index finger and in with your thumb at the top edge of the crust to make the edge straight and even. Chill the crust until you are ready to use it.

BAKING AN EMPTY PIE OR TART CRUST

To bake the crust before using it for a pie or tart, cut a disk of parchment or wax paper large enough to line bottom and side of the crust. Fill the crust with dried beans and bake the pie or tart crust on the middle rack of a preheated 350 degree oven for about 20 minutes, or until the dough is set and dull-looking. Remove paper and beans and return crust to oven if necessary to finish baking, up to about 10 or 15 minutes longer or until it is firm. Cool the baked crust in its pan on a rack before filling it.

FORMING TARTLET CRUSTS

Divide the dough into several small pieces and roll one at a time, keeping the remaining dough refrigerated. Use a plain or fluted cutter a little larger than the diameter of the tartlet pans to cut the dough, placing the disks of dough into the buttered tart pans as they are cut. Failing tiny tart pans, you may use mini-muffin pans to form tartlet shells. Press the dough firmly into the bottom and side of each little pan and arrange the lined pans on a jelly-roll pan. Chill until ready to use.

To bake the tartlet crusts in advance, fill them with dried beans and bake them on the middle rack of a preheated 350 degree oven for about 12 to 15 minutes. Cool the crusts for a few minutes, then invert the pans, beans, crust, and all. Later, after the crusts have cooled, you'll find that most of the beans have already fallen out and it is easy to remove the remaining beans. Line the baked, cooled crusts up on a jelly-roll pan and cover them loosely until time to fill them.

CHOCOLATE CUSTARD PIE

❧ ❧

THIS IS AN OLD-FASHIONED CUSTARD PIE: a pie shell filled with a rich, creamy, just-set custard. I like this best with a plain crust because to my taste it frames the chocolate filling better than a chocolate one.

1 When ready to bake the pie, set a rack in the lower third of the oven and preheat to 350 degrees.

2 To make the filling, combine the half and half and the sugar in a saucepan. Whisk once or twice to mix and bring to a boil over medium heat. Remove from heat and whisk chocolate in smoothly. Continue to whisk until chocolate is melted.

3 In a large mixing bowl, whisk the eggs with the rum and spices. Whisk in the chocolate mixture. Whisk only until mixed. You want to avoid making a lot of foam on the custard.

4 Strain the custard into another bowl and skim any remaining foam off the surface. Pour the custard into the pie shell and bake the pie for about 45 minutes, or until all but the very center of the filling is set. Cool the pie on a rack.

SERVING: Serve with whipped cream or plain.

STORAGE: Keep the pie at a cool room temperature until it is served, then cover and refrigerate leftovers.

MAKES ONE 9-INCH PIE, ABOUT 8 SERVINGS

CHOCOLATE CUSTARD

2½ cups half and half (or 1¼ cups each milk and cream)

⅓ cup sugar

5 ounces bittersweet chocolate, cut into ¼-inch pieces

4 large eggs

1 tablespoon dark rum

¼ teaspoon ground cinnamon

⅛ teaspoon ground cloves

One 9-inch pie crust made from Plain Sweet Dough, page 470, unbaked

VARIATION

CHOCOLATE BANANA CUSTARD PIE: Make sure your bananas are ripe and dotted with brown sugar spots. Reduce cream to 2 cups. Slice 2 or 3 large bananas into the pie shell before pouring in the custard cream. After baking, cool and chill pie and top with sweetened whipped cream and chocolate shavings.

OLD-FASHIONED
CHOCOLATE CREAM PIE
Chocolate Meringue Pie

THIS IS A CLASSIC, THOUGH NO ONE seems to agree whether it should be covered with whipped cream or meringue. I like the idea of the meringue for this rich pie, but there are instructions for using whipped cream following the recipe if you prefer that topping.

1 To make the filling, mix the sugar and cornstarch in a heavy, nonreactive saucepan. Mix in the milk and place over low heat, stirring constantly with a wooden spoon until the custard thickens and comes to a boil. Remove pan from heat.

2 Whisk the eggs together in a small bowl, then whisk in about a third of the hot custard mixture. Whisk the egg mixture back into the hot custard mixture and return to a boil, stirring constantly. Remove from heat again, stir in the chocolate and vanilla until chocolate is melted and mixture is smooth. Scrape the cream into a bowl, press plastic wrap against the surface, and chill until it is cold or you are ready to assemble the pie.

3 When ready to assemble the pie, set a rack at the middle level of the oven and preheat to 400 degrees. Spread the cooled filling in the cooled pie shell.

4 To make the meringue, bring a small pan of water to a boil. Lower heat so the water simmers. Combine egg whites, sugar, and salt in a heatproof bowl. Place bowl over pan of simmering water and whisk gently for about

CHOCOLATE FILLING

⅓ cup sugar

3 tablespoons cornstarch

2 cups milk

3 large eggs

6 ounces bittersweet chocolate, cut into
    ¼-inch pieces

2 teaspoons vanilla extract

One 9-inch pie crust made from
    Dark Sweet Chocolate Dough,
    page 470, baked

MERINGUE

4 large egg whites

⅔ cup sugar

Pinch salt

2 minutes, until egg whites are hot (about 140 degrees) and sugar has dissolved. Remove bowl from pan.

5 Whip meringue on medium speed until it has cooled and is able to hold a shape. But it should not be dry. Distribute spoonfuls of the meringue all over the top of the pie, then use the back of a spoon or a small offset metal spatula to spread the meringue evenly. It should cover the top of the pie and touch the edges of the crust all around. Here and there, bring up the surface of the meringue so that it has swirled peaks. Place the pie on a cookie sheet and bake for about 5 to 10 minutes, until the meringue is colored evenly. Cool on a rack.

SERVING: Serve in wedges; it needs no accompaniment.

STORAGE: Keep the pie at a cool room temperature until serving time—it tastes best if it is served after it has cooled on the day it is baked. Cover and refrigerate leftovers.

MAKES ONE 9-INCH PIE, ABOUT 8 SERVINGS

BLACK BOTTOM PIE

THIS IS A COMBINATION OF RECIPES given to me by several friends, among them Miriam Brickman and Allen Smith. The whole point of the pie, as far as I can determine, is to contrast chocolate and vanilla in one shell. I have substituted a chocolate pastry dough shell for the typical one made from chocolate cookie crumbs.

1 To make the fillings, mix the sugar and cornstarch in a heavy, nonreactive saucepan. Add the milk and place over low heat, stirring constantly with a wooden spoon until the mixture thickens and comes to a boil. Remove from heat. Whisk the eggs together in a small bowl, then whisk in about a third of the hot custard mixture. Whisk the egg mixture back into the hot custard mixture and return to a boil, stirring constantly.

2 Divide the cream evenly between two bowls. Stir the chocolate into one of the bowls and keep stirring until it melts. Stir the vanilla into the other bowl. Press plastic wrap against the surface of both creams and refrigerate them until they are cold or you are ready to assemble the pie.

3 When ready to assemble the pie, spread the cooled chocolate filling in the cooled pie shell.

4 Whip the cream and fold it along with the optional rum into the vanilla cream. Spread it over the chocolate filling in the pie shell and top with the chocolate shavings.

CHOCOLATE AND VANILLA FILLINGS

½ cup sugar

⅓ cup cornstarch

3 cups milk

3 large eggs

6 ounces bittersweet chocolate, cut into
    ¼-inch pieces

2 teaspoons vanilla extract

One 9-inch pie crust made from
    Dark Sweet Chocolate Dough,
    page 470, baked

1 tablespoon dark rum, optional

¾ cup heavy whipping cream

FINISHING

Chocolate shavings, page 525

SERVING: Serve in wedges; it needs no accompaniment.

STORAGE: Keep the pie refrigerated until serving time—it tastes best if it is served on the day it is baked. Cover and refrigerate leftovers.

MAKES ONE 9-INCH PIE, ABOUT 8 SERVINGS

CHOCOLATE RICOTTA TART

⁓ ᗡ ᕽ ⁓

THIS TYPICAL ITALIAN DESSERT is often served as an Easter specialty in southern Italy though it is excellent at any time of the year. The flavorings vary slightly according to the region, and toasted slivered almonds and grated lemon and orange zest are sometimes included. The dough here is a plain one, which accents the chocolate filling better.

1   Set a rack in the lower third of the oven and preheat to 350 degrees.

2   To make the filling, beat ricotta by hand until smooth. Stir in sugar, sift in the cocoa, then stir in the eggs, one at a time. Stir in remaining ingredients, being careful not to overmix.

3   To assemble, cut off and reserve one third of the dough. Roll the remaining two thirds into a 14-inch disk and line the prepared pan with it. Allow the dough to hang over the edge of the pan.

4   Pour in the ricotta filling and smooth it.

5   Roll the remaining dough into a 10 × 14-inch rectangle, then cut it into ten strips, 1 inch wide and 14 inches long. Paint the strips with the beaten egg. Paint the rim of the dough on the pan lightly with the beaten egg and, using the egg as glue, stick five strips of dough diagonally across the top of the pie. Stick the other five diagonally across the first to form a lattice. Trim away any overhanging dough and push the dough on the top rim back into the pan so there is no raised rim of dough.

6   Bake for about 45 minutes, or until puffed and slightly firm in the center. Cool in the pan

RICOTTA FILLING

32 ounces ricotta cheese

⅔ cup sugar

½ cup alkalized (Dutch process) cocoa powder

6 eggs

2 teaspoons vanilla extract

½ teaspoon ground cinnamon

1 cup (6 ounces) finely chopped milk chocolate or milk chocolate chips

2 batches Plain Sweet Dough, page 470

EGG WASH

1 egg, well beaten with a pinch of salt

One 9- or 10-inch-diameter layer cake pan, 2 inches deep, buttered

on a rack before unmolding. To unmold, cover the pan with a flat plate or cutting board and invert. Remove the pan. Replace the pan with a platter and invert again. Remove top platter or board.

STORAGE: Keep loosely covered at room temperature on the day it is prepared. Wrap and refrigerate leftovers.

MAKES 10 TO 12 SERVINGS

CHOCOLATE BANANA CREAM TART

THIS MELTING DESSERT COMBINES a lightened chocolate pastry cream with bananas and whipped cream.

1 To make the filling, bring the milk and sugar to a boil in a saucepan. Dissolve the cornstarch in a little water and beat in the yolks. Beat the boiling milk into the yolk mixture. Add yolks to the pan and whisk over low heat until boiling and thickened. Remove from heat and stir in chocolate to melt it. Scrape into a bowl. Press plastic wrap against the surface and chill to set.

2 To finish the filling, whip the ½ cup cream and fold into the cooled chocolate mixture. Slice the bananas and fold them into the chocolate filling, then spread evenly in the cooled tart shell.

3 Whip the 1 cup heavy whipping cream with the 2 tablespoons sugar and the vanilla and spread over the surface of the filling. Cover with the chocolate shavings.

SERVING: Keep the tart refrigerated until time to serve it. Cut small wedges—this is a rich dessert.

STORAGE: Cover and refrigerate leftovers.

MAKES ABOUT 8 SERVINGS

CHOCOLATE FILLING

1 cup milk

¼ cup sugar

2 tablespoons cornstarch

3 egg yolks

4 ounces semisweet chocolate, cut into
    ¼-inch pieces

¾ cup heavy whipping cream

3 large bananas

1 batch Dark Sweet Chocolate Dough,
    page 470, lining a 9- or 10-inch tart
    pan, baked and cooled

FINISHING

1 cup heavy whipping cream

2 tablespoons sugar

1 teaspoon vanilla extract

Chocolate shavings, page 525

WHITE CHOCOLATE STRAWBERRY TART

THE WHOLE BERRIES garnishing this tart lend it an elegant and dramatic air.

1   To make the white chocolate filling, combine the white chocolate pieces with the butter in a heatproof bowl. Place over a pan of hot, but not simmering, water and stir to melt. Remove from the hot water and stir in the cream a little at a time. Keep stirring until the mixture is very smooth. Press plastic wrap against the surface and chill to set the filling.

2   To finish the filling, combine the egg whites and sugar in a heatproof bowl and place over a pan of simmering water. Whisk gently until the egg whites are hot and the sugar is dissolved. Remove the egg whites from the simmering water and use an electric mixer on medium speed to beat until whites are cool and have increased in volume. Meanwhile, beat filling to lighten it and beat in the kirsch. Fold the meringue into the filling and spread in the cooled tart shell.

3   Dip the berries in the prepared white chocolate. Place the coated berries on a paper-lined pan. Refrigerate to set white chocolate. Arrange the dipped berries on the filling. Sprinkle a few white chocolate shavings in the center.

WHITE CHOCOLATE FILLING

8 ounces white chocolate, cut into ¼-inch pieces

4 tablespoons (½ stick) unsalted butter

½ cup heavy whipping cream

2 large egg whites

¼ cup sugar

1 tablespoon kirsch

1 batch Dark Sweet Chocolate Dough, page 470, lining a 9- or 10-inch tart pan, baked

FINISHING

12 ounces white chocolate, melted and cooled

2 pints strawberries

White chocolate shavings, page 525

SERVING: Cut the tart into wedges for serving.

STORAGE: Cover and refrigerate leftovers; return to room temperature for an hour before serving.

MAKES ABOUT 8 SERVINGS

CHOCOLATE
BROWNIE TART

~⊙ ⊙ ⊙~

LIKE A RICH BROWNIE BAKED inside a chocolate crust, this tart proves you can't be too thin, too rich, or have too much chocolate in one dessert.

1 Set a rack in the lower third of the oven and preheat to 350 degrees.

2 Bring a pan of water to a boil and remove from heat. Combine chocolates and butter in a heatproof bowl and place on the pan of water. Stir occasionally until melted. Remove bowl from pan of water.

3 In a large mixing bowl, whisk eggs with salt and sugar. Whisk in chocolate and butter, then with a rubber spatula, fold in flour and nuts. Scrape the filling into the prepared crust.

4 Bake for about 30 minutes, until well risen and firm. Cool on a rack.

SERVING: Unmold tart and serve sweetened whipped cream on the side.

STORAGE: Keep covered at room temperature.

MAKES ONE 9- TO 10-INCH TART, ABOUT 8 SERVINGS

BROWNIE FILLING

2 ounces semisweet chocolate, cut into ¼-inch pieces

2 ounces unsweetened chocolate, cut into ¼-inch pieces

8 tablespoons (1 stick) unsalted butter

2 large eggs

Pinch salt

1 cup firmly packed dark brown sugar

½ cup all-purpose flour

1 cup pecan or walnut pieces, coarsely chopped

1 batch Dark Sweet Chocolate Dough, page 470, lining a 9- or 10-inch tart pan, unbaked

CHOCOLATE
COCONUT TART

THIS RICH, STICKY tart is like a chocolate coconut version of a pecan pie.

1   Set a rack in the lower third of the oven and preheat to 350 degrees.

2   Combine corn syrup and sugar in a saucepan and stir well to mix. Place over medium heat and bring to a boil. Off heat, stir in chocolate and butter until melted.

3   In a mixing bowl, whisk together eggs, salt, and rum. Whisk in chocolate mixture until smooth. Stir in coconut.

4   Scrape the filling into the prepared crust and smooth the top. Bake for about 40 to 45 minutes, until well risen and firm. Cool on a rack.

SERVING: Unmold tart and serve with sweetened whipped cream on the side.

STORAGE: Keep leftovers covered at room temperature.

MAKES ONE 9- TO 10-INCH TART,
ABOUT 8 SERVINGS

CHOCOLATE COCONUT FILLING

1 cup dark corn syrup

¼ cup sugar

4 ounces bittersweet chocolate, cut into
    ¼-inch pieces

4 tablespoons (½ stick) unsalted butter

3 eggs

Pinch salt

2 tablespoons white rum

One 7-ounce bag sweetened shredded
    coconut

1 batch Dark Sweet Chocolate Dough, page 470, lining a buttered 9- or 10-inch tart pan, unbaked

CHOCOLATE ALMOND TARTLETS

A SIMPLER TOPPING THAN the suggested marzipan hearts for these chocolate tartlets could be fresh raspberries and a sprinkling of confectioners' sugar.

1 Set a rack at the middle level of the oven and preheat to 350 degrees.

2 To make the chocolate almond filling, use an electric mixer to beat together the almond paste, sugar, and yolk until smooth. Beat in butter, scrape bowl and beater(s), and beat in egg. Continue beating until light. Sift and stir in flour and cocoa.

3 Fill a pastry bag fitted with a ½-inch plain tube (Ateco #6 or #806) with the chocolate almond filling and pipe into lined pans to about three-fourths full.

4 Bake the tartlets 20 to 25 minutes, until dough is baked through and filling is set. Cool in pans and unmold.

5 While the tartlets are baking, prepare the chocolate cream. Bring cream to a boil, remove from heat, and add chocolate pieces. Allow to stand several minutes, then beat smooth. Leave at room temperature to set. When cream is set, put it into a pastry bag with a medium star tube and pipe a large rosette onto each cooled tartlet.

CHOCOLATE ALMOND FILLING

4 ounces almond paste

¼ cup sugar

1 egg yolk

4 tablespoons (½ stick) unsalted butter, softened

1 egg

2 tablespoons flour

2 tablespoons alkalized (Dutch process) cocoa powder

1 batch Cocoa Cookie Dough, page 469, lining twenty-four 2-inch tartlet pans, unbaked

CHOCOLATE CREAM

½ cup heavy whipping cream

8 ounces semisweet chocolate, cut into ¼-inch pieces

MARZIPAN

4 ounces almond paste

1 cup confectioners' sugar

2 tablespoons light corn syrup

Red or pink food color

6 To make the marzipan, combine almond paste, sugar, and corn syrup in food processor and pulse to mix. Knead smooth by hand. As you knead, add a small amount of the coloring. Roll marzipan out to a layer ¼ inch thick and cut heart shapes out of it. Top each rosette with a marzipan heart.

SERVING: These are great on a platter for a buffet with a few other desserts, or as the only dessert after a fancy meal. They need no accompaniment.

STORAGE: Cover and refrigerate leftovers.

MAKES TWENTY-FOUR 2-INCH TARTLETS

CHOCOLATE ORANGE CHEESE TART

⁓ᗧ ᗤ⁓

THIS TART, WHICH IS like a rich chocolate orange cheesecake, never fails to please.

1 Set a rack in the lower third of the oven and preheat to 350 degrees.

2 Use an electric mixer on lowest speed to beat cream cheese and sugar smooth. Add eggs, one at a time, scraping bowl and beater(s) well after each addition.

3 Combine chocolate, orange zest, and orange liqueur and stir well to mix. Scrape chocolate mixture into cheese mixture and beat only enough to combine evenly. Scrape the filling into the prepared crust and smooth the top.

4 Bake for about 35 to 40 minutes, until slightly puffed and firm everywhere but in the very center. Cool on a rack.

SERVING: Unmold tart and serve in wedges.

STORAGE: Wrap and refrigerate leftovers.

MAKES ONE 10-INCH TART, ABOUT 8 SERVINGS

CHOCOLATE ORANGE CHEESE FILLING

16 ounces cream cheese, at room temperature

½ cup sugar

2 large eggs

3 ounces unsweetened chocolate, melted

1 teaspoon finely grated orange zest

3 tablespoons orange liqueur

1 batch Dark Sweet Chocolate Dough, page 470, lining a buttered 10-inch tart pan, unbaked

CHOCOLATE
RASPBERRY TARTLETS

~⦾ ᧭ ⦿~

Dark chocolate and raspberry are a classic combination, and just as good with the milk or white chocolate variations that follow the recipe.

1 To prepare the chocolate filling, bring cream, butter, and corn syrup to a boil, remove from heat, and add chocolate. Allow to stand several minutes to melt, then beat smooth, beating in raspberry liqueur. Leave at room temperature to set.

2 To assemble, spoon or pipe chocolate filling into tartlet shells to fill them. Arrange 3 or 4 raspberries on each tartlet. Dust with confectioners' sugar right before serving.

Serving: Serve the tartlets as dessert or after dinner with coffee.

Storage: Keep the finished tartlets at a cool room temperature on the day they are served. Cover and refrigerate the leftovers. For advance preparation, freeze the baked pastry shells between sheets of wax paper in a tin or other container with a tight-fitting cover.

Makes twenty-four 2-inch tartlets

FILLING

½ cup heavy whipping cream

1 tablespoon unsalted butter

1 tablespoon light corn syrup

6 ounces bittersweet chocolate, cut into
    ¼-inch pieces

1 tablespoon raspberry liqueur or
    eau de vie

1 batch Cocoa Cookie Dough, page 469,
    lining twenty-four 2-inch tartlet pans,
    baked and cooled

1 half-pint basket fresh raspberries

FINISHING

Confectioners' sugar

CHOCOLATE CARAMEL
PECAN TARTLETS

~୨ ୧ ୧~

THIS CARAMEL GANACHE filling is enriched—as if it needed it—with chopped toasted pecans.

1   To prepare the chocolate filling, combine the sugar and water in a saucepan and stir well to mix. Place over medium heat and, stirring occasionally, allow the sugar to color to a deep amber. Be careful not to let the sugar get too dark and bitter. To test, drop a little of the caramel onto a piece of white paper—it should just be a dark amber color. Off heat, add cream a little at a time—be careful, the sugar may splatter. Return pan to heat, add butter, and return to a boil. Remove from heat and add chocolate. Allow to stand several minutes, then beat smooth. Whisk in rum, if desired. Allow to set at room temperature. After the filling is cooled, fold in the chopped pecans.

2   To assemble, spoon or pipe in chocolate filling to fill shells. Arrange a pecan half on each.

SERVING: Serve the tartlets as dessert or after dinner with coffee.

STORAGE: Keep the finished tartlets at a cool room temperature on the day they are served. Cover and refrigerate leftovers. For advance preparation, freeze the baked pastry shells between sheets of wax paper in a tin or other container with a tight-fitting cover.

MAKES TWENTY-FOUR 2-INCH TARTLETS

FILLING

⅓ cup sugar

1 teaspoon water

½ cup heavy whipping cream

1 tablespoon unsalted butter

6 ounces bittersweet chocolate,
    cut into ¼-inch pieces

2 teaspoons dark rum, optional

I cup toasted pecan pieces, coarsely
    chopped, about 3 ounces

1 batch Cocoa Cookie Dough, page 469,
    lining twenty-four 2-inch tartlet pans,
    baked and cooled

FINISHING

Toasted pecan halves

CHOCOLATE CHEESE TARTLETS

~☙ ❧~

THESE FUN TARTLETS WERE INSPIRED by Maida Heatter's bull's eye cheesecake, with alternating rings of plain and chocolate cheesecake batter. Here the tartlet shells are filled with plain batter, then a chocolate batter is piped into the center, so there are two different cheesecake flavors in the same little tart.

1   Set a rack at the middle level of the oven and preheat to 350 degrees.

2   To make the filling, use an electric mixer to beat together the cream cheese and sugar on low speed until smooth. Beat in the eggs, one at a time, mixing just until smooth. Scrape down bowl and beater(s) often to avoid lumps. Beat in the vanilla.

3   Remove ½ cup of the batter to a small bowl and stir in the melted chocolate.

4   Pipe or spoon plain cheesecake batter into each pastry-lined pan, filling it about half full. Put the chocolate batter into a pastry bag fitted with a small plain tube (Ateco #2 or #3). Insert the tube about ¼ inch down into the center of the plain batter in each filled tartlet. Pipe out a dab of the chocolate batter and withdraw the tube, leaving a chocolate circle in the center of the plain batter.

5   Bake the tartlets at 325 degrees for about 25 minutes, until dough is baked through and filling is set. Cool in pans and unmold.

CHEESECAKE FILLING

12 ounces cream cheese, softened

⅓ cup sugar

2 large eggs

1 teaspoon vanilla extract

1 ounce unsweetened chocolate, melted

1 batch Cocoa Cookie Dough,
    page 469, lining twenty-four
    2-inch tartlet pans, unbaked

SERVING: Serve tartlets as dessert or after dinner with coffee.

STORAGE: Keep the finished tartlets at a cool room temperature on the day they are served. Cover and refrigerate leftovers. For advance preparation, freeze the baked pastry shells between sheets of wax paper in a tin or other container with a tight fitting cover.

MAKES TWENTY-FOUR 2-INCH TARTLETS

General Techniques for
Truffles and Dipped
and Molded Chocolates

Truffle Techniques

FORMING TRUFFLES: Whipped truffle ganache should be firm enough so that it holds its shape easily. If the ganache is too loose, the truffles will flatten when they are piped out. If this happens, stir the ganache over cool, not iced, water and rewhip briefly. Repeat if necessary. Pipe truffles onto a parchment-lined pan using a ½-inch plain tube (Ateco #6 or #806). In warm weather, chill the pan before you start piping. To pipe, hold the bag so that the tube is about ½ inch above the pan, and perpendicular to it. Squeeze once, gently, so that as the ganache emerges onto the pan it forms a ball with a slightly flattened bottom. Release pressure and twist a little to detach flow. Pipe the next center about 1¾ inch away from the previous one. Chill centers thoroughly before you attempt to enrobe them.

ENROBING TRUFFLE CENTERS: If the center is to be enrobed but not later encrusted, have a bowl of tempered chocolate ready (see pages 384–385). Place truffle center, right side up, on the surface of the tempered chocolate. Use a dipping fork to press the top of the center gently to submerge it in the chocolate. Slide fork under the flat side of truffle in the chocolate. Gently lift upward until the fork and bottom of truffle come to the top surface of the chocolate. Shake fork gently up and down to shake excess chocolate off truffle's surface. Keep the fork in contact with the surface of the chocolate. This helps to pull excess chocolate off truffle's surface. Lift fork off surface of chocolate and tilt it slightly, so that truffle hangs slightly off the edge of the fork. Scrape fork bottom against the rim of the bowl as you lift the truffle out of the bowl and deposit it on a paper-lined pan. To make a spiked surface, allow chocolate to set slightly, then roll truffle across a rack using a fork. Move the fork in a series of loops to make the truffle move across the rack and pull points in the chocolate covering.

ENROBING AND ENCRUSTING TRUFFLE CENTERS: When truffle centers are to be enrobed and rolled in cocoa, confectioners' sugar, or ground nuts, follow this two-person procedure. Set up work surface with the pan of centers on far left, then the bowl of tempered chocolate to its right, and a pan of sifted cocoa or sugar to its right, arranged so one of the short sides is against the edge of the work surface. To its right arrange a clean paper-lined pan for finished truffles. (This is if dipper is right-handed. If you are left-handed, start the series at the right and move left.) The first person picks up a center in his left hand; lays his right hand flat against the surface of the tempered chocolate to coat his palm; puts center in his right hand and closes his hand to coat the center with chocolate, then deposits it into a pan of cocoa at end of the pan closest to edge of work surface. The second person uses a fork to roll the truffle in the cocoa, pushing it to the far end of the pan, where the truffles are left until the coating sets. After a quantity have been coated, the second person lifts truffles with a fork to a paper-lined pan. After all the truffles are coated, they should be placed in a strainer, a few at a time, and shaken over the pan of cocoa to remove excess. They are then lifted from the strainer and placed in a storage pan. This step is only necessary when encrusting with cocoa or confectioners' sugar, not if ground nuts are used.

TECHNIQUES FOR MAKING DIPPED CHOCOLATES

FORMING THE SHEET OF CENTER MIXTURE

1 Whip ganache until cooled, but still pourable and beginning to hold its shape. Line the bottom of a jelly-roll pan with a flat sheet of plastic wrap or parchment; chill pan.

2 Pour ganache onto the pan to a depth of ⅜ to ½ inch. With a small offset spatula, shape the edges of the sheet as straight as possible, so that the ganache is a neat 10-inch square. Chill to set.

3 Remove sheet from refrigerator and spread a *very thin* coat of tempered chocolate over the ganache, using a small offset spatula. This coating and the one on the other side makes the center mixture easy to cut and dip at room temperature. Return to refrigerator to set.

4 Invert the pan so the chocolate-coated side of the sheet is down on a clean, chilled, paper-lined pan and spread a thin layer of chocolate on the side now up. Chill until needed.

Cutting Centers from the Sheet

1 Slide sheet of center mixture to a chilled cookie sheet or the back of a chilled jelly-roll pan. Position the pan near the stove; heat a sharp knife briefly in a flame or over a heating element, then, using a ruler to keep width uniform, cut the sheet into ¾- to 1-inch strips. Wipe the blade clean after each cut and reheat the blade before each cut.

2 When all the strips have been cut, cut across them at ¾- to 1-inch intervals to make squares, rectangles, diamonds, or triangles. Keep centers at a cool room temperature before dipping. You could also use a heated 1-inch cutter with a simple shape, such as a circle, to cut centers. Heat cutter in a flame or over a heating element before each cut and wipe after every cut.

Dipping Cut Centers

1 To make plain dipped centers, set up work surface with the pan of centers on the far left, then the bowl of tempered chocolate and a clean, chilled, paper-lined pan at right. Again, reverse if you are left-handed.

2 With left hand, place a center on surface of the chocolate in the bowl. With the fork held in the right hand, press the center into the chocolate so that the top of the center is at the top surface of the chocolate and is not completely submerged. Slide the fork into the chocolate and under the center and turn the center over so the coated side is now uppermost.

3 Withdraw the fork from under the center and with the side of the fork, sweep the excess chocolate from the top of the center in one movement, slide the fork back under the center, then shake the fork gently up and down to shake the excess chocolate off the dipped center. Keep the fork in contact with the surface of the chocolate, which helps to pull excess chocolate off.

4 Lift the fork off the surface of the chocolate, and tilt it slightly, so the dipped center hangs slightly off the edge of the fork. Scrape the fork bottom against the rim of the bowl as you lift it out and deposit the dipped chocolate on the paper-lined pan.

5 Use the side of the fork to score a decorative line on the surface of the chocolate and/or place a shred of a nutmeat or crystallized flower on it. Or, streak the surface of the dipped chocolates with a contrasting chocolate piped through a very fine opening in a paper cone.

TECHNIQUES FOR MAKING SOLID MOLDED CHOCOLATES

PREPARING MOLDS: Buff cavities in molds with cotton or a very soft, clean cloth. Leave molds at room temperature before filling.

FILLING MOLDS

1 Fill the cavities with tempered chocolate either using a large paper cone or by spreading chocolate onto the surface of plaque with an offset spatula, then sweeping excess into the bowl of chocolate.

2 Once the cavities have been filled, tap the bottom of the plaque against the work surface or tap the sides of the plaque with a rolling pin or the handle of a large wooden spoon to settle the chocolate into the cavities and eliminate air bubbles.

3 Scrape plaque surface clean with an offset spatula, sweeping excess into the bowl of chocolate. Set plaques aside until contents set.

UNMOLDING: After chocolate has set, turn the plaque over onto a clean, paper-covered pan and the chocolates will fall out easily.

CLEANING MOLDS: Run through dishwasher cycle. Drain well. Store upside down.

TECHNIQUES FOR MAKING FILLED MOLDED CHOCOLATES

PREPARING MOLDS: Buff the cavities in the molds with cotton or a very soft, clean cloth. Leave molds at room temperature before filling.

FORMING SHELLS

1 Fill the cavities with tempered chocolate either using a large paper cone, or by spreading chocolate on the surface of the plaque with an offset spatula, then sweeping away the excess into the bowl of chocolate. Tap the bottom of the plaque against the work surface or tap the sides of the plaque with a rolling pin or the handle of a large wooden spoon to settle the chocolate in the cavities and eliminate air bubbles.

2 Turn the plaque over the bowl of chocolate and tap gently on the bottom and sides of the plaque so that the excess chocolate drains into the bowl. Turn right side up, and scrape the surface clean with an offset spatula, sweeping the excess into the bowl of chocolate. Put the plaques aside to set the shells.

FILLING

1 Use a paper cone or pastry bag fitted with a ¼-inch plain tube to fill shells. Be sure the filling in the cavities has a flat top surface and does not come to a point or rise higher than the shell. The easiest way to do this is to make sure the point of the cone or tube is inserted only about ⅛ inch into the shell and held steady while the cone or bag is squeezed.

2 When filling is at the proper level, release pressure on the bag and pull the tip away with a sideways motion to avoid leaving a point.

SEALING IN FILLING

1 With an offset spatula, spread a layer of tempered chocolate over the plaque, so the chocolate covers the areas over the filling.

2 Scrape the surface clean with an offset spatula, sweeping the excess into the bowl of chocolate. Set plaques aside to set the bottoms.

UNMOLDING: After the chocolate has set, turn the plaque over onto a clean, paper-covered pan and the chocolates will fall out.

ALMOND CLUSTERS

⁀⌣ ⌣⌣

THESE SIMPLE CONFECTIONS ARE a good way of using up the last bit of tempered chocolate left over after dipping or coating other centers.

1 In a bowl, combine chocolate and almonds. Stir thoroughly with a rubber spatula to coat almonds completely.

2 With a teaspoon, quickly drop 1½-inch mounds on the prepared pans and leave to set. For a different look, drop the clusters directly into pleated paper cups. If it is warm in the room, refrigerate the clusters briefly.

STORAGE: Place clusters in a tin or plastic container with a tight-fitting cover and keep at a cool room temperature for up to a month.

MAKES ABOUT 30 CANDIES

VARIATIONS

COCONUT CLUSTERS: Substitute lightly toasted sweetened shredded coconut for the almonds. Make free-standing clusters or drop them into paper cups, as above.

WALNUT-RAISIN CLUSTERS: Substitute equal parts of lightly toasted walnut pieces and dark raisins for the slivered almonds.

HAZELNUT CLUSTERS: Substitute blanched, toasted, crushed hazelnuts for the slivered almonds.

PECAN CLUSTERS Substitute lightly toasted pecan pieces for the slivered almonds.

8 ounces tempered dark, milk, or white chocolate, pages 384–385

8 ounces (about 2 cups) lightly toasted slivered almonds, cooled

2 cookie sheets or jelly-roll pans lined with parchment or foil

PISTACHIO CLUSTERS: Substitute whole, blanched, lightly toasted pistachios for the slivered almonds.

MACADAMIA CLUSTERS: Substitute unsalted, lightly toasted, crushed macadamias for the slivered almonds.

CARAMELIZED ALMOND OR HAZELNUT CLUSTERS: Coat the nuts with caramel before continuing with the recipe.

TRUFFLES

PROBABLY INVENTED BY SWISS CONFECTIONERS during the last half of the nineteenth century, chocolate truffles have become a well-known and popular confection during the last quarter of the twentieth century. Cocoa-dusted truffles are supposed to imitate the aromatic fungus that grows under the ground in Périgord and Piedmont, but many truffles are also finished in other ways. Truffles may be encrusted with toasted nuts, grated chocolate, or confectioners' sugar, or they may even be left plain to show off their shiny chocolate coating. I usually recommend coating truffles with something—it can help hide the fact that the chocolate used for coating them is not in perfect temper.

Truffles are a practical chocolate confection to prepare if you don't feel like expending a lot of effort. The process of making the center mixture is easy and foolproof and forming the centers requires only a little care. Coating the truffles, especially if you use the quick tempering method (see "When you realy need to temper," page 385) is a breeze. You'll enjoy preparing these as much as you will eating them.

TRUFFES CHAMPAGNE
Champagne Truffles

THE CHAMPAGNE IN THIS truffle refers to Fine Champagne, a grade of cognac.

1 Combine cream, butter, and corn syrup in a nonreactive pan and bring to a simmer over low heat. Remove from heat and allow to cool 5 minutes.

2 Add cream mixture to chocolate and whisk smooth. Whisk in cognac and rum.

3 Cool center mixture 2 to 3 hours at room temperature, until it reaches about 80 degrees.

4 Use an electric mixer on medium speed to whip the mixture for about a minute, until it lightens in color. Spoon it into a pastry bag fitted with a ½-inch plain tube (Ateco #6 or #806). Pipe ¾-inch balls onto the prepared pan. Chill the centers for at least an hour.

5 To coat the truffles, melt the chocolate, temper it according to the instructions on pages 384–385, or allow it to cool to about 90 degrees. Coat truffles, according to directions on page 489, rolling in cocoa.

6 Roll finished truffles in a strainer over a piece of wax paper to remove excess cocoa. Lift truffles from strainer so excess cocoa remains behind. (Sift cocoa through a fine strainer to remove any bits of chocolate and it may be reused.)

CENTER MIXTURE

½ cup heavy whipping cream

2 tablespoons (¼ stick) unsalted butter

1 tablespoon light corn syrup

9 ounces semisweet, bittersweet, or milk chocolate, melted

1 tablespoon cognac or other fine brandy

1 tablespoon dark rum

COATING

12 ounces semisweet or bittersweet chocolate

2 cups alkalized (Dutch process) cocoa powder

2 cookie sheets or jelly-roll pans lined with parchment or foil plus a small roasting pan for the cocoa

STORAGE: Place truffles in a tin or plastic container with a tight-fitting cover and keep at a cool room temperature for up to a week.

MAKES ABOUT 35 TO 50 TRUFFLES, DEPENDING ON SIZE

PECAN BOURBON TRUFFLES

THE SWEETNESS OF THE BOURBON and the pecans is a perfect counterpoint for the bittersweet chocolate, and the contrast makes for an enticing truffle.

1 To make the center mixture, bring the cream to a boil and pour over the chocolate; whisk smooth. Whisk in the butter, corn syrup, and bourbon.

2 Cool the mixture to 80 degrees or until thickened.

3 Use an electric mixer on medium speed to whip the mixture about a minute, until it lightens in color. Then whip in the ½ cup chopped pecans. Spoon into a pastry bag fitted with a ½-inch plain tube (Ateco #6 or #806). Pipe ¾-inch balls onto the prepared pan. Chill the centers for at least an hour.

4 To coat the truffles, melt the chocolate, temper it according to the instructions on pages 384–385, or allow it to cool to about 90 degrees. Coat truffles, following directions on page 489, rolling them in the chopped pecans.

STORAGE: Place truffles in a tin or plastic container with a tight-fitting cover and keep at a cool room temperature for up to a week.

MAKES ABOUT 35 TO 50 TRUFFLES, DEPENDING ON SIZE

CENTER MIXTURE

½ cup heavy whipping cream

9 ounces semisweet chocolate, melted

2 tablespoons (¼ stick) butter

1 tablespoon dark corn syrup

2 tablespoons bourbon

½ cup chopped lightly toasted pecans, about 2 ounces

COATING

16 ounces semisweet chocolate

8 ounces chopped toasted pecans

2 cookie sheets or jelly-roll pans lined with parchment or foil plus a small roasting pan for the pecans

VARIATION

HAZELNUT RUM TRUFFLES: Replace the pecans in recipe with hazelnuts that have been toasted, blanched (see page 381), and chopped. Replace the bourbon with dark rum.

ALL-PURPOSE TRUFFLES

❧

USE THIS RECIPE TO MAKE plain truffles from any type of chocolate. Fruit, liquor, liqueur, and other varieties follow.

1 To make centers, combine cream, butter, and corn syrup in a nonreactive pan and bring to a simmer over low heat. Remove from heat and allow to cool 5 minutes.

2 Add cream mixture to chocolate and whisk smooth.

3 Cool center mixture about 2 to 3 hours at room temperature, until it reaches about 80 degrees.

4 Whip the mixture using an electric mixer on medium speed, for about a minute, until it lightens in color. Spoon mixture into a pastry bag fitted with a ½-inch plain tube (Ateco #6 or #806). Pipe ¾-inch balls onto prepared pan. Chill the centers for at least an hour.

5 To coat the truffles, melt the chocolate, temper it according to the instructions on pages 489, or allow it to cool to about 90 degrees. Coat truffles, using your hand to cover truffles with chocolate (see page 384–385), depositing them into a pan of sifted cocoa.

6 Roll finished truffles in a strainer over wax paper to remove excess cocoa. Lift truffles from strainer and leave excess cocoa behind. (Sift cocoa through a fine strainer to remove any bits of chocolate and it may be reused.)

CENTER MIXTURE

½ cup heavy whipping cream

2 tablespoons unsalted butter

1 tablespoon light corn syrup

8 ounces semisweet, bittersweet, or milk chocolate, melted

COATING

12 ounces semisweet or bittersweet chocolate

2 cups alkalized (Dutch process) cocoa powder

2 cookie sheets or jelly-roll pans lined with parchment or foil plus a small roasting pan for the cocoa

STORAGE: Place truffles in a tin or plastic container with a tight-fitting cover and keep at a cool room temperature for up to a week.

MAKES ABOUT 35 TO 50 TRUFFLES, DEPENDING ON SIZE

ESPRESSO TRUFFLES

THESE DELICATE TRUFFLES COMBINE the rich flavors of coffee and chocolate, accented with a bit of cinnamon.

1   Combine cream, butter, and corn syrup in a nonreactive pan and bring to a simmer over low heat. Remove from heat and allow to cool 5 minutes.

2   Add cream mixture to chocolate and whisk smooth. Mix together espresso with cinnamon and rum and whisk in.

3   Cool center mixture 2 to 3 hours at room temperature, until it reaches about 80 degrees.

4   Use an electric mixer on medium speed to whip the mixture about a minute, until it lightens in color. Spoon into pastry bag fitted with a ½-inch plain tube (Ateco #6 or #806). Pipe ¾-inch balls onto a pan covered with parchment or wax paper. Chill the centers for at least an hour.

5   To coat the truffles, melt the chocolate, temper it according to the instructions on pages 384–385, or allow it to cool to about 90 degrees. Coat truffles according to directions on page 489, rolling them in confectioners' sugar.

6   Roll finished truffles in a strainer over a piece of wax paper to remove excess sugar. Lift truffles from strainer so that excess sugar remains behind. (Sift sugar through a fine strainer to remove any bits of chocolate and it may be reused.)

CENTER MIXTURE

½ cup heavy whipping cream

2 tablespoons (¼ stick) unsalted butter

1 tablespoon light corn syrup

8 ounces semisweet or bittersweet chocolate, melted

2 tablespoons instant espresso coffee

½ teaspoon ground cinnamon

1 tablespoon dark rum

COATING

12 ounces semisweet or bittersweet chocolate

2 cups confectioners' sugar

2 cookie sheets or jelly-roll pans lined with parchment or foil plus a small roasting pan for the confectioners' sugar

STORAGE: Place truffles in a tin or plastic container with a tight-fitting cover and keep at a cool room temperature for up to a week.

MAKES 35 TO 50 TRUFFLES, DEPENDING ON SIZE

RASPBERRY CHOCOLATE TRUFFLES

⤳⤳

THESE TRUFFLES HAVE AN EXQUISITE raspberry scent. The raspberry puree here makes more than you need for the recipe, but the remainder may be used for flavoring butter cream or as a dessert sauce.

1 To make the raspberry puree, combine berries and sugar in a saucepan and bring to a simmer over medium heat. Allow to simmer about 15 minutes, until thickened. Puree in blender, then strain to remove seeds. Let cool.

2 To make the center mixture, bring the cream to a boil in a saucepan and remove from heat. Add all at once to chocolate and whisk smooth. Whisk in remaining ingredients in order, then cool to 80 degrees.

3 To form the truffles, use an electric mixer on medium speed to beat about a minute, until it lightens in color. Spoon into a pastry bag fitted with a ½-inch plain tube (Ateco #6 or #806) and pipe ¾-inch balls onto a parchment or foil-lined pan. Chill the centers.

4 To finish the truffles, grate milk chocolate in a food processor fitted with the grating blade. Place grated chocolate in the roasting pan. Melt the dark chocolate, temper it according to the instructions on pages 384–385, or allow it to cool to about 90 degrees, and coat the centers. With a fork, roll them through the grated milk chocolate, according to directions on page 490.

MAKES ABOUT 70 TRUFFLES, DEPENDING ON SIZE

RASPBERRY PUREE
One 10-ounce package frozen raspberries
½ cup sugar

CENTER MIXTURE
⅓ cup heavy whipping cream
16 ounces semisweet chocolate, melted
1 tablespoon butter
⅓ cup raspberry puree, see Step 1
1 tablespoon light corn syrup
1 tablespoon framboise
   (raspberry eau de vie)

FINISHING
8 ounces milk chocolate
8 ounces dark chocolate

2 cookie sheets or jelly-roll pans lined with parchment or foil plus a small roasting pan for the grated chocolate

VARIATION

CASSIS TRUFFLES: Replace the frozen raspberries with 1 cup frozen or bottled cassis puree and cook it with the sugar until thickened as with the raspberry puree. Use ⅓ cup of the resulting puree in the truffle center. Replace the raspberry eau de vie with crème de cassis. Enrobe the truffles in white chocolate and roll them in grated white chocolate.

PISTACHIO MARZIPAN TRUFFLES

THIS IS A PARED-DOWN VERSION of a rich Viennese confection called a Mozartkugel. Try to find the greenest pistachios possible so both the inside and the outside of the truffles will be brightly colored.

1   To make the centers, bring the cream to a boil and remove from heat. Whisk cream into chocolate. Whisk smooth, then whisk in extract, butter, and corn syrup. Cool the mixture to 80 degrees or until thickened.

2   To make the pistachio marzipan, place the blanched pistachios, still warm, in the bowl of a food processor. Process for a long time, scraping down frequently, until they form a paste. Pulse in the almond paste, then the confectioners' sugar. Add corn syrup as necessary, keeping the marzipan fairly soft. Remove from processor and knead smooth. Divide the marzipan into three pieces and roll each into a cylinder 12 inches long. Flatten ropes and roll them 2 inches wide.

3   Beat center mixture on medium speed about a minute to lighten and then spoon into a pastry bag fitted with a ½-inch plain tube (Ateco #6 or #806). Pipe down the center of each strip of marzipan. Bring the long sides of each piece of marzipan up around the ganache and press marzipan together along the center top of the ganache, enclosing it. Don't worry if the marzipan doesn't cover perfectly or completely. Cut each roll into ¾-inch lengths. Chill if necessary, then roll pieces into balls between the palms of your hands.

CENTER MIXTURE

½ cup heavy whipping cream

8 ounces bittersweet chocolate, melted

1 teaspoon almond extract

1 tablespoon butter

1 tablespoon light corn syrup

Pistachio Marzipan

8 ounces (about 2 cups) warm blanched
    pistachios, see page 381

4 ounces almond paste

1 cup confectioners' sugar

2 to 3 tablespoons light corn syrup

COATING

16 ounces semisweet or milk chocolate

16 ounces blanched pistachios, chopped

2 cookie sheets or jelly-roll pans lined with parchment or foil, plus a small roasting pan for the pistachios

502

PERFECT COOKIES, CAKES AND CHOCOLATE

4 To coat the truffles, melt the chocolate, temper it according to the instructions on pages 384–385, or allow it to cool to about 90 degrees. Coat truffles, according to directions on page 489, rolling them in a pan of the chopped pistachios. Remove to a paper-lined pan and chill to set coating.

STORAGE: Place truffles in a tin or plastic container with a tight-fitting cover and keep at cool room temperature for up to a week.

MAKES ABOUT 60 TRUFFLES

503

CHOCOLATE

NUTMEGS

⁓⦾⦿⁓

THESE SPICE-SCENTED TRUFFLES ARE the creation of Hans Tschirren, proprietor of the beautiful Confiserie Tschirren in Berne, Switzerland. During my recent visit, he kindly gave me this recipe and the cinnamon variation that follows.

1 Combine cream, butter, corn syrup, and nutmeg in a nonreactive pan and bring to a simmer over low heat. Remove from heat and allow to cool 5 minutes.

2 Strain cream mixture into chocolate (to remove pieces of nutmeg) and whisk smooth.

3 Cool center mixture 2 to 3 hours at room temperature, until it reaches about 80 degrees.

4 Use an electric mixer on medium speed to whip the mixture. Spoon into a pastry bag fitted with a ½-inch plain tube (Ateco #6 or #806). Pipe ¾-inch olive shapes, to resemble whole nutmegs, onto the prepared pan, holding the bag at a 45-degree angle to the pan with the tube touching the paper. Squeeze and pull the tube toward you about an inch, then release pressure and pull away. Chill the centers for at least an hour.

5 To coat the truffles, melt the chocolate, temper it according to the instructions on pages 384–385, or allow it to cool to about 90 degrees. Sift the cocoa and confectioners' sugar into a roasting pan and stir in the nutmeg. Continue to stir the mixture together until it is evenly mixed. Coat truffles according to directions on page 489.

CENTER MIXTURE

½ cup heavy whipping cream

2 tablespoons (¼ stick) unsalted butter

1 tablespoon light corn syrup

1 teaspoon freshly grated nutmeg

8 ounces semisweet chocolate, melted

COATING

12 ounces semisweet or bittersweet chocolate

1 cup alkalized (Dutch process) cocoa powder

1 cup confectioners' sugar

2 teaspoons freshly grated nutmeg

2 cookie sheets or jelly-roll pans lined with parchment or foil, plus a small roasting pan for the cocoa mixture

6 Roll finished truffles in a strainer over a piece of wax paper to remove excess cocoa mixture. Lift truffles from strainer so that excess cocoa and sugar remains behind.

STORAGE: Place truffles in a tin or plastic container with a tight-fitting cover and keep at a cool room temperature for up to a week.

MAKES ABOUT 40 TRUFFLES

PERFECT COOKIES, CAKES AND CHOCOLATE

VARIATIONS

CINNAMON STICKS: Replace the ground nutmeg in both the center mixture and the coating with the same amounts of ground cinnamon. Pipe the whipped center mixture into long cylinders, as wide as the opening in the tube you are using to pipe, down the length of the prepared pan. Chill and cut the centers into 1½-inch lengths. Coat with chocolate and cinnamon-scented cocoa and confectioners' sugar.

EARL GREY TRUFFLES: Replace the nutmeg in the center mixture with 2 teaspoons best quality Earl Grey tea leaves. Pipe the truffles into ¾- to 1-inch balls. Omit the nutmeg in the coating and just use cocoa and confectioners' sugar.

LEMON TRUFFLES: Replace the nutmeg in the center mixture with the grated zest of 2 large lemons. Pipe the truffles into ¾- to 1-inch balls. Coat the truffles with milk chocolate and plain confectioners' sugar.

Sugar-Based Confections

THIS SECTION INCLUDES SOME of the most popular candies of all caramels and butter crunch. Most of these recipes require cooking sugar to a temperature above the boiling point. Although cooking sugar can be complicated, if you follow these rules you shouldn't have any problems.

- Have a good, accurate candy thermometer. Use the type that looks like a ruler, at right, not the type with a stem and a round dial at the top. A ruler-type candy thermometer can touch the bottom of the pan and still give an accurate reading.

- Choose a dry day to cook sugar. Sugar absorbs moisture from the air very easily and many a batch of fondant has been ruined by excess humidity. If you must cook sugar in a humid climate, use only half the amount of cream of tartar or corn syrup called for in the recipe.

- Stir to help dissolve sugar up to boiling point, then cease stirring to avoid unwanted crystallization that agitation may cause.

- Use a metal spoon, not a wooden one that may contain odors or flavors of other foods it was used for.

- Be sure the sugar is dissolved before the mixture reaches the boiling point—this makes all the difference, for example, between smooth or grainy fondant.

- Use low heat to bring sugar to the boiling point, then raise heat to cook the syrup to the desired temperature.

- Always have a bowl of ice water handy to verify the consistency of the sugar syrup, to help ease burns, and to dip the bottom of the pan in to stop further cooking.

- Use a stainless-lined pan that has a copper or aluminum base. Do not use an all-stainless or tin-lined copper pan. The stainless pan conducts heat unevenly and the tin lining of the copper pan melts at high temperatures.

CHOCOLATE CARAMELS

~⌒⌒⌒~

THESE DELICATE, CHEWY TREATS are a little tricky to prepare—you need an accurate candy thermometer. I think they are best when dipped in chocolate, although they may also be wrapped, as is, in cellophane.

1 Combine cream, corn syrup, sugar, and salt in a saucepan. Bring to a boil. While mixture is coming to a boil occasionally wash sugar down sides of pan with a clean brush dipped in hot water to prevent sugar crystals from accumulating there and causing the batch to crystallize. Stir often.

2 When it comes to the boil, stop stirring and insert candy thermometer. Cook to 220 degrees.

3 Remove from heat and add butter and chocolate, allow to stand 2 minutes to melt, then stir to combine and replace on heat. Cook to the soft ball stage—until a teaspoonful of the mixture dropped into a cup of ice water forms a soft ball—240 degrees.

4 Pour mixture into prepared pan and allow to stand at room temperature until completely cool.

5 Unmold onto a cutting board and use a sharp knife to cut into ¾ × 1½-inch pieces. Dip or wrap.

2 cups heavy whipping cream

1 cup light corn syrup

2 cups sugar

Pinch salt

16 tablespoons (2 sticks) unsalted butter

8 ounces bittersweet or semisweet chocolate, cut into ¼-inch pieces

Tempered chocolate for dipping, pages 384–385, or cellophane for wrapping

One 9 × 13 × 2-inch pan, buttered and lined with buttered foil

STORAGE: Store dipped or wrapped caramels in a tin or plastic container with a tight-fitting cover and keep at a cool room temperature for up to a week.

MAKES ABOUT ONE HUNDRED
3/4 × 11/2-INCH CARAMELS

CHOCOLATE PECAN CARAMEL CLUSTERS

～☙ ❧～

THESE CONFECTIONS ARE worth their trouble.

1 Combine the sugar, corn syrup, and water in a large saucepan and place over medium heat. While mixture is coming to a boil, occasionally wash sugar down sides of pan with a clean brush dipped in hot water and stir often. Insert candy thermometer and cook to 305 degrees. Remove pan from heat and swirl in butter (be careful, the sugar will boil up in the pan), then add hot cream, a little at a time. Add salt and vanilla and return pan to heat. Insert thermometer and cook to 248 degrees. Remove from heat and allow to stop bubbling. Pour caramel into the prepared 9 × 13 pan and cool to room temperature. Wrap in plastic and continue cooling overnight.

2 To form the candies, drop half tablespoons of tempered chocolate onto the parchment-lined pan to form puddles about 3 inches apart. As soon as each chocolate is poured onto the paper arrange 4 pecan halves on each puddle.

3 Turn caramel pan over onto a cutting surface, remove foil and cut candy into twenty-four 2-inch squares. Roll each square into a ball then center it over a chocolate puddle and flatten it on top of the pecans. Drizzle remaining tempered chocolate over caramel on each candy.

CARAMEL

2 cups sugar

1 cup light corn syrup

¼ cup water

4 tablespoons (½ stick) butter

2 cups heavy whipping cream, scalded

½ teaspoon salt

2 teaspoons vanilla extract

FINISHING

16 ounces bittersweet or semisweet chocolate, tempered, pages 384–385

About 100 pecan halves

One 9 × 13 × 2-inch pan, buttered and lined with buttered foil plus 1 jelly-roll pan or cookie sheet covered with parchment or foil

STORAGE: Store candies in a tin or plastic container with a tight-fitting cover and keep at a cool room temperature for up to a week.

MAKES ABOUT 24 CANDIES

CREAM CARAMELS

These rich caramels are good as is, dipped in chocolate, or in chocolate pecan caramel clusters.

1 Combine the water, sugar, and corn syrup in a large saucepan over medium heat. While mixture is coming to a boil, occasionally wash sugar down sides of pan with a clean brush dipped in hot water and stir often. Insert candy thermometer and cook to 305 degrees.

2 Remove pan from heat and swirl in butter (be careful, the sugar will boil up in the pan), then add hot cream, a little at a time. Add salt and vanilla and return pan to heat. Insert thermometer and cook to 248 degrees. Remove from heat and allow to stop bubbling.

3 Pour caramel into prepared pan and allow to cool to room temperature. Wrap in plastic and continue cooling overnight.

4 Cut the caramel into ¾ × 1½-inch rectangles and wrap in cellophane or dip in tempered chocolate.

⅓ cup water

4 cups sugar

2 cups light corn syrup

4 ounces (1 stick) unsalted butter

4 cups heavy whipping cream, scalded

½ teaspoon salt

1 tablespoon vanilla extract

Cellophane for wrapping or tempered chocolate for dipping, pages 384–385

One 9 × 13 × 2-inch pan, buttered and lined with buttered foil

Storage: Store caramels in a tin or plastic container with a tight-fitting cover and keep at a cool room temperature for up to a week.

Makes about one hundred
3/4 × 11/2-inch caramels

OLD-FASHIONED BUTTER CRUNCH

❧

ALWAYS A POPULAR CONFECTION, butter crunch successfully and enticingly combines chocolate, nuts, and sugar.

1 To make the butter crunch mixture, melt the butter in a saucepan. Remove from heat and stir in sugar, corn syrup, and water. Cook, stirring occasionally, until the mixture reaches 300 degrees on a candy thermometer. Remove from heat, stir in almonds, and pour out into prepared pan, spreading the mixture with the back of a spoon to fill the pan.

2 Before the butter crunch hardens, but when it is firm enough to handle, turn it out onto a large parchment-covered cutting board and peel away the foil. Allow the butter crunch to cool completely.

3 To finish the butter crunch, wipe the top surface of the candy with a damp paper towel to remove excess butter and allow to dry a few minutes. Have another cutting board or the back of a jelly-roll pan ready to turn the candy over onto.

BUTTER CRUNCH MIXTURE

16 tablespoons (2 sticks) unsalted butter

1½ cups sugar

3 tablespoons light corn syrup

3 tablespoons water

1 cup toasted almonds, chopped, about 4 ounces

TOPPING

12 ounces semisweet chocolate, tempered, pages 384–385

1 cup toasted almonds, chopped, about 4 ounces

One 12 × 18-inch pan, buttered and lined with buttered foil, plus 2 large cutting boards, jelly-roll pans, or cardboard pieces, covered with parchment

4 Use a small offset metal icing spatula to spread half the tempered chocolate quickly over the butter crunch. Scatter half the chopped almonds over the chocolate. Cover this finished surface with a piece of parchment paper or foil and place another cutting board or the back of a large jelly-roll pan on the paper. Turn the candy over onto the second board or pan. Remove top board and paper and quickly spread with remaining tempered chocolate and scatter on remaining almonds (it isn't necessary to wipe the second side because it wasn't against a buttered surface). Refrigerate for 20 minutes to set chocolate.

5 Break the butter crunch into 2-inch pieces.

STORAGE: Store candy in a tin or plastic container with a tight-fitting cover and keep at a cool room temperature for up to a week.

MAKES ABOUT 3 POUNDS CANDY

511

These luscious liquids are among chocolate's crowning glories. Rich, gleaming sauces are treats to be savored in conjunction with plain desserts or to put rich ones over the top.

HOT FUDGE SAUCE

This is one of those really rich hot fudge sauces that hardens as it hits ice cream. It's great to use as the sauce for a brownie sundae!

1 Combine water, corn syrup, and sugar in a nonreactive pan and bring to a boil, stirring often, until all the sugar crystals have melted. Boil 1 minute without stirring.

2 Remove from heat and add the salt and the chocolate. Allow to stand 2 minutes until chocolate has melted, then whisk smooth.

3 Sift the cocoa into a mixing bowl and stir in enough of the liquid mixture to make a paste, then stir the cocoa paste smoothly back into the syrup.

4 Whisk in the remaining ingredients.

5 Store the sauce in a tightly covered jar in the refrigerator. Reheat opened jar over simmering water before serving.

MAKES ABOUT 2 CUPS

¼ cup water

1 cup light corn syrup

1⅓ cups sugar

¼ teaspoon salt

4 ounces unsweetened chocolate, coarsely chopped

½ cup alkalized (Dutch process) cocoa powder

4 tablespoons (½ stick) unsalted butter

¼ cup heavy whipping cream

1 tablespoon vanilla extract

PERFECT COOKIES, CAKES AND CHOCOLATE

CHOCOLATE SAUCE

⎯⎯ ౨ ౿ ⎯⎯

THIS IS AN EASY AND DELICIOUS sauce to serve whenever a chocolate sauce is needed. It goes perfectly with ices and frozen desserts as well as with soufflés or any warm desserts.

1 Combine the cream, sugar, and corn syrup in a saucepan and place on low heat. Bring to a boil, stirring often.

2 Off heat, add chocolate and shake pan to submerge chocolate in hot liquid. Let stand 3 minutes until chocolate has melted, then whisk smooth.

3 Whisk in salt and vanilla.

4 Store the sauce in a tightly covered jar in the refrigerator. Reheat over simmering water before serving.

MAKES ABOUT 2 CUPS

1 cup heavy whipping cream

⅓ cup sugar

⅓ cup light corn syrup

12 ounces bittersweet chocolate, cut into
   ¼-inch pieces

Pinch salt

2 teaspoons vanilla extract or strong liquor, such as rum or brandy

CHOCOLATE SYRUP

⚯

THIS IS A GREAT, EASY chocolate syrup, perfect for drizzling on ice cream or to use for making a quick chocolate drink.

1 Combine the water, sugar, and corn syrup in a saucepan and place on low heat. Bring to a boil, stirring often.

2 Off heat, add chocolate and shake pan to submerge chocolate in hot liquid. Let stand 3 minutes until chocolate has melted, then whisk smooth.

3 Whisk in salt and vanilla.

4 Store the sauce in a tightly covered jar in the refrigerator. Use the syrup as it is or reheat over hot water before serving.

MAKES ABOUT 11/2 CUPS

½ cup water

¼ cup sugar

⅓ cup light corn syrup

10 ounces bittersweet chocolate, cut into
   ¼-inch pieces

Pinch salt

2 teaspoons vanilla extract

VARIATION

CHOCOLATE FOUNTAIN SYRUP: Use this to make a chocolate egg cream or ice cream soda, page 520.

Decrease amount of chocolate to 8 ounces and increase sugar to ½ cup for a slightly thinner and sweeter syrup.

CRÈME ANGLAISE

THIS IS A FOOLPROOF METHOD for making this tricky sauce. The key to preparing a successful crème anglaise is organization. Have all utensils and ingredients ready before you start.

1 Before you start the crème anglaise, embed a heatproof bowl securely in another, larger bowl filled with ice. Place a fine wire-mesh strainer in the top bowl (if you have a conical French wire-mesh chinois, use it. If not, any fine strainer will do).

2 Combine the half and half and sugar in a nonreactive pan. Whisk once or twice, then place over low heat and bring to a boil. In the meantime, whisk the egg yolks in a bowl, just enough to make them liquid.

3 When the liquid boils, whisk about one third of it into the yolks. Return the remaining liquid to low heat and when it is about to boil again, whisk in the yolk mixture. Begin whisking before you pour in the yolk mixture or you'll scramble the yolks. Continue whisking for about 10 seconds—there will be a great burst of steam. It will not look very thick, but it will be visibly thickened, and you will feel a greater resistance on the whisk as the cream thickens.

4 Immediately remove the pan from the heat, still whisking constantly, and strain the sauce into the chilled bowl. Whisk for a minute or so after it has been strained.

2 cups half and half or 1 cup milk and 1
    cup heavy whipping cream
½ cup sugar
6 large egg yolks
2 teaspoons vanilla extract

5 Leave the sauce over the ice bath until it cools to room temperature, then whisk in the vanilla. Pour the sauce into a bowl, cover tightly with plastic wrap, and refrigerate immediately. Use the sauce within 24 hours.

MAKES ABOUT 3 CUPS

HOW TO FLAVOR CRÈME ANGLAISE

Use the following flavors in addition to the vanilla extract.

LEMON: Add the grated zest of 2 lemons to the pan before bringing the liquid to a boil.

ORANGE: Add the grated zest of 2 oranges to the pan before bringing liquid to a boil; add 1 tablespoon orange liqueur with the vanilla.

CINNAMON: Add 2 crushed cinnamon sticks to the pan before bringing the liquid to a boil. At the boil, remove from heat and allow to stand 15 minutes. Bring back to a boil and continue with recipe—the cinnamon will be strained out after the sauce is cooked.

Coffee: Replace ½ cup of the half and half with ½ cup very strong prepared coffee.

Vanilla Bean: Omit the vanilla extract. Add a vanilla bean, split lengthwise, to the pan before bringing the liquid to a boil. (After the bean is strained out, rinse it and let it air-dry for a few hours. Wrap in plastic and store in the freezer—you may use it again.)

Chocolate: Bring ½ cup milk to a boil and remove from heat. Add 6 ounces bittersweet chocolate cut into ¼-inch pieces to the hot liquid. Let stand a few minutes and whisk smooth. Whisk into cooled crème anglaise before refrigerating.

Liqueur: Whisk 2 tablespoons liquor or sweet liqueur into the crème anglaise before refrigerating it.

BEVERAGES

WHAT COULD BE BETTER ON A COLD night than a cup of hot chocolate or cocoa? I like to distinguish between the two because hot chocolate should be made with solid chocolate, whereas hot cocoa is made with cocoa powder—an easier and less rich drink than hot chocolate.

With the advent of the espresso craze in the past few years, cold chocolate drinks have also come into their own. There are recipes for hot chocolate drinks as well as old-fashioned soda fountain specialties in this chapter.

SANDRA CHURCH'S ADULT HOT COCOA

⁓ ୧ ୨ ⁓

My friend Sandra Church, who created the role of the young Gypsy Rose Lee in *Gypsy* during its first Broadway run, jokes that enough of this hot cocoa will make anyone want to strip!

1 Combine the sugar, cocoa, and coffee in a nonreactive pan and whisk in the cream until the mixture is smooth.

2 Whisk in the water, a little at a time, whisking smooth after each addition.

3 Place over low heat and cook, whisking often, until mixture is foamy and almost boiling (it will release large amounts of steam).

4 Remove from heat, whisk in cognac, and pour into warmed demitasse cups. Serve immediately.

Makes 3 or 4 demitasse servings

3 tablespoons sugar

3 tablespoons deluxe cocoa powder, such as Pernigotti or Valrhona

1 tablespoon instant espresso coffee powder

⅓ cup heavy whipping cream

1 cup boiling water

2 tablespoons cognac or brandy

2 teaspoons vanilla extract or strong liquor, such as rum or brandy

CHOCOLATE CALIENTE
Mexican Hot Chocolate

〜♃♃〜

WHEN THE CONQUISTADORES FIRST ARRIVED in Mexico during the sixteenth century, chocolate was served exclusively as a beverage. The beans were roasted and ground, then combined with honey, almonds, and spices and served hot. The type of chocolate used for this beverage survives today in the round tablets of flavored Mexican chocolate usually available in the Hispanic foods section of most markets.

To make an authentic pot of Mexican hot chocolate, you will need a *molinillo*, a carved wooden whip with rings around the handle that is rolled between the palms of the hands to aerate the mixture while it is heating. An ordinary wire whisk is, however, a good substitute. Heat cups before beginning preparation.

1 Combine milk and water in a nonreactive saucepan and bring to a simmer.

2 Remove from heat and add chocolate. Allow to stand several minutes to melt chocolate, then whisk smooth.

3 Return pan to low heat and whisk constantly until hot chocolate is near a boil and very foamy. Pour into heated cups and serve immediately.

2 cups milk
3 cups water
8 ounces Mexican chocolate,
    finely chopped

MAKES ABOUT 11/2 QUARTS,
ABOUT 6 LARGE PORTIONS

CHOCOLATE EGG CREAM

❧ ᓚ ᓗ

A NEW YORK SODA-FOUNTAIN INSTITUTION, the egg cream is famous for containing neither eggs nor cream. The foamy mixture of chocolate syrup, milk, and seltzer makes a refreshing and satisfying drink. The proportions here are only a guide—feel free to increase or decrease them to taste.

1 Combine the chocolate fountain syrup and the milk in the glass. Stir well to mix.

2 Pour in the seltzer slowly and carefully so the drink doesn't overflow. Stir once or twice with a long spoon and drink through a straw.

VARIATION

CHOCOLATE ICE CREAM SODA: Before adding seltzer, add 2 scoops of chocolate ice cream. Add seltzer and stir once or twice. Serve with a straw and a long spoon. If you use vanilla ice cream (or a scoop each of vanilla and chocolate ice cream), you will make a black and white soda.

MAKES 1 LARGE DRINK

3 tablespoons sugar

3 tablespoons deluxe cocoa powder, such as Pernigotti or Valrhona

¼ cup Chocolate Fountain Syrup, page 514

⅓ cup milk

Cold seltzer (not club soda)

1 tall 12-ounce glass, ideally an old-fashioned soda fountain glass

CHOCOLATE PLASTIC

❧ ෨ ൭ ☙

THIS DECORATING PASTE–SIMILAR IN SOME of the ways it is used to marzipan–makes lovely, dramatic cake decorations. Use it as you would marzipan to wrap an entire layer or roll cake, or to fashion ruffles and ribbons for delicate decorations.

1   Use a rubber spatula to stir the corn syrup thoroughly into the chocolate. Be sure to scrape the sides of the bowl to incorporate any unmixed chocolate clinging there.

2   Scrape the chocolate plastic out onto the prepared pan and spread it so that nowhere is it more than ⅓ inch thick. Draw the plastic wrap up around the chocolate to cover it completely.

3   Allow the chocolate plastic to set at a cool room temperature or in the refrigerator. In any case, wait several hours before using it.

MAKES ABOUT 11/4 POUNDS OR ENOUGH
TO DECORATE 2 OR 3 DESSERTS,
DEPENDING ON THEIR SIZE

⅔ cup light corn syrup

16 ounces semisweet chocolate, melted

1 cookie sheet or jelly-roll pan covered
    with plastic wrap

WORKING WITH CHOCOLATE PLASTIC

MAKING CHOCOLATE RIBBONS, RUFFLES, AND CIGARETTES

Follow these general instructions for rolling out ribbons from chocolate plastic.

1 Lightly dust the work surface and chocolate plastic with sifted cocoa powder.

2 Divide the batch into four pieces and pound each piece of the chocolate plastic with a rolling pin to soften it and make it pliable.

3 Shape each piece into a cylinder about 4 inches long, then flatten with the rolling pin or heel of your hand into approximately a 4-inch square. Lightly dust again with the sifted cocoa powder and roll each into a thin ribbon.

4 Or use a pasta machine to roll into thin ribbons. Pass each of the four pieces through every other setting, from the widest down to the next to last. (If it is extremely cool in the room, you might be able to pass the ribbons through the last setting. The result is a wonderfully thin, almost transparent ribbon.)

5 Use the ribbons to encircle a cake. Pleat some of the ribbons into ruffles for a beautiful effect (*right*), and cover the entire top of a cake with concentric circles of them.

6 Or mass the entire batch of chocolate plastic together, roll it out thinly, and use it to cover a cake or roll. Then dust it lightly with sifted cocoa powder.

7 To make cigarettes to decorate cakes or desserts, take a 3 × 5-inch piece of ribbon and roll it up tightly from one of the long ends (*right*).

MAKING LEAVES AND FLOWERS

1   To make leaves from the chocolate plastic, roll it out with the rolling pin or pasta machine, and cut into 1¼-inch-wide ribbons (*right*). Cut ribbons across to make diamonds, then press side angles in so sides curve into leaf shapes (*far right*).

2   To make carnations, roll out the chocolate plastic with a rolling pin or pasta machine, then cut it into ribbons 1 inch wide and 12 inches long. With the point of a paring knife, make cuts ¼ inch apart and ½ inch deep down one of the long sides of the ribbon, so the ribbon looks like a fringe

(*above left*). Begin from one of the short ends and roll up the uncut edge. When the whole fringe has been rolled up, hold the carnation between thumbs and forefingers of both hands and press in right under where the slashes end, to make the carnation open (*above right*). Pinch or cut away the excess chocolate plastic under the flower. Carnations are very effective when made in a variety of chocolate colors and massed together,

3   To make roses, proceed as above, rolling 12-inch-long ribbons. Then use a round cutter about 2 to 2½ inches in diameter to cut out petals (*top left*). Make conical rose bases by pressing the scraps together (*top right*), then wrap the petals around the base, as in the illustrations (*bottom left and right*). As in nature, make a closed bud first, then assemble several open petals around it,

4 To make bell-shaped flowers such as morning glories or petunias, shape about a ½-tablespoon piece of chocolate plastic into a sphere. Point one end, to make a cone with a curved end opposite the pointed one. Use a pencil or an awl to make a hole in the center of the shape from the rounded end. Revolve the awl around in the rounded end to enlarge the opening. Then withdraw it and use your fingertips to pinch the edges thinner. Pinch the pointed end to make it thinner. For a morning glory, open up the open end of the flower so that it is almost perpendicular to the pointed stem and pinch the thin edge in four places equidistant around the flower. For petunias, make a similar shape but more closed and pinch and frill the edge of the petals with your fingertips.

5 To make 4- and 5-petaled flowers, divide a tablespoon-size piece of chocolate plastic into four or five pieces. Form each into a sphere, then point one end of the sphere to make a cone with a rounded end and a pointy one. Press between fingertips to flatten to a teardrop shape. Repeat with the other pieces to make other petals. Mass the petals together at the pointy bases and press the bases together to keep the flower intact. Make a small sphere and flatten it, placing it in the center of the petals. Open the petals out and curve them slightly to give the flower some expression.

CHOCOLATE SHAVINGS

MANY OF THE RECIPES IN THIS BOOK call for chocolate shavings. A single one is perfect to decorate the top of a small tart or the center of a whipped cream rosette; multiples can cover the top of a cake, pie, tart, or large cookie, or the sides or entire outside of a cake.

Place the chocolate on the prepared pan. Use a paper towel to hold the chocolate and grate it with the largest holes (not the slices) on the box grater. To use the food processor, fit the machine with the grating blade provided with the machine. Break the chocolate into ½-inch pieces and stuff into the feed tube. Turn on the processor and let the chocolate pass through the grating blade. Pour the shavings from the processor bowl into a lidded container for use or storage.

TO MAKE SHAVINGS WITH A VEGETABLE PEELER: Hold the chocolate with a paper towel and pass the vegetable peeler over the narrowest side of the chocolate. The chocolate will curl up like wood shavings.

TO USE A MELON BALL SCOOP, COOKIE OR BISCUIT CUTTER, OR MINIATURE TART PAN: Position the bar of chocolate on the paper-covered jelly-roll pan and hold it down with a paper towel. Scrape the melon-ball scoop or other instrument toward you, across the surface of the chocolate. You will get curved shavings. Continue until the chocolate breaks apart and the surface can no longer be shaved.

4 ounces semisweet, milk, or white chocolate, preferably in a block cut from a large bar

Any of the following implements: box grater, food processor fitted with grating blade, old-fashioned vegetable peeler, melon-ball scoop, round cookie or biscuit cutter, or a miniature tart pan

1 jelly-roll pan lined with parchment or wax paper to catch the shavings

STORAGE: Keep the shavings in the lidded container in the refrigerator until needed. Leftover shavings keep in the refrigerator indefinitely.

NOTE: Any chocolate left over from making shavings may be used for another purpose. Wrap in foil and store with your other chocolate.

MAKES ABOUT 1 CUP SHAVINGS, ENOUGH FOR THE TOP OR SIDES OF ONE 10-INCH CAKE

INDEX

542